VERTICAL MARKETS AND COOPERATIVE HIERARCHIES

Vertical Markets and Cooperative Hierarchies

The Role of Cooperatives in the Agri-Food Industry

Edited by

Kostas Karantininis
*Royal Veterinary and Agricultural University,
Copenhagen, Denmark*

and

Jerker Nilsson
*Swedish University of Agricultural Sciences,
Uppsala, Sweden*

 Springer

A C.I.P. Catalogue record for this book is available from the Library of Congress.

ISBN-10 1-4020-4072-5 (HB)
ISBN-13 978-1-4020-4072-6 (HB)
ISBN-10 1-4020-5543-0 (e-book)
ISBN-13 978-1-4020-5543-0 (e-book)

Published by Springer,
P.O. Box 17, 3300 AA Dordrecht, The Netherlands.

www.springer.com

Printed on acid-free paper

The Image of Triptolemos by Greg Morgan (www.morgangreg.co.uk. http://www.morgangreg.co.uk/)
used with permission from Bioversity International (formerly known as IPGRI) who commissioned
the original image

This publication is based on the presentations made at the European Research Conferences
(EURESCO) on "Vertical Markets and Cooperative Hierarchies: The Role of Cooperatives in the
International Agri-Food Industry – A EuroConference on Agri-Food Cooperatives in the New
Millennium: Competition & Organisation" (Bad Herrenalb, Germany, 12–16 June 2003) and
"Vertical Markets and Cooperative Hierarchies: The Role of Cooperatives in the International Agri-
Food Industry – A EuroConference on the Strategies and Organisation of Agri-Food Cooperatives:
Quality Assurance and Vertical Coordination" (Chania, Greece, 3–7 September 2004) organised by
the European Science Foundation and supported by the European Commission, Research DG,
Human Potential Programme, High-Level Scientific Conferences, Contract HPCF-CT-2000-00172.
This information is the sole responsibility of the author(s) and does not reflect the ESF or
Community opinion. The ESF and the Community are not responsible for any use that might be
made of data appearing in this publication.

Essays in Memory of
Professor Konstantinos Oustapassidis
Aristotle University of Thessaloniki, Greece

KONSTANTINOS OUSTAPASSIDIS 1951–2001

Konstantinos Oustapassidis was born in Alonia, Pierias, a small town in Northern Greece. Son of immigrants from the Black Sea, he grew up speaking the "pontiaki" dialect and being very proud of his heritage. He went to high school in nearby Katerini and then to Thessaloniki. He received his B.Sc. degree in agriculture from the Aristotle University of Thessaloniki (AUTh), in 1974. After completing his military service, he got his first job at ELVIZ, a Greek Feedstuff Firm, and attended the Graduate Business School of Thessaloniki where he received his second degree in 1979. He joined the Department of Agricultural Economics at AUTh in 1981 as a Scientific Research Associate. In 1984 he received a competitive national scholarship to pursue his PhD at Oxford University. After spending three years at Oxford he ompleted his PhD degree in 1987, and returned to AUTh and followed the tenure track until he became Full Professor of Agricultural Economics and Cooperatives in 1998. He also taught at the University of Thessaly, the University of Macedonia, and the Mediterranean Agronomic Institute of Chania. He served as chief financial officer of the Property Management Corporation of AUTh, and was a member of the Greek Antitrust Committee from 1995 to 2000. He passed away while on duty, among his colleagues, during a faculty meeting in the spring of 2001.

Professor Oustapassidis was one of the founders of modern industrial organization and cooperative studies in Greece. His teaching and research was on theoretical and empirical industrial organization, and cooperatives. He was dedicated and personally involved in student advising and in research collaborations with his colleagues. He will be remembered affectionately for his passion and dedication to scholarly research, his curiosity and pursuit of ideas, and his intellectual generosity.

SELECTED BIBLIOGRAPHY OF K. OUSTAPASSIDIS

Collins, A., S. Butt, and K. Oustapassidis. 2001. "Below Cost Legislation and Retail Product: Evidence from the Republic of Ireland." *British Food Journal* 103(9):607–622.

Vlachvei, A., I. Ananiadis, and K. Oustapassidis. 2001. "Selling Expenses and Profit Margins in Greek Wine Industry." *European Research Management and Business Economics.*

Notta, O and K. Oustapassidis, K.2001. "Profitability and Media Advertising in Greek Food Manufacturing Industries.". *Review of Industrial Organization.* 18:15–126.

Oustapassidis, K., A. Vlachvei. and O. Notta. 2000. "Efficiency and Market Power in Greek Food Industries." *American Journal of Agricultural Economics.* 82:623–629.

Oustapassidis, K. and A. Vlachvei. 1999. "Profitability and Product Differentiation in Greek Food Industries." *Applied Economics* 31:1293–1298.

Oustapassidis, K., K. Vlachvei, and K. Karantininis. 1998. "Growth of Investor Owned and Cooperative Firms in Greek Dairy Industry." *Annals of Public and Cooperative Economics* 69(3):399–417.

Oustapassidis, K. 1998. "Performance of Strategic Groups in the Greek Dairy industry." *European Journal of Marketing,* 32:962–973.

Vlachvei, A. and K. Oustapassidis. 1998. "Advertising, Concentration and Profitability in the Greek Food Manufacturing Industries" *Agricultural Economics.* 18:191–198.

Oustapassidis, K., and O. Notta. 1997. "Profitability of Cooperatives and Investor-Owned Firms in the Greek Dairy Industry." *Journal of Rural Cooperation* 25(1):33–43.

Oustapassidis, K., and K. Giannakas. 1996. "Product Development and Conduct in a Competitive Food Market: The Case of the Greek Sausage Industry" Proccedings of the 4th International Conference "Economics of Innovation: The Case of Food Industry", Catholic University of Piacenza, June 10–11, Piacenza, Italy, Physica-Verlag p. 275–294

Oustapassidis, K. 1995. "The Impact of EU Accession on Exports by Greek Agricultural Co-operatives: An Approach Based on Pooling Time Series and Cross-Sectional Data." *Oxford Development Studies* 23:197–205.

Oustapassidis, K., A. Sergaki, and G. Baourakis. 1995. "The Economic Development of the Greek Agricultural Marketing Co-operatives", "Stochastic Models and Data Analysis". Kluwer Academic Publishers, Norwell, USA.

Oustapassidis, K., A. Sergaki., A. Vlachvei., and G. Baourakis. 1995. "Market Shares of Farm Co-operatives in Greece, Before and After Accession to the EC." *Journal of Rural Cooperation* 23:17–29.

Oustapassidis, K. 1992. "Diversification, Size and Growth of the Greek Co-operative Unions." *European Review of Agricultural Economics* 19:85–96.

Oustapassidis, K. 1992. "Economies of Scale in Agricultural Marketing Co-operatives: The Case of the Greek Unions." *Journal of Rural Cooperation* 20:127–38.

Oustapassidis, K. 1988. "Structural Characteristics of the Agricultural Co-operatives in Britain." *Journal of Agricultural Economics* 39:231–42.

Oustapassidis, K. 1987. "Economic Development and Structure of the Agricultural Co-operative Unions in Greece", Ph.D. Thesis, Oxford University.

Oustapassidis, K. 1986. "Greek Agricultural Co-operatives: Radical Change or Trend Recognition?", *Oxford Development Studies* 15:216–39.

TABLE OF CONTENTS

PREFACE xi

I. THE COOPERATIVE: BETWEEN MARKET AND HIERARCHY
 1. Cooperatives: Hierarchies or Hybrids? 1
    Claude Ménard
 2. The Network Form of the Cooperative Organization –
    An Illustration with the Danish Pork Industry 19
    Kostas Karantininis
 3. Networks, Innovation and Performance – Evidence from a Cluster
    of Wine Cooperatives (Languedoc, South of France) 35
    *Yuna Chiffoleau, Fabrice Dreyfus, Rafael Stofer &
    Jean-Marc Touzard*

II. GOVERNANCE
 4. Conversions and Other Forms of Exit in U.S. Agricultural
    Cooperatives 61
    Fabio R. Chaddad & Michael L. Cook
 5. The Structure of Marketing Cooperatives – A Members' Perspective 73
    Nikos Kalogeras, J.M.E. Pennings, Gert van Dijk & I.A. van der Lans
 6. Agency and Leadership in Cooperatives – Endogenizing
    Organizational Commitment 93
    Murray Fulton & Konstantinos Giannakas

III. INTERNAL ORGANIZATION
 7. Lock-in of Farmers in Agricultural Cooperatives – Reviving the
    Effect of Exit by Means of Constitutional Amendments 115
    Søren Vincents Svendsen
 8. Two Vignettes Regarding Boards in Cooperatives versus
    Corporations – Irrelevance and Incentives 137
    George Hendrikse
 9. Regulation, Governance and Capital Structure in Cooperatives 151
    Anastassios Gentzoglanis

IV. CONDUCT
 10. Cooperative Forward Integration in Oligopsonistic Markets –
     A Simulation Analysis of Incentives and Impacts 169
     Jeffrey S. Royer

11. European Dairy Cooperative Strategies – Horizontal Integration
    versus Diversity 195
    Laurence Harte & John J. O'Connell
12. Sales Distortion in Heterogeneous Cooperatives 213
    Peter Bogetoft & Henrik Ballebye Olesen
13. Do Consumers Care about Cooperatives? A Franco-Swedish
    Comparative Study of Consumer Perceptions 225
    Jerker Nilsson, Philippe Ruffio & Stéphane Gouin

V. PERFORMANCE
14. The Horizon Problem Reconsidered 245
    Henrik Ballebye Olesen
15. The Horizon Problem in Agricultural Cooperatives –
    Only in Theory? 255
    Erik Fahlbeck
16. Performance of Cooperatives and Investor-Owned Firms:
    The Case of the Greek Dairy Industry 275
    Ourania Notta & Aspassia Vlachvei

PREFACE

Some writers argue that cooperative business has existed almost as long as mankind itself, thereby referring to how people in ancient Egypt, Babylonia, China and Greece solved joint problems. People have always experienced advantages by joining forces. However, the formal way of organizing cooperatives is a 19th century phenomenon.

The pioneering cooperatives were, however, very different from the cooperative firms of the 20th century, not to speak about the cooperatives of the 21st century. As the market conditions change the business firms, among them the cooperative enterprises have to adapt. This is an eternal truth.

During the last decade or so, considerable changes have taken place in the market places in the Western countries. The power balance between the manufacturers and the retailers is shifting to the advantage of the latter, as the retail chains are passing through a process of consolidation, globalization, and centralization. The agricultural policies in the Western economies are successively being liberalized. The food processing industry responds to these changes by globalization and extreme large-scale operations.

The cooperatives' adaptation to these changes is presently so extensive and so radical, that one may even get the impression that the pace of change has never been so rapid in cooperative history. The most powerful market strategies demand much capital, and so, new financial solutions are being developed. Likewise, new governance structures are coming. In some cases, newly established cooperatives try to identify market niches to exploit, whereby they often take on unconventional organizational set-ups. Otherwise, the most striking structural change is consolidation, and such of different kinds; mergers, also across national boundaries, alliances with other cooperatives or firms with other ownership structures, acquisitions of other firms, and also organizational forms that seem to be a mixture of cooperative and investor-owned business forms.

The issues hinted at above were the themes of two scientific conferences, organized by the editors of this book. They took place in Bad Herrenalb, Germany, in June 2003, and in Crete, Greece, in September 2004. The theme of both conferences was "Vertical Markets and Cooperative Hierarchies", i.e., the same as the title of the present book. The participants to the two conferences were most of the world's leading scholars on agricultural cooperative business. Hence, it is easy to guess that this book is composed of a number of contributions to the conferences and, in a couple of cases, with contributions from researchers who had intended to participate but were prevented from coming.

The book consists of five parts. The first one, COOPERATIVES BETWEEN MARKETS AND HIERARCHIES, expands the view of the agricultural cooperative business form by adopting the concepts of hybrids and networks. *Claude Ménard* places the cooperative organizational form within the continuum between markets and hierarchies. Cooperatives are viewed as a hybrid form. This opens new avenues in research about the cooperative organizational form. *Kostas Karantininis* suggests that cooperatives can be regarded as a network, nested conceptually in the market – hybrid – hierarchy continuum. The network of interlocking directorates of the Danish pork industry provides an illustration. *Yuna Chiffoleau, Fabrice Dreyfus, Rafael Stofer* and *Jean-Marc Touzard* map an advisory network of French wine cooperatives, thereby providing arguments for networks' role in innovation and, most importantly, on the participating cooperatives' governance structure.

The second part of the book is devoted to issues of GOVERNANCE. What do cooperatives do when they succeed and when they fail? This is a good starting question when examining governance in cooperatives. *Fabio Chaddad* and *Michael Cook* review exit strategies. They find that mergers and, to some extent, acquisitions are more common among agricultural cooperatives, rather than conversions to IOFs, or liquidations and bankruptcy. Agricultural cooperatives tend to maintain their cooperative structure, whereas cooperative organizations in other sectors more often change their business form or simply dissolve. *Nikos Kalogeras, Joost M.E. Pennings, Gert van Dijk* and *Ivo A. van der Lans* surveyed members of Dutch marketing cooperatives to reveal what kind of a cooperative they desire. The results show a demand for a more market-oriented management and an internal structure closer to an IOF, rather than the traditional proportional type. These two chapters concern management strategies and members' opinions about cooperative structures. *Murray Fulton* and *Konstantinos Giannakas* challenge the view that members' opinions decide the management strategies and the structural characteristics of the cooperative. While members demand high commitment and good performance by hired managers, they themselves may not be committed enough to their cooperative so as to attract and maintain top management performance.

INTERNAL ORGANIZATIONAL ISSUES are treated in the book's third part. *Søren V. Svendsen* adopts a political science approach, arriving at the conclusion that cooperatives should change their constitutional structure to allow for more exiting. This would improve the collective bargaining position of farmers and could potentially control management conduct. *George Hendrikse* seems to challenge this view by showing that the cooperative structure at large might be irrelevant. However, the financial structure might be important in that it limits the ability of rent extracting activities by management. *Anastassios Gentzoglanis* shows that the governance structure of the cooperative is the reason for differential performance between cooperatives and IOFs.

Four papers examine the CONDUCT OF COOPERATIVES Three distinct strategic choices by cooperatives are analyzed: vertical integration, horizontal integration and product differentiation. Using a standard oligopsonistic model, *Jeffrey Royer* shows that vertical integration is a strategic choice for a cooperative in non-competitive market structures. *Laurence Harte* and *John O'Connell* find that vertical integration does not necessarily result in higher prices for the farmers. Irish dairy cooperatives constitute the empirical basis, and European parallels are drawn. *Peter Bogetoft* and *Henrik Ballebye Olesen* argue that the choice to differentiate products depends on the composition of the membership. If most members are conventional producers it is unlikely that the cooperative will chose to differentiate their product. *Jerker Nilsson, Philippe Ruffio* and *Stéphane Gouin* investigate why only few cooperatives use the concept of "cooperative" as an element in their branding strategy. They hypothesize that this is so because less scrupulous firms might free-ride if "cooperative" were a positive brand element. After a survey among French and Swedish consumers the authors reject this idea and suggest alternative explanations. The above four studies cast some light on the extent to which cooperatives behave differently from IOFs. Most importantly, they raise questions about the survival of cooperatives as a distinct business form.

The last part of the book focuses on COOPERATIVE PERFORMANCE. The classical question of the horizon problem in cooperatives is dealt with both theoretically and empirically in two papers. By allowing for full equity redemption, *Henrik Ballebye Olesen* challenges the conventional view that the horizon problem leads to under-investment in cooperatives, showing over-investment instead. According to a survey conducted by *Erik Fahlbeck,* cooperative members in Sweden do not consider the horizon problem as a significant impediment to efficient business in their cooperatives. Do cooperatives perform/behave different than investor-owned firms? *Ourania Notta* and *Aspassia Vlachvei* scrutinize data from Greek dairy firms with different organizational forms. The evidence is clearly in favor of the IOFs. This may be the result of the Greek setting, but it may also indicate a general handicap of the cooperative organizational form.

A large number of researchers adhered to the call for papers to be presented at the two conferences. After screening by the two conference organizers a total of 74 papers were presented at the conferences, as well as 13 posters. Together with a few papers, submitted by researchers who were unable to attend the conferences, the number of potential book chapters amounted to nearly 100. Out of these, the two conference organizers (book editors) selected 24 that should be subject to scrutiny through anonymous peer reviewing. Whenever there was a disagreement between at least one of the two editors and the reviewer the paper was submitted to a third reviewer. Through this process, the 16 chapters, included in this book, were chosen.

The editors are very grateful to a number of skilled researchers who helped with selecting papers and advising the authors to improve the quality of the submissions. The editors, however, remain the residual claimants of any errors and omissions that the authors themselves have not already claimed. The contribution of the following who served as referees is hereby deeply acknowledged:

David Barton, Kansas State University, USA;
Niels Blomgren-Hansen, Copenhagen Business School, Denmark;
Thrainn Eggertsson, University of Iceland, and New York University, USA;
Michael Gertler, University of Saskatchewan, Canada;
Geir Gripsrud, Norwegian School of Management, Norway;
Werner Grosskopf, University of Hohenheim, Germany;
Brent M. Hueth, Iowa State University, USA;
Svend Hylleberg, University of Aarhus, Denmark;
Saara Hyvönen, University of Helsinki, Finland;
Michael Kirk, Philipps-University Marburg, Germany;
Peter G. Klein, University of Missouri, USA;
Rainer Kühl, University of Giessen, Germany;
Carl Johan Lagerkvist, Swedish University of Agricultural Sciences, Sweden;

Ole Øhlenschlæger Madsen, University of Aarhus, Denmark;
S.W.F. (Onno) Omta, Wageningen UR, the Netherlands;
Lars Otto, the Royal Veterinary and Agricultural University (KVL), Denmark;
Brian Oleson, University of Manitoba, Canada;
H. Christopher Peterson, Michigan State University, USA;
Jörg Raab, University of Tilburg, the Netherlands;
Bruce L. Reynolds, University of Virginia, USA;
Roger Spear, Open University, UK;
Michael E. Sykuta, University of Missouri, USA;
Angelo Zago, University of Verona, Italy;
Kim Zeuli, University of Wisconsin, USA.

Thanks are forwarded to John Bird, University of California Berkeley, who has corrected the language of the contributions.

The editors acknowledge, without implication, the funding given by the NORMA OG FRODE S. JACOBSENS FOND. Without its generous support, this book would not have been produced.

Berkeley and Aarhus in May 2006

Kostas Karantininis   Jerker Nilsson

Research Professor, Royal Veterinary   Professor of Cooperative Business,
  and Agricultural University,   Swedish University of Agricultural
  Copenhagen, Denmark   Sciences, Uppsala, Sweden
Visiting Scholar, University of   Visiting Professor, University of
  California, Berkeley, USA   Aarhus, Aarhus, Denmark

CHAPTER 1

COOPERATIVES: HIERARCHIES OR HYBRIDS?

CLAUDE MÉNARD[*]

Centre ATOM, University of Paris (Panthéon-Sorbonne), France

Abstract. Recent developments in organization theory about arrangements that are neither markets nor hierarchies provide an opportunity to reconsider the nature of cooperatives and their fundamental characteristics. The concept of "hybrids" developed by transaction cost economics to encapsulate the properties of these arrangements may be particularly relevant in that it provides a theoretical framework in which to embed cooperatives among other modes of governance. This paper goes in that direction and proposes a characterisation of different regimes among cooperatives, establishing a typology grounded in theory. An important result of this approach is that it challenges standard competition policies towards cooperatives.

1. INTRODUCTION

The importance of cooperatives as a mode of organization cannot be overestimated. In the European Union (as it was in 2000) they represented over 130,000 firms, with more that 2,500,000 employees and 85,000,000 members.[1] They often have a very significant market share, particularly in the agrifood sector (from 30% in France to 83% in the Netherlands), in banks and credit unions (from 25% in the Netherlands to 35% in Finland), and in retailing activities (over 25 millions members in 1996).[2]

Of course, economists have long been aware of that importance. There is substantial literature on cooperatives, and significant contributions have been published recently about changes in their status and the challenges that these changes represent (Cook, 1995). However, and this is somehow paradoxical, there is not much about the nature of cooperatives as modes of organization. In the standard economic literature they tend to be considered as relatively strange animals, in that they depend on an allocation of property rights that do not fit well within the traditional dichotomy between markets (with autonomous and distinct property rights of parties involved in exchange) and firms (with property rights unified within a legally well defined structure). Clearly, cooperatives do not fit well within this framework.[3]

The emergence in the late 1980s and the 1990s of a substantial body of research on organizational arrangements that are neither markets nor hierarchies may provide an opportunity to reconsider the nature of cooperatives and to shed light on some of their major characteristics. It may also help revisiting public policies, particularly

1

K. Karantininis & J. Nilsson (eds.), Vertical Markets and Cooperative Hierarchies, 1–17.
© 2007 *Springer.*

competition policies, in order to reconsider approaches that do not capture the essence of cooperatives, establishing policies that either park cooperatives in a special (favored) status, or want to put them in the same basket as fully integrated firms. Recent debates about the legal status of cooperatives in the European Union illustrate.

The concept of "hybrids" has been proposed, particularly by economists grounding their analyses in transaction costs theory, to encapsulate properties of the family of arrangements that have characteristics significantly distinct from those underlying market exchanges while they also differ substantially from those presiding at the organization of transactions within integrated firms. Therefore, a question naturally comes to mind: would this concept be appropriate for characterizing cooperatives?

In what follows, I explore this question. Section 2 introduces very briefly the theoretical framework underlying the concept of "hybrid" in a transaction cost perspective. Section 3 examines what differentiates hybrid arrangements from integrated firms. Section 4 discusses if these traits suit some fundamental properties observed in cooperatives. Section 5 develops arguments as to why this characterization matters and may challenge existing public policies. Section 6 concludes with a call for more research in this direction.

2. ANALYTICAL FRAMEWORK: A SHORT REMINDER

The observation that there exist ways for organizing transactions among economic units that maintain distinct property rights while they share a significant subset of their rights of decision is not new. Without going back to the "industrial district" identified by Marshall (1920), franchising began to attract some attention in the late 1970s (Rubin, 1978; see also Brickley and Dark, 1987). However, it was in the second half of the 1980s and the 1990s that a growing literature, initially based in managerial sciences and sociology, focused on networks and similar modes of arrangements (Thorelli, 1985; for a pioneering survey, see Grandori and Soda, 1995). In my view, the introduction of the concept of "hybrid" by Williamson in 1991 (1996, Ch. 4)[4] represents a major step forward in that it embedded the large set of empirical observations on different arrangements in a theoretical framework that provided an explanation to their existence and gave coherence to their characteristics.

The model Williamson proposed and that I summarize here with some minor changes is based on transaction cost economics, which lies at the core of new institutional economics. A preliminary question that is often raised with that approach and which deserves attention is: Why attach so much importance to transactions? Why use transaction costs as a point of entry for analyzing organizations? Does it mean neglecting, even abandoning the crucial concept of costs of production, thus turning away from the structuring role that technology often plays? Coase (1998) provides an answer, in my view a very convincing one, to this legitimate question. Transactions matter because their organization under different types of arrangements and under the umbrella of institutions that make them more or less easily happen determines the capacity of economic activities to develop and take advantage of the division of labor and of specialization. In that sense, the choice of a mode of organization for arranging transactions, which is the transfer of rights among parties to an activity of production or exchange, is crucial. And costs that result from this choice largely establish, beside the technological factors, how these activities will be structured and, therefore, the turf on which production (and its costs) develops.

As is now well known, Williamson went a step further in the direction opened by Coase, with a contribution that made the transaction cost approach operational. His powerful intuition, which was later developed in a heuristic model (Williamson, 1985, ch. 4; Riordan and Williamson, 1985), is that a few characteristics or "attributes" of transactions, namely their frequency (F), the uncertainty (U) surrounding their arrangement, and the specific investments (AS) they require, determine their costs. This relationship between transaction costs and the attributes of transactions can be expressed functionally as:

$$TC = f (F, U, AS)$$
$$- \quad + \quad +$$

with signs indicating the direction in which transaction costs vary when the related variable increases. The next step in building the model consists of linking the choice of a mode of governance (GS) to these costs and, therefore, implicitly to the attributes of the transactions at stake. We can summarize these links in Figure 1:

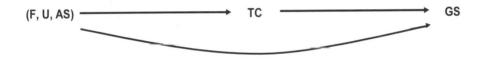

Figure 1. Relationship between characteristic, costs, and governance of transactions

Under some simplifying assumptions, particularly the idea that in choosing a mode of governance, agents intend to minimize their costs, Williamson expressed these relationships in what is often called the heuristic model, explaining the trade-off between organizing a transaction within the firm ("hierarchy") and relying on markets for doing so.

A few years later (Williamson, 1991 [1996, ch. 4]), he extended the model in order to encapsulate organizational arrangements that were neither hierarchies nor markets, and labeled them "hybrids". Taking the specificity of assets (or investment) as the key variable that explains the choice among alternative modes of organization (a proposition already substantiated by several econometric tests: see a review in Joskow, 1988), he developed an analysis in which increasing costs of governance for market transactions leaves the way to interfirm agreements before ending up in vertical integration when mutual dependence becomes so strong that it puts these agreements at too high a risk.[5] Since the model is now well known, I do not reiterate its details here. I stick to its geometric representation, summarized in Figure 2, in which the trade-off between the three alternative modes of organization is indicated in bold lines, with the lower envelope showing the most adapted mode for the corresponding level of investments specific to the transaction(s) at stake.

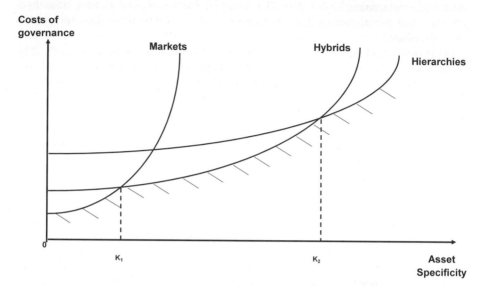

Figure 2. Modes of governance. Source: adapted from Williamson, 1996, p. 108

Based on propositions derived from this model, hundreds of tests have been published, most of them supporting the predictions made by the theory (for surveys and discussions, see Joskow, 2005, and Klein, 2005). However, in order to go further and to provide a full explanation of why one mode of organization is preferred over another for certain transactions,[6] it is necessary to make one more step and explore the internal characteristics of these different modes. In other terms, their respective advantages (and costs) must be assessed. From a technical point of view, this comparative approach raises important difficulties (Gibbons, 2003; Joskow, 2005). One condition it must fulfill is the careful examination of the properties of each mode along lines that allows comparisons. Initial progress in that respect focused on firms (see Ménard, 2005a). More recent research have contributed to a better knowledge of some basic properties of hybrid arrangements. In order to discuss whether cooperatives belong to that mode of organization or not, I now turn to a review of some of these distinct properties.

3. WHAT DIFFERENTIATES HYBRIDS FROM HIERARCHIES?[7]

At first sight, the arrangements that have been identified as "hybrids" in the literature form a strange collection. They extend from subcontracting to franchise systems, collective trademarks, partnerships, alliances, and so forth. The vocabulary itself tends to reflect this uncertain state of affairs: beside hybrids, which is the term I use in what follows because it refers to a well defined theoretical framework (see above), we find more descriptive expressions such as "symbiotic forms", "clusters", "supply chain", "networks". However, notwithstanding the apparent heterogeneity of this "bestiary", the combination of a transaction cost perspective with what we have learned from the empirical literature delineates some fundamental properties.

The central characteristic of hybrids is that they maintain distinct and autonomous property rights and their associated decision rights on most assets, which makes them different from integrated firms; however, they simultaneously involve sharing some strategic resources, which requires a tight coordination that goes far beyond what the price system can provide and thus makes them distinct from pure market arrangements. The former aspect translates into the legal status of hybrids: parties to these arrangements hold decision rights in last resort. The later aspect translates into common governance for a more or less significant segment of activities of the partners involved: hybrids look like a coalition of interests. This mix of autonomy and interdependence defines the three pillars of hybrids: they pool resources, they coordinate through contracts that provide a framework, and they combine competition with cooperation. Let me briefly review these three complementary dimensions.

Three complementary dimensions

Whatever the form hybrid arrangements take, they implement forms of interdependence through joint investments. Keep in mind the example of franchising. Hybrids develop because markets are perceived as unable to adequately bundle the relevant resources and capabilities while integration would reduce flexibility and weaken incentives. Looking for rents provides the foundation for accepting the mutual dependence created through investments specific to the relationship, whether these specific assets consist of equipment, human capabilities, or a brand name. However, this pooling of resources is restricted to specific transactions and concerns only some of the assets owned by the parties. Several consequences and problems follow. First, choosing partners is a key issue. Hybrids are selective, not open systems: partners' identity matters. Second, the complexity of decomposing tasks among partners and of coordinating across organizational boundaries requires joint planning and governance for monitoring the agreement. Third, the existence of an adequate information system among parties accepting to pool part of their resources is central to the survival of hybrids.[8] However, the inevitable asymmetries among partners maintaining autonomous rights and the risks of capture of some strategic information periodically threaten the continuity of the relationship.

To summarize, pooling resources in hybrids requires that partners accept losing part of the autonomy they would have in a market relationship without benefiting from the capacity to control that a hierarchy could provide. Hence a first problem for hybrids is: how can they secure the coordination of interdependent investments without losing the advantages of decentralized decisions?

This problem is partially solved through contracts. Relational contracting provides a framework for creating "transactional reciprocity". The resulting cooperation carries advantages but entails risks. Advantages can be expected from extended market shares, transfer of competencies, and sharing scarce resources (for example, financial ones). However, contracts are incomplete and subject to unforeseeable revisions since they contribute to organize transactions involving specific investments that are often plagued by uncertainties (for example, joint investments in R&D projects). We have a typical transaction cost problem here. Contrary to what agency theory predicts, the features of contracts are not continuously refined in order to obtain an "optimal contract" that would encapsulate all required adaptation. As shown by recent studies on franchising (Lafontaine and Shaw, 1999), contracts are not tailored to suit the exact characteristics of transactions at stake. Plainly, this would be too costly and the source of too many rigidities. Rather, contracts provide a relatively simple and uniform framework. Hence, a second problem that is recurring among hybrids: what governance to adopt for securing contracts against opportunistic behaviors while minimizing costly or even impossible renegotiations?

This difficulty is amplified by the importance of competitive pressures, which comes from two sources. First, partners in hybrid agreements often compete against each other on segments of their activities. This can take different forms. The agreement can have provisions that recurrently make partners competing, as in subcontracting. Notwithstanding restrictions (geographical, etc.), hybrids may have overlapping strategies, for example, they may target customers from the same subset. Parties may also cooperate on some activities, such as joint R&D projects, and compete on others. Second, hybrids usually compete with other modes of organization, including other hybrids. The standard neoclassical explanation of hybrids as rent seekers shows its limits here. Hybrids tend to develop in highly competitive markets in which pooling resources is viewed as a way to deal with significant uncertainties and survive. However, this competitive environment may have a highly negative side effect for hybrids: if joint investments required in an arrangement are moderately specific, partners may be tempted to switch among arrangements, making them highly unstable. Again, the implementation of an internal mode of regulation and control is a key issue. Hence a third problem for hybrids is: what mechanism can be designed for efficiently disciplining partners and solving conflicts while preventing free-riding?

These three dimensions clearly suggest that there are important regularities underlying the apparent heterogeneity of hybrids. These regularities are rooted in the way partners are dealing with the mutual dependence created by the specificity of some of their investments; by the need to guarantee some continuity in their relationship and, therefore, the frequency of transactions at stake; and by the importance of containing contractual hazards and reducing uncertainties. They do so with the mix of competition and cooperation that characterizes and plagues hybrids. Because they cannot rely on prices or on hierarchy to discipline themselves, partners need specific devices for dealing with the problems identified above. What are these mechanisms and what is the logic behind the choice of specific ones?

Variety in governance

Hybrid arrangements develop when specific investments can be spread over partners without losing the advantages of autonomous decisions, while uncertainties are consequential enough to make pooling an advantageous alternative to markets. However, the combination of specific assets and consequential uncertainties generates risks of opportunistic behavior and miscoordination. If only one aspect (or attribute) is present, the governance leans towards contract-based arrangements, close to a market form. When the two attributes combine, the governance becomes much more authoritarian. Therefore, I submit that *it is the combination of opportunism, or the risk of opportunism, and of miscoordination, or the risk of miscoordination, that determines the governance characterizing hybrids.* Let me develop briefly before applying this proposition to the analysis of cooperatives.

One way to deal with the three problems identified in the previous subsection is to rely heavily on contracts. A well known mechanism for disciplining partners while facilitating coordination is the contractual embedment of restrictive provisions. Restrictions delineate the domain of action of partners, limiting their autonomy and identifying areas in which collective decisions must prevail. There is an abundance of literature on vertical restrictions, much less on horizontal ones. The emphasis is usually on their consequences on prices and how it can distort competition. This interpretation misses what is often the main goal of these provisions – to restrict free-riding while facilitating coordination. This point was made 20 years ago by Williamson (1985, pp. 183–189) on the Schwinn case. It has been largely substantiated, for example by numerous studies on supply chain systems, particularly in the agrifood sector in which traceability and quality control have became major issues (Ménard and Valceschini, 2005). This role of contractual restrictions as an efficient tool of governance remains underexplored. However, we already know enough to be aware of the limits of contracts in that respect. First, restrictive provisions often produce conflicts among parties, particularly with respect to their interpretation. Second, they generate suspicion among competition authorities who see them as sources of collusion. Third, their allocation effects are difficult to evaluate and monitor, so partners tend to rely on other mechanisms.

The tension between contractual hazards and the expected gains from investments in interdependent assets provides strong incentives to turn to more powerful modes of coordination than market-based contracts. This is what our theoretical framework predicts. However, we have to go a step further and check if our model can help understanding the specific forms this coordination takes. Using several empirical studies, including some I have been associated with, I have submitted in several papers (Ménard, 1996; 1997 [2005]; 2004) that hybrid organizations tend to produce specific modes of internal governance, which I have suggested be called "authorities" to emphasize their difference from "hierarchies". These devices provide the cornerstone in the architecture of hybrids. Their main characteristic is the pairing of the autonomy of partners with the transfer of subclasses of decisions to a distinct entity in charge of coordinating their actions. The presence of hierarchical elements in contractual agreements has been noted before (Stinchcombe 1990, chap. 6). However, what I want to emphasize here is the existence of specific organizational devices intentionally designed by partners for monitoring their network and for controlling their actions. The authority transferred to these devices involves intentionality and mutuality, maintaining some symmetry among participants.

Empirical studies suggest that the more or less centralized power of these authorities depends on the degree of mutual dependence among partners and on the complexity and turbulence of the environment in which a hybrid monitors transactions. Let me illustrate with two polar cases. Raynaud [1997] studied a group of millers who created a brand name for high-quality bread in France. Members of this arrangement use only selected wheat from which they produce first rank flour that they dispatch to franchised bakers that agree to strict rules. However, there are risks of opportunistic behavior among partners. First, they may be tempted to free-ride in delivering lower quality flour. Second, some millers are competing: they supply the same geographical area and have a strong incentive to attract as their customers as many bakers as possible. In order to monitor this arrangement, complex internal governance has been implemented. Requirements regarding the inputs, quality control, and the monitoring of contracts are delegated to an autonomous entity, created by the millers and that owns the brand name. The millers have also created an internal "court", with delegates operating as private judges for solving conflicts. In this stylized case, the hybrid arrangement coordinates partners who are on a par. Sauvée [2002] has exhibited a very different model with a significant asymmetry among partners. In the case he studied, a private firm has developed a brand name of canned vegetables of high quality. Inputs are provided by farmers under contracts that contain detailed requirements and provisions. So far, this is quite standard. The interesting point is that because of its success the firm was rapidly confronted to the high transaction costs of monitoring thousands of contracts and farmers. In order to solve this problem, a complex organization was implemented, with growers grouped in several distinct arrangements delegating the negotiation of contracts and the numerous adjustments they require to a joint committee. Surprisingly, this powerful committee was formerly dominated by the growers with four delegates, while the firm has two representatives. It plays a key role, filling the blanks in the contracts, organizing transactions, and negotiating the distribution of quasi-rents.

Numerous variations of such arrangements could be described. They all substantiate the idea that hybrid organizations have architecture of their own, distinct from markets or hierarchies. At one end of the spectrum, close to markets, hybrids rely on trust. Decisions are decentralized and a loose coordination operates through mutual "influence" and reciprocity. The resulting relationship is not purely informal: it tends to be highly codified in order to guarantee continuity in the transactions and is often in the hands of key players. Palay (1985) has provided a pioneering study in that respect, showing the role of dedicated managers in charge of monitoring agreements among partners in the rail freight sector. At the other end of the spectrum, some hybrids are close to a hierarchy. Parties keep legally distinct property rights and may even compete on segments of their activities. However, a significant domain of decisions is coordinated through a quasi autonomous entity, which operates as a private bureau with attributes of a hierarchy. Joint ventures provide an illustration. Between these polar cases, other forms of "authority" develop. "Relational networks" have been extensively analyzed by sociologists and scholars in organization theory. Because of the significance of contractual hazards they confront, these arrangements need tighter coordination and control than trust, with formal rules and conventions framing the relationships among partners. Examples have been studied by Greif (1993) and Powell (1996), among others. When uncertainty is even more significant and interdependent assets more important, more constraining structures of governance develop, often under the leadership of one party. The pioneering study of Eccles (1981) on the construction industry provides a good illustration, with one firm establishing its authority either because it holds specific competences or because it occupies a key position in the sequence of transactions.

To summarize, hybrid arrangements tend to develop specific modes of governance with significant variances in the degree of control over partners, depending on the degree of uncertainty and the nature and degree of specific investments required by the transactions at stake. If we come back to Figure 1, these forms correspond to those associated to values between K_1 and K_2, with an increasing intensity in the centralization of their governance.

4. CAN COOPERATIVES BE UNDERSTOOD AS HYBRID FORMS?

I now turn to a most difficult question: is this analysis relevant to better understand cooperatives? The question is challenging for at least two reasons. First, there is so much diversity among cooperatives that finding a unified theoretical framework for explaining this diversity and encapsulating the various properties of the arrangements involved is not an easy task. Second, and above all, I am not at all a specialist on cooperatives. In what follows, I rely heavily on contributions from colleagues who are much more knowledgeable than I am, particularly Cook (1995), Cook, Chaddad and Iliopoulos (n.d.), Hendrikse and Veerman (2001), Hendrikse and Bijman (2002), as well as on discussions with participants at the Chania Conference.[9] Therefore, the exploration proposed in this section is very tentative.

In order to discuss the question of whether or not cooperatives are hybrids, I refer to the characteristics identified above.[10] Let us start with the central issue of the status of property rights and their relationship to decision rights. In that respect, there is a wide variety of arrangements among cooperatives. At one end of the spectrum, close to market relationships, we have cooperatives in which property rights and decision rights are separated. In this case, cooperators formerly hold "shares" in a cooperative and receive benefits according to its performance. They behave very much like small shareholders operating through financial markets, with very little control over the governance of the cooperative. Retailing and marketing cooperatives are often of that type. They process and sell products through market-type relationships; those buyers who are cooperators have very little or no control over the governance. Hence, decision rights are largely isolated from property rights: one can consider that cooperators in such cases are related to the cooperative through quasi-market forms of contracts. At the other end of the spectrum, we have cooperatives owned and governed by their shareholders, as is often the case with cooperatives grouping producers (or growers in agriculture). This type of arrangement tends to coordinate tightly the activities of its members, deciding the variety of goods or services, fixing quantities to be produced, negotiating with potential buyers, etc. The example of *Savéol,* which provides an umbrella to three cooperatives and dominates the market for fresh tomatoes in France, is a case in point (Sauvée, 1997; Ménard and Valceschini, 2005). Cooperatives with close membership or that are quasi-integrated fall into this category. We are almost in the case of classical hierarchies (Bonus, 1986). Between these polar cases, we find a large number of cooperatives, particularly the traditional, multipurpose cooperatives that coordinate a network of partners, most of them being cooperatives themselves that maintain the autonomy of their property and decision rights. For example, *Cana,* a French cooperative that operates in the poultry sector, covers a network of cooperative-partners from growers to chicks and food suppliers as well as slaughterhouses. Obviously the internal mode of governance of these widely distinct arrangements varies significantly, depending on closeness between the allocation of property rights and the allocation of decision rights. However, almost all cooperatives share something that makes them different from integrated firms as well as from pure market relationships: the one-person, one-vote rule, whatever the size of one's contribution.[11] This is a characteristic they share with many hybrid arrangements, in which decision-making rights are allocated on a par. (See the example of the millers in Section 3.)

Let us now turn to the three dimensions that I have identified as pillars of hybrid arrangements, in order to exhibit what properties are shared or not by cooperatives. (1) *Pooling resources.* This is surely an aspect which is one of the fundamental motivations for organizing cooperatives. However, it exists with very variable intensity, so that mutually dependent investments are more or less consequential. What theory predicts in these circumstances is that the degree and importance of specific assets shared by cooperators should determine the intensity in selectivity of members as well as the intensity in control over their activities. (2) *The significance of contracts* among cooperators (to the exclusion of contracts with outside partners). Again, the intensity of contracting varies widely according to the type of cooperatives. Contracts tend to be particularly detailed, with important provisions and sanction clauses in cooperatives that need to tightly coordinate the actions of their members and/or that must strictly control quality, as with growers or dairy milk cooperatives. They are much less specific and can even be almost pure formalities when it comes to agreements among members with no idiosyncratic investments in the cooperative, as with retailing and marketing cooperatives. Again, our theoretical framework allows making predictions about the characteristics of contracts depending on the specificity of assets that cooperators are pooling; for example, duration of contracts should be much shorter in the later case while in the former case they are either long term, or short term and automatically renewable. (3) *Competition conditions.* They also change significantly according to the type of cooperatives.

The need to tightly control free-riding, when specific assets are at stake, and to restrain the autonomy of decisions of partners when the reputation of the whole depends on respect for requirements by each party to the agreement, seriously reduces competition among members. In these situations, tight coordination through formal governance prevails, while competition among members is much more frequent in market-oriented cooperatives that monitor weakly specific assets, that is, assets easily redeployable from one type of activity to another.

Based on these casual evidences that need to be substantiated and tested by the specialists in the field, our model suggests the following application of the arrangements identified in Figure 2 to various types of cooperatives (See Figure 3).

If we take the degree of specificity of investments made by cooperators in their cooperative as a key variable (uncertainty should be added in a more developed model), transaction cost theory predicts that costs of governance tend to increase with the increase in asset specificity, but at a different rate according to the organizational arrangement, with the costs of using markets increasing more rapidly than hybrids which also increases more rapidly than hierarchies when investments connected directly to the relationship become significantly more idiosyncratic. When it comes to cooperatives what this means is that the more easily redeployable assets are held by cooperators in their cooperative, and the closer we are to market arrangements, as with retailing or marketing cooperatives. Symmetrically, the more specific to the transactions organized by a cooperative are the assets detained by cooperators, the tighter the coordination should be, bringing into the arrangement a form of governance that is very close to full integration. Different modes of organizing cooperatives fall in between, as suggested by Figure 3. And there are cases when investments are so specific to the transactions monitored by the cooperative that it is structured and governed very much like a classic integrated firm.

This suggested typology obviously needs to be discussed and tested. The emphasis on the degree in the specificity of investments for determining the mode of hybrid governance must be substantiated by theoretical arguments and must be assessed through empirical studies. Moreover, uncertainty is certainly another key variable in organizing transactions that should be introduced in the model. The advantage of focusing on the variable "specific investments" is that it puts at the forefront of the analysis of cooperatives the interdependence between the degree of selectivity in membership and the intensity required in the control of decision rights on one hand, and the importance of the degree of coordination needed on the other hand, in order to determine the mode of governance that can efficiently monitor the type of transactions at stake. More importantly, it provides a theoretical framework for examining and classifying cooperatives, which allows predictions that can be tested and challenged.

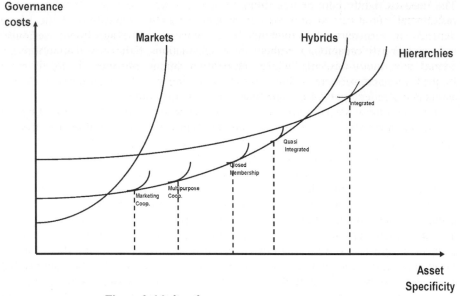

Figure 3. *Modes of governance among cooperatives*

5. WHY DOES IT MATTER?

It is legitimate to question why the development of this approach to cooperatives should matter. My answer is twofold: it might be highly relevant, for positive as well as for normative reasons. I am mostly emphasizing the second aspect here.

On the positive side, the examination within a well defined theoretical framework of factors that determine the mode of governance of cooperatives should help understanding better their differentiated characteristics and properties. More precisely, finding a model that allows characterizing the nature and variety of the different modes of organization that exist among cooperatives should provide important insights for understanding why one form emerges and predominates for certain types of activities. The transaction cost approach developed in the previous sections might shed light on two important issues: What are the attributes of transactions a cooperative wants to organize that can explain why a specific arrangement fits these attributes better than another one? And what makes organizing transactions among cooperators more adequate, and therefore more successful, than using market relationships or integrating within a unified firm?

Referring to adequate concepts for answering these questions may also have important consequences in a normative perspective. If there is economic explanation, grounded in solid theory, why do so many cooperatives have the characteristics of hybrids, and why among the variety of hybrid arrangements do cooperatives adopt specific forms and choose different modes of governance? The answers may provide indications about what type of cooperative should be chosen for organizing specific types of transactions.

Adequate answers to the questions raised above also involve policy issues. If a substantial subset of cooperatives are hybrid arrangements that exist because they provide the most relevant arrangement for the type of transactions they are organizing, and if this capacity to arrange these transactions efficiently depends, under identifiable conditions, on the implementation of mechanisms of coordination, control, and discipline over the members involved, the resulting governance may challenge standard competition policies. This brings into the picture the ongoing debate about the status of cooperatives that should prevail in the European Union.[12]

Standard competition policies are based on a theory of competition grounded in the dualism between markets and firms ("hierarchies"). In principle, firms are allowed to freely develop their activities so long as they conform to some "rules of the game", mainly: (i) they respect certain principles in their interactions, a major principle being that they do not build coalitions (rule #1); and (ii) their activities do not threaten "normal" market structures, that is, structures that guarantee the continuity of competition. Therefore, developing strategies that generate market power over a certain threshold is prohibited (rule #2). Confronted with these benchmarks, most cooperatives (with the possible exception of retailing cooperatives) represent a challenge to the two basic rules, particularly rule #1. Indeed, they clearly form a coalition of legally autonomous actors. And they often do so in order to capture part of the market. An important consequence, now argued in many instances of the European Union, is that with respect to the theory in which competition policies are grounded, cooperatives are anomalies tolerated for political reasons, but that sound economic policies should prohibit.

This way of positing the problem tends to ignore the very reason why there exist non-standard arrangements like cooperatives and, more generally, hybrid forms. In Sections 2 and 3, I have explained why, in a transaction costs perspective, modes of organizing transactions legitimately develop that are based on neither market relationships nor hierarchy, and why these modes tend to adopt inter-firms or inter-units coordination that impose some discipline and constraints on parties to the agreement. What happens when competition policies are implemented that ignore the 'raison d'être' of these non-standard arrangements? What are the consequences of ignoring the logic that explains hybrids in terms of minimization of transaction costs? Let me briefly discuss the issue through two stylized examples.[13]

First, what happens if arrangements of the hybrid types are prohibited, for example, to the motive that they represent a coalition of independent actors? If we refer to Figure 2, this means suppressing hybrids, so that the lower envelope of the curve corresponding to the degree of specific investments in the domain $[K_1, K_2]$ is eliminated. The result is that transactions are organized either under market arrangements (when assets have a specificity lower than K_1) or within integrated firms (when specificity of assets involved is higher than K_1). This means that costs of governance for the entire domain defined by $[K_1, K_2]$ are higher than they would have been if hybrids would have been allowed. Higher social costs result.

A second stylized example corresponds to a situation in which competition authorities (or other public entities) who do not properly understand the role of hybrids in a competitive environment would impose specific restrictions on their activities (that is, restrictions that are not imposed on market transactions nor on transactions that are organized by a firm, for example, regarding advertising). Such constraints translate into higher costs of governance for hybrids, which shifts their representative curve upwards. As a result, there may be more room for market transactions on the left side (K_1 is moved slightly to the right), and there is much more room for transactions organized under the umbrella of integrated firms (K_2 is moved to the left). The consequence is that an entire area in which transactions could have been advantageously arranged by hybrids are now transferred to less efficient modes of organizations. Again, social costs result.

To summarize, the ignorance of the specific nature of cooperatives or, more generally, of hybrid arrangements have important consequences that are misunderstood and need further exploration. This is a typical example of how the institutional environment may have a substantial impact on what modes of organization are chosen and on the consequences of these choices on economic efficiency and social welfare.

6. CONCLUSION

This paper has explored some properties of cooperatives in the light shed by a new institutional approach, with the conceptual apparatus of transaction costs at the core. There are three main messages from this very preliminary examination.

First, we need a theoretical framework for understanding much better the nature of cooperatives. The standard neo-classical approach that captures the essence of organizations through a production function performs very poorly in that respect. Similarly, the principal-agent approach does not explain why cooperatives exist and the specific forms they adopt. On the other hand, recent developments in transaction costs economics suggest very fruitful perspectives and provide powerful tools for going further in that direction.

Second, there are strong incentives for studying more carefully the observable characteristics of cooperatives in terms of modes of governance. On the positive side, it may help us understand why and when certain modes are preferred to others. On the normative side, it may suggest ways of determining which forms should be chosen, or should be modified in what direction, in order to fit with the properties of transactions that need to be organized.

Third, the analysis developed above suggests that there is an urgent need for policy makers and for competition authorities to introduce transaction costs issues in their reasoning. It is no more possible to build policies and regulation based on the simplistic trade-off between markets and integrated firms. And using in a rather scholastic way provisions of political arrangements, like article 81 of the Rome Treaty, to justify derogations in favor of hybrids and related arrangements cannot be considered satisfying anymore. Indeed, recent theoretical developments suggest that hybrids and similar arrangements are not "derogatory" – they are at the very heart of a dynamic market economy. In that respect, the theoretical and political status of cooperatives should be reexamined in a much more positive perspective.

NOTES

* I would like to thank Michael Cook, George Hendrikse, Kostas Karantininis, Jerker Nilsson, and participants to the Chania Conference on "Vertical Markets and Cooperative Hierarchies: The Role of Cooperatives in the International Agri-Food Industry" for the incentives they provided, the information they delivered, and the comments they shared with me. I alone remain responsible for errors and/or misleading ideas.

1 These data are from 1996 and have been published in "Statistics and Information on European Cooperatives." International Cooperative Alliance, Geneva, December 1998.

2 Rapport Annuel du Conseil Supérieur de la Coopération, Paris, 2000, pp. 120–121

3 This discrepancy was already noted by Alchian and Demsetz (1972) and is also discussed by Hansmann (1988). However, Cook et al. (n.d.) note that there is an increasing interest for organizational issues in the study of cooperatives in the post-1990 period (see their observation 4, p. 23).

4 Actually the notion of hybrid was already at work in Williamson (1985) but was considered a transitory and relatively unstable mode of organization. For an analysis of Williamson's evolution on this, see Ménard (2005c).

5 Contractual hazards increase when specific investments create mutual dependence because of an underlying assumption (explicitly made): agents tend to behave opportunistically and to take advantage of this dependence.

6 That is, how is it that hybrids or integrated firms can monitor contractual hazards better than markets when there are more specific investments and/or more uncertainty?

7 This section draws from Ménard (2004).

8 Hybrids have even been qualified as "*a cooperative game with partner-specific communication*" (Grandori and Soda [1995] p. 185).

9 "Vertical Markets and Cooperative Hierarchies", Chania (Crete), September 3–7, 2004. Several contributions to this conference are included in this book. Cook et al. (n.d.) review several papers, explicitly focusing on three alternative interpretations of cooperatives, as firms, as coalitions, and as a nexus of contracts. Several aspects of their analysis overlap with mine, although there are also significant differences.

10 In looking at cooperatives as hybrids, I adopt a distinctly different view from Bonus (1986), who considered cooperatives as pure business enterprises, as well as from Staatz (1989), who looked at cooperatives from a pure agency perspective.

11 There are exceptions to this general rule, which is one of the reasons why the status of cooperatives as distinct from firms is challenged. For an analysis of these changes in ownership status, see Hendrikse and Veerman (2001).

12 The issue is also debated in the U.S., although to my knowledge the Capper-Volstead Act has not really been challenged so far.

13 The following analysis is developed extensively in Ménard (2005b), with specific examples provided by recent decisions of competition authorities.

REFERENCES

Alchian, A.A. and H. Demsetz. 1972. "Production, Information Costs and Economic Organization." *American Economic Review* 62(5):777–795.

Bonus, H. 1986. "The Cooperative Association as a Business Enterprise: a Study in the Economics of Transactions." *Journal of Institutional and Theoretical Economics* 142(3):310–399.

Brickley, J. A. and F. H. Dark. 1987. "The Choice of Organizational Form: the Case of Franchising." *Journal of Financial Economics* 18(2):401–420.

Coase, R. H. 1998. "New Institutional Economics." *American Economic Review* 88(2):72–74.

Cook, M.L. 1995. "The Future of US Agricultural Cooperatives: A Neo-institutional Approach." *American Journal of Agricultural Economics* 77:1153–1159.

___. and C. Iliopoulos. 2000. "Ill-defined Property Rights in Collective Action: The Case of US Agricultural Cooperatives." In C. Ménard, ed. *Institutions, Contracts and Organizations. Perspectives from New Institutional Economics.* Cheltenham: E. Elgar, pp. 335–348.

___., F. R. Chaddad, and C. Iliopoulos. n.d. "Advances in Cooperative Theory since 1990: A Review of Agricultural Economics Literature". Working Paper, University of Missouri-Columbia.

Eccles, R. 1981. "The Quasifirm in the Construction Industry." *Journal of Economic Behavior and Organization* 2(4):335–357.

Gibbons, R. 2003. "Team Theory, Garbage Cans and Real Organizations: Some History and Prospects of Economic Research on Decision-making in Organizations." *Industrial and Corporate Change* 12(4):753–797.

Grandori, A. and G. Soda. 1995. "Inter-firm Networks: Antecedents, Mechanisms and Forms." *Organization Studies* 16(2):183–214.

Greif, A. 1993."Contract Enforceability and Economic Institutions In Early Trade: The Maghribi Traders." *American Economic Review* 83(3):525–547.

Hansmann, H. 1988. "The Ownership of the Firm." *Journal of Law, Economics and Organization* 4(2) :267–304.

Hendrikse, G.W.J. and C.P. Veerman. 2001. "Marketing Cooperatives: An Incomplete Contract Perspective." *Journal of Agricultural Economics* 52(1):53–64.

___. and W.J.J. Bijman. 2002. "Ownership Structure in Agrifood Chains: The Marketing Cooperative." *American Journal of Agricultural Economics* 84(1):104–119.

Joskow, P. 1988. "Asset Specificity and the Structure of Vertical Relationships." *Journal of Law, Economics and Organization* 4(1):95–117.

___. 2005. "Vertical Integration." In C. Ménard and M. Shirley, eds. *Handbook of New Institutional Analysis.* Springer, pp. 319–348.

Klein, P. 2005. "The Make-or-Buy Decisions. Lessons from Empirical Studies." In C. Ménard and M. Shirley, eds. *Handbook of New Institutional Analysis.* Springer, pp. 435–464.

Lafontaine, Francine and Kathrin Shaw (1999) "The Dynamics of Franchise Contracting: Evidence from Panel Data." *Journal of Political Economy.* 107:1041–1080.

Marshall, A. 1920. *Principles of Economics.* 8th ed. London: MacMillan. Reprint 1969

Ménard, C. 1996. "On Clusters, Hybrids and other Strange Forms. The Case of the French Poultry Industry." *Journal of Institutional and Theoretical Economics* 152(1):154–183.

___. 2004. "The Economics of Hybrid Organizations." *Journal of Institutional and Theoretical Economics* 160(3):345–376.

___. 2005a "A New Institutional Approach to Organization." In C. Ménard and M. Shirley, eds. *Handbook of New Institutional Analysis.* Springer, pp. 281–318.

___. 2005b. "The Inadequacy of Competition Policies: A New Institutional Approach." In M. Oppenheimer and N. Mercuro, eds. *Law and Economics: Alternative Economic Approaches to Legal and Regulatory Issues.* New York: M.E. Sharpe, pp. 27–54.

___. 2005c. "Oliver Williamson and the Economics of Hybrid Organizations." in M. Augier, J. March and D. Teece (eds.), *Title not yet determined,* Oxford: Oxford University Press, in press.

___. 1997/2005. "Le Pilotage des Formes Organisationnelles Hybrides", *Revue Economique* 48(2):741–751. English translation: "The Governance of Hybrid Organizational Forms." In C. Ménard, ed. *The International Library of New Institutional Economics.* Cheltenham: Edward Elgar, vol. IV, pp. 105–113.

___. and M.M. Shirley. 2005. *Handbook of New Institutional Economics,* Berlin-Boston-Dordrecht-New York: Springer.

Ménard, C. and E. Valceschini. 2005. "Institutions for Governing Agriculture and Rural Areas." *European Review of Agricultural Economics,* in press.

Palay, T.M. 1985. "Avoiding Regulatory Constraints: Contracting Safeguards and the Role of Informal Agreements." *Journal of Law, Economics, and Organization* 1(1):155–175.

Powell, W. 1996. "Inter-organizational Collaboration in the Biotechnology Industry." *Journal of Institutional and Theoretical Economics* 152(1) :197–215.

Raynaud, E. 1997. Propriété et exploitation partagée d'une marque commerciale: aléas contractuels et ordre privé. PhD dissertation, Université de Paris (Panthéon-Sorbonne).

Riordan, M. and O. Williamson. 1985. "Asset Specificity and Economic Organization. "*International Journal of Industrial Organization* 3(4):365–378.

Rubin, P. H. 1978. "The Theory of the Firm and the Structure of the Franchise Contract." *Journal of Law and Economics* 21(1):223–234.

Sauvée, L. 1997. "Managing a Brand in the Tomato Sector: Authority and Enforcement Mechanisms in a Collective Organization." *Acta Horticulturae* 536:537–554

__. 2002. "Governance in Strategic Networks." Working Paper, ISAB: Beauvais.

Staatz, J. M. 1989. *Farmer Cooperative Theory: Recent Developments*. Washington DC: U.S. Department of Agriculture, ACS Agr. Coop. Service Research Rep. 84.

Stinchcombe, A. 1990. *Information and Organizations*. Berkeley: University of California Press.

Thorelli, H.B. 1986. "Networks: Between Markets and Hierarchies." *Strategic Management Journal* 7(1):37–51.

Williamson, O.E. 1991. [1996] "Comparative Economic Organization: The Analysis of Discrete Structural Alternatives." *Administrative Science Quarterly* 36(2):269–296. Reproduced in *The Mechanisms of Governance*. Oxford: Oxford University Press.

__. 1985. *The Economic Institutions of Capitalism*. New York: The Free Press-Macmillan.

CHAPTER 2

THE NETWORK FORM OF
THE COOPERATIVE ORGANIZATION

An Illustration with the Danish Pork Industry

KOSTAS KARANTININIS*

Institute of Food and Resource Economics (FØI),
The Royal Veterinary and Agricultural University (KVL), Copenhagen, Denmark

Abstract. Cooperative organizations may develop networks, in order to reduce transaction costs, to facilitate knowledge transfer and exchange of resources, and be competitive. The pork industry in Denmark evolved along a path of cooperation and networking. The evolution is path-dependent with roots in the Grundtvig and the *folkehøjskolen* movement in the late 1800s. Today, the Danish pork industry is characterized by three levels of networks, beyond the family farm: the primary cooperative, the federated structure and the policy network. All four levels are interlinked via a nexus of director interlocks.

1. INTRODUCTION

The cooperative form of business has been part of economic life for more than 150 years. Yet its growth and success is not monotonic through time, and it varies between countries and between sectors of the economy. The literature on this issue is extensive and parallels that of similar studies in the general economics and business literature, studying success or failure, and the "boom or bust" of cooperative development and other governance structures over time. Among the factors contributing to these developments usually cited are institutions, such as property rights and contract law, and public policy, along with general factors characterizing the overall business environment.[1]

Although the published work on cooperatives has closely followed the theoretical and methodological developments in the general economic doctrine, such as game theory, industrial organization, information economics, and transaction cost economics, it is lagging behind in what has become a vast and dynamic literature on networks. With few exceptions, the network aspect of cooperatives has not been given the attention that this business form deserves. In particular, the position of a cooperative in its overall business environment and the relations a cooperative

K. Karantininis & J. Nilsson (eds.), Vertical Markets and Cooperative Hierarchies, 19–34.
© 2007 *Springer.*

establishes with its membership and with other organizations has barely been theoretically examined.

Cooperatives do not operate in isolation or in a business vacuum. Like most firms in today's business environments they form relationships with other firms (cooperatives and investor-owned firms): partnerships, coalitions, strategic alliances, federated structures, and other, more complex forms. Cooperatives may participate in policy networks at local, regional, national and international levels.

In this essay, the Danish pork industry is used as an illustrative example. Denmark has a self-sufficiency rate of 490% in pork. It exports around 80% of its production and is the largest EU exporter of pig meat to non-EU countries, and the largest exporter of pig meat to Japan. How can the Danish pork industry achieve such a remarkable performance in spite of its relative cost disadvantages?

Several researchers point to the high degree of coordination within the Danish pork industry.[2] They emphasize the flexibility and adaptability of the system, and attribute this to the "integrative" and "cooperative" characteristics of the Danish pork industry. However, the Danish pork industry is neither the only industry that is highly integrated, nor is it the only one that has large segments organized as cooperatives. The Smithfield and Tyson company models in the USA are highly integrated systems in the pork industry – even more so than the Danish. Cooperatives dominate many other industries in several other countries (e.g. the Netherlands, France, and Ireland). Hence, neither of the two attributes (integration and cooperation) are answers to the question. What is unique about the organization of the Danish pork industry? On both theoretical and empirical grounds, the relevant questions concerns how the "system" coordinates.

The aim of this essay is to promote the following hypothesis: Cooperatives gain significant advantages if they are organized as networks. Cooperative networking has been neglected by researchers of both cooperatives and networks. However, the number and complexity of the variables and concepts of this hypothesis makes the testing difficult – and beyond the scope of this short essay. Instead, I lay out here some theoretical foundations behind this claim. Furthermore, by highlighting its network characteristics I use the Danish pork industry as an illustrative example, and I propose an agenda for future research in this area.

In the next section I sketch some theory based on transaction cost economics (TCE) and economic sociology. In Section 3 the Danish pork industry serves to illustrate the theory. Some implications are drawn and the need for further research is suggested in Section 4, and in Section 5 conclusions are drawn.

2. THEORY

2.1 Conceptual foundations of network theory

A single body of network theory does not yet exist. Instead, there are three large bodies of literature where the concept of "network" is employed (albeit quite liberally): Transaction cost economics, economic sociology, and industrial economics.

The economic sociology literature (Powell and Smith-Doerr, 1994) distinguishes two main approaches to the study of networks. The first uses networks as an analytical device, while the second views networks as a form of governance. While the former has progressed to develop some concrete, quantitative methodological tools, the latter consists of a broad range of (mainly empirical) studies which do not comprise a coherent body of theory.

Research in social networks claims that network forms allow participating firms to acquire *knowledge*, gain *legitimacy*, manage *resource dependencies*, and improve *economic performance* (Podolny and Page, 1998). Furthermore, network organizations are able to create a *"macroculture"* of network social interaction (Jones *et al.*, 1997). Macroculture, in particular, refers to the way an organization views the world and organizes itself. It is a system of widely shared assumptions and values comprising industry-specific professional knowledge that guide actions and create typical behavior patterns among independent entities (Jones *et al.*, 1997). In a certain sense, this is a concept similar to *social capital*, which also refers to trust, norms, the rule of law, and social integration – features that can improve the efficiency of society by facilitating coordinated action for mutual benefit (Putnam, 1995; Burt, 2000).

In the core foundation and operationalization of social networks lies the concept of *embeddedness* (Granovetter, 1985; Granovetter, 1982). Embeddedness refers to the degree of social location of network participants and is measured in terms of "depth" or the "degree of connectivity" associated with established relationships among the network participants (Thompson, 2005). Most important to the functioning of networks is "structural embeddedness," which concerns the material quality and structure among actors and how these actors relate to third parties[3] (Granovetter, 1992). Structural embeddedness promotes economies of time, integrative agreements, Pareto improvements in allocative efficiency, and complex adaptation (Uzzi, 1997).[4]

The structural embeddedness concept, with its efficiency attributes, leads naturally to a theory of network governance of a cost-economizing nature. This is also what transaction cost economics does, although it does not explicitly refer to the embeddedness concept. However, the fundamental difference between the two approaches to networks is that while sociologists base network formations on *trust*, *cooperation*, and *reciprocity*, transaction cost economists attribute network governance (like the other two forms of governance) to the combined effect of *opportunism* and *bounded rationality* (Williamson, 2005; Thompson, 2005).

To transaction cost theorists, networks fall into the *hybrid* category, the continuum between markets and hierarchies (Williamson, 1991; Ménard, 2004; Masten, 1996). These three forms of governance have different capacities in *adaptation*[5] and *coordination*. In the transaction cost framework, hybrids are not unique organizational forms, but rather a diverse collection of relationships, and are created because they are fit to adapt to changes in the institutional environment (Williamson, 1991). Ménard (2005) argues that, in order to safeguard exchange, to support adaptation, and to coordinate transactions, hybrid forms rely on *"three pillars"*: *pooling* of resources (for example joint investments), coordination through *relational contracts*, and combinations of *competition and cooperation*. To elaborate, in order to support the governance of their relations, and in addition to "intentional safeguards" of bilateral contracting, hybrids rely on a number of less formal safeguards. Four of these non-intentional safeguards are most important (Williamson, 2005): *societal trust, institutional environment, spontaneous supports, and multi-party governance (associations)*. Networks, then, are defined as those forms of hybrid governance which rely extensively on the latter two for support: spontaneous mechanisms and/or the use of associations (Williamson, 2005).

Spontaneous mechanisms include *competition, reputation effects*, and *informal organizations* (Williamson, 2005). You will recall that the mix of competition and cooperation constitutes one of Ménard's "three pillars" of the hybrid form. Associations are multi-party governance supports, which may take the form of *supplier associations, franchising, labor organizations, restrictive membership* organizations, and *cooperatives*.

So far we have examined the sociological and TCE approaches to networks. Can the twain meet? Jones, *et al.*(1997) attempt to integrate the two approaches by highlighting the following network features of the TCE: *Demand uncertainty, high human asset specificity, complex task* performance, and *frequent exchange*. In this context, networks emerge as a form of governance that has advantages over markets and hierarchies in that they are able to simultaneously adapt, coordinate and safeguard exchanges.

Two characteristics of cooperatives are significant in the functioning of the network: the reliance of the cooperative on *reciprocity* and *trust*, and its *path dependence*. These two characteristics, along with the *interlocking directorates* are keys to understanding the success of the network.

2.2 The cooperative network governance

The network nature of the cooperative form can be seen at two levels: First, with respect to its farmer members; and second, the inter-organizational network – the participation in federated structures and other inter-organizational networks along with other cooperatives and investor-owned firms.

At the first level, the cooperative is a mechanism that combines the high powered incentives of the market with the benefits of collective action (Williamson, 2003). Ménard (2005) classifies cooperatives as hybrids, because they *pool resources*, use contracts for *coordination*, and combine *competition with cooperation* (the "three pillars").

What is of more interest here is the inter-organizational network and whether the cooperative has any advantage in forming and/or participating in such networks. An inter-firm network is a mode of regulating interdependence between firms which is different from the aggregation of these units within a single firm and from coordination through market signals (Grandori, 1995). It is suggested that 'solidarity', 'altruism', 'loyalty', 'reciprocity', and 'trust' best summarize the reasons why networks exist and function (Thompson, 2005). The latter two of these pre-requisites are of importance here, especially in a dynamic context. The cooperative is created and evolves in a certain "path". Although members retain their independence, "reciprocity" and "trust" within a membership determine the evolutionary path of the cooperative.

Path dependence is important in that the common historical experiences of the cooperators are forming mutually consistent expectations that permit coordination of individual behaviors without centralized direction (David, 1994). This "easiness" in coordination based on the certain evolutionary path of the cooperative which has created a certain *macroculture* is one key factor we stress when discussing the Danish case.

2.3 Interlocking directorates

Interlocking directorates occur when a person affiliated with one organization sits on the board of directors of another organization (Mizruchi, 1996). Interlocking directorates are probably the most studied forms of inter-organizational influence – especially in the economic sociology literature.[6] In the context of networks, interlocking directors are the actual human "vessels" through which information flows within the network. Besides their role as information channels, it has also been argued that interlocks (a) act as a mechanism of inter-firm collusion and cooperation; (b) enable firms to monitor each other; (c) are a mechanism for personal career advancement; (d) are a source of legitimacy; and (e) are a source of information about business practices.[7]

Interlocked directors also play a representational role, representing their organization, firm, or certain assets, knowledge, information, experience and credibility acquired in the past and the present (Halinen and Tornroos 1998). As such, they are the main carriers of "organizational memory" and serve as "boundary-spanners" which in essence link the organization with its environment (Jemison, 1984).

2.4 The conceptual framework

Since a single body of network theory does not exist, we need to draw from various theories in order to develop a conceptual framework to encompass the network of an industry in its entirety. We see the network from different "focal" organizations each time: the farm, the cooperative, the federated structure, the policy network. Figure 1 is an illustration of the position of the farm within the network: The *farm* (**F**), the *cooperative* (**C**), the federated structure (*macrohierachy*) (**M**); and the *policy network* (**P**). The circles are divided in nine sectors numbered in Roman numerals. The solid parts of the circle indicate total independence and spot market transactions, whereas the dashed circle indicates some form of integration or other interaction beyond impersonal pure market transactions. The nine sectors represent nine different governance structures. Let us examine each focal organization, its position in the network, and some governance structures.

The farm. In their quest for efficiency, economic agents (in this case pork producers) are able to focus on some of their core competences by outsourcing other activities that they consider more peripheral to their own capabilities. While the

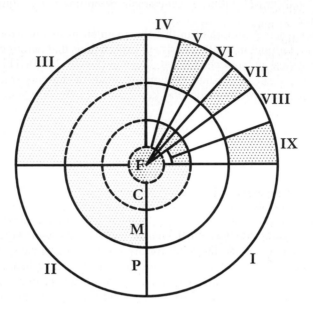

Figure 1. The Farm in the Network

the market, relational contracts, or network relations for their outsourcing. In the standard TCE framework, the choice is based on minimization of total costs (production plus transaction costs). As such, the network then becomes a rational strategic choice of the farmers, since it provides goods and services more efficiently than other forms of governance. The network within which the farmer operates consists of fellow farmers, the cooperative, the federated structure, and the policy network.

The cooperative is not only the downstream (or upstream in case of supply cooperatives) firm that processes the product delivered by its members. It not only takes advantage of economies of scale and market power. The cooperative also coordinates – hence, it provides more efficiency to its members and to the entire industry. It may also exploit its relatively central position in the industry by creating or facilitating further production and provision of services to its members in an efficient manner. In sector **I** a typical farm **F** is related to a cooperative **C**. Furthermore, the cooperative can form or participate in federated structures and/or policy networks, advancing the interests of its members.

The federated structure. Federative organizations are entities in which independent organizations (e.g. firms) join together to form a mutually owned unit which performs some functions for – and coordinates some activities of – the founding organizations (Jonnergård, 1993). Federated organizations provide services to member cooperatives or directly to their farmer members. In sector **II**, the cooperative has formed a federated structure **M**. The Danish Bacon and Meat Council (Danske Slagterier, or DS) is such an organization. The federated structure can become very central in the network. In this capacity it may produce services, or may outsource them, or may integrate further to subsidiaries that produce the goods and services in question.

The policy network (Pappi and Henning 1998; 1999). A policy network consists of farmers as members of various industry organizations, such as the cooperatives, the federated structures, and other associations. Their role is mainly to influence policy at local, national, and international levels. However, sometimes they may provide services, such as advisory services, to their members. The Danish Agricultural Council (Landbrugsrådet) is such an organization. The Danish pork industry could fit into sector **III**, where the cooperative, *Danish Crown* and the federated structure, *the Danish Bacon and Meat Council* (DS), are involved in a policy network **(P)**.

In the northeast quadrant six other forms are illustrated. In sector **IV,** there is the "neoclassical" farm **(F),** selling in the spot market and not involved in any kind of network. In sector **V,** the cooperative is involved directly in a policy network **(P),** without any federated structure in between. Sectors **VI** and **VII** illustrate a vertical integrated firm which is involved in primary production (shown with the radii lines penetrating into the farm level) as well as processing and other activities. It may or may not be involved in a policy network. Hedegaard Food, an egg producing integrator, may fit in sector **VII**. In sectors **VII** and **IX** a farm is selling to an independent firm who may or may not be involved in a policy network. Danpo and Rose Poultry, both broiler firms, may fit into **sector IX,** for example.

The final piece in this puzzle is how the entire network is coordinated and by whom. In smaller networks, there is usually a "hub" organization that plays this role (for example, the cooperative, or the federated structure). The hypothesis here is that instead of a single person or single organization, the entire network is coordinated via a nexus of leading farmers, interlocked in the various directorates. Secondly, the network − through its long (and successful) history − has developed a "macroculture" of mutual understanding and trust that is easier to coordinate than it would have been without the network.

3. THE DANISH PORK INDUSTRY AS A NETWORK: AN ILLUSTRATION

In this section, the theory presented above is used to analyze the variety of organization forms through which the Danish pork industry has acquired adaptation and coordination. Following Ménard (2005) we categorize these activities into pooling and coordination (Table 1).

3.1 The cooperative

On July 14, 1887, five hundred farmers formed the first cooperative slaughterhouse in Horsens, Denmark. Today, 90% of all the pigs (a total of 22 million heads) in Denmark are slaughtered, processed and distributed by two cooperative slaughterhouses: Danish Crown (85%) and Tican (5%). The *pooling* of resources by Danish Crown is accomplished through, first, investments in slaughterhouse plants

(Danish Crown operates six state-of-the-art facilities). Secondly, Danish Crown is vertically integrated into a number of subsidiaries, many of whom are multinational entities (Table 1).

While hog producers remain autonomous in their primary production, the cooperatives *coordinate* the production, logistics, distribution and quality of the activities via *relational contracts*. They have established, for example, a "code of practice", where farmers who comply with certain quality and animal welfare standards receive a premium (Karantininis and Vestergaard Nielsen 2004). Similar contracts are in place for farmers who produce specialty pigs.

The slaughterhouses have followed a consistent path of merger activities. In 1983 there were 17 slaughterhouses, while today there are only two. It is important to realize that it is only very recent that there exist two cooperative slaughterhouses. Twenty years ago, the degree of cooperation through networking between the then 17 firms was not much different of what is today. They had a federated structure, participated in a policy network and shared interlocked directors.

Table 1: Pooling and Coordination by Danish Crown and DBMC

DANISH CROWN		DANISH BACON AND MEAT COUNCIL	
POOLING	COORDINATION	POOLING	COORDINATION
DC SUBSIDIARIES	**RELATIONAL CONTRACTS**	**DS SUBSIDIARIES**	**COMMITTEES**
Food Processing			• National Committee For Pig Breeding
• Tulip		**SEA**	
• Tulip UK	**Code of Practice**	(Sales & Export	• Danish Meat Research Institute
• Plumrose (USA)	(Premium for Quality)	Association for breeding pigs)	
Trading			• **INITIATIVES**
• ESS Food	**Contracts for Specialty Pigs**	**SPF**	• Genetics
• Emborg Foods		(Transport of	• Meat Quality
• DAT Schaub		Pathogen-Free Pigs)	• Traceability Systems
Other			• On-farm quality assurance
• DBC-UK (Wholesale)		**Hatting-KS**	
• SFK-FOODS		(Semen)	• Specialty Pigs
(Food Ingredients)			• Eradication of Salmonella
• SFK-Meat Systems (Technology)			• Reduction of Growth Hormones
Six Slaughter Plants			

Source: Various Annual Reports by DC and DBMC

3.2 The federated cooperative structure

The Danish Bacon and Meat Council (DS) is a federative organization (Figure 2). It is, however, different from most traditional federated cooperative organizations,

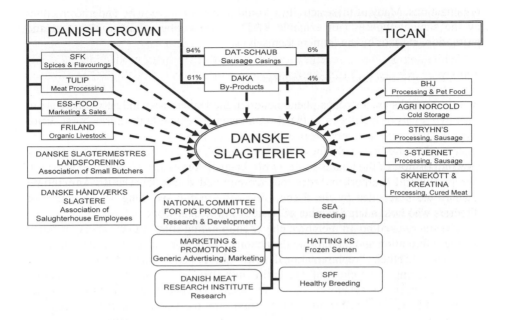

Figure 2. *The Danish Pork Industry*

where the member organizations are usually cooperatives from the same level of production (for example retail cooperatives forming a federated procurement federation). The members of the Danish Bacon and Meat Council are not only the two slaughterhouses. Several other firms related to the pork chain participate as B-members (with no voting rights).[8] The A-members of the board are from Danish Crown and Tican.

DS has three main tasks: a. Research and development, covering all areas from primary production to slaughtering and processing, including breeding, feeding, housing systems, animal welfare, the environment, food safety, meat quality, and automation. b. Sales promotion and information. c. Service, disease prevention and control: health management, combating diseases, meat inspection, legal advice and market support.

To facilitate these tasks DS operates several committees and organizations (Table 1). Furthermore, DS is *pooling* by vertically integrating into breeding via three subsidiaries (Table 1).

DS and its members constitute a solid inter-organizational network. In this, DS has a pivotal role in the *coordination* of the pork industry (Hobbs, 2001). DS has taken many initiatives (Table 1). These initiatives are credible, as they develop trust by the customers, because they were undertaken by a recognized and representative industry-wide body. Also, these actions reduce agency costs since buyers of Danish pork do not need to undertake their own monitoring activities (Hobbs, 2001).

By undertaking these activities, directly or indirectly (through its subsidiaries), DS removes a large burden of transaction and agency costs from its member organizations. Many of these activities would otherwise have to be undertaken either by the slaughterhouses (for example R&D in processing, generic marketing and promotion, etc.), or by the farmers themselves.

3.3 Policy networks and board interlocks

Board interlocks are a striking phenomenon in the Danish pork industry. There are at least two levels of interlocks, at the pork industry level and at the agricultural sector level. Figure 3 is a network chart of the board compositions of the Danish pork industry, where DS is clearly the most central node.[9] At the sector level, we can see the composition of the boards of the entire Danish Agricultural Council in Figure 4. The portions of the pork industry that are embedded into the Danish Agricultural Council are delineated by the dashed line. As we can see there are a number of directors who hold a large number of positions in this network.

The interlocked board members play a cooperating role, among others, of transferring information and monitoring the actions and performance of the other firms in the chain. In their "representational role" these board members represent the knowledge, and the values of the entire industry, and guarantee the continuity, legitimacy and homogeneity of values and ideas. The capabilities and social capital developed by these directors are valuable, non-tangible, non-copyable resources, and constitute a major source of the competitive advantage of this industry.

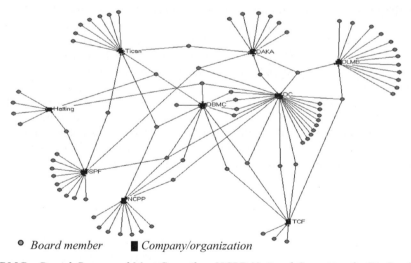

○ *Board member* ■ *Company/organization*

DBMC *Danish Bacon and Meat Council* **NCPP** *National Committee for Pig Production*
DLMB *Danish Livestock and Meat Board* **DC** *Danish Crown (Slaughterhouse)*
Tican *Tican (Slaughterhouse)* **TFC** *Tulip Food Company (Processing)*
Hatting *Hatting KS (Breeding)* **SPF** *sales and distribution of healthy pigs*
DAKA *(processing of pork by-products)*

Figure 3. *Board Interlocks in the Danish Pork Industry*

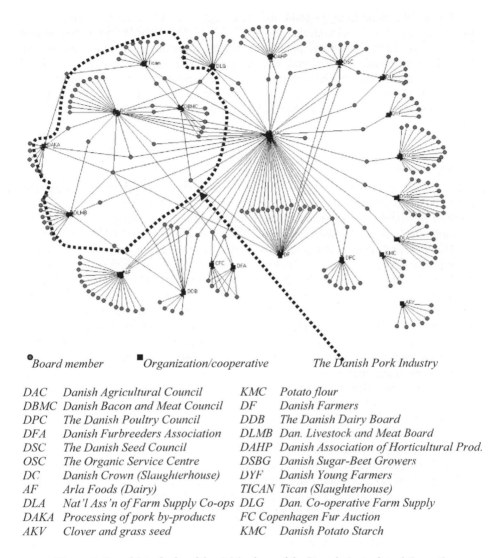

Board member   *Organization/cooperative*   *The Danish Pork Industry*

DAC	Danish Agricultural Council	KMC	Potato flour
DBMC	Danish Bacon and Meat Council	DF	Danish Farmers
DPC	The Danish Poultry Council	DDB	The Danish Dairy Board
DFA	Danish Furbreeders Association	DLMB	Dan. Livestock and Meat Board
DSC	The Danish Seed Council	DAHP	Danish Association of Horticultural Prod.
OSC	The Organic Service Centre	DSBG	Danish Sugar-Beet Growers
DC	Danish Crown (Slaughterhouse)	DYF	Danish Young Farmers
AF	Arla Foods (Dairy)	TICAN	Tican (Slaughterhouse)
DLA	Nat'l Ass'n of Farm Supply Co-ops	DLG	Dan. Co-operative Farm Supply
DAKA	Processing of pork by-products	FC	Copenhagen Fur Auction
AKV	Clover and grass seed	KMC	Danish Potato Starch

Figure 4. *Board Interlocks of the A-Members of the Danish Agricultural Council*

3.4 Path dependency and macroculture

After the severe decline of world wheat prices after 1870, Denmark turned from exporter to an importer of wheat (Kindleberger, 1951). Unlike Germany, France and Italy who pursued protectionist policy through export subsidies and tariffs, Denmark changed from an exporter of wheat into an importer. This happened at the same time that Danish agriculture turned from grains production to animal husbandry. It is in this time that the cooperative slaughterhouses and creameries emerged in Denmark.

Around the same time, in 1844, the "folk high school" movement originated in Denmark, by N.F.S. Grundtvig (Borish, 1991). The schools provided liberal education to mainly the rural population not in scientific agriculture per se, but instead in language, history, and economic life. The schools created a national awareness and strong social cohesion which contributed to the development of organizational knowledge and the development of a macroculture. These assisted to the organization of the strong cooperative movement (Kindleberger, 1951; Borish, 1991).

4. IMPLICATIONS FOR FUTURE RESEARCH

What we see above is the unfolding of an argument on how a single, integrated, centralised and influential entity can be efficient. This may challenge the common view of monopolies in general, and may enhance the logic and philosophy of, for example, the Capper-Volstead act of the USA (Sexton and Iskow, 1993).

This approach is inter-disciplinary. It draws from literature about both economic organization and strategy as well as from economic sociology. First, it shifts the unit of analysis. It is no longer the firm of the neoclassical paradigm, nor is it the transaction of the new institutional doctrine. The unit of analysis becomes either the "relationship", or the "organization". This calls for new theories, new methodologies and new data. In terms of theory, the economic sociology is rich. What is reviewed in this essay is only a fraction of the existing theoretical literature. Sociologists have also developed methods that will enrich an economist's tool box. Social network methods are quantitative and well developed, especially for the analysis of inter-personal and inter-firm networks.[10] Finally we need a new type of data: relational data. These are hard to get and one can not (with rare exceptions) rely on secondary data. This limits the analysis substantially.

Many research questions emerge from this approach, this is a non-exhaustive list:

A. The exact role of the interlocked directors remains unknown. What do these people do, how do they coordinate, and what role(s) do they play in the system?

B. What implications does this system have to farmers? How are farmers affected by these relationships in terms of their profitability, freedom of choice, voice and exit?

C. Other mechanisms developed within the network, such as relational contracting, and their implications to producers, and industry performance.

D. What is the trade-off between efficiency and market power? Does the network focus on transaction cost economizing and production efficiency, or is it taking advantage of its position as a monopolist entity?

E. The disintegration of the pork farms and the reliance on the network to provide, processing, marketing, R&D, genetics, etc. has implications on the farm costs in a way similar to the implications of disintegration on slaughterhouse mergers. It is possible, however, that this has the opposite result: i.e. the disintegration may result into a smaller efficient size and hence on the survival of the family farm.

F. Similarly at the processing level, we see what may appear as a paradox: If the network has advantages, why do slaughterhouses merge instead of relying on the network (and hence externalize some agency and transaction costs)? Through the network the slaughterhouses have managed to externalize a number of activities that otherwise they would have to undertake internally, such as R&D, genetic improvement, generic advertising and promotion. This is in accordance with Williamson's (1975) argument for vertical integration and dis-integration. It is also similar to the franchising argument, where the franchisees transfer a particular resource or right to the franchisor in order to avoid free riding on the brand name (Brickley, Dark and Weisbach, 1991).

Is networking the reason of the success of the Danish pork industry? We have not even attempted to research this question – it is beyond the scope of this essay. There is, however, some indication that networks are at least part of the answer. A recent study (Hobbs, 2001, p. ix) concluded that the cooperative organizations in the Danish pork industry have managed to facilitate the flow of information to reduce transaction costs, increase efficiency, enhance product quality, and respond to quick demand changes.[11] These are precisely the benefits of the network form of governance. In this essay we provide the ground work, though further research is needed to prove the link between network governance and economic performance.

5. CONCLUSIONS

A review of the literature on networks suggests that networks create competitive advantages by reducing transaction costs, and by facilitating knowledge transfer and exchange of resources. The Danish pork industry fits into this framework. From their early development in the 1800s the cooperative slaughterhouses were developed as a response to high powered incentives from the international environment, economizing on transaction costs and providing coordination and incentives to their farmer members. Their organizational success was founded on strong social cohesion and organizational knowledge created initially through the network of the "Folk high school". The cooperative slaughterhouses were able to grow, and to integrate, into processing and exports. At the same time, the cooperative slaughterhouses created a federated structure, which pursued R&D, genetics, generic promotion and advertising. The pork industry was also well represented into powerful professional political organizations such as the Danish Agricultural Council. These arrangements removed a lot of activities from the slaughterhouses and farmers onto the network.

Is this the reason of the success of the Danish pork industry? I have not attempted to provide a formal test of this hypothesis – it was beyond the scope of this exploratory essay. There is however, some indication that this may be true. The studies by Hobbs (2001) in the Danish meat industry and by Henriksen (1999) in the Danish dairy industry indicate that cooperative networks are instrumental to facilitate performance and efficiency in the agrifood chains.

NOTES

* I am especially indebted to Jerker Nilsson for having the patience to read, re-read and tirelessly make suggestions for improvement of my original text. An anonymous referee has provided constructive comments and criticism. Jesper T. Graversen provided technical assistance and valuable insights. I have benefited from discussions with seminar and workshop participants in Copenhagen, Bad Herrenalb, Chania, Berkeley, Stanford, and San Paolo. I am particularly indebted to Oliver Williamson and James March, and I apologize if I haven't been able to incorporate their suggestions and comments fully. I hold none of the above responsible for misinterpretations, errors and omissions herein.

[1] A review of this literature is not appropriate here. See LeVay 1983; Csaki and Kislev 1993; Sexton and Iskow 1993; Nilsson and van Dijk 1997; Cook, Iliopoulos and Chaddad, 2004).

[2] Schrader, and Boehlje 1995; Hobbs, Kerr and Klein, 1998; Hobbs 2001; Hayenga, 1998; 1999; Nilsson and Büchmann Petersen, 2001.

[3] Zukin and DiMaggio (1990) suggest four forms of embeddedness: (a) Structural, which concerns the material quality and structure among actors; (b) Cognitive; (c) Cultural; (d) Political. The first form – Structural Embeddedness – concerns mostly economic exchange and is of interest here.

[4] The embeddedness effect is, however, U-shaped: the positive effects of embeddedness are undermined by the fact that firms may become "insulated" within the network and fail to develop mechanisms to adapt to exogenous shocks. After a certain peak, embeddedness can derail economic performance. The negative effects of embeddedness may occur due to: (a) an unforeseeable exit of a core network player; (b) a rationalization of the markets; (c) overembeddedness (Uzzi 1997).

[5] Williamson (1991) identifies two types of adaptations: A-type (autonomous), which markets are more fit to handle, and C-type (cooperative) to which hybrids are better fit.

[6] The debate and consequently the literature on interlocks began after a 1913 Congress report by the "Pujo Committee" in the U.S.A. identified interlocks as a problem in the early 20th century (Dooley, 1969).

[7] Haunschild and Beckman 1998; Mizruchi 1996; Mizruchi and Stearns 1988; Mintz and Schwartz 1983; Burt 1980; Dooley 1969.

[8] These include GØL (a sausage firm); Tulip (a meat processing firm, which is also a subsidiary of Danish Crown); DAT-Schaub (sausage casings, also Danish Crown subsidiary), and others (Figure 2).

[9] The composition of the board of DS: Danish Crown (eight board members, including the chairman and one managing director); Tican (three members, including the vice-chair and one managing director); and one member from the National Committee for Pig Production. Nine out of the twelve members of the board are farmers (including the chair and vice-chair), whereas three members are from management.

[10] See for example the software UCINET which was used to create the network diagrams in this chapter (Borgatti, 1992).

[11] Henriksen (1999) advances a similar hypothesis for the Danish dairy industry: cooperative dairies were developed to avoid hold-up problems by creameries.

REFERENCES

Borgatti, S., M.G. Everett, and L.C. Freeman. 1992. "UCINET IV Network Analysis Software." *Connections* 15:12–15.

Borish, S.M. 1991. *The Land of the Living.* Nevada City, CA: Blue Dolphin Publishing.

Brickley, J.A., F.H. Dark, and M.S. Weisbach 1991. "An Agency Perspective on Franchising." *Financial Management* 20:27–35.

Burt, R.S. 1980. "Cooptive Corporate Actor Networks – A Reconsideration of Interlocking Directorates Involving American Manufacturing." *Administrative Science Quarterly* 25:557–82.

Burt, R.S. 2000. "The Network Structure of Social Capital." *Research in Organizational Behavior* 22:345–423

Cook, M.L., C. Iliopoulos, and F.R. Chaddad. 2004. "Advances in Cooperative Theory since 1990: A Review of Agricultural Economics Literature." In Hendrikse, G.W.J. ed. *Restructuring Agricultural Cooperatives*, Rotterdam: Erasmus University:Press, pp. 65–89.

Csaki, C., and Y. Kislev., ed. 1993. *Agricultural Cooperatives in Transition.* Boulder, etc: Westview Press.

David, P.A. 1994. "Why are Institutions the Carriers of History? Path Dependence and the Evolution of Conventions, Organizations and Institutions." *Structural Change and Economic Dynamics* 5(2):205–20.

Dooley, P.C. 1969. "Interlocking Directorate." *American Economic Review* 59:314–23.

Grandori, A. and G. Soda. 1995. "Inter-Firm Networks: Antecedents, Mechanisms and Forms." *Organization Studies* 16(2):183–214.

___. 1985. "Economic-Action and Social-Structure – the Problem of Embeddedness." *American Journal of Sociology* 91:481–510.

Granovetter, M. 1992. "Problems of Explanation in Economic Sociology." N. Nohria, and R. Eccles ed. *Networks andOorganizations: Structure, Forms and Action.* Boston: Harvard Business School Press, pp 25–56.

___. 1982. "The Strength of Weak Ties: A Network Theory Revisited." In P.V. Marsden, and N. Lin, ed. Beverly Hills: Sage Publications (UMI Books on Demand, Michigan), pp. 105–31.

Halinen, A., and J.-E. Tornroos. 1998. "The Role of Embeddedness in the Evolution of Business Networks." *Scandinavian Journal of Management* 14(3):187–205.

Haunschild, P.R., and C.M. Beckman. 1998. "When do Interlocks Matter?: Alternate Sources of Information and Interlock Influence." *Administrative Science Quarterly* 43:815–44.

Hayenga, M.L. 1998. "Global Competitiveness of the U.S. Pork Sector." Working Paper, Department of Economics, Iowa State University.

___. 1999. "Structural Changes in the Pork Production and Processing Industry of the U.S. and Other OECD Countries: Major Trends and Issues.", Working paper, Dept. of Economics, Iowa State University.

Henriksen, I. 1999. "Avoiding lock-in: Cooperative Creameries in Denmark, 1882 – 1903." *European Review of Economic History* 3:57–78.

Hobbs, E. 2001. "Against All Odds – Explaining the Exporting Success of the Danish Pork Co-operatives." Centre for the Study of Cooperatives, University of Saskatchewan.

Hobbs, J.E., W.A. Kerr, and K.K. Klein. 1998. "Creating International Competitiveness Through Supply Chain Management: Danish Pork." *Supply Chain Management* 3(2):68–78.

Jemison, D. 1984. "The Importance of Boundary Spanning Roles in Strategic Decision-Making. *Journal of Management Studies* 21:131–52.

Jonnergård, K. 1993. "Federative Organizations: The Effects of Double Binding Contracts." *Scandinavian Journal of Economics* 9:211–24.

Jones, C., W.S. Hesterly, and S.P. Borgatti. 1997. "A general Theory of Network Governance: Exchange Conditions and Social Mechanisms." *Academy of Management Review* 22:911–45.

Karantininis, K. and T.V. Nielsen. 2004. "Hold-Up and the Implementation of Code of Practice by Agri-Food Cooperatives." Proceedings, 6th International Conference on Chain and Network Management.

Kindleberger, C.P. 1951. "Group Behavior and International Trade." *Journal of Political Economy* LIX(1):30–46.

LeVay, C. 1983. "Agricultural Co-operative Theory – A Review." *Journal of Agricultural Economics* 34:1–44.

Masten, S.E. 1996. "Introduction." *Case Studies in Contracting and Organization.* In S.E. Masten ed. New York, Oxford: Oxford University Press.

Ménard, C. 2004. "The Economics of Hybrid Organizations." *Journal of Institutional and Theoretical Economics* 160(3):345–76.

__. 2006. "Cooperatives: Hierarchies or Hybrids?". Chapter 1, This volume.

Mintz, B. and M. Schwartz. 1983. Financial Interest-Groups and Interlocking Directorates. *Social Science History* 7:183–204.

Mizruchi, M.S. 1996. "What do interlocks do? An Analysis, Critique, and Assessment of Research on Interlocking Directorates." *Annual Review of Sociology* 22:271–98.

__, and L.B. Stearns. 1998. "A Longitudinal-Study of the Formation of Interlocking Directorates." *Administrative Science Quarterly* 33:194–210.

Nilsson, J., and S. Büchmann Petersen. 2001. "The Rationale of Traditional Cooperatives – The Case of Danish Crown." In Borgen, S.O. ed. *The Food Sector in Transition – Nordic Research.* NILF Report 2001-2. Oslo.

Nilsson, J., and G. van Dijk. 1997. *Strategies and Structures in the Agro-food Industries.* Assen, the Netherlands: Van Gorcum & Comp.

Pappi, F.U., and C.H.C.A. Henning. (1999). "The Organization of Influence on the EC's Common Agricultural Policy: A Network Approach." *European Journal of Political Research* 36:257–81.

__. 1998. "Policy Networks: More than a Metaphor ?" *Journal of Theoretical Politics* 10(4):553–75.

Podolny, J.M. and K.L. Page. 1998. "Network Forms of Organization." *Annual Review of Sociology* 24:57–76

Powell, W.W., and L. Smith-Doerr. 1994. "Networks and Economic Life." In N.J. Smelser, and R. Swedberg, ed. *The Handbook of Economic Sociology,* Princeton, New York: Princeton University Press.

Putnam, R.D. 1995. "Bowling Alone: America's Declining Social Capital." *Journal of Democracy* 61: 65–78.

Schrader, L.F., and M. Boehlje. 1995. "European Models for Cooperative Coordination in the Pork Sector.". Paper presented at AAEA Symposium *The Role of Farmer Cooperatives in the Changing U.S. Pork Industry,* Indianapolis, 7–9 August.

Sexton, R.J., and J. Iskow. 1993. "The Competitive Role of Cooperatives in Market-Oriented Economics: A Policy Analysis." In C. Csaki, and Y. Kislev, ed. *Agricultural Cooperatives in Transition,* Boulder, etc: Westview Press, pp. 55–83.

Thompson, G.F. 2005. *Between Markets and Hierarchy – The Logic and Limits of Network Forms of Organization.* Oxford: Oxford University Press.

Uzzi, B. 1997. "The Sources and Consequences of Embeddedness for the Economic Performance of Organizations: The Network Effect." *American Sociological Review* 61:674–98.

Williamson, O.E. 1991. "Comparative Economic-Organization – the Analysis of Discrete Structural Alternatives." *Administrative Science Quarterly* 36:269–96.

__.. 1975. *Markets and Hierarchies: Analysis and Antitrust Implications – A Study in the Economics of Internal Organization.* New York: The Free Press.

__. 2005. "Networks – Organizational Solutions to Future Challenges." In T. Theurl, ed. *Economics of Interfirm Networks.* Tubingen: Mohr Siebeck.

__. 2003. "Transaction Cost Economics and Agriculture – An Excursion." In G. v. Huylenbroeck, and G Durant, ed. *Multifunctionality Agriculture: A New Paradigm for European Agriculture and Rural Development.* Amsterdam: Elsevier B.V.

CHAPTER 3

NETWORKS, INNOVATION AND PERFORMANCE

Evidence from a Cluster of Wine Cooperatives (Languedoc, South of France) *

YUNA CHIFFOLEAU

National Institute for Agronomic Research, Dept. of Sciences for Action and Development, UMR Innovation, Montpellier, France

FABRICE DREYFUS

National School for Higher Studies in Agronomics, UMR Innovation, Montpellier, France

RAFAEL STOFER

National Institute for Agronomic Research, Dept. of Sciences for Action and Development, UMR Innovation, Montpellier, France

JEAN-MARC TOUZARD

National Institute for Agronomic Research, Dept. of Sciences for Action and Development, UMR Innovation, Montpellier, France

Abstract. This paper combines economics and economic sociology to assess the role of local inter-firm networks in innovation dynamics and economic performance in a cluster of cooperatives. Focusing on the exchanges of advice between managers, our study is based on 31 cooperatives in southern France. Using both sociometric and economic data, we find correlations between cooperatives' relational, innovation and economic scores. The cooperatives' specificity, however, questions the results obtained in different settings. The network analysis may thus ground a comprehensive interactionist approach to cooperatives, but may also offer tools to renew their governance strategies.

K. Karantininis & J. Nilsson (eds.), Vertical Markets and Cooperative Hierarchies, 35–59.
© 2007 *Springer.*

1. INTRODUCTION

Agricultural cooperatives have played a crucial role in French agriculture develop-ment, especially in processing and marketing activities. Since the end of the 70s, they have contributed more than 50% of farming output in sectors including milk, meat, cereals and wine (Mauget and Koulytchizky, 2003). However, internationali-zation of markets, quantitative and qualitative changes in consumers' demand, CAP reforms and new waves of technology prompt agricultural cooperatives to change their products, technology and organization (Coté, 2001). In the last two decades, "innovation" has been presented as the key factor for the continuation of coopera-tives' development, becoming the main issue aimed by their managers at social sciences researchers (Draperi and Touzard, 2003).

Thus, most of the current economic, sociological and management studies on French agricultural cooperatives are exploring the features and conditions of "innovation" in these organizations, focusing on strategic alliances (Guillouzo et al., 2002; Filippi, 2002), cooperative governance (Mauget and Forestier, 2001; Lambert, 2003) or social capital management (Chiffoleau, 2004). They all suggest that technical or organizational changes in the cooperatives mostly depend on their ability to develop learning processes and relevant networks at both local and sectorial levels.

In parallel, recent works on clusters and industrial districts stress the key role of local inter-firm networks in both individual and collective performances, thus defining highly competitive firms and areas (Porter, 1998; Antonelli et al., 2002). Scholars point out that local networks favor strategic information flows and then facilitate small firms' cognitive capacities, innovation and performance (Carbonara, 2002). In most of these analyses, however, inter-firm relations are theoretically supposed, rather than practically demonstrated, or are restricted to institutional and financial ties.

Following these two sets of studies, we propose to assess the influence of local and informal inter-firm networks on innovation and economic performance of cooperatives. Considering innovation as a cognitive and interactive process, we assume the crucial role of information flows and, more specifically, of advice exchanges between the cooperatives' managers. Our contribution is based on a case study in the Languedoc region (South of France) where wine cooperatives manage 75% of the production and implement technical and organizational innovations in order to produce quality wines. They constitute geographical concentrations of small firms, identified as clusters (Chiffoleau et al., 2003). Using both sociometric and economic data, we will show how advice network analysis provides tools to improve economic approaches to innovation in these wine cooperatives, thus proposing a fruitful link between economics and economic sociology (Swedberg, 2003) for a more general interpretation of changes in agricultural cooperatives.

The paper is organized as follows. The second section presents theoretical issues in innovation and the roles of networks in clusters, stressing the promising contribu-tion of economic sociology for agricultural cooperatives studies. In the third section we present the material and the method of our fieldwork on Languedoc wine cooperatives. Both economic and networks data are presented in the fourth section, and then correlated with wine cooperatives' innovation and performances data. Empirical, theoretical and operational contributions of the research are discussed in the last section.

2. THEORETICAL BACKGROUND

2.1. Innovation within clusters: a relational and cognitive issue

Over the past two decades, there has been an increasing interest in geographical concentrations of specialized small firms, not only by economic geographers but also by economists and policymakers (Saxenian, 1994; Amin, 1999). Inspired by Marshall's definition of an "industrial district" (1891), many concepts have emerged from this newfound focus, but Porter's work on "clusters" has proved by far to be one of the most influential. According to Porter, a cluster refers to "a geographic concentration of small and medium-sized firms acting in the same branch, both competing and cooperating, and showing a high level of collective and individual economic performance" (Porter, 1998). The Californian wine industry constitutes a famous example of a cluster, whose efficiency is supposed to be linked with a high degree of interaction between the firms. In the context of a knowledge-based economy, social scientists working on clusters assess innovation as a local learning process (Giuliani, 2003), relying on both intra-firm and inter-firm interactions.

These studies on clusters thus meet the development of innovation economics. In that research field, there has indeed been increasing evidence that close interactions among firms are the major determinant of technological development and competitiveness (Lundvall, 1993). Assuming an interactionist approach, innovation could be defined as a non-linear process that leads to a structural change in an economic organization (its products, technologies, rules or frontiers) and is mostly based on the cumulative and path-dependent creation of knowledge (Cohendet et al., 1998). Innovation thus supposes learning by doing, using and interacting. As spatial proximity between firms may be linked with a higher probability of interactions, we have a basic explanation as to why clusters can facilitate innovation and allow the production of specific assets (Porter, 1998; Storper and Harrison, 1991).

But the "cluster effect" on innovation and performance cannot be explained only by the "agglomeration effect". It also relies on local institutions and networks, built through these interactions between the firms and/or inherited from the local community. Local networks are supposed to both stimulate competition and facilitate trust and control, allowing combinations of economies of scale and scope (Amin, 1999), reductions of transaction costs (e.g. for local labor markets; Carlsson, 1997), solving of principal-agent problems (Mistri, 1999) or access to "local public goods" (Bellandi, 2002). But which kinds of networks are efficient when innovation and performance are challenged? Economists focus on several kinds of links as financial ties or formal relations sustaining collective action (Bijman, 2003). They also point out the role of informal and cultural ties, suggested by Marshall (1891) through the notion of "atmosphere", but without having any tools to explore these local relationships. A call is thus made to sociologists to proceed with the identification of the relevant networks in such phenomena.

2.2. The perspectives opened by economic sociology

Economic sociology may be mobilized to progress in the understanding of the relations between inter-firm networks and innovation processes in clusters. The concept of "embeddedness", as first invoked by Polanyi (1944), then specified by Granovetter (1985), refers to the process by which social relations shape firms' economic actions and results, highlighting and specifying social mechanisms that mainstream economic schemes overlook or mis-specify. Uzzi, for instance, shows how firms' entanglement into social ties, also called "relational embeddedness", constitutes a "social exchange system" which offers opportunities to the firms and increases their economic performance up to a threshold where the positive effect reverses itself (Uzzi, 1996). Another scholar, Burt, highlights the links between a firm's innovations and performance on the one hand, and its "position" in the socio-economic system in which it is involved on the other. Positions are assessed as specific relational profiles[1] towards others: whereas firms in the same position are likely to behave (and innovate) in the same manner (Burt, 1987), those managing "structural holes" (i.e. unconnected contacts) are expected to be more competitive, due to their control of information flows (Burt, 1992).

Moreover, as innovation proceeds from a cognitive process, it prompts us to refer to sociologists who are trying to combine networks and knowledge issues in their analysis. In the current context of uncertainty about markets, Callon highlights the role of "socio-cognitive networks" that are developed by firms. In these networks, bridging firms and their environment, information and values are produced and exchanged, thus favoring the cooperative building of new products fitted with consumers (Callon, 1998). As far as action is concerned, when routine is insufficient and new practices have to be implemented, Lazega underlines the exchanges of advice between "peers", belonging to the same professional community and developing the same activities (Lazega, 2002). Advice is indeed more than information: it involves the link people make between information and its (past and potential) application and, as such, is closer to action. Moreover, as advice is laden with trust and value, it may be capitalized on as a useful form of knowledge (Cross *et al.*, 2001). Finally, according to Lazega, exchanges of advice allow peers not only to master their activity when routine practices are challenged, but also to coordinate their actions with their colleagues, thus promoting a collective capacity for innovation that may benefit every member of the professional community.

Within a cluster coping with economic uncertainty, amongst all the kinds of ties that may be developed by firms, the advice network between managers may then be assessed as the basic form of inter-firm cooperation and the essential condition of innovation and competitiveness. However, advice relations shape an informal hierarchy insofar as people usually refer to others they assess as having a higher status than themselves (Lazega, 2001). The advice network provides crucial resources for innovation and performance, as well as building a system for the distribution of power and authority throughout the social system (Blau, 1964).

2.3. Clusters: alternative organizational forms for agricultural cooperatives?

We assume that agricultural cooperatives constitute suitable case studies for the economic and sociological research agenda on clusters and innovations. The specific role of cooperatives has been mentioned in a few empirical studies on agri-food districts or clusters (SYAL, 2002), pointing out their capacity to better control the cluster by local familial capital (Becattini, 1991) or their "territorial anchorage" (Zimmerman, 1998), which refers to a strong relationship with the geographical area and local communities, based on cooperatives' material and immaterial investments but also on members' local involvement (Draperi and Touzard, 2003).

Economic arguments for the involvement of cooperatives in networks or clusters have been suggested in studies on federal cooperatives (Lazzarini et al., 2001) or strategic alliances in the agri-food sector (Nilsson and Van Dijk, 1997; Guillouzo et al., 2002). Belonging to networks and clusters could allow small and medium cooperatives, in particular, to share skills and advice, making up, in part, for their difficulties in obtaining external funding for a specific R&D department.

More general studies on the organization and strategies of cooperatives also suggest that cooperative's specific status, values, rules, patronage or origin of its directors influence its management practices and alliances, explaining for instance why cooperatives are more inclined to cooperate with other cooperatives than with investor-owned firms (Mauget and Koulytchizky, 2003). So on the one hand, agricultural cooperatives should take specific advantage of belonging to clusters, while on the other hand these clusters may be influenced by the specific characteristics of the cooperatives.

More recently, research on personal interdependencies between cooperatives (Gargiulo, 1993; Bijman, 2003; Chiffoleau et al., 2003) or interlocking directorates (Karantininis, 2003; Filippi and Triboulct, 2003) has been developing, leading to fruitful collaborations between institutional economics and economic sociology.

Thus, a more systematic analysis of the involvement of cooperatives in clusters is called for by cooperative managers exploring organizational alternatives, as well as by social scientists concerned by the link between clusters and innovations or by the future of these organizations. We note that clusters including agricultural cooperatives may have three general forms: i) cooperatives within a cluster dominated by investor-oriented firms, ii) cooperatives as hierarchical clusters themselves (through federal marketing cooperatives), or iii) clusters of cooperatives, where cooperatives are dominant within the agricultural area and not driven by one firm. In this paper we focus our analysis on a cluster of cooperatives, exploring how informal inter-firm networks could benefit innovation and performance.

3. MATERIAL AND METHOD

3.1. Presentation of the empirical field: the wine cluster of Beziers (Languedoc)

Our empirical investigation has been carried out in a geographic area located around the city of Beziers, 70 kilometers by 40 kilometers wide. In the 1970s this area was considered to be the core of the Languedoc table wine industry (Auriac, 1983).

Ninety percent of its wine was basic, priced according to its alcohol level, and processed and marketed by 45 village cooperatives' cellars that had reached a dominant position (80% of the local wine production in 1979). In 2002, the area still specialized in wine (around 85% of local agri-food production) and cooperatives have kept their marketing share (Touzard, 2002). Nevertheless, the local wine industry is radically changing. Vine growers and their cooperatives are following divergent paths. Some of them try to keep producing table wine, but the majority engages in "innovation trajectories" which consist of a large diversity of combinations of new activities (along the processing chain but also in tourism and local development), new wines ("appellation wines" or "cultivar wines"), new internal rules and marketing alliances (Touzard, 2000).

In 2003, the area includes 31 cooperative cellars (14 have been involved in mergers since 1988). They are very diverse in terms of size, specialization and innovation dynamics (Table 1). Small wine estates and wineries, institutions dedicated to the wine industry (e.g. oenological centre), 11 second step marketing cooperatives, suppliers (e.g. bottles production) and wine merchants are also located in the Beziers area. Some of them have been recently attracted by the development of quality wines.

Table 1. Main characteristics of the 31 wine cooperatives in the cluster of Beziers

	average	minimum	maximum	total	% area
Volume (hectoliters)	76 200	8 790	431 000	2 362 300	78 %
Turn over (1 000 €)	4 365	460	19 000	135 320	75 %
Vineyard (hectares)	1 026	180	5 277	31 830	77 %
Number of members	265	55	1 444	8 230	95 %
AOC wine (hectoliters)	12,5 %	0 %	73 %	194 400	71 %
Variety wine (hectoliters)	27 %	0 %	63 %	611 400	82 %
Table wine (hectoliters)	49 %	7 %	81 %	1 249 800	80 %

This area presents the apparent characteristic of a "cluster" as defined by Porter: geographical concentration of specialized small firms, formal institutional ties and a long common history materialized through shared values and rules, testified by historians and experts (Gavignaud-Fontaine and Michel, 2003).

3.2. Collection of economic and technological information

The economic and technological information on cooperative cellars was extracted from the regional census of wine cooperatives in 2002, and included the 31 cooperatives of the Beziers area. It yielded, through direct inquiry, detailed economic and technical information for years 2000 and 2001 (Touzard, 2002). We completed this information by the evaluation of wine cooperatives' accounts since 1994 (Laporte and Touzard, 1998), and assigned 1994 as the "starting situation" for our analysis. Eventually, the 31 cooperatives have been entered in a database combining structural criteria, indicators of innovation, and ratios of economic performance.

(a) Structural criteria describe the size and the specialization of the cooperatives: number of members, volume, turnover, and ration of table wine or AOC wine in the overall production...

(b) Indicators of innovation are related with new production or processing technologies (cooling system, pneumatic press, stainless steel tanks, environment-friendly production, aging in barrels...), organizational changes (certifications, grape grading, differentiated payment system) and marketing innovations (bottling, new packaging, selling point). A global score has been given to each cooperative, computed simply by summing up the number of elementary innovations implemented. Three categories have been made, rating high, medium and low score innovative cooperatives.

(c) As far as economic performance is concerned, we adopted three criteria: i) cooperative turnover growth between 1994 and 2001; ii) average members' income per hectare of grape, which is a key issue for the sustainability of both members' farms and cooperative firm (Touzard *et al.*, 2000); iii) average price of the wine sold by the cooperative, expressing its capacity to add value. These three economic criteria portray complementary indicators of performance for traditional farmer-owned cooperatives, which are both firms competing in the agri-food sector and associations of members remunerated through the payment for their agricultural delivery.

3.3. Collection of relational information

In order to structure the collection of relational data, we delineated six strategic domains where elementary innovations are implemented and advice is exchanged between the managers (Chiffoleau, 2001):

(a) grape production and wine-making (technical process issues);
(b) grape grading and payment system (organizational innovation);
(c) merging and formal alliances with other cooperatives;
(d) marketing (product innovation, pricing strategy, contracts, new selling point ...);
(e) human resources (staff and members) management;
(f) landscaping and involvement in local development.

In December 2002 we inquired into the advice networks of both the CEO and the chairpersons of all the cooperatives located in the Beziers area, which represented 67 people.[2] Assuming a "cluster" hypothesis, we supposed that the Beziers area was delineating managers' networks boundaries.[3] People were asked to tell to whom they have given and asked advice for each of the six identified innovation domains during the last two campaigns (2001, 2002). Following the methodology usually developed in network analysis (Degenne and Forsé, 1994), each interviewee was first asked to explain his/her links with each of the 66 other cooperatives' managers, a priori included in the network. Of course, in a second step they were asked about their respective links with persons outside the 66 managers' set and/or the Beziers geographic area. Data has also been produced about their possible collection of strategic information from professional press, technical books, trade fairs, travels, etc. Finally, qualitative questions have been developed to assess the point of view of the interviewee on its cooperative, and on the relevance of each innovation domain. Interviews have been recorded and used for interpretation and control of the relational data.

3.4. Principles of network data processing

The elaboration of the final database required a specific statistical processing of the relational data in order to characterize the advice networks. Relations have been aggregated at the cooperative level, assuming a complementarity between CEO and chairman ties. Network analysis provides scores or categories that enable us to characterize the cluster as well as each cooperative:

(a) "Density index" refers to the ratio between the current ties and all possible ties within the cluster,
(b) "out-degree score" measures the number of asking-advice relations, in each domain and in total,
(c) "in-degree score" measures the number of giving-advice relations, in each domain and in total,
(d) "External openness index" indicates the weight of relations outside the set of the 31 cooperatives' managers,
(e) "Prestige score" proceeds from the difference between giving- and asking-advice relations,
(f) "betweenness centrality score" refers to Burt's structural holes theory and evaluates the propensity of the cooperative to be a compulsory intermediary between others within the cluster,
(g) "profiles" (i.e. approximation of structural equivalence, cf. 2.3) are identified as specific sets of relations with others, taking into account both given and asked ties in and out of the 31 cooperatives' managers,
(h) "cliques" feature sub-groups of cooperatives highly connected (n=1) on at least 3 themes.

The final database includes all these relational scores and positions[4] and the structural, innovation and economic indicators, allowing correlation tests and multivariate analyses.

4. RESULTS

4.1. Innovation and performance in the wine cluster

Firstly, statistical analyses have been made on economic and innovation criteria, without taking into account relational data. These aimed at testing the possible relationships between size, specialization, innovation scores and economic perform- ances in the cluster of cooperatives (Table 2):

(a) The size of the cellars (volume, turnover, number of members) is not corre- lated with any innovation and performance criteria.

(b) The specialization in "appellation wines" ("AOC") is correlated with a specific set of innovations (aging in barrels, wide range of wines, bottling, direct selling) and two performance ratios (wine price and turnover growth): this identifies a technological model that allows the firm to develop through the territorial specification of wine, but it has no specific positive impact on farmer income.

(c) Among all elementary innovations, only one is correlated with economic efficiency: the level of grape grading. This indicates the role of these new rules, distinguishing the quality levels of grape deliveries according to specific criteria. They radically change the relationships between the farmers and their cooperative, for all kinds of cooperative sizes and specialization.

(d) However, combinations of complementary elementary innovations are correlated with all economic performance criteria. We test this proposition with different scores, adding the occurrence of elementary changes. This result is confirmed by a step-by-step multiple regression analysis run on the 365 Languedoc wine cooperatives (Chiffoleau *et al.*, 2003).

Then, the first statistical analysis shows that cooperatives are innovating within the cluster and that innovation seems to be efficient whenever it combines elementary innovative items. Nevertheless, the difficulty of identifying structural factors of innovations and performances prompts us to investigate the role of social factors and particularly of inter-firm networks.

Table 2. Linear correlations between structural data, innovation and performance

	Farmer income per hectare	Farmer wine price	Turn over growth	Innovation score
Volume (hectoliters)	0.31	-0.04	-0.03	0.03
Turn over (1 000 €)	0.34	0.24	0.19	0.21
Number of members	-0.02	0.27	-0.04	0.05
AOC wine (hectoliters)	0.20	0.80**	0.65**	0.53**
Variety wine (hectoliters)	-0.02	-0.36*	-0.26	-0.12
Table wine (hectoliters)	-0.10	-0.51**	-0.36*	-0.54**
Area in grape classification	0.46*	0.50**	0.38*	0.32
Score of innovation	0.26	0.61**	0.51**	1.00**

*$p < 0,05$; **: $p < 0,01$

4.2. General characteristics of the advice networks

Secondly, we proceeded with the relational data in order to describe the advice networks:

(a) Three-quarters (74%) of the cooperatives' advice relations (concerning the six domains of innovation) are developed within the network boundaries that we defined a priori (i.e., a set of 67 cooperative managers in Beziers area): the empirical data thus confirm the realist approach we assumed by supposing the geographic area as a social entity concentrating personal relations. As ties are also based on the common activity (wine production), it tends to prove the existence of a "cluster". Besides, beyond the dense "peers" networks, relations with other kinds of actors are mainly connected with local institutions or firms, thus strengthening the evidence of a cluster feature. There are also very few cooperatives connected to long distance advisers or involved with professional travels or lectures.

(b) From a total number of 1 072 inter-individual relations declared by managers, ¾ are of intra-status, that is, CEO to CEO or chairman to chairman. This proves a high degree of "homophily" of the advice networks at the inter-individual level of analysis. However, considering the inter-firm level, advice relations link very diverse cooperatives, in terms of size or wine specialization.

(c) The density of chairmen and CEO networks (21% and 17%) is lower than the density of inter-cooperative networks (33%), implying mainly different advisers for chairmen and CEO in each cooperative. This may be a source of complementarity or disturbance.

(d) However, the density varies according to the domain of advice (Table 3). Advice on matters of grape and wine production techniques, as well as on grape grading, are the most developed (density up to 20%) whereas issues about alliances or landscaping are very little discussed.

Table 3. *Networks density according to innovation domains (Ucinet)*

Domain of innovation	grape production and wine-making	grape grading and payment system	merging, alliances with other coopera-tives	marketing	human resources management	landscaping
Network density	20%	25%	11%	14%	11%	6%

These results are consistent with our observations on the role of grape grading (see Section 4.1). But our qualitative approach also points out the different perceptions of managers concerning each domain: technical issues are entering into routines, whereas alliances or commercial items are highly strategic, inducing rivalries and confidentiality. Landscaping is assessed as a secondary item, whereas human resources are evoked as "the most important domain", but for which "there are no efficient solutions".

(e) The density of advice networks is correlated with the size of the cellars, but little influenced by the institutional involvement of managers and cooperatives (Table 4): CEOs who belong to the regional CEO professional union are more involved in advice exchange than the others, but only for technical and marketing issues; the commitment in one of the 11 second step marketing cooperatives has no impact on network density, except for two or three cases according to the domain of advice. Then, in our case study, formal relations between cooperatives, usually assessed by economists as the essential form of cooperation between managers, do not explain the structure of advice networks.

Table 4. *Correlations between size, institutional involvement and in-degree scores*

	Giving-advice relations for human resource	Giving-advice relations for marketing	Giving-advice relations for landscaping	Giving-advice relations for vine and grape	Giving-advice relations total
Volume of wine production 2001	**0,49***	0,34	0,12	**0,48***	**0,45***
% of wine sales to federated cooperatives	-0,21	-0,28	-0,00	-0,26	-0,25
Involvement in directors union	0,33	**0,38***	0,18	**0,50***	**0,49***

* $p < 0,05$

4.3. Relational scores, positions and sub-groups within the cluster

(a) From in-degree and out-degree scores, one domain at a time or all categories combined, we can identify polyvalent vs. specialized "experts" (See Appendix). Cooperatives 1 and 16, for instance, give advice on every theme and ask for it on relatively few, emerging as polyvalent prestigious advisers. Cooperative 20 has a high score of prestige, but mainly due to its advice-giving relations in technical domains (Figure 1). Other cooperatives do not emerge as prestigious but with a high betweenness centrality, such as cooperative 18, whereas others distinguished themselves by their network openness, such as cooperative 9. This leads to the identification of several roles in the cluster that we can compare with economic or innovation data.

(b) As shown in Table 5, five profiles were then identified, taking into account all advice relations.

Above all, according to Burt's theory, these profiles may distinguish cooperatives likely to behave in the same manner, especially relative to innovation. This calls for the identification of human resources, landscaping and commercialization as the current strategic areas where new practices may be implemented, and that are therefore likely to differentiate firms in the near future.

Table 5. *Advice relational profiles within the cluster of cooperatives (factorial analysis)*

Profile	1	2	3	4	5
Cooperatives	1,11,22,24,25	18,21,28	2,3,6,8,10,13,17, 19,27	4,5,7,9,14,15,16, 20, 23,29,30,31	12
Main characteristics of the relational profile	Ask and give advice in landscaping, do not ask any advice in human resources	Ask advice in human resources and grape grading	Ask advice on commercialization, alliances and grape production	Give advice on grape production and grading, and on human resources	Isolated

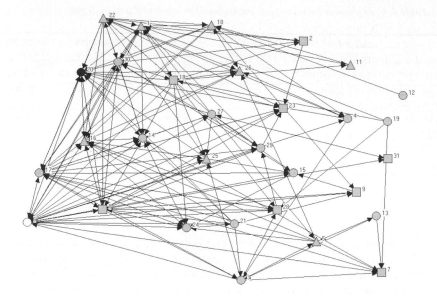

Figure 1. *Advice network between cooperatives about grape and wine production*

☐ Low score of innovation   ◯ Medium score   △ High score
In black: the highest in-degree score; in white: the highest out-degree score

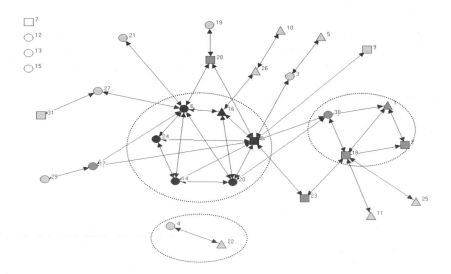

Figure 2. *Cliques within the cluster assessed through thematic advice networks(graph theory)*

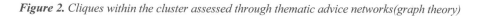

(c) Firms of the same relational profile are not assumed to be directly linked. A second approach to the cluster is to identify cliques, as sub-groups of cooperatives that are highly interconnected. Two cliques may be identified: the first one is quite dense and gathers the cooperatives 14, 16, 8, 24, 20 and 6, while the second is weaker and consists of cooperatives 1, 2, 18 and 30 (Figure 3). These two cliques appear as groups of geographically close firms, mainly belonging to a common federal cooperative (Figure 3).

More generally, cooperatives may be classified into six types according to their level of direct connectivity with others in the cluster (Table 6).

Table 6. Firms' direct connectivity with the other cooperatives in the cluster (graph analysis)

1	2	3	4	5	6
Cooperatives involved in a high density clique	Cooperatives in a medium density clique	Cooperatives involved in a strong bilateral relation	Bridges between cliques	Cooperatives in periphery of the cliques, weaker connection	Cooperatives very little connected to others or isolated
6,8,14,16,20,24	1,2,18,30	4,22	17,23,28	3,5,9,10,11,19,21, 25,26,27,29,31	7,12,13,15

A firm's inclusion in a clique may either limit or stimulate its innovative capacity, according to the degree of social pressure and competition inside the group (Burt, 1992), whereas bridges between cliques may allow them to benefit from their strategic position.

4.4. Networks structure, innovations and performances

In order to identify possible relationships between the managers' networks, the innovation dynamics and the performances of their cooperatives, we proceeded with a second correlation test completed by a general discriminant analysis.

(a) As shown in Table 7, we find significant correlations between relational scores and technical or organizational innovations implemented in cooperatives:

- Considering the elementary innovations, there is no correlation between the implemented innovation and the scores in the advice network related to the domain of this innovation. However, we note a correlation between the request for marketing advice and the practice of grape grading, and between the request for landscaping advice and the development of direct selling and bottling. For each domain, it seems that the main innovators are not the main advisers, but that implemented innovations call for new domains of innovation, then for advice-seeking.

- We specify these relationships by a discriminant analysis run on the three categories of innovation score that we defined: low, medium and high (see Figure 2). Low innovation score cooperatives may be identified by their advice request in human resources (an urgent issue for them?), but some of them have few interactions; high innovation score cooperatives have specific requests on "new" domains of innovation (such as landscaping), but only some of them provide advice on

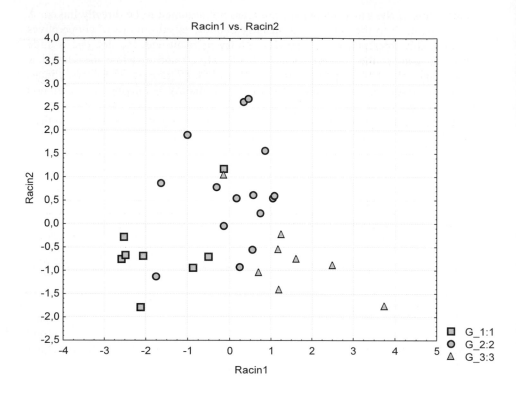

Figure 3. *Discriminant analysis of low, medium, high innovation score cooperatives*
(G1, G2, G3)
Racin 1: out-deg human resources (- 0,42), out-deg landscaping (+ 0,32), betweenness score (- 0,29), prestige (+ 0,22); Racin 2: out-deg marketing (+ 0,29), out-deg landscaping (- 0,29), out-deg alliance (+ 0,22), out-deg ext (+ 0,22)

innovative domains for which they are supposed to have capacities; medium innovation score cooperatives are more involved in advice exchanges than the others, especially in the technical and marketing domains. Thus, progressive adoption of innovations seems to be linked with different behaviors in matter of advice exchange and with different network structures.

(b) We find few significant correlations between relational scores and economic performances (Table 7):

- The strongest correlations are found between performances in 1994-95 and the giving of advice in marketing, alliances or landscaping (in 2002). Thus, previous economic performance seems to still influence current advice networks.

- 2000–2001 farmers' income per hectare is only correlated with advice giving in landscaping, while the 2000–2001 average wine price is negatively correlated with advice request in human resources. The turnover evolution is positively correlated with the advice request in landscaping.

Table 7. Correlations between cooperatives innovations, performance and network scores

	ask advice human re-source	give advice human re-source	ask advice mar-ket	give advice mar-ket	ask advice land-scap-ing	give advice land-scap-ing	ask advice vine and grape	give ad-vice vine and grape	pres-tige score	be-tween-ness score
% direct selling	-0,20	-0,10	-0,16	-0,21	**0,38***	-0,03	0,14	-0,04	-0,07	0,35
% grape grading	0,04	-0,12	**0,37***	-0,03	0,34	0,28	0,28	0,23	0,11	0,07
Range of wine	-0,09	-0,01	-0,20	-0,19	**0,42***	-0,11	0,21	0,03	-0,11	-0,18
Score innova-tion	**-0,43***	0,27	-0,08	0,33	0,26	0,24	0,11	0,35	0,29	-0,20
Wine price 2001	**-0,39***	-0,31	-0,09	-0,11	0,15	0,27	-0,01	-0,15	0,06	-0,29
Output/ ha 1994	0,05	0,02	-0,05	**0,48***	0,06	**0,44***	-0,18	0,35	0,23	-0,07
Output/ ha 2001	-0,11	-0,14	-0,01	0,26	0,14	**0,48***	-0,05	0,15	0,06	-0,06
Turnover growth	0,07	-0,13	0,14	-0,11	**0,49***	0,22	**0,37***	0,06	-0,26	0,05

Thus, economic performance seems to be influenced by (or to influence) few relational scores, mainly those that are more highly correlated with innovation scores. Specific positions in the network, materialized by openness, prestige or betweenness scores, seem to have no significant effect, whereas they are often presented as key factors for innovation and performance.

(c) Finally, we test the possible influence of relational profiles and degrees of connectivity on innovation and performance by a general discriminant analysis (Table 8).

- The involvement of cooperatives in a dense clique or a strong dyad is only discriminated by the average wine price in 1994–95. This "past" effect is clear for the dyad (group 3) which associates two elitist AOC cooperatives, having also high scores of innovation and turnover growth.[5] The two central cliques (group 1 and 2) and their peripheral connections (group 5) seem to be very close as far as economic and innovation scores are concerned. The three cooperatives playing a bridge role in the cluster (group 4) are not taking economic advantage of their position. So, except the elitist dyad, the involvement in sub-groups seems to have no influence on innovation or economic differentiation in the cluster.

- Relational profiles seem to have more effects on innovation and performances. Four of them are statistically discriminated by both innovation score and turnover growth. Profile 1 is characterized by the highest score of innovation and performance. At the other extreme, profile 2 is discriminated by the lowest innovation score and wine price growth, and profile 4 (medium innovation score) by the lowest turnover growth. Profile 3 presents scores that are very close to cluster averages.

- No dependence between the firms' profiles and type of connectivity in the cluster can be found, expressing that numerous profiles are associated with each cohesive clique or degree of connectivity. The cohesive sub-groups seem to be spaces of information sharing, rather than spaces of strategic differentiation, except in the case of the dyad where the two cooperatives stimulate each other to innovation and better performance.

Table 8. *Innovation and performance scores for each connectivity group and each relational profile, significant variable in discriminant analysis (*: $p <0.05$)*

	Income per hectare 94–95	Income per hectare 00–01	Farmer wine price 94–95	Farmer wine price 00–01	Turn over growth	Innova- tion score
High density clique (G:1)	18500	21644	278*	280*	116	5
Medium density clique (G:2)	22222	21712	276*	288*	106	5
Bilateral relation (G:3)	20050	21304	436*	443*	150	7
Bridges between cliques (G:4)	21700	17528	295*	255*	107	3
Periphery of the cliques (G:5)	18030	20752	278*	331*	103	6
Low connected (G:6)	19747	21641	284*	306*	116	5
Profile 1	18753	21134	295	328*	127*	7*
Profile 2	20766	20430	275	265*	114*	3*
Profile 3	19102	21200	278	309*	111*	5*
Profile 4	19698	20776	297	316*	100*	5*
Average 31 coopera- tives	19375	20887	291	312	111	5

5. DISCUSSION

5.1. Features of a cluster of cooperatives

Advice relations between managers have proven to be an essential component of the cooperatives cluster: these geographically close firms both cooperate and compete by giving, diffusing or asking for at least some advice, more among themselves than with external actors. They thus assume different roles in the cluster and are connected through different relational sub-structures, like cliques. Moreover, the number and structure of the advice relations appears to depend on the position of the cooperative in a trajectory of innovation: moderately innovative cooperatives are the most involved in local collective learning processes, while cooperatives with low and high scores of innovation have a dual behavior (specific involvement vs. isolated strategy). Advice networks thus express and contribute to the cooperatives' path dependency and differentiation within the cluster.

Furthermore, the wide diffusion of advice about grape and wine production may explain incremental improvements in most of the firms and confirms the recognition by regional and national experts on this area as one of the most advanced in these technical domains. In that sense, advice networks between cooperatives produce collective assets from which each firm eventually benefits, as argued as a positive "cluster effect" by Porter (1998). Nevertheless, as far as human resources or marketing are concerned, the relative lack of relations between managers reveals a strong competition for new markets development, strengthening the power of the traders' oligopoly. Thus, through these local networks, combination of rivalry and cooperation seems to be efficient for technical innovation but non-efficient for marketing innovation.

Our analysis also shows the overlap between informal advice relations and some institutional relations, as typically belonging to a marketing cooperative or managers' union. The two identified cliques, for instance, clearly overlap with formal producers' groups, often accused to be "empty structures" designed with the only aim of beneficiating from public subsidies. In these cases, beyond their formal dimension, these groups distinguish themselves by a specific collective project which, according to them, makes them closer whereas they were not particularly linked before. Furthermore, beyond these few cliques, cooperatives' advisers appear to vary according to the domain of innovation. This prompts us to consider a renewed approach to expertise and leadership in a cluster facing the "economy of quality" context. As radical and multidimensional innovations may be performed both in value chains and territories (Allaire, 2002), that stimulates cooperatives to develop complementary skills and networks. It illustrates the principle of "distributed cognition" highlighted by cognitive science in organizational settings (Conein, Jacopin, 1994).

5.2. From network positions to innovation and performance of cooperatives

So far as innovation and performance are challenged, economic sociologists point out specific positions in social networks. However, in our study case, prestige or betweenness centrality, for instance, are not significantly linked with high levels of innovation and competitiveness. Several hypotheses may be argued, linked with the specificity of wine cooperatives and their managers:

(a) Cooperative managers do not really act and react as the highly strategy-oriented agents, considered by Burt, Uzzi or Lazega. They are not involved in a constant quest for relevant social relationships, and may be neither able nor inclined to use their strategic positions in networks for the interest of their cooperatives. This prompts us to consider both cultural and human capital issues. Indeed, Lazega stresses the need for a "strategic culture" in the efficient building and management of a relevant social capital (2001), whereas Burt points out the impact of training (1992). In the Beziers cluster, only a few cooperative managers, including presidents and CEO, have been trained in firm management;

(b) The exchanged advice has a low quality level and/or is not directly useful. It may express a high level of competition between cooperative managers, reluctant to share "what works here". The numerous historical references to petty local quarrels, as well as the low level of inclusion of the more competitive cooperatives in the networks, strengthen this hypothesis. However, in one case, a director coming from Bordeaux and managing a very efficient cooperative would like to integrate but is rejected by others who are locally born and established. Human capital and psychology also condition the capacity to be aware and able to share practices or projects;

(c) The advice network between managers is not the most relevant nor efficient social network related to firms innovation and performance. As a cooperative consists of both an enterprise and an association, we chose to assess the networks of its president and CEO, but the board of directors, or even the basic members, could be more efficient at obtaining some information. Indeed, our previous works showed the role of part-timers in the development of innovations (Chiffoleau, 2001). Moreover, our current works suggest the impact of another network, built by marketing ties and partnerships with market professionals, ranging from wholesalers to wine writers.

In that sense, the wine cooperative specific feature questions the works developed in economic sociology about links between networks and innovation. However, Podolny, studying the Californian wine cluster characterized by Porter, obtained results more consistent with the hypotheses of network specific positions and management in strategies explanation (Benjamin and Podolny, 1999). Thus, as the Californian cluster is managed by investor-owned firms, the results issued from the Beziers one may be resolutely linked with the specific functioning and types of leaders of its cooperative organizations.

5.3. Beyond innovation and performance, the challenges of social status and authority

According to Blau (1964) and Lazega (2001), advice relations within a professional community shape the informal hierarchy of power, as well as building social status and authority positions, both due to the authority dimension of knowledge (Conein, 2003) and higher status recognition when asking for advice from someone. In our case, the most competitive and innovative cooperatives do not emerge as particularly prestigious whereas some with low levels of competitiveness do. Consistent with Lazega's results, our discussions with managers highlight that some of them are preoccupied with their social status: some of the most efficient clearly consider the others as "below them" and do not even want compliance from them, preferring to build and stabilize their status in other networks. The competitive dyad, for instance, belongs to a club of "big wine producers" gathering cooperatives from the more prestigious vineyards of Bordeaux and Côtes-du-Rhône. On the other hand, managers of cooperatives of low competitiveness recognize that they try to compensate for low performances by giving advice on alliances that they often envisage as a solution to their difficult situation, or by spreading advice that they obtain from the cluster, even if they do not apply it in their own cooperative.

In the Beziers area, the early involvement of the cooperative in the quality revolution appears to be the source of managers' social status assessment, more than cooperatives' economic assets or results alone. Indeed, the accumulation of experience and the improvement of the wines' reputations (awards, prices) progressively improve managers' identities and status inside the cluster, even if the cooperatives' economic results and prestige (i.e. balance between giving- and asking-advice relations) has not really grown. Taking into account the role of managers' social status in the real economic dynamics seems relevant in the case of small "village cooperatives", embedded in social relations based on strong rivalries between individuals and communities. It could also help to understand decisions and behaviors in other forms of cooperatives and organizations, as suggested by Lazega (2001).

5.4. From Languedoc cellar cooperatives to agricultural cooperatives forms and governances

Beyond correlation tests and results, the advice network analysis, combined with a precise assessment of economic assets, allows a better understanding of the professional community of wine cooperatives' managers in the South of France. It also contributes to the theoretical understanding of the evolution and functioning of "traditional village cooperatives" and, more widely, questions the specific conditions of agricultural cooperative development, throughout renewed governance strategies based on relevant networks dynamic management.

(a) We show that local advice networks and clusters play a key role in the innovation dynamics of small cooperatives. Clusters are a locus for the sharing of experiences, at least in technical domains, when both the small size of the firm and the legal constraints of traditional cooperatives are limiting for the founding of research-development activities. In this case, networking proceeds from both inherited local constraints and explicit strategies, combining economic calculation, interactions for social status building and conformity to "cultural norms". In other kinds of agricultural cooperatives or industries, networking is also relevant (Bijman, 2003), but could have a different rationality and structure: advice networks seem to be rather institutionalized when cooperatives are integrated in a federation or group, for instance, structured through regular managers meetings; networks seem to proceed from more explicit economic strategies in the case of formal alliances with investor-owned firms (Guillouzo *et al.*, 2002); management training and clear sharing of functions between the CEO and the chairman also have a strong influence (Lambert, 2003). Nevertheless, we argue that in the current context of multidimensional innovations in agri-food supply chains, local or regional inter-firm networks have common issues and principles for various kinds of agricultural cooperatives. A wider range of complementary advice is required, but this should also be adapted to local conditions and the higher "site specificity" of the assets, when cooperatives and farmers invest in quality production and origin marketing, or are both challenged by new issues about rural development.

(b) We confirm that local networks and clusters have specific characteristics when agricultural cooperatives are concerned. These characteristics are particularly pronounced in the case of a "cluster of traditional cooperatives", but are convergent with observations made in other forms of clusters and agricultural cooperatives. We note that both cooperative patronage and the agricultural origin of the board of directors can explain specific relational practices, for example, dedicated more to the building of a social status in local community than to the improvement of the cooperative's economic performance. It could also explain why the advice is rather oriented to agricultural innovation than questioning marketing issues. Furthermore, the "territorial anchorage" of these organizations globally increases the cluster geographical stability, even if the relational structure and positions are evolving. Common cooperative values, rules and culture have also been highlighted by our interviewees as driving their propensity to cooperate with other cooperatives, rather than with investor-owned firms.

(c) Finally, our results bring out conclusions in the matter of cooperative governance. Advice exchange contributes to innovation and performance at the individual and cluster level, but also to the building of social status and quality models (distinction between "AOC wines" vs. "cultivar wines" cooperatives). As such, advice networks assume diverse essential functions. They are strategic tools that may be built and not only inherited, and simultaneously allow collective learning and firms' identity preservation (Cross et al., 2002). Hence, this is a key issue for cooperatives dealing with few R&D resources and competing with investor-owned firms. The challenge, then, is for cooperatives' managers and boards to include advice networking and clustering in their governance strategies. That calls for the development of collective action at the cluster level in order to both strengthen advice exchanges between local firms and institutions (about marketing innovations in particular), and to develop and coordinate advice networks outside the area. Our research team is developing feedback sessions to favor such a dynamic: networks structures are locally presented and discussed, revealing the potentialities that could be valorized, suggesting new forms of relational management and thus contributing to a better governance of this wine region.

6. CONCLUSION: TOWARDS AN INTERACTIONIST APPROACH TO AGRICULTURAL COOPERATIVES

Assessing the structure of real interactions between managers of wine cooperatives in Languedoc may be a comprehensive interactionist way to analyze agricultural cooperative trajectories, highlighting both economic and social mechanisms of innovation and networking. The advice network analysis contributes both to the specification of agricultural cooperatives' strategies and to the identification of its embeddedness in local relations, institutions and culture; networking remains globally linked with the position of the cooperatives in trajectories of innovation, even if strategic choices and quests for advice could be influenced by individual social status building and rivalries between communities or social groups. Our empirical analysis thus shows the need for an interdisciplinary approach to assess the social dynamics underlying changes and collective action in cooperatives. This approach calls for an interactionist model of the cooperative, inspired by current research in economic sociology, institutional economics and evolutionary economics. The cooperative could be construed as a set of interaction systems, concerning either production routines or innovation processes, and oriented to both the inside (managers and members) and outside (cluster and industry) of the firm. It thus calls for further investigation, comparing various forms of agricultural cooperatives into the concrete relationships that may efficiently connect local resources and global markets, from an "ethical trade" perspective, for instance, based on cooperative founding values (Chiffoleau *et al.*, 2004).

NOTES

* We thank Alain Degenne (CNRS Lasmas Caen) for his generous help in network analysis.
[1] These profiles have to be understood in reference to Lorrain and White's research equating structural equivalence with competition and social influence (1971). As structural equivalence refers to identical ties with third parties in a network and needs computerization to be assessed, Burt portrays two actors as structurally equivalent in degrees, insofar as they possess similar relations with others, thus sharing a similar relational profile.
[2] One of the cooperatives is managed by seven executive directors.
[3] According to Laumann *et al.* (1983) discussing "the boundary specification problem in network analysis", we thus assumed a "realist approach". We construed the Beziers area as a social entity to which most of the people are aware to belong and which delineates their personal networks. Moreover, as scholars stress relations between "peers" in innovation processes, we also focused on one kind of actor, defined by his/her occupation (cooperative manager), even if the interviewee could refer to other kinds of actors in his/her advice-seeking strategy.
[4] The scores have been calculated by the software "Ucinet", the profiles have been done through a factorial analysis and the cliques have been identified with the graph theory.
[5] Even if one of them appears statistically with a medium innovation global score, its innovations are numerous but more dedicated to marketing, whereas the score is calculated on elementary changes both in production and marketing.

REFERENCES

Allayer, G. 2002. "L'économie de la qualité, en ses secteurs, ses territoires et ses mythes". *Géographie, Economie et Sociétés* 4:155–180.

Amin, A. 1999. "An Institutional Perspective on Regional Economic Development". *International Journal of Urban and Regional Research* 23:365–378.

Antonelli, C., J.L. Gaffard, and M. Quere. 2002. "Interactive Learning and Technological Knowledge: The Localised Character of Innovation Processes". In S. Rizzello, ed. *Cognitive development in economics*. London: Routledge.

Auriac, F. 1983. *Système économique et espace*. Paris: Economica.

Becattini, G. 1991. "Italian Industrial Districts: Problems and Perspectives". *International Studies of Management and Organization* 21:83–89.

Bellandi, M. 2002. "External Economies and Local Public Goods in Clusters and Industrial Districts". Working paper, Universita di Firenze, Italy, 25 p.

Benjamin, B., and J. Podolny. 1999. "Status, Quality and Social Order in the California Wine Industry". *Administrative Science Quarterly* 44:563–589.

Bijman, J. 2003. "Multiple Interdependencies: Applying the Netchain Approach to Cooperative Restructuring". Paper presented at the EURESCO Conference on Vertical Markets and Cooperative Hierarchies, Bad Herrenalb, Germany.

Blau, P. 1964. *Exchange and Power in Social Life*. New York: John Wiley.

Burt, R.S. 1987. "Social Contagion and Innovation: Cohesion versus Structural Equivalence". *American Journal of Sociology* 92:1287–1335.

Burt, R.S. 1992. *Structural Holes. The Social Structure of Competition*. London: Harvard University Press.

Callon, M. 1998. *The Laws of the Markets*. London: Blackwell Publishers.

Carbonara, N. 2003. "Innovation Processes within Geographical Clusters: A Cognitive Approach". *Technovation* 24(1):17–28.

Carlsson, B. 1997. *Technological Systems and Industrial Dynamics*. Boston: Kluwer Academic Publishers.

Chiffoleau, Y. 2001. "Réseaux et pratiques de l'innovation en milieu coopératif". Thèse de Doctorat en Sociologie, Université Paris V - René Descartes.

Chiffoleau, Y. 2004. "Learning through Networks: The Development of Environment-friendly Viticulture". *Technovation*, 25(10):1193–1204.

Chiffoleau, Y., F. Dreyfus, R. Stofer, and J.M. Touzard. 2003. "Re-conversion of Cooperative Wine Cellars in Languedoc-Roussillon: The Confrontation of Three Approaches". Paper presented at International Cooperative Alliance Congress, Victoria, British Columbia, Canada, 28–31 May.

Chiffoleau, Y, F. Dreyfus, and J.M. Touzard. 2004. "Fair Trade and Ethical Projects: New Challenges For Wine Cooperatives ?" Paper presented at International Cooperative Alliance Research Conference, Segorbe, Spain, 6–9 May.

Cohendet P., P. Llerena, H. Stahn, and G. Umbhauer. 1998. *The Economics of Networks*. Berlin: Springer Verlag.

Conein, B. 2003. "Communautés epistémiques et réseaux cognitifs : coopération et cognition distribuée". *Revue d'Economie Politique: économie des communautés médiatées*, 20 p.

Conein, B. and B. Jacopin. 1994. "Action située et cognition: le savoir en place". *Sociologie du Travail* 4: 475–500.

Coté, D., dir. 2001. *Les holdings coopératifs: évolution ou transformation définitive?* Bruxelles: DeBoeck Université.

Cross R., S.P. Borgatti, and A. Parker. 2001. "Beyond Answers: The Different Dimensions of Advice Networks". *Social Networks* 23(3):115–135.

Cross, R., S.P. Borgatti, and A. Parker. 2002. "Making Invisible Work Visible: Using Social Network Analysis to Support Strategic Collaboration". *California Management Review* 44(2):25–46.

Degenne, A., and M. Forsé. 1994. *Les réseaux sociaux*. Paris: Armand Colin.

Draperi, J.F., and J.M. Touzard, eds. 2003. *Coopératives, territoires et mondialisation*. Paris: L'Harmattan / IES.

Filippi, M. 2002. "Les sociétés coopératives agricoles: entre ancrage territorial et integration economi-que". *Etudes et Recherche sur les Systèmes Agraires* 33:25–38.

Filippi, M., and P. Triboulet. 2003. "Modalité d'exercice du pouvoir dans le contrôle mutualiste". *Cahiers du GRES* 12.

Gargiulo, M. 1993. "Two-step Leverage: Managing Constraint in Organisational Politics". *Administrative Science Quaterly* 38:1–19.

Gavignaud-Fontaine, G., and H. Michel, eds. 2003. *Vignobles du Sud (XVIe – XXe siècle)*. Montpellier: Université Paul Valery.

Giuliani, E. 2003. "Beyond Localisation: The Role of Knowledge Communities in Wine Clusters". Paper presented at Regional Studies Association Conference, April 2003, Italy, Pisa.

Granovetter, M. 1985. "Economic Action and Social Structure: The Problem of Embeddedness". *American Journal of Sociology* 91(3):481–510.

Guillouzo, R., P. Perrot, and P. Ruffio. 2002. "Alliance stratégiques et structuration des groupes coopératifs agricoles ». *Revue Internationale de l'Economie Sociale* 285:63–74

Karantinis, K. 2003. "Cooperative Networks". Chapter 2 in this book, pp. 19–35.

Lambert, F. 2003. "Entre liberté d'action et coercition: le gouvernement des coopératives". In J.F. Draperi and J.M. Touzard, eds. *Coopératives, mondialisation et territoires*. Paris: L'harmattan-IES, pp. 233–251.

Laporte, J.P., and J.M. Touzard 2001. "Les coopératives vinicoles de l'Hérault". *Agreste série données*, Ministère de l'Agriculture 6:13–19.

Laumann, E. O., P.V. Marsden, and D. Prensky. 1983. "The Boundary Specification Problem in Network Analysis". In R. Burt and M. Minor, eds. *Applied network analysis: A methodological introduction*. Beverly Hills, Sage, pp.18–34.

Lazega, E. 2001. *The Collegial Phenomenon: The Social Mechanisms of Cooperation among Peers in a Corporate Law Partnership*. Oxford: Oxford University Press.

Lazega, E. 2002. Réseaux et capacité collective d'innovation : l'exemple du brainstorming et de sa discipline sociale. In N. Alter, dir. *Les logiques de l'innovation*. Paris: La Découverte: Coll. Recherches.

Lorrain, F,. and H.C. White. 1971. "The Structural Equivalence of Individuals in Social Networks". *Journal of Mathematical Sociology* 1:49–80.

Lundvall, B.A 1993. "Exploring Inter-firm Cooperation and Innovation: Limits of the Transaction-cost Approach". In G. Grabher G., ed. *The embedded firm*. London: Routledge.

Lazzarini, S.G., F.R. Chaddad, and M.L. Cook. 2001. "Integrating Supply Chain and Networks Analysis". *Journal of chain and networks science* 1(1):7–22.

Mauget, R., and M. Forestier. 2001. "De la coopérative au groupe coopératif: quelle gouvernance?" *Revue Internationale de l'Economie Sociale* 279:26–37.

Mauget, R., and S. Koulytchizky. 2003. Un siècle de développement des coopératives agricoles en France. In J.F. Draperi and J.M. Touzard, eds. *Coopératives, mondialisation et territoires*. Paris: L'Harmattan-IES, pp. 51–76.

Marshall, A. 1891. *Principles of Economics*. London: McMillan.

Mistri, S. 1999. "Industrial Districts and Local Governance". *Human System Management* 18(2):9–27.

Nilsson, J., and G. Van Dijk, eds. 1997. *Strategies and Structures in the Agro-food Industries*. Assen: Van Gorcum.

Porter; M.E. 1998. "Clusters and the New Economics of Competition". *Harvard Business Review* 76(6):77–90.

Saxenian, A. 1994. *Regional Advantage: Culture and Competition in Silicon Valley and Route 128*. Cambridge: Harvard University Press.

Storper, M., and B. Harrison. 1991. "Flexibility, Hierarchy and Regional Development: The Changing Structure of Industrial Production Systems and their Forms of Governance in the 1990s". *Research Policy* 20(5):407–422.

Swedberg, R. 2003. *Principles of Economic Sociology*. Princeton: Princeton University Press.

SYAL, 2002. *Systèmes agro-alimentaire localisés*. Workshop Cd-rom, Montpellier: CIRAD.

Touzard, J.M.. 2000. "Coordination locale, innovation et Régulation, l'exemple de la transition vin de masse – vin de qualité". *Revue d'Economie Régionale et Urbaine* 3:589–605.

Touzard, J.M. 2002. "Recensement des caves coopératives: diversité des stratégies et des résultats économiques". *Agreste LR*, Ministère de l'Agriculture, octobre 2002, 12 p.

__., A. Bouchier, F. Jarrige, and J. Wadrawane. 2000. "Méthodes de segmentation de trajectoires et analyse évolutionniste". *Cahiers scientifiques de l'OCVE* 3.

Uzzi, B. 1996. "The Sources and Consequences of Embeddedness for the Economic Performance of Organizations: The Network Effect". *American Sociological Review* 61:674–698.

Zimmerman, J.B. 1998. "De la proximité dans les relations firmes territoires: nomadisme et ancrage territorial". *Revue d'Economie régionale et urbaine* 2:211–230.

APPENDIX. NETWORK SCORES OF COOPERATIVES IN THE BEZIERS CLUSTER

	vine-wine		clas-pay		comm		alliances		hum res		landscaping		Total		prestige	centrality	outext	Openness outext/out+outext	position	connection
	out	in	out	in	out	in	out	in	out	in	out	in	out	in	in-out					
1	9	10	13	14	1	10	0	10	0	3	7	4	30	51	21	1,75	9	9,3	1	2
2	4	3	7	3	5	6	2	0	0	1	0	2	18	10	-8	0	10	10,6	3	2
3	7	6	5	8	6	6	6	3	0	0	0	2	24	25	1	5,3	9	9,4	3	5
4	4	4	8	4	1	3	0	2	0	0	0	1	14	14		0	5	5,4	4	3
5	6	3	4	7	1	4	18	3	2	1	0	1	11	19	8	0	7	7,6	4	5
6	18	13	19	15	21	5	6	3	0	3	4	2	82	41	-41	18,8	12	12,1	3	1
7	0	7	6	10	1	4	12	4	5	0	0	0	13	25	12	0	6	6,5	4	6
8	11	6	11	9	12	3	0	2	0	2	0	2	51	24	-27	32,3	9	9,2	3	1
9	1	4	0	5	0	5	0	2	0	0	0	0	1	18	17	0	7	14,0	4	5
10	8	5	6	5	8	4	3	3	0	0	3	3	22	20	-2	0	7	7,3	3	5
11	3	2	3	0	3	0	2	1	0	1	1	0	15	9	-6	0	3	3,2	1	6
12	3	0	0	2	1	0	3	0	0	0	0	1	5	0	-5	0	8	9,6	5	6
13	3	1	3	15	3	2	5	2	0	0	0	2	12	8	-4	0	7	7,6	3	1
14	6	12	11	5	4	6	1	4	2	4	4	3	32	43	11	0,84	12	12,4	4	6
15	2	6	9	14	1	4	1	3	0	5	4	1	13	22	9	0	11	11,8	4	1
16	8	13	7	9	1	7	5	5	2	4	0	1	19	46	27	10,9	11	11,6	4	4
17	13	10	5	1	15	4	4	3	13	1	7	3	41	31	-10	6,05	9	9,2	3	1
18	4	0	16	16	7	6	0	5	0	1	0	2	61	29	-32	13,5	14	14,2	2	4
19	3	15	10	1	4	2	4	0	0	4	7	2	22	6	-16	0	7	7,3	3	2
20	7	1	10	16	4	9	0	6	9	0	0	2	21	52	31	8,7	6	6,3	4	5
21	13	5	13	3	0	2	2	2	0	0	0	0	29	8	-21	0	12	12,4	2	3
22	0	7	8	5	7	2	2	1	9	1	12	2	36	16	-20	0	9	9,3	1	4
23	2	9	5	8	1	4	2	4	0	2	0	3	14	27	13	4,9	8	8,6	4	1
24	2	7	9	10	6	6	0	5	0	1	5	3	17	35	18	0,77	7	7,4	1	5
25	4	7	1	8	2	6	5	1	0	2	6	4	20	33	13	0	7	7,4	1	5
26	4	3	9	2	9	4	3	4	0	1	0	1	18	23	5	5,3	9	9,5	4	5
27	10	7	9	5	0	6	6	4	0	2	0	2	34	18	-16	5,3	7	7,2	3	4
28	4	3	9	10	2	5	1	4	8	0	1	1	22	22	0	6,05	9	9,4	4	5
29	5	5	5	2	2	6	2	4	3	2	2	2	18	29	11	0	9	9,5	2	2
30	10	8	12	14	7	7	4	5	1	4	4	4	36	42	6	15,8	13	13,4	4	5
31	2	2	2	4	1	2	1	2	0	1		0	6	11	5	0	7	8,2	4	5

CHAPTER 4

CONVERSIONS AND OTHER FORMS OF EXIT IN U.S. AGRICULTURAL COOPERATIVES

FABIO R. CHADDAD

Ibmec Business School, São Paulo, Brazil

MICHAEL L. COOK

Department of Agricultural Economics, University of Missouri-Columbia, USA

Abstract. This paper discusses exit strategies in U.S. agricultural cooperatives. Compared to other mutual organizations, liquidations and conversions have not been common in U.S. agriculture. We attribute this phenomenon to the "stickiness" of the cooperative organizational form in agriculture. Hypothesized factors that lead to this conclusion include existence of considerable economic incentives for the continued role of cooperatives, low member pecuniary incentives to pursue an exit strategy, and lack of disruptive institutional and market changes. We conclude that if property right constraints continue to be ameliorated with selective incentives and innovative structures, producers will be more likely to invest in cooperatives.

1. INTRODUCTION

Since the 1960s, an increasing number of scholars have debated the challenges and opportunities faced by agricultural cooperatives in light of agricultural industrialization. Given the dynamic nature of structural change in the process of agricultural industrialization, some authors have predicted the demise of the traditional cooperative structure (e.g., Helmberger, 1966; Holmström, 1999). Contrasting to this view, others have suggested that cooperatives would become farmers' integrating agency and provide them an "offensive" structure for value creation and capture in the global food chain (e.g., Abrahamsen, 1966; Royer, 1995; Cook, 1997).

Emerging as a response to market failures and transaction costs in agricultural markets, traditional cooperatives have been instrumental in providing market access and competitive returns to independent producers in the U.S. during the twentieth century. Since the 1980s agricultural crisis, however, cooperative organizations have increasingly faced survival challenges. Fulton (1995) has observed that forces

K. Karantininis & J. Nilsson (eds.), Vertical Markets and Cooperative Hierarchies, 61–72.
© 2007 *Springer.*

external to the cooperative – including technological change and increasing member individualism – would emerge as obstacles to cooperative development in North America.

Additionally, Cook (1995) has argued that the economic benefits brought about by traditional cooperatives in ameliorating the negative economic impacts of market failures might be surpassed by the producers' costs of transacting with the cooperative. These transactions costs result from the vaguely defined property rights structure of agricultural cooperatives and manifest themselves as conflicts over residual claims and decision control among cooperative stakeholders. Three strategic choices were identified as viable for cooperative leaders: the option to exit either the sector or the organizational form, the option to continue strategically and structurally with moderate changes, or the option to shift to a more radical strategy-structure form. The latter two strategic options have been dealt with in previous work (e.g., Cook and Chaddad, 2004; Cook and Iliopoulos, 2000, 1999). This paper discusses exit strategies in U.S. agricultural cooperatives.

2. EXIT STRATEGIES OF U.S. AGRICULTURAL COOPERATIVES

Exit strategies include liquidations, mergers and acquisitions, and conversions. Recently a number of large multipurpose cooperatives have filed for bankruptcy, including Tri Valley Growers, Agway and Farmland Industries. In each case, they had high degrees of member heterogeneity. Their ownership rights were misaligned with use, control, investment incentives, and benefit distribution. The high degree of misalignment violated most laws of optimal organizational design. This observation does not suggest there were not other external and internal forces that might have led to their financial failure, but rather point out that their organizational architecture was misaligned.

The most common exit strategy for U.S. agricultural cooperatives has been through mergers and acquisitions. According to a USDA report, there have been 777 cooperative unification activities including mergers (66 percent) and acquisitions (34 percent) between 1989 and 1998 (Wadsworth, 1999). Recent empirical work has found that capital constraints significantly affect cooperative consolidation activity (Richards and Manfredo, 2003). In other words, cooperatives facing financial challenges might decide to join another cooperative in order to realize scale and scope economies and thereby avoid being forced to liquidate.

The third exit option – conversion or, as increasingly found in the literature, demutualization (Birchall, 2001) – has not been common in U.S. agriculture. Conversion refers to changes in the ownership structure of user owned and controlled organizations from a cooperative (or mutual) to a for-profit, proprietary organization. As a result of demutualization, residual claim and control rights are reassigned among stakeholders with implications to firm behavior and performance. In particular, cooperative membership rights are converted to unrestricted common stock ownership rights in a corporate organization. Most frequently, demutualization is followed by public listing, which allows the firm to acquire additional risk capital from outside investors.

Notwithstanding vaguely defined property right constraints and exogenous challenges, there have been only a few cases of U.S. agricultural cooperative conversions to a corporate structure. In the 1980s, four agricultural cooperatives converted to an investor-oriented form of organization – Rockingham Poultry Marketing Cooperative, American Rice, Capitol Milk Producers Cooperative, and American Cotton Growers. In addition, two cooperatives – Gold Kist and Land O'Lakes – offered shares of subsidiary corporations to the public.

Schrader (1989) analyzes the restructuring decision of the six agricultural cooperatives that partially or wholly converted in the 1980s. He advances the hypothesis that, "the nature of patron's equity in cooperatives may predispose high performance cooperatives to restructure as investor-oriented firms" (p. 41). If the market value of a successful cooperative exceeds its book value, members with limited patronage horizons can realize the value of their cooperative shares only by selling or converting the business. Schrader's case study analysis provides support to this "equity liquidation" hypothesis as "members voted to sell when offered a price reflecting market value of the going business" (p. 50).

Collins (1991) puts forth two additional hypotheses to explain the cooperative conversions documented in Schrader (1989): the "cost-of-equity" hypothesis and the "corporate acquisition" hypothesis. The cost-of-equity hypothesis suggests that conversions will occur if the risk premium required by diversified outside investors is lower than the premium required by cooperative members. In other words, there might be an investor demand for cooperative stocks associated with conversions. Alternatively, the corporate acquisition hypothesis suggests that the primary impetus for conversion emerges from acquisitive companies particularly if members have limited patronage horizons. Based on case study evidence, Collins (1991) concludes that agricultural cooperative conversions appear to be driven by cost-of-equity considerations – that is, "cooperatives will find a way to issue public equity if their equity is extremely attractive to the investing public" (p. 329). However, alternative hypotheses are not fully discarded: conversions may occur because cooperatives are "easy prey" to corporate takeovers or as a result of liquidity restrictions on members' ownership rights. The case study evidence analyzed by Collins (1991) lends partial support to the hypothesis that conversions are driven by the need to acquire equity capital from investors that cooperative members are unwilling or unable to contribute.

Following a relatively "quite" decade, conversion activity among U.S. agricultural cooperatives resumed in the early 2000s. Recent examples include the transition to a limited liability corporation (LLC) form of organization by South Dakota Soybean Processors, U.S. Premium Beef and Golden Oval Eggs. In addition, Calavo Growers, Gold Kist and Dakota Growers Pasta converted to C-corporations with subsequent public listing in the first two cases. Rather than converting to a corporate structure, U.S. agricultural cooperatives actively pursued non-traditional equity capital acquisition schemes in the 1990s by means of a series of organizational innovations. Chaddad and Cook (2004a) examine these emerging cooperative models from an ownership rights perspective and argue that they represent significant departures from the traditional cooperative model. Their analysis also suggests that ameliorating financial constraints in agricultural cooperatives generally entail some degree of organizational redesign rather than the extreme solution of conversion.

In contrast to agriculture, demutualization has been occurring at a fast rate in many industries since the 1980s. Mutual financial exchanges, insurance companies, and savings and loan associations have converted *en masse* to publicly listed companies in the U.S. Differently from mutual organizations in these industries, anecdotal evidence suggests a forced, continuous, evolutionary, reluctant, and piecemeal transformation of the traditional cooperative structure. This paper thus poses the question: what prevents wholesale conversions of the cooperative organizational form in agriculture? To address this question, we first document waves of demutualization and briefly review the literature examining the economics of organizational structure changes that have occurred in the savings and loan, insurance, and financial exchange industries in the U.S. since the 1980s.

3. THE ECONOMICS OF CONVERSIONS

Demutualization has been occurring at a fast rate in many U.S. industries since the 1980s. Interestingly enough, conversion activity occurs in waves in specific industries following some institutional or market change that alters the "rules of the game." As mutuals converted *en masse* to corporate forms, economists have used the available data from these "natural experiments" to study the determinants, motivations and consequences of demutualization. Chaddad and Cook (2004b) document these waves of demutualization and provide a critical analysis of the literature with the emphasis on empirical studies. As an introduction we review their main findings plus add a new section on ownership structure changes in member-owned financial exchanges.

3.1 Conversions in the Savings and Loan Industry

Savings and loan (S&L) mutual associations are user-owned organizations with residual claims restricted to depositors. They were originally formed in the U.S. to promote thrift among the poor and specialized in providing residential mortgages. Mutual S&L associations dominated the U.S. thrift industry until the 1980s when they controlled 73 percent of total industry assets (Cordell, MacDonald and Wohar, 1993). In the early 1980s, industry deregulation and interest rate volatility fostered increased competition in deposit markets with significant reductions in participants' margins. Increased industry rivalry was particularly harmful to mutual associations because of their dependence on internally generated capital. The Garn-St. Germain Depository Act of 1982 liberalizing chartering provisions and subsequent post-conversion anti-takeover rules introduced by the Federal Home Loan Bank Board (FHLBB) provided strong incentives for mutual-to-stock conversions. As a result, 762 mutuals converted to stock associations between 1975 and 1989, raising over $11 billion in external equity. This wave of conversions continued into the 1990s and now stock associations control over 90 percent of the thrift industry's assets.

The rapid and drastic organizational change in the U.S. thrift industry has been subject to empirical scrutiny by economists examining the causes and effects of mutual conversions to corporate charter. Empirical studies of conversion activity include: (i) Hadaway and Hadaway (1981) examine the demutualization of 29 mutual S&L associations that converted to stock associations before 1978; (ii) Masulis (1987) analyzes 205 completed conversions in the S&L industry between 1974 and 1983; (iii) Cole and Mehran (1998) examine the stock price performance and ownership structure of a sample of 94 thrifts that converted from mutual to stock ownership between 1983 and 1987; and (iv) Cordell, MacDonald and Wohar (1993) examine a large sample of mutuals, chartered stocks, and mutual-to-stock conversions that occurred in the 1980s.

Taken together, these applied studies of conversions in the S&L industry suggest that mutual-to-stock conversions are often associated with efficiency gains, as converting mutuals mitigate equity capital constraints and pursue aggressive growth. Financial performance is improved possibly because agency costs between managers and stockholders are attenuated. In general, the literature neglects potential distributional effects related to conversions.

3.2 Conversions in the Insurance Industry

The U.S. insurance industry is comprised of several organizational forms, including stock and mutual insurance companies, reciprocals, fraternals, and Lloyd's associations (Mayers and Smith, 1988). Mutual insurers have been organized as a reaction against excessive market power by for-profit insurers (Smith and Stutzer, 1995). Since mutual insurance companies are owned by their customers (i.e., the policyholders), their major benefit is the attenuation of policyholder-stockholder agency conflicts (Fama and Jensen, 1983).

The insurance industry has recently witnessed a wave of demutualizations, as 34 property-casualty and 17 life-health mutual insurers decided to convert during the 1990s (Viswanathan and Cummins, 2003). Since the 1999 passage of the Gramm-Leach-Bliley Act, which repealed the Glass-Steagall Act, mutual insurance companies have been exposed to increased competition from diversified financial companies with access to public equity markets. Subsequently, mutual life insurance "giants" – including Prudential, MetLife, and John Hancock – converted to stock companies in the late 1990s. Following these conversions, the share of the U.S. life insurance industry held by mutual companies decreased to approximately 15 percent, down from 50 percent as recently as 1986 (Gorski and Cohen, 2002).

Interestingly enough, stock insurers have converted to mutual ownership in the past. Mayers and Smith (1986) examined 30 stock insurance companies converting to a mutual form between the years 1879 and 1968 and concluded that, "changing from a stock to a mutual ownership structure is on average efficiency-enhancing" (p. 95). Subsequent studies of mutual-to-stock conversions in the U.S. insurance industry include: (i) McNamara and Rhee (1992) examine the pre- and post-conversion performance of 33 life insurers that demutualized between 1902 and 1984; (ii) Cagle, Lippert and Moore (1996) study the demutualization of

27 property-liability insurers and examine whether efficiency gains or wealth
transfers among stakeholders motivate the decision to convert; (iii) Carson, Forster
and McNamara (1998) examine a sample of 26 life insurers that demutualized from
1902 to 1995; (iv) Mayers and Smith (2000) examine 98 property-casualty mutual
insurance companies converting to stock charter between 1920 and 1990; and
(v) Viswanathan and Cummins (2003) examine the determinants of conversions in
the insurance industry.

These empirical studies also suggest that changes in the ownership structure of
insurance companies are efficiency enhancing. Stock insurers have adopted the
mutual form of organization in order to reduce agency costs between policyholders
and stockholders. Mutual insurers, on the other hand, have converted to a for-profit
status when imperfect access to capital constrains growth and agency costs between
policyholders and managers are high. The evidence also suggests that strategic
decisions regarding growth and business lines also influence the choice of insurer
ownership structure.

3.3 Financial Exchanges

Financial exchanges – including stock, commodity and derivative exchanges – have
different ownership structures, ranging from state ownership to for-profit corporations controlled by investors. Customer owned and controlled cooperatives and
nonprofit companies have historically prevailed as the main form of ownership
among financial exchanges (DiNoia, 1999). In other words, the major customers of
exchange services – financial intermediaries, issuers of listed securities, brokers,
dealers and institutional investors – are commonly the member-owners of exchanges. Customer-owned exchanges are operated as self-regulatory organizations
with members contributing their time to governance and self-regulation to make
exchanges more effective and profitable (Karmel, 2000). Customer ownership has
been the dominant governance structure because exchanges have historically
enjoyed monopoly power and the costs of ownership have been relatively low
(Hansmann, 1996).

The 1990s, however, saw a wave of demutualization among financial exchanges.
In 1993, the Stockholm Stock Exchange became the first mutual stock exchange to
convert to a corporate form and was subsequently followed by stock exchanges in
Helsinki, Copenhagen, Amsterdam, Milan, Australia, Iceland, Singapore, Athens,
Hong Kong, Toronto, London, and Paris. In the U.S., both the NYSE and NASDAQ
are in the process of conversion. Among derivative exchanges, the London International Financial Futures and Options Exchange (LIFFE) separated ownership shares
from trading rights opening the door to outside investor capitalization. In the U.S.,
the Chicago Mercantile Exchange (CME) became the first financial exchange to
convert its membership rights into shares of common stock that trade separately
from exchange trading rights. The IPO of CME Holdings Inc. – the parent company
of the 105-year-old CME – occurred in December 2002. The Chicago Board of
Trade (CBOT) is undergoing a major restructuring process that might eventually
lead to its demutualization.

According to Williamson (1999), many factors are behind the current wave of demutualization among financial exchanges, including: (i) technological changes that allow the development of electronic trading platforms; (ii) increased competition from existing exchanges and new entrants forming electronic trading networks; and (iii) increased cross-border investment flows that result in increased consolidation of existing exchanges. Electronic trading systems erode traditional exchanges' natural monopolies thereby putting downward pressure on trading spreads. The author argues that cooperative ownership has some disadvantages in adjusting to these dynamic market conditions due to its governance structure. In particular, consensual decision making and lack of capital prevent mutual exchanges from being sufficiently flexible to respond to technological and market changes. Additionally, different exchange members are affected unevenly by electronic trading competition.

Hart and Moore (1996) propose a conceptual model based on the property rights theory of the firm to explain organization structure changes among financial exchanges. The model contrasts the cooperative structure with "outside ownership" in which residual claims are not bundled with trading rights. The authors suggest that two factors critically determine the relative performance of cooperative and outside ownership: membership heterogeneity and degree of competition. More specifically, outside ownership becomes relatively more efficient when membership becomes more heterogeneous and when the exchange faces increasing levels of competition. Their theoretical results suggest that mutual exchanges decide to convert when diversity of interests among members increases collective decision making costs and when there is less scope for outside owners to exploit their market power position.

3.4 Observations

In analyzing the literature on the economics of organization structure changes, Chaddad and Cook (2004b) proffered a set of observations that inform the future role of cooperative organizations in agriculture. First, waves of demutualization often follow disruptive institutional changes which increase industry rivalry and negatively affect profits. Second, organization structure changes are in general efficiency enhancing, as the economic performance of converted firms improves after demutualization. One cannot rule out, however, that conversions are partly motivated by self-interested managers and directors. Third, demutualization helps converting mutuals to alleviate perceived financial constraints, access additional sources of equity capital, and thus reduce dependence on internally generated capital. Fourth, limited horizon cooperative members might have a positive perspective on demutualization as a way of having access to accumulated surplus and reserves. Fifth, demutualization is often related to weak governance systems with ineffective member control. Very large cooperatives with heterogeneous memberships are, therefore, serious candidates for conversion unless they implement tight governance mechanisms to safeguard member control. Sixth, demutualization is creating cooperative-corporate hybrid arrangements that enable cooperatives to acquire permanent capital from members and outside investors while maintaining member control. And lastly, institutional innovation might prevent future waves of demutualization especially if they provide sufficient organizational flexibility for cooperatives to remain user owned and controlled businesses.

4. THE STICKINESS OF THE COOPERATIVE FORM IN U.S. AGRICULTURE

To date, a very limited number of U.S. agricultural cooperatives have opted to convert to an investor-oriented structure but an increasing number is seeking to ameliorate property rights constraints by means of organizational innovations (Chaddad and Cook, 2004a). We attribute this phenomenon to the "stickiness" of the cooperative organizational form in agriculture. We cannot help but ask the question – what prevents wholesale conversions in agriculture as observed in other industries that were once dominated by the cooperative (or mutual) form? Hypothesized factors which lead to this query are postulated.

The first marked difference with other industries is that there still remain considerable economic incentives for the continued role of cooperatives in agriculture. In particular, high degrees of temporal and physical asset specificity expose agricultural producers to potential holdup situations. According to the incomplete contract theory of the firm, the assignment of control rights (and hence ownership) is dictated by *ex ante* investment incentives of contracting parties. The theory predicts that residual rights of control are assigned to agents making relationship specific investments whose quasi rents are under risk from holdup behavior. Based on this rationale, Hendrikse and Bijman (2002) analyze the impact of ownership structure on firm investment in the context of agrifood chains and show the conditions under which the marketing cooperative is the most efficient ownership structure.

In addition to exposure to holdup situations, increasing levels of concentration and non-market vertical coordination mechanisms in agriculture suggest that handlers and processors continue to exert considerable market power relative to producers. It is, therefore, beneficial for farmers to bypass the market and conduct transactions through a cooperative because markets are not competitive due to market power of buyers and/or suppliers, missing input or output markets, asymmetric information leading to quality uncertainty problems, and post-contractual opportunistic behavior of buyers. In these cases, it might be hypothesized that the generic reason producers form cooperatives is to "protect" the value of current farm assets. This cooperative formation reasoning is defined as defensive (Cook and Chaddad, 2004).

As the process of agricultural industrialization marches on giving impetus to the continued role of cooperatives as "defensive" institutional arrangements, farmers are increasingly aware of the importance of residual rights of control in safeguarding the value of their farm assets and cooperative residual claims. Perhaps not surprisingly, U.S. agricultural cooperatives in general have stronger corporate governance systems relative to mutual organizations in other industries. For example, the separation of board chairmanship and chief executive roles is a common practice among U.S. agricultural cooperatives. Anecdotal evidence suggests that producers are keen on exerting control over managers' decisions (Cook, 1994).

Even in the cases where economic benefits to "defensive" collective action arrangements are decreasing and/or cooperative organization costs are increasing – primarily due to increased member heterogeneity – agricultural cooperative members have low pecuniary incentives to pursue some form of exit strategy. This is so because in general U.S. agricultural cooperatives maintain low levels of unallocated equity and reserves in their balance sheets. In other words, there is a limited number of cases where Schrader's (1989) "equity liquidation" hypothesis might hold true. In addition, there are high costs of pursuing an exit strategy which might lead to organizational inertia and unwillingness to change (Nilsson, 1997). An additional explanation of the impact of cooperatives' defensive role is that they represent a competitive yardstick by inhibiting monopoly rents from being extracted from their respective industries. As a result, competitive firms may be forced to exit the industry leaving U.S. agricultural cooperatives to exist with spatial monopolies and monopsonies. These market positions are facilitated by the pro-cooperative institutional environment embodied in legal structures such as the Capper Volstead Act.

When internal transaction costs and/or exogenous competitive forces are sufficiently high, cooperative leaders have attempted to adapt the traditional cooperative structure by means of selective incentives. These selective incentives are organizational responses to internal conflicts over residual claims and control rights. As cooperative memberships become increasingly heterogeneous, selective incentives need to be constantly monitored and modified. Recently the demand to organize "offensive" types of cooperatives has gone beyond the internally determined redesign of organizational incentives and structure. In the mid 1990s Iowa adopted its Chapter 501 to allow the formation of cooperatives that were exempt from rather restrictive corporate farming laws. In 2001, the Wyoming legislature passed a new cooperative statute that allows a cooperative to be organized with both patron and non-patron ownership rights. During the 2003 legislative session, Minnesota created a cooperative law, Chapter 308B, which authorizes outside equity in cooperatives in return for limited voting rights in order to facilitate more flexible financing alternatives for cooperatives. Numerous other states have similar legislation under study, suggesting that the institutional environment relating to producer collective action is under reform. The flexibility embedded in the user-ownership-control-and-benefit definition of U.S. agricultural cooperatives and in the evolving institutional environment enables cooperative leaders to ameliorate property rights constraints without having to pursue some form of drastic exit strategy.

Lastly, but no less importantly, agriculture has not yet witnessed disruptive institutional and/or market changes that significantly altered incentives for cooperative leaders to pursue exit strategies. For example, U.S. agricultural cooperatives continue to receive public policy support in the form of securities waivers, limited immunity to antitrust laws, single taxation and favorable access to credit. Other things being equal, given no significant disturbances at the institutional environment level – i.e., the "rules of the game" do not change – one should not expect drastic restructuring of institutional arrangements or organizations (Williamson, 1991).

5. THE FUTURE OF U.S. AGRICULTURAL COOPERATIVES REVISITED

Since the 1960s, scholars have been predicting the end of the agricultural cooperative form of business organization in the United States. Yet, these organizations demonstrate a strong capacity to survive, especially relative to other forms of U.S. mutuals. We have attempted to explain why this might be in the previous sections. In addition to the aforementioned arguments, we proffer the following hypothesis as a potential research agenda. There exists an acknowledged economic and public policy need for a cooperative form of business organization in a dynamic economic environment where introductions of new technologies, trade liberalization, and organizational change create rapid and dramatic shifts in market structure. These economic and public policy arguments suggest that collective action in agriculture would serve the public good when: (i) a transaction is supported by specific investments on both sides of the exchange having widely different economies of scale; (ii) shared risk through relational contracts can be accomplished; (iii) high frequency transactions requiring long term commitment in an uncertain environment exist; (iv) holdup and opportunistic behavior prevention is needed in declining markets; (v) producers recognize asset-specificity-driven opportunism in the early stages of technology adaptation; (vi) farmers mutually vertically integrate to internalize externalities imposed by trading partners, particularly where reputation and quality assurance are concerned; and (vii) politically-derived redistribution of property rights is granted, earned or extracted from public policy. In conclusion, if property right constraints continue to be ameliorated through innovative selective incentive regimes, producers will be more likely to invest in defensive and offensive oriented cooperatives.

REFERENCES

Abrahamsen, M.A. 1966. Discussion: Government Regulations and Market Performance – Problems in Research and Future Roles for Agricultural Cooperatives. *Journal of Farm Economics* 48:1439–1443.

Birchall, J. 2001. *The New Mutualism in Public Policy*, London: Routledge.

Cagle, J.A.B., R.L. Lippert and W.T.Moore. 1996. Demutualization in the Property-Liability Insurance Industry. *Journal of Insurance Regulation* 14:343–369.

Carson, J.M., M.D. Forster and M.J. McNamara. 1998. Changes in Ownership Structure: Theory and Evidence from Life Insurer Demutualizations. *Journal of Insurance Issues* 21:1–22.

Chaddad, F.R. and M.L. Cook. 2004a. Understanding New Cooperative Models: An Ownership-Control Rights Typology. *Review of Agricultural Economics* 26:348–360.

Chaddad, F.R. and M.L. Cook. 2004b. The Economics of Organization Structure Changes: A U.S. Perspective on Demutualization. *Annals of Public and Cooperative Economics* 75:575–594.

Cole, R.A. and H. Mehran. 1998. The Effect of Changes in Ownership Structure on Performance: Evidence from the Thrift Industry. *Journal of Financial Economics* 50:291–317.

Collins, R.A. 1991. The Conversion of Cooperatives to Publicly Held Corporations: A Financial Analysis of Limited Evidence. *Western Journal of Agricultural Economics* 16:326–330.

Cook, M.L. 1994. The Role of Management Behavior in Agricultural Cooperatives. *Journal of Agricultural Cooperation* 9:42–58.

__. 1995. The Future of U.S. Agricultural Cooperatives: A Neo-Institutional Approach. *American Journal of Agricultural Economics* 77:1153–1159.

__. 1997. Organizational Structure and Globalization: The Case of User Oriented Firms. In , J. Nilsson and G. van Dijk, eds., *Strategies and Structures in the Agro-Food Industries.* Assen, The Netherlands: Van Gorcum, pp. 77–93.

__. and F.R. Chaddad. 2004. Redesigning Cooperative Boundaries: The Emergence of New Models. *American Journal of Agricultural Economics* 86:1249–1253.

__. and C. Iliopoulos. 1999. Beginning to Inform the Theory of the Cooperative Firm: Emergence of the New Generation Cooperative. *The Finnish Journal of Business Economics* 4:525–535.

__. and C. Iliopoulos. 2000. Ill-defined Property Rights in Collective Action: The Case of Agricultural Cooperatives. In C. Ménard, ed., *Institutions, Contracts, and Organizations: Perspectives from New Institutional Economics.* London: Edward Elgar Publishing Ltd., pp. 335–348.

Cordell, L.R., G.D. MacDonald and M.E. Wohar. 1993. Corporate Ownership and the Thrift Crisis. *Journal of Law and Economics* 36:719–756.

DiNoia, C. 1999. Customer-Controlled Firms: The Case of Stock Exchanges. Working Paper No.2, R.L. White Center for Financial Research, Wharton School.

Fama, E.F. and M.C. Jensen. 1983. Separation of Ownership and Control. *Journal of Law and Economics* 26:301–325.

Fulton, M. 1995. The Future of Canadian Agricultural Cooperatives: A Property Rights Approach. *American Journal of Agricultural Economics* 77:1144–1152.

Gorski, L. and M.A. Cohen. 2002. Life in the Public Eye. *Best's Review – Life/Health* 103:22–29.

Hadaway, B.L. and S.C. Hadaway. 1981. An Analysis of the Performance Characteristics of Converted Savings and Loan Associations. *Journal of Financial Research* 4:195–206.

Hansmann, H. 1996. *The Ownership of Enterprise.* Cambridge, MA: The Belknap Press of Harvard University Press.

Hart, O.D. and J. Moore. 1996. The Governance of Exchanges: Members' Cooperatives versus Outside Ownership. *Oxford Review of Economic Policy* 12:53–69.

Helmberger, P.G. 1966. Future Roles for Agricultural Cooperatives. *Journal of Farm Economics* 48:1427–1435.

Hendrikse, G. and J. Bijman. 2002. Ownership Structure in Agrifood Chains: The Marketing Cooperative. *American Journal of Agricultural Economics* 84:104–119.

Holmström, B. 1999. The Future of Cooperatives: A Corporate Perspective. *The Finnish Journal of Business Economics*, 4:404–417.

Karmel, R.S. 2000. Turning Seats into Shares: Implications of Demutualization for the Regulation of Stock and Futures Exchanges. Working Paper, Brooklyn Law School.

Masulis, R.W. 1987. Changes in Ownership Structure: Conversions of Mutual Savings and Loans to Stock Charter. *Journal of Financial Economics* 18:29–59.

Mayers, D. and C.W. Smith. 1986. Ownership Structure and Control: The Mutualization of Stock Life Insurance Companies. *Journal of Financial Economics* 16:73–98.

Mayers, D. and C.W. Smith. 1988. Ownership Structure across Lines of Property-Casualty Insurance. *Journal of Law and Economics* 31:351–378.

__. and C.W. Smith. 2000. Ownership Structure and Control: Property-Casualty Insurer Conversion to Stock Charter. Working Paper No.FR00-15, The Bradley Policy Research Center, University of Rochester.

McNamara, M. and S.G. Rhee. 1992. Ownership Structure and Performance: The Demutualization of Life Insurers. *Journal of Risk and Insurance* 59:221–238.

Nilsson, J. 1997. Inertia in Cooperative Remodeling. *Journal of Cooperatives*, 12:62–73.

Richards, T.J. and M.R. Manfredo. 2003. Cooperative Mergers and Acquisitions: The Role of Capital Constraints. *Journal of Agricultural and Resource Economics* 28:152–168.

Royer, J.S. 1995. Potential for Cooperative Involvement in Vertical Coordination and Value-Added Activities. *Agribusiness: An International Journal* 11:473–481.

Schrader, L.F. 1989. Equity Capital and Restructuring of Cooperatives as Investor-Oriented Firms. *Journal of Agricultural Cooperation* 4:41–53.

Smith, B.D. and M. Stutzer. 1995. A Theory of Mutual Formation and Moral Hazard with Evidence from the History of the Insurance Industry. *Review of Financial Studies* 8:545–577.

Viswanathan, K.S. and J.D. Cummins. 2003. Ownership Structure Changes in the Insurance Industry: An Analysis of Demutualization. *Journal of Risk and Insurance* 70:401–437.

Wadsworth, J.J. 1999. *Cooperative Unification: Highlights from 1989 to Early 1999*. Washington, DC: USDA Rural Business Cooperative Services, Research Report 174.

Williamson, C. 1999. Structural Changes in Exchange-Traded Markets. *Bank of England Quarterly Bulletin* 39:202–204.

Williamson, O. 1991. Comparative Economic Organization: The Analysis of Discrete Structural Alternatives. *Administrative Science Quarterly* 36:269–296.

CHAPTER 5

THE STRUCTURE OF MARKETING COOPERATIVES

A Members' Perspective[*]

NIKOS KALOGERAS

Dept. of Marketing & Consumer Behavior, Wageningen University, The Netherlands
Dept. of Agricultural & Consumer Economics, University of Illinois at Urbana-Champaign, Illinois, USA

JOOST M. E. PENNINGS

Dept. of Agricultural & Consumer Economics, University of Illinois at Urbana-Champaign, Illinois, USA
Dept. of Marketing & Consumer Behavior, Wageningen University, The Netherlands

GERT VAN DIJK

Dept. of Marketing & Consumer Behavior, Wageningen University, The Netherlands
The Netherlands Institute for Cooperative Entrepreneurship (NICE), Nyenrode University, The Netherlands Business School, Breukelen, The Netherlands

IVO A. VAN DER LANS

Dept. of Marketing & Consumer Behavior, Wageningen University, The Netherlands

Abstract. This paper examines marketing cooperatives' (MCs') structure from a members' perspective. We support the notion that the utility that members derive from the attributes of MC's structure enhances our insight in members' commitment. Using a conjoint experimental design, we elicit the utility that producers attach to attributes of a MC. These attributes are related to the cooperative's internal organizational structure and strategic behavior. The results of 120 producers of a Dutch horticulture cooperative show that the selected cooperative attributes are significant drivers of members' utility. In particular, members attach high importance to strategic attributes and prefer a more individualized cooperative structure.

73

K. Karantininis & J. Nilsson (eds.), Vertical Markets and Cooperative Hierarchies, 73–92.
© 2007 *Springer.*

1. INTRODUCTION

Many agricultural cooperatives have modified their organizational structures because of changes in agricultural policy (Sexton, 1990), technology and member individualism (Fulton, 1995), consumer concerns about food quality and safety (Meulenberg, 2000), and globalization (Cook, 1997).

In response to the changing economic environment, the structure of many cooperatives and the relationships with their members have changed considerably after the 1990s. Today's cooperatives have changed or are considering a change in their corporate governance operations, equity structures, benefits allocation mechanisms, and strategic business behavior. During this transition process cooperatives abandon their passive service-oriented role and move towards an active customer-oriented role (van Dijk and Mackel, 1991) by adopting more "member-investor"-oriented (Cook and Chaddad, 2004) and/or "individualized" (van Bekkum, 2001) organizational structures.[1] However, the effect of these structural changes for cooperative members' commitment and satisfaction has raised questions for scholars and practitioners.

Members' dissatisfaction seems to have increased as new forms of governance and strategic behavior have led producers to question whether cooperatives are acting in their best interest (Fulton, 1999). Active participation and member loyalty are crucial for the success of the cooperatives (Hakelius, 1996). Hence, attention is centered on the member firms and the question that emerges is how one can evaluate the cooperative's organization structure in the light of members' commitment. Failure to identify and evaluate members' preferences for cooperative structure's elements may result in declining market shares (Fulton and Gibbings, 2000) and financial pressures (Anderson and Henehan, 2002). Cooperative quality might be perceived to be low when members believe that the elements of its structure do not capture their economic incentives. The source of this perceived quality is the overall utility (members' preferences) that members derive from patronizing the cooperative (Fulton and Giannakas, 2001).

The research question addressed in this paper is how members evaluate the aspects that make up a cooperative structure and that are hypothesized to be important for members' commitment. Information about these structural aspects may be crucial for the management of cooperatives. Cooperative policies that provide members of the cooperative organization with additional benefits (e.g., to invest further down the supply chain) to those being provided collectively may solve collective action problems (Olson, 1971) such as opportunistic behavior of members to deliver their produce to an investor-owned firm (IOF) if they are given the incentive (better price) (Sexton and Sexton, 1987). Cotterill (2001) calls for empirical advances (i.e., solid case studies and quantitative analysis of real world applications) beyond the conceptual stage to study membership commitment. Therefore, the empirical study of the overall utility that individual members attach to structural aspects, which are directly linked to the degree that the cooperative is perceived to act as an agent that captures their economic interests, is a challenging task.

We propose an empirical research design that identifies the aspects of marketing cooperative's (MC's) structure that drive the utility of its members. Following Hendrikse and Veerman (1997) and Bijman (2002), we define the various aspects that make up the structure of a MC as *attributes*[2]. Based on previous research that dealt with market-driven cooperatives (e.g., Staatz, 1987a; Cobia, 1989; Peterson and Anderson, 1996; Nilsson and van Dijk, 1997; Sykuta and Cook, 2001; Kyriakopoulos, Meulenberg, and Nilsson, 2004) we propose that the cooperative structure consists of two classes of attributes: organizational attributes (cooperative's internal structure) and strategic behavior attributes. The control, equity formation and benefit allocation mechanisms are the three organizational attributes of the cooperative's internal structure. The strategic behavior attributes are related to the cooperative's strategic choices in developing and implementing a plan for success in the market place. We investigate the utility that members derive from these two classes of attributes that make up the MC's structure and that are hypothesized to be important for members' commitment. The empirical study concerns a Dutch horticulture MC, the VTN/The Greenery.

The paper is structured as follows. First, the methodology and model to study cooperative structures based on members' preferences are specified. Second, the formation of the VTN/The Greenery's structure is discussed. Third, the study's design is described in detail. The presentation of the results and a discussion on them follow. Finally, managerial implications of the results are mentioned and suggestions for further research are made.

2. METHODOLOGY AND MODEL

Applied research in agricultural economics and marketing should confront models with micro-level data to investigate the drivers of behavior of market participants (e.g., producers) (Brorsen and Irwin, 1996). In the economic and management sciences literature the use of measurement-based models and methodologies that are rooted in behavioral economics are emerging to study empirically the utility that individual decision makers derive from the attributes of a product, service or organization (Schoemaker, 1982; 1993, Little, 1986). In the context of this study a behavioral methodology may be properly used to examine the utility that individual members derive from the attributes of a MC's structure. The assessment of this utility demands the consideration of subjective values (Keeney and Raiffa 1972; 1993). Hence, the application of a suitable methodological approach, which allows the measurement and analysis of multi-attribute preferences, should consider how preference measurement parameters are elicited from the members' (subjects') holistic evaluative responses (overall utility) to different combinations of all the attributes. Statistical methods should then be applied to estimate the contribution of the attributes (and their levels) to the overall utility that members derive from a particular cooperative structure.

We use conjoint analysis to determine members' preferences for MC structures. Conjoint analysis is a multivariate market research technique which allows for the evaluation of the relative importance of a product's/service's attributes using preference ratings (Green and Wind, 1975). In contrast to expectancy-value models that utilize compositional approaches, conjoint methodology is based on a decompositional approach, in which subjects judge a set of "full profile" descriptions. Full profiles are constructed as combinations of levels of all attributes (one per attribute). They are bundles of attributes that make up the product, service or, in the context of this study, the structure of the cooperative. This approach, which is based on some type of a composition rule (i.e., additive or multiplicative), results in a set of part worths (i.e., values) for individual attributes that are most consistent with the subject's overall preferences (Green and Srinivasan, 1978).

The use of conjoint analysis is grounded in the basic utility framework and assumes that decision-makers derive utility from the attributes of a product or service (Green and Srinivasan, 1990). In this study it is assumed that the levels of the selected MC attributes contribute in an additive way to the members' overall utility as given in equation (1):

$$P_{ik} = \alpha_i + \sum_{j=1}^{m} \sum_{l=1}^{L_j} \chi_{klj} p_{ilj} \tag{1}$$

where: i) P_{ik} is the preference of member i for profile k, which represents a hypothetical cooperative structure ii) a_i is a member-specific intercept term (to be estimated), iii) m is the number of attributes, iv) L_j is the number of levels of attribute j, v) x_{klj} is profile k's value of a dummy variable for level l of attribute j, and equals to 1 if the attribute j of profile k holds level l and $x_{klj} = 0$ otherwise, vi) p_{ilj} is the (to be estimated) utility (part worth) that level l of attribute j has for member i. The formulation simply assumes that the members add-up the values for each attribute (the part-worths) to assess the total value (sum of part-worths) for a combination of attributes that describes a cooperative's profile.

In order to examine the behavioral aspects of subjects' (members') decision making process there is a need for a case study (Vazsonyi, 1990). In agribusiness research the use of case studies generates a robust and comprehensive array of knowledge (Sterns, Schweikhardt, and Peterson, 1998). We estimate the conjoint model specified in (1) using experimental data collected from members of a Dutch MC operating in the horticultural sector. This research design allows us to examine the relative importance of a MC's organizational and strategic attributes.

3. DECISION CONTEXT: VTN/THE GREENERY

An example of a MC in which members have a prominent influence in the collective organizational structure and strategy is The Greenery (TG) which is a distribution, sales and marketing company of fresh produce (fruits and vegetables) established and operating in The Netherlands. The shares of the TG are owned by the horticultural cooperative *Voedings Tuinbouw Nederland* (VTN). The VTN/TG emerged after a merger of nine cooperative fruit and vegetable auctions in 1996. Here we discuss the reasons for the transition of the cooperative auctions into a single market-driven cooperative and the reaction of members to the transition, particularly their responses to the institutional arrangements.

3.1 From an Auction to a Marketing Cooperative

The auctions had long been the logistic centers and the locus of price formation of fruit and vegetables marketing in The Netherlands. A serious disadvantage of the auction systems was that the information flow through the supply chain was limited to price information. The information flow through the chain about delivery conditions (special quality aspects, packaging, time and quantity of delivery, assortment) was low (Bijman, 2002). In addition, transaction costs in the auction system were high, particularly for large buyers since they had to have buying agents at each auction. Because the information flow regarding quality demanded by customers was not effective in the auction system, large buyers (e.g., supermarkets) started to bypass the auction and conduct business with the larger producers directly.

As a result, the cooperative auctions were unable to keep the members loyal because solidarity among producers had disappeared. The merger of all horticultural auctions in order to achieve sufficient scale resulted in the VTN/TG. The business goal of the new organization was to rely on principles that reflect both market and production developments. The business plan involved: a) the separation of a cooperative (VTN) from the marketing company (TG) through the creation of autonomous legal entities to facilitate market-oriented strategies, and b) the appointment of professional managers to take over activities related to the organization's transition and marketing strategy (Veerman, 1998).

The organizational attributes of the new-established cooperative and the response from its members are discussed. The information presented is based on a synthesis of various sources (personal contact with VTN/TG's members; managers; and personnel, annual reports and recent studies using the VTN/TG as a case study)

3.2. The Structure of the New Cooperative

After the VTN/TG was established, both members and the leaders of the TG had considerable freedom to pursue their views. The constitution of the TG determined how business was to be conducted in the cooperative setting. The TG case is unique in that members are not as dependent on their cooperative, for instance, as are the dairy farmers or the sugar beet growers (van Dijk, 1999). The producers of fruit and vegetables are in the position to determine the product attributes themselves and, for the most part, are able to do the essential post-harvest handling as well.

3.2.1 Internal Organization of VTN/TG
There are three concepts that distinguish the attributes of cooperative's organizational structure from other businesses' structures (e.g., from an IOF): user-owner, user-controller, and user-benefit principles. Members are those persons who own, use and control the cooperative and receive cooperative benefits on the basis of their

use (Barton, 1989). Here, we discuss how these three principles were applied in forming the internal organization of the VTN/TG.

Control Relations

The VTN/TG's governance structure was developed such that the decision-making between TG and VTN is separated. In VTN, which has the legal structure of a cooperative, the ownership rights of members are exercised via regional representation (see Figure 1). The general assembly of VTN consists of 105 members of regional boards (each of 15 regions provides seven representatives). These members elect the 11 members of VTN's board of directors (BOD). VTN also has a supervisory board that consists of nine members. The cooperative VTN is the owner of TG, which has the legal structure of a limited liability company under Dutch law (BV). For the period 1998–1999, the TG was governed by a management board (six professionals) and was supervised by a board consisting of seven VTN members, other than the members in the BOD or in the Board of Supervisors of VTN. The Board of Supervisors of TG also includes non-members.

From the very beginning of the new organization's establishment members have not only exercised control rights in VTN, but they are also represented in the transaction relationship with the TG through their Product Market Advisory Committees (PMACs). These committees acquired a formal decision-making role since 1999. PMACs are co-decision making bodies for different product market combinations and discuss product transaction issues. In the PMACs both professional employees of TG and member representatives have a position. However, the formal separation in decision-making resulted in poor communication among members and the VTN's BOD regarding the control of the TG. Several times the TG's management board was involved in conflicts with PMACs concerning selling policies. Members felt that the influence on the TG's marketing policy was lost and their interests were not well represented by the governance structure of the organization (van Dijk, 1999). Many of them exited VTN at that time. In 1998 several members of the VTN's BOD and supervisory board resigned. Also, cost cutting strategies resulted in the canceling of positions of the management board of the TG.

A direct and transparent link between the VTN's Board and the TG's supervisory board was demanded by members. Hence, a new corporate governance structure was formed after 1999. Since that time the BOD's members of the VTN have become members of the board of supervisors of the TG at the same time. The supervisory board of the TG also has non-member directors, including the chairman (VTN Annual Reports 1998, 1999). Figure 1 depicts the role of various bodies with respect to these control relationships in VTN/TG in the two different periods. The number of member representatives (BOD) and professionals participating in these decision-making bodies are mentioned.

VTN Cooperative

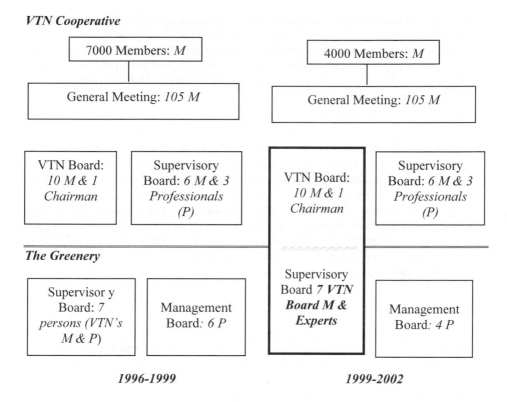

Figure 1. VTN/TG's Corporate Control.

Equity Capital

The transition from an auction to a MC organization turned out to be more costly than expected. Additional equity capital needed to come from members' "out–of–pocket" investments for financing the implementation of the marketing plan. Special financial instruments (e.g., loans) were developed in cooperation with credit organizations (e.g., Rabobank) but were not successful because of members' low willingness to invest. The TG started issuing individual ownership titles (certificates) in addition to its equity capital in 1998 (TG Annual Report, 1998). Each member received 2.5% of his average patronage the last three years before the merger. Approximately 30% of shares are represented by unallocated equity. These are called A-shares and collectively held by the VTN. The B-shares are allocated to members, who hold certificates of B-shares. The BOD of the VTN represents the control rights of both A-shares and B-shares. The income rights of B-shares are individualized (Kyriakopoulos, 2000).

Cost-Benefits Distribution

The VTN/TG's developed a cost-benefit differential system based on cross-subsidies between various groups of producers. This mechanism discriminated prices per product category to reflect market prices and differentiated cost tariffs based on the volumes delivered by the producers. This pricing mechanism resulted in complaints as members questioned the transparency of the price formation. Some groups of members (e.g., cucumber producers) formed their own producer associations that negotiate product-related issues with the TG and with food retailers.

3.2.2. Strategic Behavior of VTN/TG

The stated objective of the VTN/TG was that it would be a market-oriented company. Market-orientation implies that marketing plays a central role in organizational policies. As a result the VTN/TG planned to implement some aggressive marketing strategies, but the high costs for marketing and innovation in combination with a low solvency made the TG's marketing plan too ambitious and it could not always be executed. Marketing strategies that have been implemented include product differentiation, brand promotion, market research, product planning and innovation, logistics of high quality, and managerial expertise (TG Annual Report 2002). The market-oriented focused strategic plan was forced upon the producers by coercion (Kyriakopoulos, 2000).

3.3 Members' Response: Loss of Commitment

The members' lack of commitment because of the perceived mismatch between producers' vision and management's resulted in the exit of a considerable number of members (Bijman, 2002). Members felt that their interests were not represented in the corporate decision-making procedures and they had lost control on the marketing policy. The exit of members had a substantial impact on the financial performance of the TG as a large share of turnover was lost.

In the effort to "raise their voice" in the marketing of their produce the remaining members established producer associations. This development was also strongly stimulated by subsidies from the European Union (EU) for the establishment of marketing associations. The TG gradually acknowledged these associations and developed a "unity in diversity" policy that carries *the greenery* brand name for building a strong business image (TG Annual Report, 2002). The TG also acquired a few strong wholesale and exporting firms and integrated these with their own business units. This move towards forward integration in wholesaling activities was considered necessary for the successful implementation of its marketing strategy.

Members regularly expressed their concerns regarding the transparency in the corporate management of the organization and regarding the high uncertainty with respect to cost-benefit allocation mechanisms. Several efforts are made for the development of an organizational decision-making structure which will satisfy the members' demands and needs. In fact the organizational restructuring of the VTN/TG is an ongoing process (personal contact, 2002).

In the next section, the design of the survey is presented.

4. RESEARCH DESIGN

A survey was conducted during spring 2002/winter 2003. We used both qualitative and quantitative research techniques. Focus group discussions were held with VTN/TG's members in winter 2002. The results of these discussions were used as input for the design of conjoint data collection instrument. Below we present in detail the development of our survey instrument.

4.1. Identification of Attributes: A Focus Group Study

We identified the attributes of MC and the corresponding levels based on the literature of cooperatives. In addition we collected data of members using the focus group technique to empirically verify the attributes identified by our desk research (Braun and Srinivasan, 1975). This research design ensures that the attributes that we use in our large scale survey are based on theory and are relevant for our decision context, thereby minimizing response biases. Two focus-group sessions were conducted. Members were selected on the basis of demographic (lifetime of member's enterprise, region at which company is located), product related (nature of produce, protected or unprotected cultivation), economic (business size and structure), and the degree to which they are involved in the MC's decision making (e.g., participation in PMACs) criteria, to ensure that we had a representative sample of all members of the VTN/TG. Each session consisted of 15 members.

In both sessions members were asked to discuss the two broad categories that were assumed to drive the VTN/TG's structure. The two sessions were coordinated by an expert on cooperative policy issues and an expert on research methodology to ensure a high degree of accuracy in the arguments and opinions of interviewed members. Members identified six attributes, each with two levels, as attributes that are very important to them when choosing among different types of MCs (see Table 1). Below we explain the attributes and their corresponding levels.

Business Issue/Scope. Members argued that the VTN/TG's business scope should represent the economic interests and expectations of the members in the first place. Members indicated that the VTN/TG has to specify whether its business issue/scope is based on the development of an entrepreneurial market-oriented organization model that involves its members in a long-term relationship, or simply acts as an intermediary channel that buys and sells on behalf of its members using modern marketing methods.

Corporate Governance. In both discussions much emphasis was given to corporate decision making. This attribute was defined by members as the corporate govern-ance framework in which the control relationships of the VTN/TG are specified. Two levels were considered as the most important for this attribute. The first level considered that members have to hold most of the control decision rights. So, the BOD of VTN consists of members governing the VTN (cooperative) and the same persons supervise the managers (professionals) who take the role of board of directors of TG - the marketing company in which almost all business activities are carried out). The second level considered the need for even more corporate control by professionals. Managers govern the VTN supervised by the BOD and the TG is governed by managers who are supervised by a professional supervisory board (PSB) including external non-member professionals and the member representatives would be a minority. The PSB would be appointed and supervised by the general assembly.

Table 1. MC's Attributes and Levels Identified in Focus Group Study

Attribute	Level
Business Issue/Scope	Entrepreneurial market-oriented organization
	Intermediary organization
Corporate	*VTN*: governed by *BOD*
Governance	*TG:* governed by managers supervised by *VTN's BOD*
	VTN governed by managers supervised by *VTN's BOD*
	TG: governed by managers supervised by PSB.
Product-related Decision-Making	Members
	Managers
Financial Structure	General reserves
	Individualized equity
Members' Benefits	Product price
	Product price & return on capital
Product Quality	General grading of products
	Specific/client's grading of products

Product-Related Decision Making. Members supported that product related decision making is an attribute that should be considered apart of the corporate governance issue. The question here is: who determines the VTN/TG's transaction conditions such as price setting and sales methods? The need for transparency regarding product related issues was reported as being one of the major priorities. The two levels considered by the members were whether members of the VTN can make decisions about product-related issues or, alternatively, that professional managers (TG) who acquire a high degree of market and expert knowledge should make these decisions.

Financial Structure. Members made a distinction between the interrelated functions of collective equity's financing and the distribution of benefits attribute (i.e., equity redemption). Some members argued that they will be satisfied only if a transparent and well-defined general reserves system will be established (first level). Contrarily, some other members seemed to prefer a more individualized equity scheme and proposed equity formation based on individual certificates and member loans (second level).

Members' Benefits. Members' opinions concerning the net-income allocation mechanism were ambiguous. Many participants in both sessions felt that performance should be expressed in a product's price setting through a well-defined contract between the VTN/TG and the member (first level). But other members disagreed with this norm. Next to the product pricing mechanism they also prefer a dividend reward system (second level)

Product Quality. Finally, the critical role of product quality in the VTN/TG's marketing strategy received a lot of attention during the focus group sessions. Members complained that their products' quality is not well rewarded so they are not able to realize economic efficiency at their own farms' operations. Two main levels were identified. First, the VTN/TG may consider following a general grading line for the various buyers. This strategy may imply that price competition on the basis of efficiency in production and logistics and serving price conscious consumers. Second, the VTN/TG may follow a specific grading line for individual clients, thus focusing on a specific product market combination which may increase its competitive potential.

4.2. Conjoint Design

The number of attributes allowed us to use a full-profile conjoint design. The main advantage of a full-profile approach is that it gives a realistic description of stimuli by defining the levels of each of the factors (Green and Srinivasan, 1978). A 2 (Business Issue/Scope) × 2 (Corporate Governance) × 2 (Product-related Decision-Making) × 2 (Financial Structure) × 2 (Members' Benefits) × 2 (Product Quality) fractional-factorial main-effect-only design generated a set of eight calibration profiles. In addition, three pairs of holdout profiles were generated. We chose the fractional-factorial main-effects-only design to keep the number of profiles to be evaluated at a level that could be managed by the respondents (Green, 1974).

A pilot test consisting of eight face-to-face interviews was conducted to check the face validity and degree of comprehensiveness of the conjoint task. Based on these interviews, the wording of the survey was changed at some places. Respondents indicated that they understood the selected attributes and levels included in the hypothetical MC profiles and that they are actionable (i.e., realistic). The respondents in the pilot test expressed a desire to "build" their own VTN/TG's profile by choosing one of the two given levels of each examined attribute.

We tested first-order interactions of the pilot test's preference data.[3] No interactions were identified except for a low-level interaction between the attributes of financial structure and members' benefits.[4]

In the large-scale survey, respondents were asked to rate the eight calibration profiles according to their preferences on a nine-point rating scale, which ranged from one (least preferred) to nine (most preferred). Subsequently, the respondents were asked to choose their most preferred profile for each pair of holdout profiles, and rate the extent of their preference for that profile on a seven-point rating scale ranging from one (a little more preferred) to seven (much more preferred). The two rating scales adopted for the evaluation of conjoint profiles and holdout cases are interval and commonly used in conjoint experiments (Wedel & Kamakura, 2000). Respondents were also asked to design their preferred cooperative structure by selecting one of the two levels for each attribute.

For the large scale survey respondents were selected on the basis of their economic size (i.e., members with high annual turnovers so they are not at margin and represent the future of cooperative) and the degree of their involvement in the VTN/TG's decision-making functioning (e.g., participation in PMACs, BOD). Most interviews were conducted in conjunction with producers' meetings, which are held regularly on an annual basis in different regions all over the Netherlands. Some interviews were conducted at the farm of the respondent since they were unable to attend the meeting. A total of 120 producers participated. All interviews were held on an individual basis and they were presented to the members through a computer-assisted display.

5. RESULTS AND DISCUSSION

The results of the additive conjoint model are presented in the Table 2. The part-worth estimates (i.e., the utilities of the attribute levels) show that for the attributes of corporate governance and product related decision-making the first levels are more preferred. That is, members prefer that the BOD of VTN also supervises the TG. A similar result is found for the product-related decision-making attribute: Members prefer that they hold the control regarding decisions on transaction conditions (quantity, cost and quality of their produce). For the other two attributes of the internal structure of the VTN/TG the second levels were more preferred. That is, members prefer a more individualized equity structure based on dividend reward on their invested equity in addition to product price.

The conjoint results show that in the case of the strategic attributes members prefer to participate in an entrepreneurial market-oriented organization. This implies a business model that is responsive to market intelligence and that supports grading lines based on product quality to fulfill the wishes of its existing or potential market segments. These findings confirm the theoretical work done by van Dijk and Mackel (1991); Cook (1995); van Dijk (1999); Meulenberg (2000); and Cook and Chaddad (2004), who argue that many market-driven food cooperatives adopt more individualized organizational structures (alike IOFs) and customer-driven strategies. The regression coefficients of all six attributes (represented by average part worths (*APWs*) for each attribute level in Table 2.) indicate that the selected attributes are significant drivers of member preferences for the MC's structure, substantiating the validity of the chosen attributes in our experimental design.

In Table 2 descriptive statistics of individual part worths are also presented. The standard deviation of part worths (presented in second column of Table 2, *St.D.*, for each attribute) are relatively small compared to the estimated average values (mean) for each attribute and indicate that the *APWs* are accurate representations of members' ratings. In addition, the standard errors (second column of Table 2,

Table 2. Average Part Worths (APWs) of MC's Attributes Based on Individual Estimates (N=120)[a,b]

	APWs	Std. D.	Std.E.	Percentiles		
				25	50	75
Business Issue/Scope						
Entrepreneurial market-oriented organization	0.309*	0.560	0.051	0.000	0.250	0.625
Intermediary organization	-0.309					
Corporate Governance						
VTN: governed by BOD (members)						
TG: governed by managers supervised by *VTN's BOD*	0.183*	0.643	0.054	-0.125	0.125	0.625
VTN: governed by managers supervised by *BOD*	-0.183					
TG: governed by managers supervised by experts						
Product-Related Decision-Making						
Members	0.247*	0.636	0.058	-0.125	0.250	0.625
Managers	-0.247					
Financial Structure						
General reserves	-0.215					
Individualized equity	0.215*	0.501	0.046	0.500	-0.125	0.125
Member Benefits						
Product price	-0.213					
Product price & return on capital	0.213*	0.515	0.047	-0.125	0.125	0.500
Product Quality						
General grading of products	-0.271					
Specific/clients' grading of products	0.271*	0.571	0.052	-0.125	0.250	0.625

[a] Table 2 presents the estimated part-worth results for the selected attributes that drive members' overall utility of marketing cooperative's structure (dependent variable) based on individual estimates. The levels that have a positive MPW value are the preferred ones.

[b] We tested the predictive validity for the individual part worth estimates by computing the Tucker Coefficient (Zegers and Berge, 1985) in order to identify the degree of association between the predicted and the observed ratings of holdout pairs. The results showed that almost all individual part worths' predictive validity is satisfactory. An extra validity test using the self-constructed MC most preferred levels revealed similarity with the predicted results derived from the ratings of the calibration profile.

* $p < 0.05$.

Std.E.), are small relative to sample mean (*APW* of each attribute presented in first column of Table 2) and imply that most individual member part worths are similar to the total sample mean. So we have several indications that the *APWs* of each attributes are accurate reflections of individual members' part worths. However, looking at the part worths for different percentiles (see percentiles presented in last three columns of Table 2) some variability among individual preferences is identified. Individual member part worths vary below different percentile levels (25, 50, 75). For example, the 75th percentile (of a set of 100 numbers) for the first attribute (business issues/scope) has the value 0.625, hence 75% of the estimated part worths have a value smaller than 0.625; the median of the set is the 50th percentile. The percentile results show that the estimated conjoint model for each individual member follows a specific distribution based on his/her estimated part worths. These results indicate that individual member preferences vary in the sample. This may be due to the fact that the overall utility, which is the conceptual basis for measuring value in conjoint analysis, is a subjective judgment of preference unique to each individual.

In addition we calculated the attributes' relative importance, based on the range of the attribute part-worth estimates (see Figure 2).[5] The attributes related to the cooperative strategic behavior, business issue/scope and product quality strategy are the most important. Members attach a high importance to the business issue/scope (21.4%) and the product quality strategy (18.7 %). The attributes related to the internal cooperative structure are almost equally important except for the product-related decision-making attribute (17.2%). The attributes of the financial structure (14.9%) and members' benefits (14.8%) are less important. The corporate governance attributes has the lowest relative importance (13%). These results indicate that members consider the examined strategic attributes as very important for the MC's structure. Members prefer the VTN/TG to behave as an entrepreneurial and market-oriented organization using a market segmentation strategy based on the superior quality of its products. The last reveals their high interest for investing via collective action in forward integration in the food market supply chain. They also assign a high importance to the decision-making issues regarding the pricing, quantity and quality of their produce. This result may be caused by the fact that the TG's members were dissatisfied regarding the poor communication between members and experts on product-related and marketing issues.

Our findings confirm previous research in the cooperative literature (e.g., Shaffer, 1987; Staatz, 1987b; Schrader, 1989; Peterson and Anderson 1996; Kyriakopoulos, Meulenberg and Nilsson, 2004) that argued that cooperatives should better communicate product and service specification needs backward (member-suppliers) and forward (retailers, final consumers) in the market chain in order to create value for their members' produce. Furthermore, these results confirm recent neo-institutional economic (organizational economic and strategic management) theoretical advances (e.g., Teece, Pisano, and Shuen, 1997; Lewin and Volberda, 1999; Sykuta and Cook, 2001), namely that the competitive environment is reflected in the organizational structures and strategies of businesses.

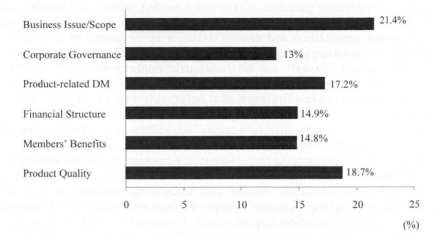

Figure 2. MC's Attributes' Importance

6. CONCLUSIONS

An implicit hypothesis in the cooperative literature is that perceived quality of the cooperative is the source of members' commitment. Perceived quality can be conceptualized as the utility that members derive from the use of the services provided by the cooperative. The perceived quality will be high when members believe that the cooperative operates on behalf of their interests as it attempts to meet the challenges posed by a competitive market place (Fulton and Giannakas, 2001). In this study we investigated a MC's structure based on the attributes that are related to the internal organization and the strategic behavior of the cooperative. This paper is the first that empirically identifies the relevance of these attributes for cooperative organizations from a member's perspective.

We developed an empirical research design to identify and evaluate the subjective utility that individual members attach to MC attributes. The empirical context is the Dutch horticultural MC, the VTN/TG, an organization that resulted from a merger of cooperative auctions. The transformation into a market-driven cooperative was confronted with a decline of members' commitment. The declining commitment of the VTN/TG members was caused by the corporate decision-making plan, product-related issues, and the transparency about cost-benefit allocations. The results show that members prefer to participate in a more entrepreneurial and market-oriented organization which will involve them in long-term relationships and develop a more direct link between its members and market segments. The high importance that members attach to product-related decision-making attributes reveals their preference for more active participation in functional operations higher up in the chain. In addition, members prefer that their MC's equity structure moves from the proportional type of financial arrangements to a more investor-oriented one. This implies that members desire that the MC distribute benefits to members' shareholdings in addition to product price. The latter is a fundamental shift from the traditional cooperative paradigm (Cook and Chaddad, 2004). The results of the empirical analysis also show that the attributes that we identified, attributes related to the internal organization and strategic behavior of the cooperative, drive members' preferences (utility) regarding the MC's structure.

The findings of this study may have managerial implications for MC's organizations. The great importance that members attach to the strategic attributes suggests that members prefer to benefit from market opportunities via the vertical integration offered by a MC. This may be an element which substantially reinforces their commitment toward cooperative participation and willingness to invest in collective actions. Such information may be utilized by cooperative policy makers when restructuring a MC. Recent research in behavioral economics shows the importance of the information revealed through market participants' preferences. Preferences are constructed, hence driven, by variables that describe the environment such as the competitive environment (e.g., see Bettman, Frances and Payne, 1998). Therefore, relying on this kind of information, managers of cooperatives may develop policies that satisfy cooperative members' demands. Likewise, members' commitment and willingness to invest in collective activities may be reinforced by adjusting internal organization and strategic behavior.

Traditionally, the theoretical study on cooperative formation involves only pricing as a unique attribute from which members derive utility. Our results clearly show that several other attributes of internal organization (e.g., product-related decision making) and the strategic behavior (e.g., product quality) of cooperatives can also significantly drive the cooperative structure, and are considered by members as more important than the attribute related to pricing policy (i.e., members' benefits). These findings may provide guidelines and fruitful thought for further theoretical research on modeling and hypothesis formation regarding cooperative structure. However, two major limitations of our research should be mentioned here. First, we conceptualized and measured attributes related to internal organization and strategic behavior of a horticultural MC. Although the focus group discussions and the pre-testing of our hypothetical MC profiles characterized the combinations of these attributes as actionable and coherent, we suggest that further empirical research should pay special attention on the design of different attribute and level combinations – in particular, by accounting for interaction effects among attributes within the existing range of cooperative models (i.e., traditional to member-investor and/or more individualized cooperative models). Second, we assumed that the membership has homogeneous preferences. We mentioned the actions undertaken by various groups of the VTN/TG's members in order to better represent their interests via the collective action. We also indicated briefly how the individual preferences vary in the sample. Our analysis did not account for the fact that members may value the attributes of the cooperative structure differently. This may be caused by differences in member firms' structure (Staatz, 1983), entrepreneurial skills (Karantinis and Zago, 2001), and risk preferences regarding operational and strategic cooperative issues (Vitaliano, 1983; Cook, 1995). The heterogeneity in members' behavior may adversely influence members' commitment when cooperatives expand and diversify (Sexton, 1986). Taking the heterogeneity of members into account is a challenging task since one has to allow the part-worth (value for an attribute) to differ across groups of members. Work is in progress to examine the impact of members' heterogeneity on cooperative structural designs.

NOTES

* The authors gratefully acknowledge all the members of the VTN/TG who participated in focus-group sessions (30), pilot test study (8), and final field study (120). We would like to thank J. Bijkerk for his help in designing the computerized interviews and the administrative personnel of the Dutch National Cooperative Council for Horticulture and Agriculture (NCR) for facilitating the data collection. Finally, the authors would like to thank the editors, an anonymous referee, Prof. M.T.G. Meulenberg, Dr. J. Bijman, and the participants of ESF Meeting held in Chania, Greece, 3–7 September, 2004, for providing valuable comments on a preliminary draft of this paper.
[1] In a "member-investor" cooperative, members' benefits are realized either through dividends distribution to shares and/or appreciability of cooperatives shares in addition to patronage. A detailed description about the different cooperative models that vary from traditional cooperatives to cooperatives inversed in an IOF (individualized business structure) is given by Cook and Chaddad (2004). van Bekkum (2001) uses an extreme classification of a collective versus an individualized structure in order to describe differences in the functionality of their organizational elements.
[2] Hendrikse and Veerman (1997) provide an example of a MC's structure as a coherent system of attributes (control, equity, wealth allocation) that brings together several subsystems of operating and functional activities (e.g., delivery rights conditions); Bijman (2002) follows recent organizational economic theory and examines whether organizational attributes for marketing fresh produce makes a coherent system in the transition from a cooperative auction to a cooperative's governance structure.
[3] The evaluation process of communicable and actionable measures determines the degree to which the attributes and levels are easily communicable for realistic evaluation and capable of being put in practice, respectively. These technical terms as well as the evaluation of first-order interactions among the attributes of a product/service are described in detail by Hair, et al., 1998 (p. 405–407).
[4] Such an interaction was somehow expected considering that the members' gains are closely related to the cooperative's net income allocation and equity redemption mechanisms. However, we kept these attributes within the conjoint design as they were stated by members participated in focus-group sessions.
[5] The range of the part-worth estimates was calculated for each attribute by taking differences between the highest and the lowest part-worth estimate. The sum of the ranges of all attributes equals to the total range. Dividing every individual attribute's range by the sum of the ranges across attributes and multiplying by 100 gives the relative importance of each attribute for members' preferences in terms of a percentage. For a more detailed description of attribute-importance calculations in conjoint analysis experiments see Hair et al., (1998).

REFERENCES

Anderson, B.L., and B.M. Henehan. 2002. "What Went Wrong at AgWay?" Fact Sheets and Extension Resources, Cornell University Cooperative Enterprise Program. Cornell University, October. Available at http://cooperatives.aem.cornell.edu/pdf/resources/agway.pdf, accessed 10 May 2005.

Barton, D. 1989. "What Is a Cooperative?" In D. Cobia, ed. Cooperatives in Agriculture, Prentice Hall, Englewood Cliffs NJ: Prentice Hall, pp. 1-20.

Bettman, J.R., L.M. Frances, and J.W. Payne. 1998. "Constructive Consumer Choice Processes." Journal of Consumer Research, 25:187-217.

Bijman, W.J.J. 2002. "Essays on Agricultural Co-operatives: Governance Structure in Fruit and Vegetable Markets." Erasmus Research Institute of Management (ERIM) PhD Series in Management 15, Erasmus University Rotterdam.

Brorsen, B.W., and S.H. Irwin. 1996. "Improving the Relevance of Research on Price Forecasting and Marketing Strategies." Agricultural and Resource Economics Review 25: 68-75.

Cobia, D., ed. 1989. *Cooperatives in Agriculture,* Englewood Cliffs NJ: Prentice Hall.

Cook, M.L. 1997. "Organizational Structure and Globalization: The Case of User-Oriented Firms." In J. Nilsson. and G. van Dijk, eds. *Strategies and Structures in the Agro-food Industries.* Assen: Van Gorcum, pp. 77-93.

____. 1995. "The Future of U.S. Agricultural Cooperatives: A Neo-Institutional Approach." *American Journal of Agricultural Economics* 77: 1153-1159.

Cook, M.L., and F.R. Chaddad. 2004. "Redesigning Cooperative Boundaries: Emergence for New Models." *American Journal of Agricultural Economics* 86: 1249-1253.

Cotterill, R.W. 2001. "Cooperative and Membership Commitment: Discussion." *American Journal of Agricultural Economics* 83: 1280-1281.

Fulton, M.E. 1999. "Cooperatives and Member Commitment." *Finish Journal of Business Economics* 4: 418-473.

____. 1995. "The Future of Canadian Agricultural Cooperatives: A Property Rights Approach." *American Journal of Agricultural Economics* 77:1144-1152.

Fulton, M.E., and J. Gibbings. 2000. *Response and Adaptation: Canadian Agricultural Cooperatives in the 21ˢᵗ Century.* Ottawa: Canadian Co-operative Association and Le Conseil Canadien de la Coopération, October.

Fulton, M.E., and K. Giannakas. 2001. "Organizational Commitment in a Mixed Oligopoly: Agricultural Co-operatives and Investor Owned Firms." *American Journal of Agricultural Economics* 83: 1258-1265.

Green, P.E. 1974. "On the Design of Choice Experiments Involving Multifactor Alternatives." *The Journal of Consumer Research* 1: 61-68.

Green, P.E., and V. Srinivasan. 1978. "Conjoint Analysis in Consumer Research: Issues and Outlook." *Journal of Consumer Research* 5: 103-123.

____. 1990. "Conjoint Analysis in Marketing: New Developments with Implications for Research and Practice." *Journal of Marketing* 54: 3-19.

Green, P.E., and Y. Wind. 1975. "New Ways to Measure Consumers' Judgements." *Harvard Business Review* 53: 107-117.

Hair, J.F., R.E. Anderson, R.L. Tanham, and W.C. Black, eds. 1998. *Multivariate Data Analysis.* Englewood Cliffs NJ: Prentice Hall.

Hakelius, K. 1996. "Cooperative Values: Farmers Cooperatives in the Minds of Farmers." PhD dissertation, Swedish University of Agricultural Sciences.

Hendrikse, G.W.J., and C. P. Veerman. 1997. "Marketing Cooperatives as a System of Attributes." In J. Nilsson and G. van Dijk, eds. *Strategies and Structures in the Agro-food Industries,* Assen: Van Gorcum, pp. 111-130.

Karantinis, K., and A. Zago. 2001. "Endogenous Membership in Mixed Duopsonies." *American Journal of Agricultural Economics* 83:1266-1272.

Keneey, R.L., and H. Raiffa. 1972. "A Critique of Formal Analysis in Public Decision Making." In A.W., Drake, R.L. Keeney, and P.M. Morse, eds. *Analysis of Public Systems.* Cambridge, MA: M.I.T. press.

____. eds. 1993. *Decisions with Multiple Objectives: Preferences and Value Tradeoffs.* New York: Cambridge University Press.

Kyriakopoulos, K. 2000. "The Market Orientation of Cooperative Organizations. Learning Strategies and Structures for Integrating Firms and Members." Ph.D. Thesis, Nyenrode University, The Netherlands Business School, Assen: van Gorsum.

Kyriakopoulos, K., M.T.G. Meulenberg, and J. Nilsson. 2004. "The Impact of Cooperative Structure and Firm Culture on Market-Orientation and Performance." *Agribusiness: An International Journal* 20: 379-396.

Lewin, A.Y., and H.W. Volberda. 1999. "Prolegomena on Coevolution: A Framework for Research on Strategy and New Organizational Forms." *Organization Science* 10: 519-534.

Little, J.D.C. 1986. "Research Opportunities in Decision and Management Sciences." *Management Science* 32: 1-13.

Meulenberg, M.T.G. 2000. "Voluntarily Marketing Institutions in Food Marketing Systems." In A. van Tilburg, H.A.J. Moll, and A. Kuyvenhoven, eds. *Agricultural Markets Beyond Liberalization.* Boston: Kluwer Academic Publishers, pp. 213-233.

Nilsson, J., and G. van Dijk, eds. 1997. *Strategies and Structures in the Agro-food Industries.* Assen: van Gorcum.

Olson, M., ed. 1971. The *Logic of Collective Action: Public Goods and the Theory of Groups.* Cambridge, MA: Harvard University Press.

Peterson, C.H., and B.L. Anderson. 1996. "Cooperative Strategy: Theory and Practice." *Agribusiness: An International Journal* 12: 371-383.

Schrader, L.F. 1989. "Economic Justification." In D.W. Cobia, ed., *Cooperatives in Agriculture.* Englewood Cliffs, NJ: Prentice Hall.

Sexton, R.J. 1990. "Imperfect Competition in Agricultural Markets and the Role of Cooperatives: A Spatial Analysis." *American Journal of Agricultural Economics* 72:709-720.

____. 1986. "The Formation of Cooperatives: A Game–Theoretic Approach with Implications for Cooperative Finance, Decision Making, and Stability." *American Journal of Agricultural Economics* 68: 214-225.

Sexton, R.J., and T.A. Sexton. 1987. "Cooperatives as Entrants." *The Rand Journal of Economics* 18: 581-595.

Shaffer, J.D. 1987. Thinking About Farmer's Cooperatives, Contracts, and Economic Coordination, In: *Cooperative Theory: New Approaches,* J.S. Royer (ed.), pp. 61-86, Washington, D.C.: USDA ACS Service, Rep. 18, July 1987.

Shoemaker, P.J.H. 1982. "The Expected Utility Model: Its Variants, Purposes, Evidence and Limitations." *Journal of Economic Literature,* 20(2): 529-563.

Shoemaker, P.J.H. 1993. "Strategic Decisions in Organizations: Rational and Behavioral Views." Journal of Management Studies, 30(Fall): 108-129.

Staatz, J.M. 1983. "The Cooperative as a Coalition: A Game Theoretic Approach." *American Journal of Agricultural Economics* 65:1984-1089.

____. 1987a. "The Structural Characteristics of Farmer Cooperatives and their Behavioral Consequences." In J.S. Royer, ed. *Cooperative Theory: New Approaches.* Washington, D.C.: U.S. Department of Agriculture, ACS Service Rep. 18, July, pp. 33-60.

____. 1987b. "Farmers' Incentives to Take Collective Action via Cooperatives: A Transaction Cost Approach." In J.S. Royer, ed. *Cooperative Theory: New Approaches.* Washington, D.C.: U.S. Department of Agriculture, ACS Service Rep. 18, July, pp. 87-107.

Sterns, J.A., D.B. Schweikhardt, and H.C. Peterson. 1998. "Using Case Studies as an Approach for Conducting Agribusiness Research." *International Food and Agribusiness Management Review* 1: 311-327.

Sykuta, M.E., and M.L. Cook. 2001. "A New Institutional Approach to Cooperatives and Contracting." *American Journal of Agricultural Economics* 83: 1273-1280.

Teece, D.J., G. Pisano, and A. Shuen. 1997. "Dynamic Capabilities of Strategic Management" *Strategic Management Journal* 18: 87-110.

Vazsonyi, A. 1990. "Decision Making: Normative, Descriptive and Decision Counseling." *Managerial and Decision Economics* 11: 317-325.

van Bekkum, O.F. 2001. "Cooperative Models and Farm Policy Reform: Exploring Patterns in Structure-Strategy Matches of Dairy Cooperatives in Protected vs. Liberated Markets." Ph.D. Thesis, Nyenrode University, The Netherlands Business School, Assen: van Gorcum.

van Dijk, G. 1999. "Evolution of Business Structure and Entrepreneurship of Cooperatives in the Horti- and Agribusiness." *Finish Journal of Business Economics* 4:471-483.

van Dijk, G., and C. Mackel. 1991. "Dutch Agriculture Seeking for Market Leader Strategies." *European Review of Agricultural Economics* 18: 345-364.

Veerman, C.P. 1998. "Ontwikkelingen Bij de Afzet van Glasgroenten." In J.T.M. Allebas and M.J. Varekamp, eds. *De Glastuinbouw in het Derde Millennium: Wendingen en Kansen,* Naaldwijk: Gemeente Naaldwijk, pp.49-55.

Vitaliano, P. 1983. "Cooperative Enterprise: An Alternative Conceptual Basis for Analyzing Complex Institutions." *American Journal of Agricultural Economics* 65:1078-1083.

Wedel, M., and W.A. Kamakura, eds. 2000. *Market Segmentation: Conceptual and Methodological Foundations* (International Series in Quantitative Marketing), 2nd edition, Dordrecht: Kluwer Academic Publishers.

Zegers, F. E., and J.M.F. ten Berge. 1985. "A Family of Association Coefficients fro Metric Scales." *Psycometrika,* 50(1): 17-24

Beside the publications referenced in the text and listed above, the following sources have been used for this study:

- *VTN Annual Reports 1998 and 1999*

- *The Greenery Annual Reports, 1998, 1999, 2000, 2001, 2002*

- Interviews with Prof. M.T.G. Meulenberg, Wageningen University, The Netherlands, September, 2001; Prof. G. van Dijk, General Director of the Dutch National Cooperative Council for Horticulture and Agriculture, Den Haag, October, 2001; A.J.M. van De Riet, Manager Co-operative Affairs, Utrecht, February, 2002 and March, 2002; Sabien Henselmans, Administrative Staff of Co-operative Affairs Office, March, 2002; Dr. O. F. van Bekkum, Senior Researcher of The Netherlands Institute for Cooperative Entrepreneurship, June, 2003, the Netherlands.

CHAPTER 6

AGENCY AND LEADERSHIP IN COOPERATIVES

Endogenizing Organizational Commitment

MURRAY FULTON

Dept. of Agricultural Economics, University of Saskatchewan, Saskatoon, Canada

KONSTANTINOS GIANNAKAS

Dept. of Agricultural Economics, University of Nebraska-Lincoln, Lincoln, U.S.A.

Abstract. The poor financial performance of a number of previously successful agricultural cooperatives appears to be connected to member commitment, which in turn is linked to the decisions made by the cooperatives' leaders. While cooperative members should have an incentive to hire leaders that promote strong organizational commitment, the evidence suggests this incentive is weaker than imagined. This paper shows that cooperatives that believe they have a well-defined and loyal membership are less likely to hire leaders that will enhance member commitment. Thus, historical success is no guarantee of future success and may in fact contain the seeds of failure.

1. INTRODUCTION

Cooperatives face the problem that while they have been formed by their members for the members' benefit, the members' commitment to the organization cannot be relied upon. Instead, the commitment by the members to the organization is conditional upon the members believing that the organization is indeed acting in their interest – i.e., that the leaders of the organization are acting as effective agents of the members (Fulton and Giannakas, 2001). This commitment is generally of vital importance to the organization and to the well being of the members – as membership commitment wanes, so does the financial and organizational health of the organization and with it its ability to provide goods and services to the members.

Examples of low member commitment and its connection to the decisions made by the cooperative can be found in some of the major agricultural cooperatives in Canada and the United States. In the past several years, a number of previously successful agricultural cooperatives have found themselves in severe financial

K. Karantininis & J. Nilsson (eds.), Vertical Markets and Cooperative Hierarchies, 93–113.

trouble. This financial trouble has been reflected in cooperatives such as Tri-Valley Growers, Farmland, Agway and the Rice Growers Association (RGA) in the United States filing for bankruptcy protection and in cooperatives such as Agricore, Dairyworld and the Saskatchewan Wheat Pool (SWP) in Canada being taken over by or converting to investor-owned firms (IOFs).[1]

The poor financial performance of these cooperatives appears to be linked to member commitment. Agway, for instance, faced declining revenues since 1990. While a portion of this decline was likely due to price decreases resulting from more intense competition, some of the decline was also likely a result of falling member commitment (Anderson and Henehan). For the SWP, one reason for reduced profitability was a substantial drop in market share – e.g., in its core grain market in Saskatchewan, the SWP's market share fell from 59 percent in 1993 to 33 percent in 2003 (Lang and Fulton). The situation was similar in RGA – in the early 1980s the cooperative handled upwards of 70 percent of the total California rice crop; at the time of its closure in 2000, it handled approximately 5 percent of the crop (Keeling).

This drop in member commitment and the poor financial performance have been directly linked to the decisions made in these cooperatives by their leaders. In their overview of what went wrong at Agway, Anderson and Henehan remark, "Managers too often selected, and poorly executed the wrong strategies to achieve profitability" (p. 11). In commenting on events at SWP, a grain industry analyst was quoted as saying that the cooperative was guilty of "poor strategic thinking" (quoted in Ewins, p. 10). Keeling concludes that "RGA's board of directors failed to actively exercise its duty to supervise the management. In turn, the management fell short of expectations to fully evaluate complex business decisions and was remiss in planning for future contingencies."

The connection between the leadership of cooperatives and the well being of its members suggests that members should have an interest in hiring leaders (and properly overseeing them once they are hired) that promote strong organizational commitment. However, the examples presented above suggest that this incentive may be weaker than imagined.

Conceptually, the members – through the individuals they elect to the board of directors – face two problems in generating leadership that will enhance their well-being. The first is an adverse selection problem – is the correct type of leader being chosen? The second is a moral hazard problem – is the leader that is chosen acting in the proper manner? Both problems appear to have been factors in the demise of the agricultural cooperatives discussed above. While the second of these problems has been examined in the cooperative literature (see, for example, Cook, 1994, 1995, Featherstone and Al-Kheraiji, 1995, and Fulton, 1999), the first has received much less attention.

The purpose of this paper is to examine why a cooperative may fail to hire the proper type of leader, and to investigate the effect of this hiring decision on member commitment to the organization and the performance of the organization. The basis for the model developed in this paper is that businesses are typically managed by a collection of key individuals in the organization that make the most important resource allocation choices (Prahalad and Bettis, 1986). These choices are guided by a dominant general management logic, namely the manner in which "managers conceptualize the business and make critical resource allocation decisions" (p. 490). In short, an organization's key leaders are extremely important in influencing the direction taken by the organization, and these decisions are guided by a dominant logic or conceptualization that is very difficult to change, particularly in the short run (Prahalad and Bettis, 1986; Bettis and Prahalad, 1995).

Given this backdrop, our analysis focuses on the incentives that a cooperative has to invest in screening its potential leaders before they are hired as to their general approach to running a cooperative business. The analysis also examines the incentives that the leaders have – once hired – to signal their management approach (i.e., their management logic). To simplify the analysis, the paper examines the decision to hire the top leader – the CEO, for instance. It is assumed that this individual would, in turn, hire the remainder of the key management group.

The key conclusion of the paper is that cooperatives are less likely to invest in screening a potential leader when they believe the leader is unlikely to undertake a signaling investment. The result is that cooperatives that provide favorable conditions for leaders to truthfully signal their type as somebody that is focused on enhancing member benefits are also the ones that are most likely to hire leaders with precisely such a focus. Given the different incentives that different cooperatives have to hire managers that will work to enhance member well being and strengthen member commitment, cooperatives can be expected *ex post* to exhibit a wide range of outcomes from highly successful organizations with strongly committed members to relatively weak organizations with low organizational commitment.

A key factor influencing the cooperative's incentive to screen its potential leaders is the nature of competition provided by other organizations supplying similar goods or services. The greater is the (perceived) difference in the organizations and the products they provide and/or the more costly it is for consumers to shift their purchases, the lower is the cooperative's incentive to screen. Thus, screening of leaders is less likely to occur in cooperatives that believe they have a well-defined and loyal membership; the implication is that these cooperatives are less likely to hire leaders that will work to enhance member commitment.

The rest of the paper is organized as follows. The next section provides an overview of the structure of the model; this overview is then followed by a formal development of the model. The implications of the model are then examined, followed by a discussion and concluding remarks.

2. OVERVIEW OF THE MODEL

The basis of the model developed in this paper is that cooperative leaders have significant power and influence when it comes to determining the direction taken by the cooperative, which in turn determines the attitude of the members toward the cooperative and hence its market share. The model used to address these issues is a composition of two simpler models – one is an adverse selection model with screening and signaling; the other is a product differentiation model. The type of leader chosen in the adverse selection model determines the "quality" of the product offered by the cooperative which then – via a product differentiation model – determines the cooperative's market share.

The underlying assumption in the analysis is that cooperative members, via the board of directors, have limited ability to influence the strategic decisions made by the senior management (e.g., CEO, CFO). This lack of power stems in part from informational and control problems present in the principal-agent relationships inherent among members, board members and senior management (see Cook (1995) for a discussion of these control problems in the context of a cooperative). This lack of influence also arises because the leaders' dominant management logic, which strongly influences their decisions, is difficult to change.

While a cooperative's board has limited power to influence the strategic direction taken by the leader once he or she has been hired, it does have the power to choose the leader, thus indirectly influencing the cooperative's actions. This power is important because potential leaders are not homogeneous, but differ in a number of important respects. For the purposes of the analysis in this paper, it is assumed that leaders differ in the dominant general management logic they bring to the organization. Specifically, it is assumed that leaders are one of two types – those that maximize the welfare of members and those that maximize the profits of the cooperative. These two types correspond roughly, on the one hand, to leaders that see their role as creating an organization that benefits the members, and, on the other hand, to leaders that see their role as creating an organization that alone is successful and profitable.

Although the different types of leaders may attempt to signal their abilities (e.g., through educational accomplishments such as advanced business degrees), these signals are not sufficient to indicate their inclination to serve the members' interests. The result is a pooling equilibrium in which both leader types are available at the going market wage (which the cooperative is unable to influence). Thus, board members are uncertain as to which type of leader they are choosing. They can, however, decide to reduce this uncertainty in period 1 by making an investment that acts as a partial screen for leader type (see Figure 1). While the nature and range of leader types, as well as the range of options open to boards, are much richer in reality than what is modeled in this paper, the distinct nature of the leader types examined serves to highlight the importance of the hiring decision made by the board.

Once a particular leader has been hired, the game moves to period 2 where the true type of the leader may or may not be revealed (see Figure 1). The revelation of type is important because member knowledge of leader type affects their commitment. More specifically, member commitment is lowered if the leader is revealed to be a profit maximizer, while member commitment is raised if the leader is revealed to be a member-welfare maximizer. If the leader type is not revealed, then members have an average degree of commitment. Leaders can affect the probability of the leader type being revealed by making an investment in a signal.

An implied assumption in the model is that the members are able to determine the type of the leader when the board of directors is not able to do so or is unable to act on this knowledge (presumably the board would fire the leaders if it was felt that they were not operating in the best interest of the cooperative and its members). This

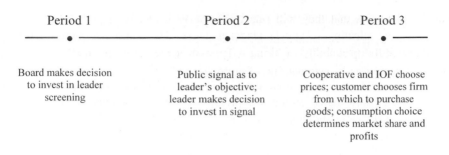

Period 1	Period 2	Period 3
Board makes decision to invest in leader screening	Public signal as to leader's objective; leader makes decision to invest in signal	Cooperative and IOF choose prices; customer chooses firm from which to purchase goods; consumption choice determines market share and profits

Figure 1. Timing of the Game

assumption reflects the fact that a board often buys into the dominant logic of the leader it hires, thus making it difficult for it to see problems when they first emerge and/or creating difficulties in firing the leader, at least in the short run. The leader is also likely to provide the board with information that supports the leader's dominant logic, thus camouflaging the leader's true type.

With member commitment determined, the cooperative then competes with an IOF in the provision of a product or service in period 3 (see Figure 1). The degree of member commitment, along with the degree to which the products of the IOF and the cooperative are differentiated in the minds of consumers, determines the prices charged by the two organizations, their market share, and the well being of the consumers. To keep the analysis simple and to focus attention on the leader of the cooperative, it is assumed that the leader of the IOF always maximizes profits.

3. THE FORMAL MODEL

Consider a mixed oligopoly in which an investor-owned firm and a cooperative compete with each other in selling a good to a group of consumers. The two firms sell products that are differentiated. This differentiation reflects differences in consumer valuation of the products supplied by the two firms (this valuation includes the price each firm charges for the product) as well as differences in the degree to which the consumers perceive the cooperative to be meeting their needs.

This latter aspect is modeled as a quality attribute q_c that is high when the cooperative is perceived to be meeting its members' needs. When q_c is high, the cooperative is assumed to be a superior organization with which to do business (Fulton and Giannakas). Thus, a high q_c corresponds to high member commitment. An in-depth examination of this product differentiation is provided in the Appendix, while the set-up of the consumer model is considered in more detail below.

In the first period, the cooperative's board of directors hires the cooperative leader (e.g., CEO). The cooperative leader makes the pricing decisions in the cooperative. The leader of the cooperative is one of two types. A Type-W leader makes pricing decisions that maximize the welfare of the members, while a Type-Π leader makes pricing decisions that result in maximum profits for the cooperative.

The board knows that they will select a Type-W leader with probability α; the probability of selecting a Type-Π leader is $1-\alpha$. The board also knows that they can increase the probability of hiring a Type-W leader from α to β ($\beta > \alpha$) by making a screening investment I (see Figures 1 and 2).

Once the leader has been hired, the game moves to period two (see Figure 1). In this period, a public signal occurs with probability μ and consumers perfectly learn the nature of the cooperative leader (see Caillaud and Tirole, 2002, for a similar set-up). The probability that this public signal does not occur is $(1-\mu)$; in the absence of this signal, consumers are uncertain as to the type of cooperative leader that is in place (and thus the type of objective the leader will pursue). One interpretation of this public signal is that outside observers trusted by the members (e.g., newspapers, trade publications, and academic institutions) are able to discern and disclose the nature of the leader. The leader can increase the probability that his/her true nature is revealed from μ to ν ($\nu > \mu$) by making a signaling investment K (see Figure 2). Alternatively, the same investment K can be used to decrease the probability that his/her true nature is revealed from μ to λ ($\lambda < \mu$). Consistent with *a priori*

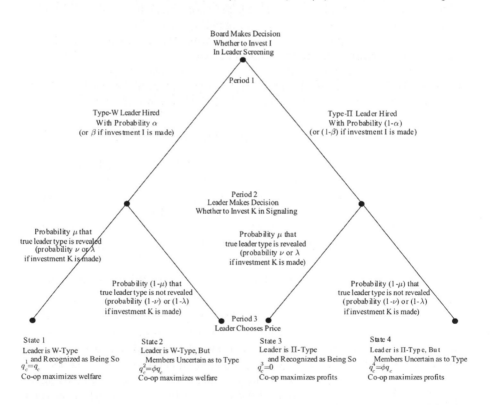

Figure 2. *Decision Tree for the Cooperative Leadership and Member Commitment Game*

expectations, it will be shown that Type-W leaders never have an incentive to decrease the probability that their true type is revealed, while Type-Π leaders never have an incentive to increase this probability.

In the third period of the game, the cooperative and the IOF set the prices for the product they are supplying (see Figure 1). The IOF always maximizes profits, while the cooperative maximizes member welfare if the leader is of Type-W and maximizes profits if the leader is of Type-Π. Figure 2 graphs the four possibilities – or states of the world – that can occur in Period 3. In state 1, the leader is of Type-W and the consumers know this – thus the cooperative maximizes member welfare and member commitment is high. In state 2, the leader is of Type-W, but the consumers do not know this – the cooperative maximizes member welfare and member commitment is average. In state 3, the leader is of Type-Π and the consumers know this – the cooperative maximizes member profits and member commitment is low. In state 4, the leader is of Type-Π and the consumers do not know this – the cooperative maximizes profits and member commitment is average.

Based on the prices chosen by the cooperative and IOF, consumers/members choose the firm from which they purchase the product and the market shares of the cooperative and IOF are determined. To solve this game, we use backward induction and start with the decision of the consumers in the last period.

3.1. Period 3 – Consumption and Pricing Decisions

The coexistence of cooperatives and IOFs that provide similar goods/services suggests that consumers differ in their willingness to pay for products supplied by cooperatives versus products supplied by IOFs. Differences in willingness to pay denote differences in the utility derived from the consumption of these products.

Consider a consumer with the following utility function:

$$U_c^s = U - p_c^s + (q_c^s - tx)$$
$$U_i^s = U - p_i^s + (q_i - t(1 - x))$$

(1)

where U_c^s and U_i^s are the net consumer benefits associated with purchasing a unit of the product from the cooperative and the IOF, respectively, in state s ($s \in \{1, 2, 3, 4\}$). The parameter U is a base level of utility, and p_c^s and p_i^s are the prices charged by the cooperative and IOF in state s. The parameter t is a non-negative utility reduction factor, while the variable x takes values between zero and one and captures heterogeneous consumer preferences (and thus, heterogeneous willingness to pay) for the product supplied by the cooperative and the IOF. The parameters q_c^s and q_i are quality parameters for the cooperative and the IOF, respectively. The quality parameter for the cooperative is state dependent, while the quality parameter for the IOF is state independent. Without loss of generality, let

$q_i = 0$. This normalization means that the quality of the cooperative is measured relative to that of the IOF.

The parameter q_c^s captures member commitment – the degree to which, in any state s, the product of the cooperative is valued more than that of the IOF when the prices charged are the same. Following Fulton and Giannakas, q_c^s indicates the perceived quality of the cooperative and the IOF as organizations. One interpretation of q_c^s is that it measures the degree to which the cooperative effectively acts as the agent of its members. Thus, the more the cooperative is perceived to act in the interests of the members, the greater is q_c^s, and the more committed are the members to their cooperative. The parameter q_c^s thus depends on the prevailing state of knowledge about the nature of the leader.

The parameter t captures the difference in utility obtained by consumers with different values of the differentiating attribute x and can be interpreted in a number of ways. One interpretation is that t is a transportation cost.[2] Higher values reflect a greater cost to consumers of shifting business between the cooperative and the IOF; the larger is t, the less responsive are consumers to changes in price. The parameter t can also be interpreted as partisanship or as an indicator of ideology (Fulton, Fulton and Giannakas). Similar to the previous interpretation, the more partisan or ideological are consumers (i.e., the larger is t), the less responsive they are to changes in price.

For tractability, the analysis assumes that consumers are uniformly distributed between the polar values of x. Each consumer buys one unit of the product and the purchasing decision represents a small share of his/her total budget. A consumer's purchasing decision is determined by comparing the utility derived from the product when it is purchased from the cooperative and when it is purchased from the IOF. In state s, the consumer with differentiating characteristic x_c^s given by:

$$x_c^s : U - p_c^s + (q_c^s - tx) = U - p_i^s - t(1-x) \Rightarrow x_c^s = \frac{1}{2} + \frac{q_c^s}{2t} + \frac{(p_i^s - p_c^s)}{2t} \quad (2)$$

is indifferent between buying from the cooperative and buying from the IOF – the utility of consuming these two products is the same. Consumers "located" to the left of x_c^s (i.e., consumers with $x \in [0, x_c^s)$) purchase from the cooperative while those located to the right of x_c^s (i.e., consumers with $x \in (x_c^s, 1]$) buy from the IOF.

When consumers are uniformly distributed with respect to their differentiating attribute x, the location of the indifferent consumer, x_c^s, also determines the market share of the cooperative. The market share of the IOF is given by $(1 - x_c^s)$. By normalizing the mass of consumers at unity, the market shares give the consumer demands faced by the cooperative, x_c^s, and the IOF, x_i^s, respectively (Mussa and

Rosen, 1978). In what follows, the terms "market share" and "demand" will be used interchangeably to denote x_i^s or/and x_c^s. Formally, x_i^s and x_c^s can be written as:

$$x_i^s = \frac{1}{2} - \frac{q_c^s}{2t} + \frac{(p_c^s - p_i^s)}{2t}; \; x_c^s = \frac{1}{2} + \frac{q_c^s}{2t} + \frac{(p_i^s - p_c^s)}{2t} \tag{3}$$

If the cooperative and the IOF charge the same price to consumers (i.e., when $p_i^s = p_c^s$), x_c^s and x_i^s depend on the magnitude of the quality parameter q_c^s. Obviously, when $q_c^s = 0$ and prices are equal, $x_i^s = x_c^s = 0.5$.

Consider now the optimizing decisions of the IOF and the consumer cooperative that are involved in a strategic price competition (i.e., they choose their prices simultaneously). The problem of the IOF is to determine, in each state s, the price of the product, p_i^s, that maximizes profits given the price of the cooperative, p_c^s, and consumer demand schedule, x_i^s. The problem of the cooperative depends on the type of leader that has been hired. A Type-W leader maximizes members' welfare, while a Type-Π leader maximizes profits.

When a Type-W leader makes the pricing decisions at the cooperative, the resulting prices and market shares for the cooperative and IOF are given as follows (see the Appendix for the derivation):[3]

$$p_i^{s*} = \frac{-q_c^s + m_i + m_c + t}{2}; \; p_c^{s*} = m_c$$

$$x_i^{s*} = \frac{t - q_c^s + (m_c - m_i)}{4t}; \; x_c^{s*} = \frac{3t + q_c^s + (m_i - m_c)}{4t} \tag{4}$$

Note that since marginal cost pricing results in a maximum market share (subject to non-zero profits) for the cooperative, these same equilibrium conditions will also prevail when the objective of the cooperative is to maximize sales (market share), again subject to non-zero profits. This equivalence between maximizing sales and maximizing member welfare will be used in subsequent analysis.

The results change when the objective of the cooperative leader is to maximize profits rather than member surplus. With a Type-Π leader making the pricing decisions for the cooperative, the Nash equilibrium outcome of the strategic price competition becomes:

$$p_i^{s*} = \frac{3t - q_c^s + m_c + 2m_i}{3}; \; p_c^{s*} = \frac{3t + q_c^s + m_i + 2m_c}{3}$$

$$x_i^{s*} = \frac{3t - q_c^s + (m_c - m_i)}{6t}; \; x_c^{s*} = \frac{3t + q_c^s + (m_i - m_c)}{6t} \tag{5}$$

The profits of the two firms are given by:

$$\pi_i^{s*} = 2t(x_i^{s*})^2; \pi_c^{s*} = 2t(x_c^{s*})^2 \tag{6}$$

Compared to when the cooperative maximizes member welfare, the change in the cooperative's objective increases p_c^s, p_i^s and x_i^s, while reducing x_c^s and consumer welfare.

The market share of the cooperative in each state of the world depends on the quality perceived by the members, which in turn depends on the type of cooperative leader that has been hired. To add some structure to the problem, assume that when a Type-W leader has been hired and the consumers know this (state 1), the perceived quality of the cooperative q_c^1 is q_c – i.e., $q_c^1 = q_c$. When a Type-Π leader has been hired and the members know this (state 3), the perceived quality of the cooperative q_c^3 is assumed to be the same as that of the IOF – thus, $q_c^3 = 0$. When the consumers do not know what type of leader has been hired (states 2 and 4), it is assumed that the cooperative is perceived to have quality ϕq_c – i.e., $q_c^{2,4} = \phi q_c$, $0 < \phi < 1$. The parameter ϕ can be interpreted as the discount that is applied to the perceived quality of the cooperative when consumers are uncertain as to the type of leader (the smaller is ϕ, the greater is the discount that is applied), or it can be interpreted as the probability of hiring a Type-W leader. Under this latter interpretation, ϕ can be presumed equal to either α if no screening has been carried out or β if screening has been carried out.

The different perceived qualities translate into different market shares in each of the four states. Table 1 summarizes these market shares under the assumption that the marginal costs of the cooperative and the IOF are identical (i.e., $m_c = m_i$).

Table 1. *Cooperative's market share under different states*

	State			
	State 1	State 2	State 3	State 4
Leader Objective	Max W	Max W	Max Π	Max Π
Perceived Quality	$q_c^1 = q$	$q_c^2 = \phi q_c$	$q_c^3 = 0$	$q_c^4 = \phi q_c$
Expected Market Share	$x_c^1 = \dfrac{3t + q_c}{4t}$	$x_c^1 = \dfrac{3t + \phi q_c}{4t}$	$x_c^3 = \dfrac{1}{2}$	$x_c^2 = \dfrac{3t + \phi q_c}{6t}$
Expected Profits	Zero	Zero	$\pi_c^3 = \dfrac{t}{2}$	$\pi_c^2 = \dfrac{(3t + \phi q_c)^2}{18t}$

3.2. Period 2 – The Coop Leader's Signaling Decision

The purpose of this section is to outline how the quality of the organization, and hence member commitment, q_c, can be linked to the behavior of the cooperative leader.

As was outlined in the discussion above, the leader can make a signaling investment in Period 2 that will increase the probability of his/her true type being revealed from μ to υ. The cost of this investment is K. In deciding whether to make this investment, the leader examines the expected benefits from doing so. These expected benefits depend on the leader type.

Consider first the case of a Type-W leader. Since this type of leader is interested in maximizing member welfare, the benefits from making the signaling investment are evaluated in terms of member welfare. Let V_W be the monetary valuation that the Type-W leader attaches to member welfare.[4] Recalling that the market share of the cooperative (x_c) maps directly onto member welfare and that μ is the probability that the true type is revealed, the expected benefits obtained by the Type-W leader when no signaling investment is made are given by:

$$E(B_W^{NS}) = \mu V_W x_c^1 + (1 - \mu)V_W x_c^2 = V_W \left[x_c^2 + \mu \left(x_c^1 - x_c^2 \right) \right] \tag{7}$$

where x_c^k is the market share of the cooperative in state k ($k = 1,2$).

The expected benefits obtained by the Type-W leader that makes a signaling investment designed to increase the probability that the leader's true type is revealed are given by:

$$E(B_W^{S_y}) = \upsilon V_W x_c^1 + (1 - \upsilon)V_W x_c^2 - K = V_W \left[x_c^2 + \upsilon \left(x_c^1 - x_c^2 \right) \right] - K \tag{8}$$

If the leader makes a signaling investment designed to lower the probability that the leader's true type is revealed, the expected benefits are given by:

$$E(B_W^{S_\lambda}) = \lambda V_W x_c^1 + (1 - \lambda)V_W x_c^2 - K = V_W \left[x_c^2 + \lambda \left(x_c^1 - x_c^2 \right) \right] - K \tag{9}$$

Since $x_c^1 - x_c^2 > 0$ (see Table 1) and $\upsilon > \lambda$, Type-W leaders will never invest in lowering the probability that their true type is revealed.

Leaders will make the signaling investment K and raise the probability that their type is revealed when the net benefits from this investment exceed the benefits when this investment is not made. Thus, the leader will find it optimal to signal when:

$$V_W \left[x_c^2 + v\left(x_c^1 - x_c^2\right)\right] - K > V_W \left[x_c^2 + \mu\left(x_c^1 - x_c^2\right)\right] \qquad (10)$$

Simplifying equation (10) gives:

$$K < V_W \left(v - \mu\right)\left(x_c^1 - x_c^2\right) \qquad (11)$$

Thus, the Type-W leader finds it optimal to signal when his/her cost K is less that the expected benefits derived from doing so. The benefits are given by the difference in market shares in states 1 and 2 weighted by V_W and multiplied by $(v - \mu)$, the change in the probability of having the leader's true type revealed. Substituting the market shares for states 1 and 2 (see Table 1) into equation (11) gives the condition under which the Type-W leader finds it beneficial to make the investment K:

$$K < \frac{V_W \left(v - \mu\right)\left(1 - \phi\right)q_c}{4t} \qquad (12)$$

Equation (12) has a number of implications. The smaller is t, the greater is the likelihood that a Type-W leader will make the investment K. Thus, the less partisan are consumers and/or the less costly it is for them to shift their business to another firm, the greater is the likelihood that the leader will make the investment. The greater is the signaling effectiveness (i.e., the greater is $(v - \mu)$) and the greater is the monetary valuation V_W attached to member welfare (or market share), the greater is the likelihood of a Type-W leader making the investment K. Type-W leaders are also more likely to make the investment K when the perceived quality q_c of the cooperative is high and when the discount applied to quality when consumers are uncertain as to the type of leader is high (i.e., ϕ is low). If the parameter ϕ is interpreted as the probability of hiring a Type-W leader, then the investment K is more likely to be made when the probability of hiring a Type-W leader (i.e., α) is presumed to be low. One implication of this relationship is that Type-W leaders are more likely to invest in a signal that reveals their true type if the board has not invested in screening at the hiring stage.

Consider now the case of a Type-Π leader. Since this type of leader is interested in maximizing profits, the benefits from making the signaling investment must be evaluated in terms of profits. Let V_Π be the monetary valuation that the Type-Π leader attaches to cooperative profits. The expected benefits obtained by the Type-Π leader when no signaling investment is made are:

$$E(B_\Pi^{NS}) = \mu V_\Pi \pi_c^3 + (1 - \mu)V_\Pi \pi_c^4 = V_\Pi \left[\pi_c^4 + \mu\left(\pi_c^3 - \pi_c^4\right)\right] \qquad (13)$$

where π_c^k is the profits of the cooperative in state k ($k = 3,4$). The expected benefits obtained by the Type-Π leader from the signaling investment designed to raise the probability that the true leader type is revealed are given by:

$$E(B_\Pi^{S_\nu}) = \nu V_\Pi \pi_c^3 + (1-\nu)V_\Pi \pi_c^4 - K = V_\Pi \left[\pi_c^4 + \nu\left(\pi_c^3 - \pi_c^4\right)\right] - K \qquad (14)$$

If the Type-Π leader makes a signaling investment designed to lower the probability that his/her true type is revealed, the expected benefits are given by:

$$E(B_\Pi^{S_\lambda}) = \lambda V_\Pi \pi_c^3 + (1-\lambda)V_\Pi \pi_c^4 - K = V_\Pi \left[\pi_c^4 + \lambda\left(\pi_c^3 - \pi_c^4\right)\right] - K \qquad (15)$$

Since $\pi_c^3 - \pi_c^4 < 0$ (see Table 1) and $\nu > \lambda$, the Type-Π leader will never invest in raising the probability that their true type is revealed.

The Type-Π leader will find it desirable to make the signaling investment K that lowers the probability that their true type is revealed when the net benefits from making this investment exceed the benefits obtained when this investment is not made. Thus, the leader will find it optimal to signal when:

$$V_\Pi \left[\pi_c^4 + \lambda\left(\pi_c^3 - \pi_c^4\right)\right] - K > V_\Pi \left[\pi_c^4 + \mu\left(\pi_c^3 - \pi_c^4\right)\right] \qquad (16)$$

Simplifying equation (16) gives:

$$K < V_\Pi \left(\lambda - \mu\right)\left(\pi_c^3 - \pi_c^4\right) \qquad (17)$$

Substituting in the expressions for π_c^3 and π_c^4 (see Table 1) gives:

$$K < V_\Pi \left(\mu - \lambda\right)\frac{\phi q_c}{3}\left(1 + \frac{\phi q_c}{6t}\right) \qquad (18)$$

The smaller is t, the more likely are the Type-Π leaders to make a signaling investment K that conceals their true type. Thus, the less partisan are consumers and/or the less costly it is for them to shift their business to another firm, the greater is the likelihood that leaders will try and conceal their true type. The greater is the effectiveness of the signal (i.e., the greater is $(\mu - \lambda)$) and the greater is the monetary valuation V_Π attached to cooperative's profits, the greater is the likelihood of a Type-Π leader making the investment K. Type-Π leaders are also more likely to make the investment K when the perceived quality q_c of the cooperative is high and when the discount parameter ϕ is high. If the parameter ϕ is interpreted as the probability of hiring a Type-W leader, then a Type-Π leader is more likely to conceal his/her true type when the probability of hiring a Type-W leader (i.e., α) is presumed to be high. One implication of this relationship is that Type-Π leaders are more likely to conceal their true type if the board has invested in screening at the hiring stage.

As was discussed above, signaling by a leader can depend on whether the board has invested in screening at the hiring stage. In order for the board's screening decision to affect the leader's signaling decision, it is necessary that ϕ be dependent on the board's screening decision. This situation can occur if the membership knows that screening was undertaken and that the probability of hiring a Type-W leader has increased, and if they then use this knowledge when determining the expected organizational quality when the leader type is unknown. Under these conditions, $\phi = \alpha$ if the board has not screened, while $\phi = \beta$ if the board has screened.

The connection between ϕ and the screening decision of the board means that the signaling decision of the Type-W and Type-Π leaders can be partitioned. For the Type-W leader, the decision to signal is made as follows:

$$K > K_W^\alpha \qquad \text{Never Signal}$$
$$K_W^\beta < K \leq K_W^\alpha \qquad \text{Signal if Board Does Not Screen; Otherwise Do Not}$$
$$K \leq K_W^\beta \qquad \text{Always Signal}$$

where $K_W^\alpha = (1-\alpha)\dfrac{V_W(v-\mu)q_c}{4t}$ and $K_W^\beta = (1-\beta)\dfrac{V_W(v-\mu)q_c}{4t}$. For the Type-$\Pi$

leader, the decision to signal is made as follows:

$$K > K_\Pi^\beta \qquad \text{Never Signal}$$
$$K_\Pi^\alpha < K \leq K_\Pi^\beta \qquad \text{Signal if Board Screens; Otherwise Do Not}$$
$$K \leq K_\Pi^\alpha \qquad \text{Always Signal}$$

where $K_\Pi^\alpha = \alpha\dfrac{V_\Pi(\mu-\lambda)q_c}{3}\left(1+\dfrac{\alpha q_c}{6t}\right)$ and $K_\Pi^\beta = \beta\dfrac{V_\Pi(\mu-\lambda)q_c}{3}\left(1+\dfrac{\beta q_c}{6t}\right)$.

3.3. Period 1 – The board's Screening Decision

In Period 1 the board of directors hires a leader. As noted above, a leader can be one of two types – Type-W or Type-Π. Recall that if no screening is carried out, the probability of hiring a Type-W leader is α, while the probability that a Type-Π

leader is hired is $1 - \alpha$. The probability of hiring a Type-W leader can be increased to β ($\beta > \alpha$) if the board makes a screening investment.

Assuming that the board of directors of the cooperative is interested in selecting a leader that will generate the highest expected market share (recall that maximizing market share will also maximize member welfare), the board has to weigh the expected benefits when no screening of the leader is carried out against the expected benefits when screening is carried out. Denote $E\left(x_W^{SC}\right)$ and $E\left(x_\Pi^{SC}\right)$ as the expected market shares when screening occurs and a Type-W leader and a Type-Π leader, respectively, are hired, and $E\left(x_W^{NSC}\right)$ and $E\left(x_\Pi^{NSC}\right)$ as the expected market shares when no screening occurs and a Type-W leader and a Type-Π leader, respectively, are hired. The board will find it advantageous to make the screening investment I if:

$$\beta E(x_W^{SC}) + (1 - \beta)E(x_\Pi^{SC}) - I > \alpha E(x_W^{NSC}) + (1 - \alpha)E(x_\Pi^{NSC}) \qquad (19)$$

The board's screening decision is greatly simplified if it is assumed that ϕ is independent of whether screening takes places. With ϕ independent of the board's screening decision, the expected market share does not depend on whether the board has made the screening investment or not – thus, $E\left(x_W^{SC}\right) = E\left(x_W^{NSC}\right)$ and $E\left(x_\Pi^{SC}\right) = E\left(x_\Pi^{NSC}\right)$. Using these two equalities and rearranging terms in equation (19) gives the condition that must hold in order for the board to invest in screening:

$$I < (\beta - \alpha)\left[E(x_W) - E(x_\Pi)\right] \qquad (20)$$

Equation (20) illustrates one of the main conclusions of the paper, namely that the greater is the expected difference in market share when a Type-W leader is hired versus when a Type-Π leader is hired (i.e., the greater is $E(x_W) - E(x_\Pi)$), the greater is the incentive to invest in screening. The economic interpretation is straightforward. The term $(\beta - \alpha)[E(x_W) - E(x_\Pi)]$ is the expected benefit of engaging in screening, while I is the cost. Screening is desirable if its benefit outweighs its costs.

Equation (20) suggests some important implications for the board's decision to screen. For instance, if the board anticipates that a Type-W leader will invest in signaling (thus raising $E(x_W)$), the board will be more likely to invest in screening. Conversely, the board will be less likely to invest in screening if it believes that a Type-W leader will not invest in signaling. The board is also less likely to invest in screening if it believes that a Type-Π leader will invest in a signal to mislead the membership as to their true type, while the board is more likely to invest in screening if it believes that a Type-Π leader will not try to mislead the membership.

M. FULTON & K. GIANNAKAS

Both of these cases indicate that information acquisition by the board is a strategic complement to information provision by the leader. The greater is the information that the leaders can be expected to provide, the greater is the likelihood that the
board will seek out information on the leader they are hiring by investing in
screening. The board is more likely to screen candidates when it is expected that the
leader will provide information because this provision of information by the leaders
increases the payoff from screening.

These results imply that if a board is observed to undertake little screening, then
it indicates that the screening cost is high and/or the addition to market share
$E(x_W) - E(x_\Pi)$ is believed to be small. The perceived addition to market share will
be small when t is believed to be large (i.e., members are expected to be unlikely to
move) and/or ϕ is high (i.e., members are expected to not discount the quality of the
cooperative when they are uncertain as to the leader's type). Thus, screening is less
likely when the cooperative believes that the members are in some way captive to
the organization, since this captivity reduces the benefit of screening.

The results derived above may change when ϕ is dependent on the board's
screening decision. Consider, for instance, the situation where ϕ is dependent on the
board's screening decision but this decision does not affect the leaders' decision to
signal. There are four such cases: Case A_ϕ – $K \leq K_W^\beta$ and $K \leq K_\Pi^\alpha$ – both leaders
signal; (b) Case B_ϕ – $K > K_W^\alpha$ and $K \leq K_\Pi^\alpha$ – the Type-Π leader signals, while the
Type-W leader does not; (c) Case C_ϕ – $K \leq K_W^\beta$ and $K > K_\Pi^\beta$ – the Type-W leader
signals, while the Type-Π leader does not; and (d) Case D_ϕ – $K > K_W^\alpha$ and
$K > K_\Pi^\beta$ – neither leader signals. Examining the case where both leaders signal (i.e.,
case A_ϕ where $K \leq K_W^\beta$ and $K \leq K_\Pi^\alpha$) in more detail, the board will invest in
screening if:[5]

$$I < \frac{(\beta - \alpha)}{12} \left[3 + \frac{q_c}{t} \left[3 + (1 - \alpha - \beta)(3\nu - 2\lambda - 1) \right] \right] \qquad (21)$$

The other three cases can easily be obtained by modifying equation (21) as follows:
The other three cases can easily be obtained by modifying equation (21) as follows:
Case B_ϕ – set $\nu = \mu$; Case C_ϕ – set $\lambda = \mu$; and Case D_ϕ – set $\nu = \mu$ and $\lambda = \mu$.

Equation (21) implies that an increase in t will reduce the likelihood that the
board screens (note that $[3 + (1 - \alpha - \beta)(3\nu - 2\lambda - 1)] > 0$). Thus, screening will be
less likely to occur in cooperatives where members are believed to be highly
partisan or where they face large costs of shifting their business to an IOF, once
again highlighting the notion that cooperatives with captive members are less likely
to screen.

Unlike the case where ϕ is independent of the board's decision, signaling by the leader can have an ambiguous effect on screening. Suppose the Type-W leader is not expected to signal (cases B and D); as equation (21) shows, the impact of replacing ν with μ depends on the sign of $(1 - \alpha - \beta)$, which may be positive or negative. A similar outcome occurs if the Type-Π leader is not expected to signal (cases C and D), since the impact of replacing λ with μ depends on the sign of $(1 - \alpha - \beta)$.

When the board's screening decision does affect the leaders' decision to signal (i.e., $K_W^\beta < K \le K_W^\alpha$ and/or $K_\Pi^\alpha < K \le K_\Pi^\beta$), the board's decision is highly case specific and is not examined here.

4. DISCUSSION

The results of this paper indicate that the level of information present in a cooperative organization, which affects the type of leader hired and the level of member commitment, is endogenously determined. Specifically, the board is generally less likely to make a screening investment when it is expected that future information levels will be low (e.g., when there is an expectation that a Type-W leader will not make a signaling investment or there is an expectation that a Type-Π leader will try to mislead). Thus, low expected levels of information in later periods will tend to lead to low levels of information in the first period, which in turn means that no action is taken to increase the probability of hiring a Type-W leader. This result occurs because low levels of information in later periods have the effect of reducing the benefits to screening in the first period, thus making screening less likely.

One consequence of the above result is that cooperative organizations that provide favorable conditions for Type-W leaders to signal their type (e.g., low levels of partisanship or ideology, high levels of valuation) also provide conditions under which it is more likely that Type-W leaders are hired. To the extent that hiring a Type-W leader gives rise to better performance, organizational success can breed organizational success. Of course, the dynamics may also work in reverse. Cooperative organizations can find that they have no incentive to reduce the probability of hiring Type-Π leaders at the same time that these Type-Π leaders have an incentive to mislead the membership as to their type.

While organizational success can breed organizational success, the continuation of this positive feedback relationship is not guaranteed. As equation (21) shows, higher values of t can reduce the incentive for the board to invest in screening. Thus, all else equal, cooperatives with relatively stable market shares may be more likely to hire a Type-Π leader than cooperatives with low initial member commitment – the result is a "resting on your laurels" effect.

Since hiring a Type-Π leader is more likely to lead to a reduction in member commitment through a reduction in the perceived quality of the organization, the result is that historical success can lead to conditions that will undermine this success. This "resting on your laurels" effect appears to have been at work in creating the difficulties experienced by cooperatives such as Agway, SWP, and RGA.[6]

This feedback effect may be particularly important if the board misinterprets the behavior of its members or the nature of member commitment. For instance, suppose a Type-W leader has successfully generated a high organizational quality – the result is that the cooperative's market share is relatively large (see equation (4)). If the board believes that this high market share is also a sign that members are loyal to the cooperative they may come to the conclusion that t is high (as equation (3) shows, the response of the cooperative's market share to a change in the cooperative's price is small if t is large), which in turn reduces the incentive for the board to invest in screening (see equation (21)). Such behavior can lead to an increased probability that a Type-Π leader is hired and thus an increased probability that the cooperative cannot maintain its high market share.

The discussion above highlights the fact that the financial performance of cooperatives is linked in important ways to member commitment. Member commitment, in turn, has a number of dimensions and is influenced by (and influences) the hiring decisions of the cooperative and the nature of the leadership within the cooperative. As this paper shows, the incentive that cooperatives have to hire leaders that promote member commitment may be limited in a number of situations. In particular, success by a cooperative can often provide the conditions under which the organization has limited incentive to screen its candidates for continued success. An examination of recent failures among a number of previously successful agricultural cooperatives using this framework is a subject for future research.

NOTES

[1] For further information on these cooperatives, see: Anderson and Henehan (2002), and Fairbairn (2003), for an analysis of Agway; Ewins (2002), and Lang and Fulton (2004) for details on Saskatchewan Wheat Pool; Goddard (2002) for an examination of Dairyworld; Torgerson (2003) for thoughts on Farmland Industries Limited; Sexton and Hariyoga (2004) for an analysis of Tri-Valley Growers; and Keeling (2004) for an examination of Rice Growers Association.

[2] See Sexton (1990) for an analysis of the impact of the spatial location of potential cooperative members on the behavior of a cooperative.

[3] The equilibrium prices and quantities presented are not dependent upon the nature of price competition between the cooperative and the IOF. Instead, the same equilibrium conditions prevail for a wide variety of price competition scenarios. For instance, the same prices and quantities result from a sequential pricing game with the leader being either the IOF or the cooperative. The reason is that the best response function of the cooperative ($p_c = m_c$) is not a function of the price charged by the IOF (Fulton and Giannakas).

[4] One source of this monetary valuation could be the cooperative's remuneration scheme. For instance, if the leader's salary was linked to member welfare, or equivalently market share, then the monetary valuation would reflect this linkage.

[5] Assuming that $\phi = \alpha$ when the board does not screen and $\phi = \beta$ when the board screens,

$$E\left(x_W^S\right) = \frac{3}{4} + \frac{v + (1-v)\beta}{4t}q_c, \qquad E\left(x_W^{NS}\right) = \frac{3}{4} + \frac{v + (1-v)\alpha}{4t}q_c, \qquad E\left(x_\Pi^S\right) = \frac{1}{2} + \frac{(1-\lambda)\beta}{6t}q_c, \qquad \text{and}$$

$$E\left(x_\Pi^{NS}\right) = \frac{1}{2} + \frac{(1-\lambda)\alpha}{6t}q_c.$$ Substituting these expressions into equation (19) and simplifying gives equation (21).

[6] See the references cited in note 1 for details.

REFERENCES

Anderson, B., and B. Henehan. 2002. "What Went Wrong at Agway?" Extension Paper, Cornell University Cooperative Enterprise Program, Cornell University. Located January 18, 2005 at http://cooperatives.aem.cornell.edu/pdf/resources/agway.pdf.

Bettis, R.A., and C.K. Prahalad. 1995. "The Dominant Logic: Rretrospective and Extension." *Strategic Management Journal* 16:5–14.

Caillaud, B., and J. Tirole. 2002. "Parties as Political Intermediaries." *The Quarterly Journal of Economics* 117:1453–89.

Cook, M.L. 1994. "The Role of Management Behavior in Agricultural Cooperatives." *Journal of Agricultural Cooperation,* 9:42–58.

Cook, M.L. 1995. "The Future of U.S. Agricultural Cooperatives: A Neo-institutional Approach." *American Journal of Agricultural Economics* 77:1153–9.

Ewins, A. 2002. "Special Report: Saskatchewan Wheat Pool." *Western Producer* May 9: 10–11.

Fairbairn, B. 2003. "Losing Sight of the Goal: Agway." Paper prepared for the CARD II Leadership Development Forums, Centre for the Study of Co-operatives, University of Saskatchewan, Saskatoon SK.

Featherstone, A. M., and Al-Kheraiji, A.A. 1995. "Debt and Input Misallocation of Agricultural Supply and Marketing Cooperatives." *Applied Economics* 27:871–78.

Fulton, M.E., and K. Giannakas. 2001. "Organizational Commitment in a Mixed Oligopoly: Agricultural Cooperatives and Investor-owned Firms." *American Journal of Agricultural Economics* 83:1258–1265.

___. 1999. "Cooperatives and Member Commitment." *Finnish Journal of Business Economics* 4:418–37.

___. 1989. "Co-operatives in Oligopolistic Industries: the Western Canadian Fertilizer Industry." *Journal of Agricultural Cooperation* 4:1–19.

Goddard, E. 2002. "Factors Underlying the Evolution of Farm-related Cooperatives in Alberta." Principal Paper, Canadian Agricultural Economics Association Annual Meeting, Calgary AB, May 30–June 1.

Keeling, J.J. 2004. "Lessons in Cooperative Failure: The Rice growers' Association experience." Working paper. Presented at the NCERA-194 Research on Cooperatives Annual Meeting, Kansas City, November 2–3.

Lang, K., and M.E. Fulton. 2004. "Member commitment and the market and financial performance of the Saskatchewan Wheat Pool." *Current Agriculture Food and Resource Issues* 5:238–252. Located at www.cafri.org.

Mussa, M., and S. Rosen 1978. "Monopoly and Product Quality." *Journal of Economic Theory* 18: 301–17.

Prahalad, C.K., and R.A. Bettis. 1986. "The Dominant Logic: A New Linkage between Diversity and Performance." *Strategic Management Journal* 7:485–501.

Sexton, R.J. 1990. "Imperfect Competition in Agricultural Markets and the Role of cooperatives: A Spatial Analysis." *American Journal of Agricultural Economics* 72:709–20.

___. and H. Hariyoga. 2004. "The Canning of Tri-Valley." *Rural Cooperatives* (September/October): 20–24.

Torgerson, R. 2003. "Farmland Industries Limited." Presentation to the Annual Meeting of the American Agricultural Economics Association and the Rural Sociological Society, Montreal, PQ, July 27–30.

APPENDIX

Utility Model

The utility functions in equation (1) are based on the assumption that the good has two attributes – the first of these is the set of physical characteristics of the good, while the second is the organization from which the good is purchased. The utility of the good is assumed to be the sum of the utilities associated with each of these two attributes.

The first component of equation (1) – the term $U - p_k$ $(k \in \{c, i\})$ – shows the net consumer benefit derived from the physical characteristics of the product after adjustment is made for the price that is paid for the product. The parameter U is a per unit willingness to pay for the physical attributes of the product. Subtracting the price of the product from this willingness-to-pay value gives the net utility associated with the physical characteristics.

The second component of equation (1) gives the willingness to pay for the type of organization at which the good is purchased – this is the component $(q_c - tx)$ for the cooperative and $(q_i - t(1-x))$ for the IOF. Recall that for a consumer with attribute x, the term tx gives the reduction in utility from patronizing the cooperative while the term $t(1-x)$ is the reduction in utility from doing business with the IOF.

Pricing Decisions

The IOF's problem can be written as:

$$\max_{p_i} \pi(p_i, p_c) = (p_i - m_i)x_i \quad s.t. \quad x_i = \frac{1}{2} - \frac{q_c}{2t} + \frac{(p_c - p_i)}{2t} \tag{A1}$$

where m_i represents the constant marginal cost associated with the supply of the product. Note that q_i is assumed to be equal to zero and that the state superscript is suppressed.

Solving the IOF's problem shows the standard result that profits are maximized at the price-quantity combination determined by the equality of the marginal revenue and the marginal cost of production. Specifically, for any p_c, the best-response function of the IOF (i.e., the profit-maximizing price of the IOF) is given by:

$$p_i = \frac{(p_c + m_i) + t - q_c}{2} \tag{A2}$$

With a Type-W leader, the problem facing the consumer cooperative is to choose the price p_c that maximizes the welfare of the consumers that patronize the cooperative subject to a non-negative profit constraint. Given the price of the IOF, p_i, and consumer demand schedule, $x_c = \frac{1}{2} + \frac{q_c}{2t} + \frac{(p_i - p_c)}{2t}$, the cooperative's problem is:

$$\max_{p_c} \; MS(p_i, p_c) = (U - p_c + \lambda)x_c - \frac{1}{2}\lambda x_c^2$$

$$s.t. \; x_c = \frac{1}{2} + \frac{q_c}{2t} + \frac{(p_i - p_c)}{2t} \text{ and } p_c \geq m_c \tag{A3}$$

where m_c is the cooperative's constant marginal cost of supplying the product.

Solving the cooperative's problem specified above shows that the optimality (Kuhn-Tucker) conditions for a maximum are satisfied when the cooperative prices its product at marginal cost, i.e., MS is maximized when $p_c = m_c$.

Solving the best response functions of the IOF and the cooperative simultaneously and substituting p_i and p_c into equation (3) gives the Nash equilibrium prices and quantities for the two competitors:

$$p_i^* = \frac{m_i + m_c + t - q_c}{2} \; ; p_c^* = m_c$$

$$x_i^* = \frac{t - q_c + (m_c - m_i)}{4t} \; ; x_c^* = \frac{3t + q_c + (m_i - m_c)}{4t} \tag{A4}$$

If both the IOF and the cooperative choose price to maximize profits, then the cooperative's best response function is similar to that of the IOF shown in equation (A2) – i.e., $p_c = [(p_i + m_c) + t + q_c]/2$. Solving the two best response functions gives the Nash equilibrium prices and quantities for the two competitors:

$$p_i^* = \frac{3t - q_c + m_c + 2m_i}{3} \; ; p_c^* = \frac{3t + q_c + m_i + 2m_c}{3}$$

$$x_i^* = \frac{3t - q_c + (m_c - m_i)}{6t} \; ; x_c^* = \frac{3t + q_c + (m_i - m_c)}{6t} \tag{A5}$$

CHAPTER 7

LOCK-IN OF FARMERS IN AGRICULTURAL COOPERATIVES

Reviving the Effect of Exit by Means of Constitutional Amendments

SØREN VINCENTS SVENDSEN

The Aarhus School of Business, Denmark

Abstract: Structural changes in the agricultural set-up challenge the value of traditional practices in cooperatives. The major sector development causes a lock-in effect for individual farmers and gives rise to non-Pareto-optimal outcomes for individual farmer members. Constitutional economics may be a theoretical source for reviving the effect of exit by addressing potential adjustments to the traditional cooperative institutional set-up and, thereby, generating more stable equilibria in collective bargaining processes between farmers. The approach focuses on voting rules, investment levels as well as individual positive and negative rights in farmers' collective actions and calls for adjustment of traditional practices in agricultural cooperatives.

1. INTRODUCTION

This article presents an analysis of the need for adjustments of procedural as well as substantial aspects of the set of rules governing agricultural cooperatives on the basis of, firstly, the coalition theoretical framework for understanding the cooperative, most notably developed and applied in this field by Staatz (1984). Secondly, the analysis will be conducted by applying insights and explanations from constitutional economic theory or, hereafter, public choice theory building primarily on the work developed by Buchanan and Tullock (1965) and Brennan and Buchanan (1980). Public choice theory is the study of non-market decisions and analysis of procedural as well as substantial aspects of collective action with the aim of protecting individual rights and reaching Pareto-efficient solutions.[1]

The background for the analysis is increasing cooperative investments with a matching need for more risk bearing capital from farmer members, as well as an ongoing structural development taking place in the food chain including stages beyond the farm gate[2] (Traill, 1998). The changes alter and modify conditions for farmer membership of agricultural cooperatives in various ways. Generally,

K. Karantininis & J. Nilsson (eds.), Vertical Markets and Cooperative Hierarchies, 115–135.
© 2007 *Springer.*

collective decisions can be expected to affect farmers differently because of different perceptions of business strategies, different transactions with the jointly owned firm and differences in personal circumstances (Hansmann, 1996). Increasing costs of membership as a result of more offensive cooperative business strategies will affect owners differently because of their different forecasts on returns, different risk preferences and costs of capital and, consequently, challenge the ability to align interests between members and generate non-stable equilibria for individual members. Therefore, the development may be detrimental to the cohesion of collective action.

Traditionally, farmer members of agricultural cooperatives have confined business activities of their joint action as a mechanism for achieving homogeneity of interests (Hansmann, 1988; Holmström, 1999). Besides, exit is a powerful tool for disciplining behavior of other persons (Hirschman, 1970). The value of exit for the individual farmer is deteriorating in light of structural changes. Consequently, individual farmer members become susceptible to the interests of powerful coalition members. This is a challenge for collective action where the ability to balance interests in the bargaining process between coalition members is important for the ability to generate outcomes that can be considered stable equilibria by all members. The assumption is that farmers should be able to confine business activities and discipline others' actions in order to align individual interests with group goals. Therefore, the need is to both institutionalize the scope of joint action and to revive the *effect* of exit by means of institutional rules for disciplining behavior of powerful coalition members. The former issue links to the substantial aspects and the latter to the procedural aspects of the constitutional or institutional set-up for agricultural cooperatives, and public choice theory is suggested to provide insights to formalize both aspects of a "cooperative constitution".

Consequently, *the aim of this article is twofold. First, it is to identify the essence of farmers' joint action in light of structural development in cooperative sectors and increasing costs of ownership. Second, given the structural conditions, public choice theory will be used to identify and analyze implications for cooperative structural features, especially by focusing on substantial and procedural aspects of a cooperative constitution in order to generate stable equilibria in joint action.* The discussion and analysis is primarily centered around investment decisions and specifically the matter of the level of earnings to be retained on a yearly basis as an increase in the risk-bearing capital of the cooperative.

The article is structured in two parts: Part one deals basically with the background for applying public choice theory on agricultural cooperatives, including an understanding of the agriculture cooperative and its structural features in addition to the assumption that changes in market conditions lead to increased costs of membership and cause potential tensions. Part two undertakes analysis of cooperative constitutional aspects, including the importance of avoiding non-Pareto-optimal outcomes of cooperative investment decisions. A tentative methodology for design of cooperative constitutions will close this part. Finally, a conclusion is presented.

2. THE ESSENCE OF AGRICULTURAL COOPERATIVES: LOCK-IN OF FARMERS IN JOINT ACTION

2.1 The agricultural cooperative: the coalition perspective

Hansmann (1999: 388) explains, that "It is common to think of cooperatives as something very different from investor-owned business corporations. But this is misleading." However, other cooperative researchers point to some distinctive features, which they argue have to be considered understanding the viability of the cooperative organization and outcomes of cooperative decision-making processes. The implications for cooperative behavior of structural features of the cooperative institutional set-up and in particular of constraints on residual claims and voting rights have often been addressed in cooperative literature (Vitaliano, 1983; Porter & Scully, 1987; Cook, 1995).

Much of this literature builds on the coalition theory: the agricultural cooperative is viewed as a coalition of members, e.g., different groups of farmers, management, board members and employees. Each coalition member has his own preferences and consequently pursues different objectives and participates only as long as benefits outweigh costs of taking part in the collective action (Staatz, 1984, 1987a). The outcome of a bargaining process is determined by the relative power of different participants in the organization. So the assumption is that the coalition member that can impose his strategy on the coalition will determine the goals and strategies of the cooperative, and institutional rules will serve as conditioning variables in order to generate stable equilibria of bargaining processes. The focus is, in other words, on intra-farmer conflicts and the different objectives of coalition members of the cooperative. Addressing intra-farmer conflicts, the focus is on situations where farmer members do not bear the full marginal cost or receive the full marginal return for their actions, and thereby, as explained by Staatz (1987a: 9), have "...an incentive to act in ways inconsistent with the long-run welfare of the cooperative or some of its members."

An outcome of a collective decision leaving some farmer members worse off would be non-Pareto optimal and cause unstable equilibria in the decision-making process. Therefore, the Pareto criterion seems crucial in relation to the challenge of "...building an organization with sufficient cohesion to withstand the disintegrating forces arising out of conflicting interests," as it is formulated by Helmberger and Hoos (1965: 184).

2.2 Balancing power by means of exit: The effect of sector structure

Hirschman (1970) points to exit, voice and loyalty as three complementary mechanisms for customers to express satisfaction and/or dissatisfaction, but the work is applicable in many other situations. In relation to collective action among farmers the point is that behavior of different member coalitions is constrained or balanced by countervailing disciplinary actions, which other members have control over, and these disciplinary actions comprise both exit and voice mechanisms (Staatz, 1983).

The lesson from Hirschman (1970) is that the relative costs of exercising disciplinary actions classified in accordance with exit or voice determine the appropriate combination of these two mechanisms to use in a specific situation for customers, cooperative members, managers or other coalition members taking part in collective action. Therefore, the implication is that exit as disciplinary action becomes more costly when the structural development leads to fewer alternative trading partners for farmers or just fewer benchmarks. The development suggests that "...there may be greater member voice in large cooperatives covering a broad geographic area than in small cooperatives where members have alternative market outlets" (Staatz, 1983: 15–16).

In light of the structural development in the food and/or cooperative sector over the last three decades cooperative members will to a larger degree have to rely on voice in their farmer controlled companies. In other words, exit becomes more costly if it is an option at all, and *farmers become locked in to the joint action.* Outcomes of decision-making processes will, in other words, be more difficult to balance by non-powerful coalition members. The development should not be lamented, though, or assessed independently of potential positive effects. Even though farmer members could be assigned more *formal* rights that make the exit option less costly, empirical and theoretical arguments are supportive of mutual obligations across farmer members and weak farmer obligations could be detrimental to the competitiveness (Staatz, 1987b).

Less opportunity to balance interests in a bargaining process can be expected to increase the influence of management as a powerful coalition member and other member groups with coinciding preferences, e.g., employees and some external stakeholders. Theoretically, the influence of management on outcome of corporate decisions relates to the separation of ownership and control in companies (Berle & Means, 1932; Ross, 1973). The assumption is that managerial objectives are variables like firm size or growth because these objectives are connected with compensation and power of managers: "One of the explanations for the pursuit of growth by corporate managers...is to achieve the nonpecuniary rewards associated with 'empire building'" (Mueller, 1989: 272).

The link between managerial objectives and cooperative behavior has long been assumed, and to some degree analyzed in cooperatives. One of the pioneers in analyzing cooperatives on the basis of organizational theory emphasized that cooperative managers may not be loyal to member preferences, seeking their own interests instead. In particular, growth maximization was suggested to be a dominant goal for management (Eschenburg, 1971). The identification of the control problem as one or more organizational weaknesses in the cooperative organizational structure emphasizes conflicting interests among (some) farmer members and management (e.g. Cook, 1995). In a comprehensive study of user owned firms it is argued that a mismatch can occur between the member organization and the business operation because of weakening member orientation in cooperatives as an effect of a higher business complexity and, consequently, more management resources and discretion over the decision-making process (Bager, 1992). More empirically oriented cooperative literature on management influence on strategies supports the general observations; managers favor capital accumulation to lower the degree of leverage, thereby increasing their own flexibility and achieving more room for "empire building" (Murray, 1983).

In light of structural development in the sector, manager discretion in determination of emergent business strategies and financing arrangements, including the level of risk bearing capital, is explained rather boldly by a CEO in an agricultural cooperative:[3] "There is no doubt that the room for cooperative managers to influence the level of retained earnings from members have increased as a result of the structural development in the sector. It has become easier to set the level of retained earnings at a higher level; the current and intended business strategies and future investment plans are a reflection of this development."

2.3 Increasing costs of ownership: Implications for joint action

Assuming room for more biased outcomes of cooperative decisions when the effect of member exit deteriorates, it would be natural to ask: Does it matter? Yes, in light of market justifications, broadly speaking, for further investments in up-and-downstream processing activities the demand for more risk bearing capital from farmers will increase and may likely provoke inherent conflicts of interests among farmers. More generally, higher farmer investments in combination with more complex organizational structures of cooperatives may provoke or increase the problems or the organizational weaknesses inherent to the cooperative organizational form[4] (Cook, 1995; Nilsson, 2001). Better specified property rights in cooperatives have been suggested to ameliorate such organizational weaknesses, and not least create higher farmer incentives for cooperative investments (Cook, 1995) because "[It] is the key to the incentive effects of ownership," and the effects are powerful because then "...[T]he decision-maker bears the full financial impact of his or her choices" (Milgrom and Roberts, 1992: 291). Consequently, it also reduces potential conflicts in a cooperative (Cook, 1995).

The positive incentive effects of better specified property rights in the sense of transferable and appreciable equity shares build on the Fisher Separation Theorem (Milgrom and Roberts, 1992). The Theorem suggests[5] that the individual member's incentive to invest will only depend on the farmer's forecast of return and on individual costs of capital or discount rate, and not on individual preferences regarding timing of consumption. Consequently, cooperative investment decisions affect farmer members differently. Milgrom and Roberts (1992:294–296) explain that group members are likely to differ on matters such as production costs, forecast on returns of investments, and costs of participation given the range alternatives. Differences between farmers are no less: members work with different resources in the very broad sense, different risk preferences and different discount rates or costs of capital (Staatz, 1987a, 1987b; Vitaliano, 1983).

To avoid costly investment decisions, decisions can be based on the preferences of the average member, thereby maximizing aggregate welfare of the group given the composition of the farmer "community" (Hansmann, 1996). It resembles LeVay's (1983) recommendation for the cooperative objective, i.e. to maximize the integrated profit composed of revenue and costs of a specific activity in the cooperative as well as costs related to the activity at individual member level. The residual return of the activity can be distributed proportionally to the individual member's patronage and capital can also be generated on a proportional basis. This allocation of costs and benefits will, in principle, fulfill the principle of equal treatment of members, which is assumed to be a precondition for the stability of the member organization (Bager, 1992). However, the outcome may not be conceived equitably and it is hardly Pareto-efficient.

Given the diversity of farmer investment preferences, the investment decision based on the average member would be optimal to only a small fraction of members (Nilsson, 2001): Some farmers would prefer and benefit more from a higher cooperative investment level, while others will lose as a result of the collective decision. The latter group may lose comparatively to other farmers who benefit more from the investment due to lower costs of capital, or they may even take a loss in nominal terms when individual costs of capital exceed the return of the investment. In both cases, the comparative competitiveness at farm level will be affected; consequently, tensions over cooperative investment decisions are likely to occur and investment plans will, inevitably, fuel inherent conflicts of interests between farmer members of agricultural cooperatives.

Increasing conflicts of interests and member heterogeneity constitute a challenge to the cooperative system and for the very fundamental reason for farmers' collective action. Farmers' reliance on vertical integration as a safeguard mechanism for transaction specific investments does only have value if the collective action is reliable. What reduces uncertainty for the individual farmer and provides incentives to make transaction specific investments *is not the vertical integration in itself*, but the farmer's expectations of future cohesion of collective action because the joint action is the safeguard of investments. It is necessary to make a distinction between vertical integration undertaken by one individual company and vertical integration accomplished by many competing firms.[6] The main advantage of farmers' collective action is, therefore, not as such the ability to protect transaction specific investments at primary level and provide farmers with incentives to make optimal investments. Rather it is the ability to design institutional rules that create homogeneity of interest and/or stable equilibria from the bargaining process in collective action, because that is the prerequisite for a future coherent cooperation, which in turn is the precondition for creating a credible safeguard of farm members' transaction specific investments. Then farmers have incentives to make transaction specific investments at primary level.

2.4 Summary: Pursuing Pareto-efficient strategies

Increasing cooperative investments affect owners differently because of different personal circumstances, e.g. different discount rates and risk preferences. Therefore, cooperative decisions concerning increasing investments and a matching need for further capital contributions from members may cause externalities.

An externality occurs in situations "...in which one individual's economic position is affected by what other individuals do with respect to consumption or production" (Furobotn and Richter, 1998: 89–90). Consequently, collective decisions could imply unintended impacts on the economic position of individuals who do not favor the passage of a specific issue. The implication of collective decisions is, in other words, that if a less than unanimity rule is required for the passage of an issue, then some participants taking part in the decision process can impose costs on other individuals who oppose the adoption of the issue because they would be made worse off by the adoption (Mueller, 1989).

A prerequisite for homogeneity of interests between farmer members could be assumed to be that outcomes of collective decisions do not make any members worse off, or the homogeneity of interests and, consequently, the stability of the member organization will be challenged and put under pressure if collective strategies do not lead to Pareto-optimal allocation of resources. So, non-Pareto-optimal solutions would be likely to increase tensions among members and cohesion of joint action deteriorates.

Therefore, it becomes essential to design institutional rules for the joint action that ensure the alignment of individual interests with group goals and constrain the ability of individual members to act inconsistently with the interests of other members. In other words, the aim is to *constrain* collective decisions to avoid non-Pareto-optimal allocation of resources because the homogencity of member interests deteriorates. Rules for collective decision-making as well as determination of the scope of collective action can be assumed to be important mechanisms for constraining collective decisions and is, consequently, analyzed in the next section.

3. COOPERATIVE CONSTITUTIONAL ASPECTS: REVIVING THE EFFECT OF EXIT

James Buchanan and Gordon Tullock (Buchanan and Tullock, 1965) have probably contributed most in the field of public choice theory, i.e. in general terms analysis of non-market decisions. The public choice theory is applying the Pareto criterion as *the* measure for allocative efficiency of decisions, i.e. an optimal situation has been reached when no one can achieve more without making someone else worse off. The Pareto optimality criterion is appropriate considering the focus of public choice theory on abuse of power and protection of individual rights.

In order to protect individual rights and secure alignment of individual interests with group goals, the challenge is to consider: a) how to make decisions that affect all members of a collective group and, b) how to design individual rights and, c) which assignments or activities to undertake within a collective community. The public choice theory is a useful approach in this respect with its distinction between procedural aspects of the decision-process and the substantial aspects concerning individual rights and scope of joint action (Mueller, 1989). The constitution constrains the range of activities that can be undertaken in a non-market setting, i.e. the constitution lays down the activities that must be conducted in a political setting, assigns the civic rights and sets the voting rules for reaching collective decision when collective solutions are appropriate. Considering the cooperative as a political institution (Hansmann, 1996), collective decisions can have unintended consequences for participants taking part in the decision-process, and the approach is applicable in this context as well.

Procedural rules affect the way of making decisions and have only indirect impact on the content of decisions, e.g. the voting rules will probably impact the set of available choices to the participants. On the other hand, substantial rules have direct implications for the content of decisions; certain decisions may be prohibited within a given collective framework based on costs/benefits analyses and/or the constitution lays down certain minimum policies and civic rights for members of the community.

In this context constitutions are considered formal rules that regulate individual property rights in a given collective setting. Constitutional aspects resemble, therefore, corporate governance mechanisms; governance defined in a broad sense as the system by which companies are directed and controlled (Shleifer and Vishny, 1997) or as institutions by which firm activities are co-ordinated (Williamson, 1996). In general terms, "Institutions include any form of constraint that human beings devise to shape human interaction" as explained by North (1990: 4), who also states that institutions can be both formal and informal. Institutions are, as explained by North (1990:24–26), formed to structure political, social and economic interaction by creating order and reducing uncertainty in human interaction and in all exchanges taking place, thereby paving the way for specialization and division of labor in society. In traditional economic theory, choice is constrained only by scarce resources and technology (Alchian and Demsetz, 1972), but in a world of uncertainty due to bounded rationality and lack of information, exchanges are costly.

Therefore, individuals form institutions to reduce transaction costs and to make human interaction predictable because costs and benefits of behavior are affected by the institutional set-up or the "rules of the game". In other words, constraining human behavior by means of formal and informal institutions is to be understood in the sense that human behavior becomes (more) predictable when some types of behavior is facilitated while others are made more costly.

3.1 Costs of constitutional rules: The Buchanan-Tullock model

Following the arguments of public choice theory a constitutional set-up should be designed on the basis of the Pareto-efficiency criteria, i.e. attempting to reach solutions where as many as possible are being left in a better position without making anyone else worse off at the lowest costs (Mueller, 1989). The Pareto-optimal equilibrium is achieved in the market, where "...individual atoms negotiate with each other until they reach a state of the economy in which no one can improve his position without hurting someone else..." (Furobotn and Richter, 1998) and under the assumption of perfect market competition, decisions will be Pareto-efficient.

The implication of following the Pareto-efficiency criterion in the design of the constitutional set-up would be to maximize the number of members of a collective group that would have to take part in a decision in order to minimize the external costs or costs of externalities; the external cost represents "...the expected loss of utility from the victory of a decision to which an individual is opposed..." (Mueller, 1989: 53). So if the constitution requires that any decision should be made unanimously by the members of the group the costs of externalities would be zero; the externalities can on the other hand be considerable if just one person – or a board of managers – according to the constitution can make decisions on behalf of a whole group of persons (Kurrild-Klitgaard, 2001).

Potential costs of externalities will be balanced against the costs of decision-making, i.e. the costs of making a marginal decision. The assumption is that the costs are increasing with the number of participants that are required (Kurrild-Klitgaard, 2001), i.e. "...the decision-time costs of achieving the required majority to pass the issue as a function of the size of the required majority" for the specific issue to be voted on (Mueller, 1989: 53). For example, if the constitution requires a qualified majority to make a decision the costs of politics will be higher than if a dictator or even a benevolent dictator can make the decision.

The external costs and costs of decision-making costs add up to the costs of interdependence. The costs of interdependence will reflect the trade-off between costs and benefits of a given number of participants in the community required to pass the issue (Mueller, 1989: 50–65). On the basis of the costs of interdependence it is possible to assess social costs and benefits of different decision-making rules as laid down by the constitution for making decisions within the political framework (Kurrild-Klitgaard, 2001). Following these considerations it becomes possible to compare political decision-making rules with alternative, non-political ways of undertaking different assignments, e.g. by using the market mechanism or, more generally, by using different kinds of contract modes or governance structures.

As for a political decision any decisions in the marketplace will imply costs, i.e. costs of decision-making and costs of externalities as a result of the decision taken by the participants in the market. The lesson from the Buchanan and Tullock model is that constraints should be imposed on the public sector's ability to produce goods and services; if the market can produce solutions to a specific issue at lower costs of interdependence compared to the costs of producing the same solution to the problem on the basis of a collective decision within a political community, the marketplace takes control of the assignments. Constraints on the public sector should, therefore, be integrated in the constitutional set-up, which then ideally will define the limits of the activities of the public sector based on a comparison between costs of interdependence and costs of using other governance structures, e.g. the market mechanism. This logic can be applied on agricultural cooperatives and will be elaborated on in the following sections.

3.2 Procedural aspects of constitution: Decision-processes and voting rules

The function of giving voting control to a group of patrons "...is not to provide a means for conveying the patron's preferences to the firm's management, but ... to prevent the firm from taking actions that will strongly disadvantage a substantial majority [of the owners]" (Hansmann, 1996: 288). Hansmann (1996: 289) emphasizes that "...the principal role of voting in firms is much as it is in most democratic governments: Not to aggregate and communicate preferences, but simply to give the electorate some crude protection from gross opportunism on the part of those in power" and the assessment is that "…where the owners of a firm are at all heterogeneous in their interests, it is common to encounter devices designed to attenuate rather than increase the refinement and force with which electoral mechanisms convey the interests of the individual owners". Actually, the latter mechanism is just another way of requiring a large majority to pass an issue but, contrary to the outcome of member voting, this solution leaves room for management discretion and owners become vulnerable.

Hansmann seems to underestimate the importance of owner or member voting, not necessarily in relation to the question of aggregation of member preferences through voting but concerning the ability to secure the interests and property rights of electorates or members. The magnitude of business activities, which is a substantial aspect of a cooperative constitution, can be assumed to be a function of the ability to generate risk-bearing member capital. Given the available capital and labor resources, management will supply a matching level of goods and services as a parallel to the work of bureaucrats and politicians (Mueller, 1989). Therefore, member voting on the level of retained earnings can be assumed to be an effective way of constraining business activities with the aim of securing Pareto-optimal solutions. Actually, the lack of member voting may explain that even though undercapitalization "…has most commonly been the focus of the literature on alternative forms of ownership, the evidence suggests, that [over-capitalization] is more important" (Hansmann, 1996: 291). Historically, limitations on business activities as a function of less complex and less risky activities and a high degree of leverage may explain farmers' willingness to delegate power to various cooperative committees and their acceptance of abandoning direct member participation in the decision-making process and member voting on specific issues.

Formally, control rights follow the one member – one voting principle as one of the cooperative principles, developed by the International Co-operative Alliance[7] (ICA) and applies in most agricultural cooperatives. The principle is often used to define the cooperative in a comparative perspective to other ownership structures (Bager, 1992) and the ICA principles "…suggest a basic set of property rights governing ownership and control of resources used by cooperatives …" (Condon, 1990: 10). The ICA's second principle concerning "Democratic Member Control" states that, in addition to the principle of equal voting rights to members, "Cooperatives are democratic organizations controlled by their members, who actively participate in setting their policies and making decisions." This rather broad and vague statement could be interpreted in line with the recommendations based on public choice theory. Reviewing interpretations of the principle of cooperative democracy and work conducted prior to review of ICA principles provides ambiguous interpretations, but not in the direction of a public choice understanding, and an analysis or even a discussion of voting rules, for example, to ensure individual rights seems not to be raised (Watkins, 1986). Rather the discussion is focused on the interpretation of the democratic influence and other voting rights besides the one member – one vote principle, e.g., allocating voting rights to individual members on a proportional basis in accordance with their patronage (Bager, 1992).

This discussion may be, at best, redundant[8] and at worst it removes attention from the important issue of applying member voting and the matching voting rules. Bager (1992) argues that the choice of the one member – one vote principle can be interpreted as a way of ensuring cohesion. At first it seems to be a fair explanation and is a widespread understanding, however, the problem is the issues that are not being addressed in this discussion, e.g., the actual practice of member voting and the types of equilibria likely to emerge from bargaining processes with powerful coalition members.

Public choice theory assumes, naturally, the equal voting power between participants of the public community and the logic matches, therefore, a common practice of agricultural cooperatives and a widespread understanding of cooperative identity. However, according to the theoretical approach other aspects of decision-making become more important to determine outcomes of decision-making processes. Application of the public choice theory on agricultural cooperatives would have various implications for decision-making and voting rules and, probably, for outcome of decisions in relation to a) member participation and b) voting rules:

Re a) Direct member participation in the decision-process
According to the Buchanan-Tullock model, multiple decision-making rules can be applied in relation to different types of political decisions. The general rule is that the number of decision-makers participating should be as high as possible without causing overly high costs of decision-making compared to the costs of externalities.

Direct member participation or member voting on various issues would, at least to some degree, conflict with the representative system in many large cooperatives; the Board of Representatives is the supreme decision-making body in relation to issues such as allocation of yearly returns and the level of retained earnings, and given the distinction between *decision control* and *decision management* (Fama and Jensen, 1983) much power rests with the Board of Directors and the Board of Management respectively.

Re b) The choice of voting rules
When a less than unanimous majority is sufficient to pass an issue concerning e.g. investment levels and the matching level of risk bearing capital required from members, there exists the possibility that some farmer members will be made worse off by the majority's decision. In relation to public good quantities and tax shares this feature of the unanimity rule made Buchanan and Tullock strongly favor the rule and, were there no costs of using this rule, it would naturally be the optimal rule since it minimizes costs of externalities (Mueller, 1989).

Collective decisions on the level of retained earnings could be made based on members' identification of different levels of retained earnings. For example, a majority of farmer members could agree on a maximum level of retained earnings via a voting procedure. So, outcome of a decision-process concerning the level of retained earnings could be set at the level which is ranked first by more than half of all farmer members or by e.g. 75% in accordance with the recommendation of public choice theory concerning adoption of tax levels. In this case, it would *not* be possible to set the level of retained earnings at a higher level without making more than 25% of the farmers members worse off due to the collective decision on the specific issue, i.e. causing externalities for a higher number of the members and, consequently, reducing the minority protection and the right to discipline others' actions via the voting procedure.

The outcome of a member voting on the level of retained earnings would probably affect the level that it would be possible to gain support for from the required majority of members. Although the costs related to the decision process itself would be low, a low level of retained earnings could lead to costly decisions in the sense that the aggregate welfare of the cooperative as a whole would not be maximized. Therefore, it would not be possible to comply with the recommendation for the cooperative objective (LeVay, 1983). The non-maximization of total returns could happen under any voting regime, e.g.: "With simple majority rule only those proposals where the benefits exceed the costs for the majority will pass. Conversely, if the costs exceed the benefits for the majority the proposal will fail" even though the community of farmers as a whole would benefit from the proposal (Anderson, 1986: 20).

Logrolling, hypothetical compensation or vote trading are ways to overcome the problems of members turning down proposals that are beneficial to the group as a whole.[9] Logrolling or compensation in accordance with the Coase Theorem (Coase, 1960) is "critical" for effective political decision making in corporations because members "can avoid costly compromises and capture long-term gains" (Holmström, 1999: 414). The argument is that *if* net benefits for the whole group are possible to derive from a proposal, logrolling would allow the benefits to be derived because members who lose because of increased costs of membership would be compensated by the members who benefit. Those members would still be better off after having compensated others by the amount of the net benefit of the proposal. So the adoption of the proposal would produce a Pareto-optimal solution, however, some members may gain a comparative advantage because they gain comparatively more than other members.

Several factors may hinder effective use of logrolling. Anderson (1986) is raising seven points to illustrate that logrolling may not operate perfectly in a cooperative setting: Misrepresentation of preferences, asymmetric and costly information, different member perceptions of costs and benefits, influence activities and transaction costs related to the actual exchange are factors that work against the application of the compensation principle. Therefore, compensation mechanisms work "relatively easy as long as the game repeats itself with sufficient regularity. When entirely new circumstances are confronted, the game changes, challenging traditional patterns. It will take time and effort to find new equilibrium. Misunderstandings will occur, leading to expensive compromises in place of long-term agreements based on trust" (Holmström, 1999: 414). Consequently, the change in sector structure and not least changing market conditions leading to more cooperative investments, which affect members differently, change the mutual game between farmers and challenge their traditional ways of reaching Pareto-efficient solutions and stable equilibria from the bargaining process.

The question is whether it is possible to find a new equilibrium and at what decision-making costs? According to the Buchanan-Tullock model the costs of decision-making are critical for the question of where to produce a solution: within the farmer community or on the market. One could argue that the Buchanan-Tullock model in this respect does not contribute with more value than what it would be possible to derive from the formula of Hansmann (1996) for efficient assignment of ownership. However, costs of decision-making both in terms of the costs of the decision and costs of the decision-making process could be kept at a low level, if the management alone, as a benevolent dictator or together with only a fraction of members, could determine the outcome of the bargaining process as a result of a more biased decision-making process due to structural development and low(er) value of the exit option as a disciplinary mechanism. The point is that the external costs could be very high and the decision-making process would not generate a stable equilibrium. Therefore, the costs of interdependence would be high and the Buchanan-Tullock would prompt another governance structure for the production of a solution to the specific assignment.

It is hardly surprising that by allocating more resources to the decision-making process it is possible to gain more member support for a proposal that would be beneficial to the group as a whole but with different impact at individual level. Cooperative literature often stresses the potential benefits of member involvement (e.g. Anderson, 1986; Bager, 1992). Involvement of members in the decision-making process could reduce misinterpretations of investment proposals and since "perceived costs and benefits are more important than the real costs and benefits" for members (Anderson, 1986: 24), management information on proposals could align members' perceived interests with group goals. Besides, logrolling and compensation between members would require member involvement and the related costs would be highly dependent on diversity of member preferences.

The costs of member involvement and logrolling to gain member support and prevent non-Pareto-optimal solutions would, according to the Buchanan-Tullock model, be dependent on the required majority to pass an issue. Thereby, the model also explicitly stresses the correlation between costs of decision making and attempts to reduce externalities for members participating in a community, and the suggestion is to compare these costs with alternative governance structures for production of a solution.

In an ideal world with zero transaction costs, alignment of interests via compensation would be possible as stated in the Coase Theorem (Coase, 1960). In a comprehensive study of different payment schemes in farmer controlled companies operating with product differentiation at farm level it is suggested that the most efficient model maximizes total integrated profit and distribute the profit on an equal basis to members (Bogetoft and Olesen, 2000). This solution is alleviated by the fact that profit in principle can be redistributed between members (Bogetoft and Olesen, 2000), and by a high degree of interdependence between farmers concerning production and decisions on the marketing of farm produce.

The same conditions do not apply (to the same degree) when it concerns investments in up- or down-stream business activities. The profit of a specific investment could be distributed equally to members in accordance with patronage and the costs, however, the costs of ownership would be incurred individually and affect owners differently. Therefore, investment proposals could easily provoke high decision-making costs, and compensation to members being worse off by the proposal would hardly be acceptable for members who gain because of low individual costs of capital. It points in the direction of reducing the ambition of farmers' joint activities and investments. The substantial aspects of a constitution explicitly address that issue and will be elaborated on in the following section.

3.3 Substantial aspects of constitution: Scope of activities of joint action and individual rights

In the work by Brennan and Buchanan (1980) it is assumed that the only effective constraints in the long term on government's desire to expand are laid down in constitutional rules targeting directly the three above-mentioned sources, which are necessary conditions for expansion. The idea of constraining and limiting the scope of cooperative activities to achieve homogeneity of interests among farmer members is not new or unique in cooperatives either. Holmström (1999: 407) clarifies that it is necessary to achieve homogeneity in agricultural cooperatives by constraints and limitations on the scope of cooperative activities and it "is a significant liability on the cooperative form of organization". The amount of risk bearing capital determines to a large degree the scope of activities possible to undertake. By emphasizing that cooperatives' "…'capital stock' is not entrepreneurial capital of a collective enterprise, but the sum of advances needed for financing anticipated transactions of individual members of the aggregate", Emelianoff (1942: 251)[10] points to an effective limitation on cooperatives. Besides, "Homogeneity of interests is assured by the fact that the cooperatives largely confine themselves to relatively simple, homogeneous commodities", as explained by Hansmann (1988: 288) and similarly by Holmström (1999). Similar considerations could be made regarding magnitude of common business activities and a matching need for retained earnings and up-front capital contributions from individual farmer members.

However, formal protection of individual rights has mainly focused on rights in relation to production and farmer autonomy at farm level, and farmer rights have been secured by means of open access and delivery rights; open access and delivery rights prevent internal opportunism in the form of hold-up situations between members (Bogetoft and Olesen, 2000). Expanding producers could be exposed to hold-up by other coalition members. It would undermine the security of joint action for transaction specific investments at farm level. Besides, it would lead to the deterioration of the individual farmer's autonomy and right to decide production level at an optimal level, which is one of the very basic motives for farmers to embed transactions in ownership (Staatz, 1984).

In addition to open access and delivery rights, farmers have traditionally applied the rule of equal treatment in relation to distribution of cooperative return in order to achieve homogeneity of interests among farmers (Emelianoff, 1942). Especially in relation to product differentiation, the principle reduces uncertainty for the individual farmer confronted not only with a private counter partner as buyer but a competitive buyer (Søgaard, 1994).

Concern about formal protection of farmers' rights in relation to the role as risk bearer and investments in the cooperative seem to have played a secondary role which is understandable in light of industry structure, exit options and historical demands for common investments in farmer controlled companies. Therefore, the traditional focus has been on user value and it has been emphasized that the significant economic difference between a cooperative and an investor owned firm is "user ownership" (Lang, 1995: 64–65). The user orientation is also emphasized by the fact that "Cooperative user-owners behave as users of the organization's goods and services on an almost daily basis. Cooperative user-owners (if current and active) behave as owner-investors only several times a year (tax day, equity redemption day, dividend day)" (Cook, 1994). It is also in this structural characteristic of the cooperative that any comparative advantages are to be identified: "The source of advantage to cooperatives has to be in user value" and "If there is an economic reason for cooperatives to survive, it is because there is something about user ownership that permits cooperatives to add value to or cut costs from the food system in ways that IOFs cannot" (Lang, 1994:64–65).

Substantial aspects of constitutional economics also encompass individual rights in addition to delimitation of common activities; a distinction between "negative" and "positive" rights is often used to structure civic rights in a community. While positive rights refer to an individual's right to receive goods and services, negative rights are those rights related to the absence of encroachment in individual property and absence of action from other persons in more general terms. Open access and delivery rights would be considered "negative" rights because such principles provide the individual farmer with autonomy. Similarly, the concept of "negative" rights could be applied in relation to capital contributions because any collective decisions on retained earnings taken by less than unanimity could imply encroachment on an individual farmer's rights and negatively affect production and investment decisions at farm level. In this respect, certainty of collective action is a precondition for optimal investment decisions made by the individual farmer and motivates him or her for vertical integration, but certainty at farm level is also conditioned by the predictability of outcomes of future collective decisions within the farmer "community". Therefore, the farmer's right to determine the most efficient allocation of capital between the farm and subsequent processing stages could be laid down in a constitution for the collective action.

3.4 Constitutional design: Tentative suggestions for methodology

The purpose of this article is not to design a constitution for agricultural cooperatives. Understanding the essence of cooperatives, the lock-in effect of farmers and the increasing costs of ownership, the lesson is that there is a need for a better clarification of the cooperative constitution or the governance mechanisms aiming at protecting individual rights by alignment of individual interests with group goals. The lesson learned by applying public choice theory is the need for constraints, broadly speaking, by means of both procedural as well as substantial rules. Procedural and substantial constraints are the safeguards of individual member rights, primarily by minimizing internal externalities of collective decisions and aiming at producing outcomes of collective decisions that affect cooperative members equally.

The traditional cooperative principles form the basis of a cooperative constitution. In other words, there is *no* need for a new constitution or another set of governing principles for coordinating farmers' economic activities, yet the substantial aspects of public choice theory may require additions. In this respect, the need is to revitalize agricultural cooperatives by going back to some basic elements and interpret the cooperative principles in such a way that they serve the basic purpose of ensuring cohesion by aligning interests between farmers. The main point is that the interpretation of the cooperative principles can be much improved in the sense of making the principles better able to ensure cohesion of the collective action amongst farmers by applying public choice or constitutional economic theory on agricultural cooperatives.

There is no formula for design of constitutions – or for adjusting existing cooperative principles – yet pursuing Pareto-optimality is a strong guideline. In the context of agricultural cooperatives the same criterion for optimality could be applied. Additionally, Williamson's (1985) methodology for assigning transactions to alternative governance structures on the basis of their transaction properties could serve as a guideline for design of constitutional limitations on cooperative behavior to avoid abuse of power or ensure Pareto efficiency, and to align individual interests with group goals. The basic idea of Williamson is that transactions should be assigned to alternative governance structures on the basis of transaction properties. Williamson (1985) argues that three properties are especially critical for determining the optimal governance structure: frequency of the transaction, uncertainty, and the most central transaction property, namely asset specificity. Each of these three transaction properties, and particularly in combination, favors adoption of an internal mechanism for co-ordination of a transaction. Besides, it is the expectation, that higher levels of uncertainty and higher degrees of asset specificity leads to "a more complex contracting environment and a greater need for post-contractual adjustments", as Royer explains (1999: 49). The party having made the transaction specific investment becomes locked in to a greater or lesser degree once starting to patronize the firm, and as explained by Hansmann (1999: 391), the patron "loses the protective option of costless exit if the firm seeks to exploit her". It gives rise to ex post market power or hold-up problems; the hold-up problem involves a redistribution of quasi-rents either where contractual incompleteness calls for renegotiations as uncertainty unfolds or as contingencies not accounted for in the contract arises.

Parallel insights to Williamson's methodology for assigning transactions to alternative governance structures could be suggested in a constitutional context. The tentative idea is: *To assign farmers' joint action to alternative constitutions on the basis of the following attributes of the joint action*:

• *The degree of lock in or dependence on the joint action for the individual farmer*. Access to exit as a tool for disciplining other members' actions being dependent on sector and industry structure determines the individual farmer's need for safeguards against internal opportunism, both in terms of procedural as well as the substantial rules serving as cooperative governance mechanisms;

- *The degree of uncertainty in relation to business conditions and market demands.* The contract between governing their internal relationships as well as individual obligations as a result of collective decisions will be incomplete since all future contingencies cannot be foreseen up front. Hence, there is need for adaptive, sequential decision making between farmer members as uncertainty unfolds and changing market demands require collective positions. The degree of market complexity and uncertainty determines the individual farmer's need for constraints on the scope of collective decisions in order to reduce uncertainty of collective action, i.e. ensure alignment of individual interests with group goals;
- *The degree of member homogeneity.* Characteristics, preferences and composition of the players of the game determine the individual farmer's need for limitations on collective decisions in order to achieve fairness and equality of joint action.

4. CONCLUSION

Coalition analyses are mainly concerned with the types of equilibria likely to emerge from bargaining processes between coalition members having different preferences, and each seeking to maximize individual utility. In the context of agricultural cooperatives the main question is whether traditional cooperative principles and practices are able to generate stable equilibria, which would be outcomes of bargaining processes where no coalition member has an incentive to change his or her behavior (Staatz, 1987a). In light of the structural development in many agricultural sectors creating less access to exit or lock-in of farmers in collective action, decision-making processes and outcomes in agricultural cooperatives are likely to be more biased. Combined with market justifications for increasing investments and, consequently, more need for risk-bearing capital, common and traditional practices in cooperatives may hardly be able to create stable equilibria.

Constitutional economics or public choice theory may be a theoretical tool for *reviving the effect of exit* by enhancing the function of the individual farmer's voice mechanism and, thereby, generating stable equilibria in the collective decision-making processes. Four main issues are identified in the theoretical approach and can be summarized as follows:

- Voting rules: The use of a less than unanimity rule can impose costs on participants to the decision and make them worse off by the passage of an issue; a large majority would be required to pass vital issues such as decisions on the level of retained earnings.
- Member voting: It follows from the logic of the focus on procedural aspects that participants of collective action should be entitled to participate directly in the decision-process and have the right to vote as individual members, at least on all major issues affecting personal wealth and consumption utility.

- Confinement of assignment and activities for joint action: The basic issue is "what not to do" by identifying core activities, e.g. concerning collection and first stage processing with the aim of maximizing the aggregate welfare and benefit from the fact that cooperative income, in principle, can be redistributed to members on an equal basis treatment.
- Individual rights in collective action: Identify positive and negative rights for collective action. Investments beyond the need to secure farmers' right to produce and deliver could be an encroachment on farmer autonomy and cause potential non-Pareto-optimal solutions.

So the main conclusion is that by adopting rules concerning member voting on vital issues, and by applying majority or less than unanimous voting rules, farmers can reduce uncertainty and create the basis for future cohesion of the collective action, which is a fundamental precondition for farmers' ability to exploit the benefits of vertical integration. Besides, by adopting rules regarding substantial aspects of the cooperative business, the available set of choices can be limited with the aim of confining business activities, thereby creating the basis for homogeneity of interests among members.

All four issues in public choice theory have been shown to be beneficial to the study of agricultural cooperatives in this article. The emphasis on the liability of the cooperative organizational form is not new, whereas *the theoretical formalization of the process of constraining activities by use of the logic and methodology of public choice theory may be*. That seems to be a major strength of this approach which also has proven to have a (much) broader applicability than the study of public choices alone.

NOTES

[1] The Pareto criterion has been developed as early as in 1906 by Vilfredo Pareto: *Manuale di Economia Politica*, the English translation: *Manual of Political Economy*, London 1971.

[2] In the context of this article, the mentioning of structural determinants and background variables are based on observations in the Danish dairy and pork industry, yet it may apply to other sectors and countries as well.

[3] Personal interview with the CEO of a Danish agricultural cooperative, March 2002, made on condition of anonymity.

[4] The alleged problems intrinsic to the cooperative organizational form are: the free rider, the horizon, the portfolio, the control and the influence costs problem (Cook 1995).

[5] The Theorem would assume a perfect functioning market for transferability of residual claims which would hardly be the case in a cooperative context.

[6] Many competing firms constitute cooperatives (Staatz, 1984). This assumption could with advantage be viewed in light of the so-called treadmill theory developed by Cochrane (1965). The treadmill theory suggests that implementation of new technology and search for low-cost production methods in agriculture result in continuous competition among farmers, and lead to cannibalism because land is the scarce resource necessary to possess to increase total income at farm level.

[7] The ICA has formulated a set of cooperative principles, which have been informed by the Rochdale pioneers. The principles are supposed to serve as governance mechanisms in cooperatives. Many agricultural cooperatives adhere to the cooperative principles (Nilsson, 1998).

[8] Concerning cooperative investment decisions, application of equal voting rights in agricultural cooperatives have not proven to make any significant influence on outcomes as compared to a situation

where voting rights would be distributed proportionally to members on the basis of individual member patronage or capital contributions as in a traditional investor owned firm (Albæk and Schultz, 1997).

⁹ E.g. Buchanan and Tullock (1965) and Mueller (1989) for elaboration on the issue of logrolling.

¹⁰ Emelianoff's contribution from 1942 can be considered a classic in cooperative economic theory.

REFERENCES

Albæk, S., and C. Schultz. 1997. "One Cow, One Vote?" *Scandinavian Journal of Economics* 99:597–615.

Alchian, A., and H. Demsetz. 1972. "Production, Information Costs and Economic Organization." *American Economic Review* 62:772–795.

Anderson, B. L. 1986. "The Impact of Democratic Control on Co-opertive Decision-Making." *Co-operatives to-day: A Tribute to Prof. dr. V. Laakkonen*. Geneva: ICA, pp. 13–43.

Bager, T. 1992. *Andelsorganisering. En analyse af danske andelsorganisationers udviklingsprocesser.* Esbjerg: Sydjysk Universitetsforlag.

Berle, A., and G. Means. 1932. *The Modern Corporation and Private Property.* New York: Macmillan Co.

Bogetoft, P., and H. Ballebye Olesen. 2000. *Afregning i andelsselskaber. Teoretiske modeller og praktiske eksempler fra slagteribranchen.* Copenhagen: DSR Forlag.

Brennan, G., and J. M. Buchanan. 1980. *The Power to Tax: Analytical Foundations of a Fiscal Constitution,* Cambridge: Cambridge University Press.

Buchanan, J. M., and G. Tullock. 1965. *The Calculus of Consent: Logical Foundations of Constitutional Democracy.* Ann Arbor: University of Michigan Press

Coase, R. H. 1960. "The Problem of Social Cost", *Journal of Law and Economics* 3:1–44.

Cochrane, W. 1965. *The City Man's Guide to the Farm Problem.* Minneapolis: University of Minnesota Press.

Condon, A. M. 1990. "Property Rights and the Investment Behavior of U.S. Agricultural Cooperatives." PhD dissertation, Virginia Polytechnic Institute and State University.

Cook, M. L. 1994. "The Role of Management Behavior in Agricultural Cooperatives." *Journal of Agricultural Cooperation* 9:42–58.

__. 1995. "The Future of U.S. Agricultural Cooperatives: A Neo-Institutional Approach." *American Journal of Agricultural Economics* 77:1153–1159.

Emelianoff, I. V. 1942. *Economic Theory of Cooperation – Economic Structure of Cooperative Organizations.* Michigan: Edwards Brothers, Inc.

Eschenburg, R. 1971. *Ökonomische Theorie der genossenschaftlichen Zusammenarbeit.* Tübingen: J.C.B. Mohr.

Fama, E.F., and M.C. Jensen. 1986. "Separation of Ownership and Control." *Organizational Economics.* London: Jossey-Bass Ltd., pp. 276–298.

Furobotn, E.G., and R. Richter. 1998. *Insitutions and Economic Theory. The Contribution of the New Institutional Economics.* Ann Arbor: University of Michigan Press.

Hansmann, H. 1988. "Ownership of the Firm." *Journal of Law, Economics and Organization* 4:267–305.

__. 1996. *The Ownership of Enterprise.* Cambridge, Massachusetts: The Belknap Press of Harvard University Press.

__. 1999. "Co-operative Firms in Theory and Practice." *Finnish Journal of Business Economics* 48:387–403 (Special Issue: The Role of Cooperative Entrepreneurship in the Modern Market Environment).

Helmberger, P.G., and S. Hoos. 1965. *Cooperative Bargaining in Agriculture.* Berkeley, California: Unversity of California, Division of Agricultural Sciences.

Hirschman, A. 1970. *Exit, Voice and Loyalty: Response to Decline in Firms, Organizations and States.* Cambridge, MA: Harvard University Press.

Holmström, B. 1999. "The Future of Cooperatives: A Corporate Perspective." *Finnish Journal of Business Economics* 48:404–417 (Special Issue: The Role of Cooperative Entrepreneurship in the Modern Market Environment).

Kurrild-Klitgaard, P. 2001. "Velstandens grundlov: Magtdeling, rettigheder og gevinstsøgning." *Politica* 33(1):41–65.

Lang, M.G. 1995. "The Future of Agricultural Cooperatives in Canada and the United States: Discussion." *American Journal of Agricultural Economics* 77:1162–1165.

LeVay, C. 1983. "Agricultural Co-operative Theory: A Review." *Journal of Agricultural Economics* 34(1):1–44.

Milgrom, P., and J. Roberts. 1992. *Economics, Organization, and Management.* Englewood Cliffs, N.J., Prentice Hall.

Mueller, D.C. 1989. *Public choice II.* Cambridge: Cambridge University Press.

Murray, G.C. 1983. "Management Strategies for Corporate Control in British Agricultural Co-operatives." *Agricultural Administration* 14.

Nilsson, J. 1998. "The Emergence of New Organizational Models for Agricultural Cooperatives." *Swedish Journal of Agricultural Research* 28:39–47.

__. 2001. "Organisational Principles for Co-operative Firms." *Scandinavian Journal of Management* 17:329–356.

North, D. 1990. *Institutions, Institutional Change and Economic Performance.* Cambridge: Cambridge University Press.

Porter, P.K., and G.W. Scully. 1987. "Economic Efficiency in Cooperatives." *The Journal of Law & Economics* 30:489–512.

Ross, S.A. 1973. "The Economic Theory of Agency: The Principal's Problem." *American Economic Review* 63:134–139.

Royer, J.S. 1999. "Cooperative Organizational Strategies: A Neo-Institutional Digest." *Journal of Cooperatives* (14):44–67.

Shleifer, A., and R.W. Vishny. 1997. "A Survey of Corporate Governance." *Journal of Finance* 52:737–783.

Søgaard, V. 1994. *Farmers, Cooperatives, New Food products.* Aarhus: The Aarhus School of Business, MAPP project no. 5.

Staatz, J. 1983. "Towards a model of decision making in farmer cooperatives." Working paper No. 6, Michigan State University, Department of Agricultural Economics.

__. 1984. "A Theoretical Perspective on the Behavior of Farmers' Cooperatives." PhD dissertation, Michigan State University, Department of Agricultural Economics.

__. 1987a. "Recent Developments in the Theory of Agricultural Cooperation." Staff paper No. 87-44. Michigan State University, Department of Agricultural Economics.

__. 1987b. "A Game-Theoretic Analysis of Decision Making in Farmer Cooperatives." *Cooperative Theory: New Approaches*, Washington, D.C.: USDA, ACS Service Report No.18, pp. 117–147.

Traill, B. 1998. "Structural Changes in the European Food Industry: Consequences for Competitiveness." *Competitiveness in the Food Industry.* London: Blackie Academic & Professional.

Vitaliano, P. 1983. "Cooperative Enterprise: An Alternative Conceptual Basis for Analyzing a Complex Institution." *American Journal of Agricultural Economics* 65:1078–1083.

Watkins, W.P. 1986. *Co-operative Principles Today & Tomorrow*. Manchester: Holyoake Books.

Williamson, O.E. 1985. *The Economic Institutions of Capitalism*. New York: The Free Press.

___. 1996. *The Mechanisms of Governance*. New York: Oxford University Press.

CHAPTER 8

TWO VIGNETTES REGARDING BOARDS IN COOPERATIVES VERSUS CORPORATIONS

Irrelevance and Incentives

GEORGE HENDRIKSE

RSM Erasmus University, Erasmus University, Rotterdam, the Netherlands

Abstract. This article addresses two observations regarding the board of directors in agricultural cooperatives. First, it is sometimes stated that cooperatives seem to behave like ordinary enterprises. Second, it is argued that cooperatives may have advantages compared to corporations with publicly exchanged shares. These observations are analyzed from complete as well as incomplete contracting theory.

1. INTRODUCTION

A widespread and important governance structure in many agricultural markets is the cooperative. For example, the European Union has 132,000 cooperatives with 83.5 million members and 2.3 million employees in 2001 (Commission of the European Communities, 2001), the United States of America has 47,000 cooperatives with 100 million members in 2001 (USDA, 2002), and China has 94,771 cooperatives with 1,193 million members in 2002 (Hu, 2005). In the EU, cooperative firms are responsible for over 60% of the harvest, handling and marketing of agricultural products, with a turnover of approximately 210,000 million euros (Galdeano, *et al.*, 2005).

This article will address a number of features regarding the governance of the board of directors in agricultural cooperatives. Governance concerns the organization of transactions, whereas a governance structure consists of a collection of rules structuring the transactions between the various stakeholders (Hendrikse, 2003). A cooperative is an example of a governance structure.[1] It is a horizontal arrangement between many independent farmers (horizontal relationship), often jointly owning an upstream input company or a downstream processor (vertical relationship). These

K. Karantininis & J. Nilsson (eds.), Vertical Markets and Cooperative Hierarchies, 137–150.

producer-owned organizations are usually not stock-listed, and have distinguishing features (Commission of the European Communities, 2001, p. 12) like

> ... an orientation to provide benefits to members and satisfy their needs, democratic goal setting and decision-making methods, special rules for dealing with capital and profit, and general interest objectives (in some cases).

A standard way of delineating a governance structure is to distinguish decision and income rights. Decision rights in the form of authority and responsibility address the question, 'Who has authority or control?'. They matter because contracts are in general incomplete, due to the complexity of the transaction or the vagueness of language. The incompleteness of contracts is completed by allocating authority to somebody to decide in circumstances not covered by the contract. Decision rights concern all rights and rules regarding the deployment and use of assets (Hansmann, 1996). For example, a cooperative has to decide how much discretion is assigned to the board of directors regarding investments. Important themes regarding authority are its allocation ('make-or-buy' decision), formal versus real authority, relational contracts, access, decision control (ratification, monitoring), decision management (initiation, implementation), task design, conflict resolution, and enforcement mechanisms. Section 3 provides a rationale for the observation by various practitioners that cooperatives and stock-listed enterprises behave in a similar way.

The concept of income rights addresses the question, "How are benefits and costs allocated?" Income rights specify the rights to receive the benefits, and obligations to pay the costs, that are associated with the use of an asset, thereby creating the incentive system faced by decision makers. For example, a cooperative has to choose a compensation package for the CEO and the other members of the board of directors. Section 4 addresses differences in compensation packages of CEOs between firms with publicly exchanged stocks and cooperatives. Other important themes regarding income rights in cooperatives are payment schemes like member benefit programs, cost allocation schemes like pooling arrangements, and the effects of horizontal as well as vertical competition.

This article is organized as follows. Section 2 introduces various ways in which simple incomplete contracts can be extended. Section 3 provides a rationale for the claim that the choice of governance structure does not matter for the incentive to invest. Section 4 claims that cooperatives may have an advantage in the design of the compensation package of a CEO compared to a corporation because its stocks are not publicly exchanged. Finally, Section 5 summarizes and concludes.

2. BEYOND SIMPLE CONTRACTS

An important issue in organizing the enterprise is the allocation of control and authority. Standard incomplete contracting indicates that the ownership of assets should be allocated to the party whose relationship specific investments are most important (Grossman and Hart, 1986). This result is determined in a three-stage game.

The allocation of decision power in the first stage of the game identifies a governance structure with a distribution of bargaining power. A distribution of bargaining power is characterized by the slope of a line thru point $(-k_f, -k_p)$ in Figure 1, where k_f (k_p) is the relationship specific investment of the farmer (processor). For example, a cooperative, i.e. a governance structure characterized by forward integration, is presented by the horizontal line thru point (-k_f,-k_p), reflecting that the farmers have all power.[2] The farmers and the processor have about equal power in the governance structure characterized by the line with slope Y. Specific investment decisions by the farmer and the processor are determined in the second stage. A higher level of specific investment entails a worsening of bargaining positions (due to hold-up in the third stage of the game) regarding the division of the surplus V. Renegotiation decisions are determined in the final stage.

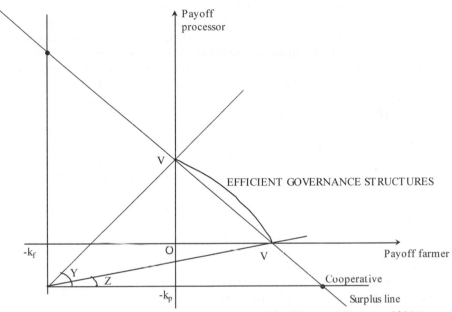

Figure 1. Two hold-up problems and governance (Hendrikse and Veerman, 2001b)

The above result of Grossman and Hart may be at odds with a basic feature of the firm. Crucial to the notion of the firm is the centralization of decision-making power, i.e. the employer, not the employee, is the owner of the firm. Similarly, the core of an agricultural cooperative is member control over the infrastructure at the downstream stage. In other words, formal ownership by the input suppliers over the downstream assets is the essential feature of a cooperative. However, bosses (and members as owners of downstream assets) are problematic from an efficiency perspective when the relationship specific investments of the employee (or the relationship specific investments at the downstream stage of production in a cooperative) are most important.

The developments in agricultural markets seem to increase the importance of specific assets at the downstream stage of production, i.e. k_p increases. This puts pressure on cooperatives in favor of market exchange. Wierenga (1997, p. 53) states that a

> ... drawback of co-operatives is that their locus of power (and perspective), even if they
> have integrated processing and distribution facilities, is close to primary production and
> far moved from the market. This does not make them very suitable for taking the guid-
> ing role in an AVAP (Agrifood Value-Added Partnership), the very purpose of which is
> to derive competitive advantage from adding those values that consumers want.

The implication seems to be to abandon the cooperative structure.

A way to deal with the problem of allocating formal decision rights to subordi-
nates, and the pessimism regarding the efficiency of the cooperative in the previous
citation, is to consider a richer class of incomplete contracts than the type of contracts
considered by Grossman and Hart. Their conceptualization of the allocation of
ownership can be viewed as a simple long-term contract. It is simple because it is non-
contingent, i.e. it is not allowed to make the allocation of authority contingent on the
circumstances or the results. Allowing contingent long-term contracts creates additional degrees of freedom to make value creating downstream activities blossom.

One way to extend simple contracts is to distinguish formal and informal or real
authority (Aghion and Tirole, 1997, and Baker *et al.*, 1999). Formal authority
resides at the top, whereas informal authority can be either centralized or decentralized. Control over the operational activities by a professional management may be
efficient when it has superior knowledge. So the efficiency of a relationship may be
enhanced by giving up some control, i.e. giving real authority away, even though the
formal control stays at the top. Hendrikse (2005) applies this idea to cooperatives.

Another possibility is to consider various long-term contracts, informal as well
as formal. Section 3 will focus on informal or relational contracts to address the
irrelevance of governance structure for investment behavior. Richer incomplete
contracts therefore create various additional degrees of freedom. This may result in
restructuring the cooperative in order to make the traditional cooperative more
responsive to market demand, rather than abandoning it.

A third possibility to create an additional degree of freedom is the introduction of a
third party (Bolton and Scharfstein, 1998). The standard analysis of the relationship
between members and the cooperative considers a two-party relationship: members (as
a group) and the management of the cooperative. In the terminology of the standard
principal-agent model, members are the principal and the Chief Executive Officer, or
the professional management, is the agent. This characterization is relevant in many
situations, but sometimes this relationship is more complicated. An example is the
relationship between the members of a cooperative and the CEO. There are usually
many small members, making it hard for them to design and choose an appropriate
contract for the manager. The standard way to overcome the coordination and
motivation problems between many members is to install a board of directors
representing the members. Installing a board of directors entails the introduction of a
third party in this relationship. Various implications are explored in Section 4.

3. IRRELEVANCE OF GOVERNANCE STRUCTURE

Governance structure, and therefore the board of directors, may not matter at all.
This observation is sometimes formulated in scientific journals as well as in
interviews with practitioners. For example, LeVay (1983, p. 5) states

... whatever the formal basis of association, co-operatives may behave no differently from other types of enterprises.

A more recent example is Nilsson (1999, p. 468) stating that

... traditional cooperatives may let some branches be run within firms that have resemblance to member-investor firms.

Similar observations are formulated CEOs of cooperatives. For example, CEO Jos van Campen of sugar cooperative Royal Cooperative Cosun in the Netherlands, as quoted by Griffioen (2004, p. 8), remarks that

More important than the governance structure are really the way people deal with each other every day at the interface between enterprise and cooperative. This is what determines whether things run smoothly or not. This way of dealing with each other, giving each other some discretion regarding their field of expertise, making clear agreements, and having sufficiently many discussion meetings to deal with problems, is much more important than the governance structure.

Similarly, CEO Hans van der Velde of Visa International EU views a cooperative as an association of parties created in order to solve a problem. He states (Klep, 2004, p. 9)

These [organizations or the allocation of decision authority] are secondary: they can always be rearranged, within every governance structure. It is much more essential that there is agreement about the problem that has to be solved. There is no discussion in Visa about whether they should be a cooperative or not. We just cooperate because it is a necessity.

These observations signal that cooperatives behave like ordinary enterprises. The main idea is that the informal structure determines to a large extent the way things really work. Frequent, informal interactions between the board and the CEO will result in similar choices across governance structures. The claim is therefore that governance structure does not matter much in the daily affairs of enterprises. A relational contracting perspective will be adopted to investigate this claim regarding the irrelevance of governance structure, and therefore the board of directors.

Informal agreements and unwritten codes of conduct (within and between enterprises) are widespread and important, due to the nature of knowledge. Knowledge, and its location, is important in enterprises. Teece (1998, p. 75) writes:

The essence of the firm is its ability to create, transfer, assemble, integrate, and exploit knowledge assets. Knowledge assets underpin competences, and competences in turn underpin the firm's product and service offerings to the market.

The nature of knowledge has changed over the course of time. Knowledge used to be explicit, or at least codifiable and transmissible in a formal and systematic language, in the past, whereas it isn't nowadays (Drucker, 1998). Knowledge which is personal, implicit, or hard to codify and express in the formality of language is called tacit knowledge. It is costly to transfer to outside parties and usually resides with a limited number of individuals. A problem regarding the tacitness of knowledge is that formalization of major components of, agreements regarding, and understandings about the relationship become impossible due to the unverifiability of this knowledge by third parties.

A governance structure consists of formal and informal rules. The formal structure is roughly described by the organizational chart, and can be represented by the decision rights of an incomplete contract in the property rights approach (Grossman and Hart, 1986). Formal decision rights allocate the right to intervene selectively, i.e. the decision rights determine who decides in circumstances not covered in formal agreements. The models in the property rights approach are usually limited to the allocation of formal decision rights in a setting where the parties interact only once. A general feature of short-run interaction is the unattractive prisoner's dilemma outcome. Underinvestment is a prominent example.

Relationships in the real world usually last more than one period. This holds of course not only within enterprises, but also between parties in a market setting. Multi-period interactions between the same parties open the possibility to build a relationship and a reputation, which might overcome the problem of underinvestment. Informal agreements or contracts and unwritten codes will be called relational contracts. The role of relational or implicit contracts is to utilize the parties' detailed knowledge of their situation in an informal way in complex or new situations. The fundamental incentive problem in relational contracts is that each party may see opportunities to increase its current returns by behavior that hurts the other party but that cannot be effectively deterred through normal, court-enforced contracts. Meaningful relational contracts therefore have to be self-enforcing, i.e. each party has to face incentives such that abiding the informal agreement is attractive.

A feature of relational contracts is that the involved parties have to decide every period about the continuation of their good behavior. Meaningful or credible relational contracts are self-enforcing when the value of maintaining a reputation for good behavior outweighs the gain from reneging on the promise. Knowledge can therefore be brought to value in a relational contract by the concern to maintain a reputation for honoring informal agreements. Meaningful relational contracts, i.e. credible informal agreements, have to be designed in such a way that the reputation of each party is sufficiently important to maintain. This can be made more precise by modeling a relational contract as an (infinitely) repeated game. It enables us to be more specific about self-enforcement and reputation.

The main result in the theory of repeated games, i.e. the Folk theorem (Fudenberg & Maskin, 1986), specifies the circumstances for relational contracts to be self-enforcing. First, the future has to be sufficiently important. If the benefit of defection is larger than the costs, then it is predicted that the relational contract will fall apart. Second, the environment is not too volatile or uncertain. A volatile environment may make the short-run gain of defection more attractive than the adherence to the long-run implicit contract. Third, the observability of decisions is important for the stability of long-term relationships. Cheating on implicit agreements becomes more attractive when the observability of decisions decreases. This argues for frequent meetings of the board of directors in order to discover the professional management's eventual deceitful or incompetent behavior in an early stage. Fourth, the history of the relationship is important. A relationship is hard to restore once it is damaged.

Farmers like the processor to take (unobservable) actions that improve the (unverifiable) value of the good in the downstream production process, regardless of the choice of governance structure. Relational contracts may be helpful in such a setting because the concern for ones reputation may induce the desirable behavior. When both parties agree on a certain course of action in an informal, self-enforcing way, then the formal aspect of the relationship does not affect the distribution of bargaining power. Every governance structure therefore induces the same distribution of bargaining power, i.e. the incentive to invest is identical in every governance structure (Baker, *et al.,* 2002). The important relational contracting result regarding the choice of governance structure is that the distribution of bargaining power is identical for all governance structures.

There is, according to this relational contracting perspective, no difference in investment behavior between various governance structures. This is depicted in Figure 2, where the upward sloping line represents the distribution of bargaining power in all possible governance structures. (The downward sloping line is again the surplus.) Notice the difference with Figure 1. Governance structure differences are captured by lines with different slopes in a setting with an emphasis on the allocation of formal decision rights (Figure 1), whereas every governance structure is characterized by the same slope in a relational contracting setting (Figure 2). For example, the governance structure cooperative is characterized by a flat line in Figure 1, i.e. the farmers have all power, whereas it is characterized by a line with a positive slope in Figure 2, representing the outcome of the frequent and informal exchange of information between the owners and the management.

Figure 2 illustrates the irrelevance of the choice of relational governance structure for the incentive to invest. However, it is incomplete because the location of the upward sloping line is not identified. Bargaining positions will distinguish different relational governance structures. They differ because the identity of the party making a promise differs between various relational governance structures. The farmers in a cooperative may promise the CEO at the processing stage of production a bonus, or to allocate capital in a certain direction. Other examples of promises are promotions, task allocations, and internal audit transfer payments. The identity of the party making a promise differs when the downstream processor is an independent contractor rather than an employee. A processor as independent contractor makes promises to farmers. For example, the processor may promise to always buy the produce of a certain group of farmers. Relational governance structures are therefore not distinguished by their distribution of bargaining power, but by their bargaining positions (Baker, *et al.,* 2002).

Promises, and therefore reputations, only mean something when they are self-enforcing because they are vulnerable to renegotiation. For example, the upstream farmers may not pay the bonus, or the downstream producer may buy his inputs somewhere else. The identity of the party tempting to renege is therefore determined by the specific relational governance structure. This is important because a key difference between a cooperative and market exchange is that the processor does not have an outside option available in a cooperative because the farmers own the downstream assets and products. The processor in a cooperative has to take the produce of the owners of his assets as inputs, whereas inputs can be bought somewhere else when he is an independent contractor. The input's value in its alternative use affects the reneging decision under independent contracting or relational

144   G. HENDRIKSE

outsourcing, but not under a cooperative or relational employment. This has an effect on the choice of (inefficient) actions to improve one's bargaining position.

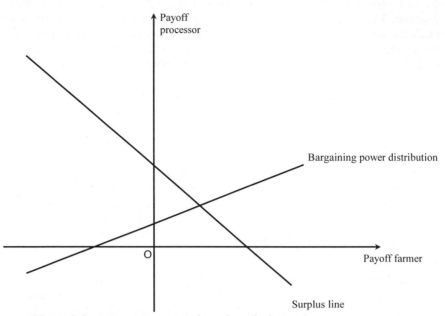

Figure 2. Incentive to invest is independent of relational governance structure

Figure 3 presents a situation where upstream ownership of the downstream assets, i.e. a cooperative, is advantageous to the farmers as well as the processor. Ownership of the downstream assets by the cooperative has the advantage of eliminating efficiency reducing activities of the processor, i.e. the surplus line shifts outward. The processor chooses surplus reducing activities in order to improve his bargaining position. To be specific, the activities (a) of the processor improve his bargaining position from 0 to P(a), but reduces the surplus from Q* to Q(a). The processor is an employee in a cooperative rather than an independent contractor because the worsening of his bargaining position is more than compensated for by the elimination of his efficiency reducing actions to improve his bargaining position.

4. CEO POWER

The lack of public exchange of the shares of cooperatives has advantages as well as disadvantages (Van Bekkum, 2004, p. 20). Advantages of a stock listing are the transferability of shares, reporting obligations, decisions are scrutinized by and published in the financial press, and the stock price is an easy measure to determine the quality of management. Disadvantages are a short-run focus, the imprecise relationship between the share price and the state of the enterprise, and a dominant focus on money.

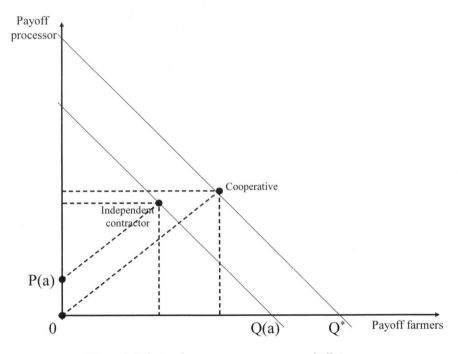

Figure 3. Relational governance structures and efficiency

It will be argued that cooperatives may have advantages compared to enterprises with publicly exchanged stocks in limiting the rent extraction tendencies in the design of the compensation package of the CEO by the CEO via the board of directors. An important aspect in this design is that there are three parties involved. LeVay (1983, p. 9) observes

> The main groupings within a co-operative are the rank and file membership, its board of directors and the management.

Figure 4 depicts the relevant players in the cooperative.

The introduction of the board of directors may not be unproblematic. Directors of the board are supposed to act in the interests of the owners, like formulating compensation packages for the CEO, in order to bring the money of the owners to value. However, from the perspective of the owners the compensation package for the CEO is often less than optimal. There are at least two reasons for this managerial power of the CEO. First, the CEO has superior information about product markets. Superior information regarding the output market may result in the choice of investment projects having a high personal value for the CEO. The lack of a stock market listing with publicly exchanged shares may prevent a situation in which bad choices become immediately visible.

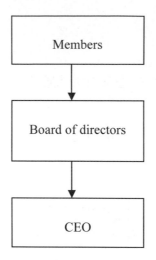

Figure 4. Members, board of directors, and CEO

Second, the CEO also probably has superior information about the compensation packages for his position. It is hard for directors to formulate an alternative payment scheme than the one proposed because they usually lack easy access to independent information and advice regarding compensation packages. Directors' limited time forces them to rely on information prepared by the human resources department of the company and compensation consultants, all having incentives to favor the CEO in the provision of information to the directors.

A number of aspects of the performance of the board of directors has been addressed, but this does not say much about the performance of the cooperative as a governance structure. A relevant question is the performance of the cooperative compared to alternative governance structures. Will the performance of the processor improve when it is governed by investors rather than members? Bebchuk and Fried (2003) address the impact of the distinction between shareholders and the board of directors in stock-listed enterprises. They argue that there is substantial scope for managerial power due to actual incentives of directors being geared towards the interests of the CEO rather than the interests of the owners.

First, board directors like to be reappointed. It entails not only an attractive salary, but also prestige and valuable business and social connections. CEOs are favored by directors of the board in the design of compensation packages because they almost always play an important role in the renomination process of directors to the board. The CEO may also have some discretion regarding the directors' compensation and perks, and a CEO may become a fellow board member in the future. Second, directors usually have only limited, or no, shares in the enterprise. Third, directors not only lack the expertise of developing an appropriate compensation package, but their concern for developing a reputation for haggling with the CEO over compensation may even discourage proposing alternatives. Finally, the market for corporate control does not work sufficiently strong to assure optimal compensation packages.

The overall implication of the incentives facing the members of the board of directors is that executives may have considerable power over their own compensation arrangements. However, governance structure choice probably serves as an important moderating variable. Hendrikse and Veerman (2001a) have identified a number of differences between cooperatives and investor owned firms. First, each member will have a considerable share of his crop processed by a particular cooperative. This financial stake provides strong motivation for members to acquire substantial information in order to evaluate policy decisions. These incentives are further enhanced by the fact that member farm level assets may be totally dependent on the success of the cooperative (no market alternatives, highly specialized technology of the cooperative, etc.). This is important for the functioning of the board of directors because the majority of the board of directors in a cooperative consists of members, whereas the financial involvement of directors of the board in a stock listed enterprise is usually (very) limited. Board directors in cooperatives therefore have stronger incentives to perform their jobs well than directors in stock listed enterprises.

Second, shares of a cooperative are not traded on the stock market. Stockholders can easily get out of the enterprise by selling their stock in the market, whereas members in a cooperative cannot. Members therefore pay more attention to the way the cooperative is being run. The lack of the market for corporate control enhances the incentives for the board of directors in a cooperative even more. Third, a similar incentive is provided by the lack of a market for inputs. The absence of a market for inputs eliminates the possibility for a cooperative to compare its own performance with those of rivals. It therefore becomes more attractive to put forth effort in the internal control system in order to compensate for the absence of the yardstick of the market. Finally, the lack of a stock listing of a cooperative precludes a source of information for the design of the compensation package of the CEO. The stock price of a cooperative cannot be used in the remuneration scheme of the CEO because there is no stock price.

According to Bebchuk and Fried (2003), managerial power is limited by three variables: outrage costs, outsiders' perception of a CEO's compensation, and "camouflage". The extent of rent-extraction by the CEO depends on how much "outrage" a proposed compensation arrangement is expected to generate among relevant outsiders. Directors and managers will try to prevent embarrassment and reputational harm in the formulation and approval of compensation schemes. Managers have a substantial incentive to obscure and try to legitimize, i.e. camouflage, their extraction of rents in order to avoid or minimize the outrage that results from outsiders' recognition of rent extraction.[3]

Cooperatives may be advantageous in limiting managerial power compared to stock listed enterprises for two reasons. First, outrage costs are likely to be higher in cooperatives than in stock listed enterprises. The considerable financial involvement of the members in the cooperative and the regular member meetings may discipline the compensation package awarded to the CEO. Second, the lack of a stock listing is often considered a disadvantage of cooperatives because a stock price summarizes a lot of varied information. However, a stock listing is not necessarily advantageous for the design of an executive compensation package. An example is a conventional option plan when the market or sector rises substantially. It does not benchmark and therefore fails to filter out industry and general market trends.

5. SUMMARY AND FURTHER RESEARCH

This article has addressed two observations regarding the board of directors in agricultural cooperatives. First, it is sometimes stated that cooperatives seem to behave like ordinary enterprises. A relational contracting perspective is put forward to model this claim. All governance structures turn out to entail the same bargaining power distribution in a relational contracting setting, because the parties informally establish the same outcome in every governance structure. Governance structure is therefore irrelevant from an investment incentive perspective. However, they differ in their bargaining positions. Second, it is argued that cooperatives may have advantages compared to firms with publicly traded shares in limiting the rent extraction tendencies in the design of the compensation package for the CEO. The lack of publicly traded shares of cooperatives may be advantageous for the board in cooperatives in bargaining with the professional management.

This article is to be positioned at the level of governance in the classification scheme of Williamson (2000).[4] A few aspects of the governance structure cooperative have been addressed, but much work remains to be done, even along the lines explored in this article. For example, the irrelevance of governance structure can be formulated from other perspectives. Suppose that the organization has adopted a certain, simple formal structure. It will be apparent that this structure will channel its activities in a certain direction, and will respond by adding, or structuring, the bylaws in ways to counter the undesirable effects of this direction. These theoretical exercises are various ways to formulate the claim made regarding the irrelevance of governance structure, but data will determine whether governance structure matters or not. Similarly, the three-tier approach in Section 4 can be extended in various ways. For example, a cooperative is often characterized as a society of members and an economic entity. The impact of the organization and representation of the society of members in a cooperative as compared to the organization and representation of shareholders in a corporation did not receive detailed attention, but it may have an effect on the behavior of the board of directors. Another aspect of the membership in cooperatives is that they are owners with a vested interest, taking the entire portfolio of farm activities into account when they exercise their ownership rights in a particular cooperative. Finally, the focus of attention in this article is on the board in cooperatives versus corporations. This asks for a sequel with the CEO at the center of the analysis. Cook (1994) is already an informative contribution.

NOTES

[1] Other examples are investor-owned enterprises, worker-controlled firms, franchises, mutuals, joint ventures, networks, and public enterprises.

[2] The vertical line thru point $(-k_f,-k_p)$ represents the governance structure backward integration, whereas the 45° line represents the governance structure market exchange.

[3] An example is the use of compensation consultants for reasons of legitimization. Consultants may supply useful information and contribute expertise on the design of compensation packages, but they can also help in camouflaging rents because they have strong incentives to use their discretion to benefit the CEO. Evidence suggests that compensation consultants are often used to justify executive pay rather than to optimize it. For example, consultants argue that pay should be related to performance when things go well, whereas they focus on peer group pay when firms do poorly. Other examples of camouflage are gratuitous goodbye payments to departing executives, and stealth compensation practices like pension plans, deferred compensation, post-retirement perks, and consulting contracts.

[4] Embeddedness, Institutional environment, Governance, and Resource allocation are distinguished. Research regarding the relationship between the Institutional environment and cooperatives is actual, given the transition in Eastern Europe and China. The relationship between Resource allocation and cooperatives has always received considerable attention due to the Common Agricultural Policy in Europe, and similar policies elsewhere.

[5] A specific illustration is the architecture choice model of Sah and Stiglitz (1986). A hierarchy compensates for its large number of type I errors by choosing lower screening levels for its bureaus, whereas the polyarchy corrects for its large number of type II errors by increasing its screening levels.

REFERENCES

Aghion, P. and J. Tirole. 1997. "Formal and Real Authority in Organisations." *Journal of Political Economy* 105(1):1–29.

Baker, G., R. Gibbons and K.J. Murphy. 1999. "Informal Authority in Organisations." *The Journal of Law, Economics, & Organisation* 15(1):56–73.

Baker, G., R. Gibbons and K.J. Murphy. 2002. "Relational Contracts and the Theory of the Firm." *Quarterly Journal of Economics* 2002, 117(1):39–84.

Bebchuk, L.A. and J.M. Fried. 2003. "Executive Compensation as an Agency Problem." *Journal of Economic Perspectives* 17(3):71–92.

Bolton, P. and D.S. Scharfstein. 1998. "Corporate Finance, the Theory of the Firm, and organizations." *Journal of Economic Perspectives* 12(4):95–114.

Commission of the European Communities. 7.12.2001. *Co-operatives in Enterprise Europe.* Draft Consultation paper, Brussels.

Cook, M.L. 1994. "The Role of Management Behavior in Agricultural Cooperatives." *Journal of Agricultural Cooperation* 9:42–58.

Drucker, P. 1999. "Knowledge-Worker Productivity: The Biggest Challenge." *California Management Review* 41(2):79–94.

Fudenberg, D. and E. Maskin. 1986. "The Folk Theorem in Repeated Games with Discounting or with Incomplete Information." *Econometrica* 54(3):533–554.

Galdeano, E., J. Cespedes, and M. Rodriguez. 2005. *Productivity and Quality – Environmental Changes in Marketing Cooperatives: An Analysis of the Horticultural Sector.* presented at the XIth Congress of the European Association of Agricultural Economics, Copenhagen.

Griffioen, C. 2004 "We Moeten Ons Steeds Opnieuw Blijven Waarmaken". *Cooperatie* 579:8–9.

Grossman, S.J. and O. Hart. 1986. "The Costs and the Benefits of Ownership: A Theory of Vertical and Lateral Integration." *Journal of Political Economy* 94(4):691–719.

Hansmann, H. 1996. *The Ownership of Enterprise*, Cambridge: The Belknap Press of Harvard University Press.

Hendrikse, G.W.J. 2003. "Governance of Chains and Networks: A Research Agenda." *Journal on Chains and Network Sciences* 3(1):1–6.

__. 2005. Contingent Control Rights in Agricultural Cooperatives. in T. Theurl and E.C. Meijer (Eds.), *Strategies for Cooperation,* Shaker Verlag, 385–394.

__. and C. P. Veerman. 2001a. "Marketing Cooperatives and Financial Structure: A Transaction Costs Economics Analysis." *Agricultural Economics* 26:205–216.

__. and C.P. Veerman. 2001b. "Marketing Co-operatives: An Incomplete Contracting Perspective." *Journal of Agricultural Economics* 52(1):53–64.

Hu, Y. 2005. *Cooperatives as Systems of Attributes: A Study on China's Cooperatives.* RSM Erasmus University.

Klep, L. 2004." Cooperatie is Belangrijk: Gezamenlijk een Probleem Oplossen." *Cooperatie* 577:8–10.

LeVay, C. 1983. "Agricultural Co-operative Theory: A Review." *Journal of Agricultural Economics* 34:1–44.

Nilsson, J. 1999." Co-operative Organisational Models as Reflections of the Business Environments." *The Finnish Journal of Business Economics* 4:449–470.

Sah, R.K. and J.E. Stiglitz. 1986. "The Architecture of Economic Systems: Hierarchies and Polyarchies." *American Economic Review* 76(4):716–727.

Teece, D. 1998. "Capturing Value from Knowledge Assets." *California Management Review* 40(3):62–78.

USDA. 2002. *Agricultural Cooperatives in the 21st Century.* Rural Business-Cooperative Service, Cooperative Information Report 60.

Van Bekkum, O.F. 2004. De Cooperatieve Beursgang. *Cooperatie* 580:20–23.

Wierenga, B. 1997. *Competing for the Future in the Agricultural and Food Channel.* in Wierenga, B. *et al.* (eds.), Agricultural Marketing and Consumer Behavior in a Changing World, Dordrecht: Kluwer Academic Publishers.

Williamson, O.E. 2000. "The New Institutional Economics: Taking Stock, Looking Ahead." *Journal of Economic Literature* 38(3):595–613.

CHAPTER 9

REGULATION, GOVERNANCE AND CAPITAL STRUCTURE IN COOPERATIVES[*]

ANASTASSIOS GENTZOGLANIS

University of Sherbrooke, Faculty of Business Administration, Department of Finance & CEREF (Center for the Study of Regulatory Economics and Finance), Sherbrooke, Quebec, Canada, and University of Crete, Greece[**]

Abstract. Capital structure efficiency is viewed as contributing to good financial performance. According to the traditional arguments, cooperatives have difficulties in getting an optimal capital structure. This paper argues that *governance rules* may explain their less efficient performance. By combining the arguments of the political model of governance and the traditional theory of regulation, a unified approach is developed that makes the link between regulatory governance and capital structure explicit. It is argued that the heterogeneity of cooperatives' members may result in powerful coalitions and in a sub optimal capital structure. The evidence gathered from the empirical literature confirms these results.

1. INTRODUCTION

In the last decade or so a new organizational and competitive environment has emerged after the adoption of major structural reforms, regulatory and market liberalization policies by many developed and developing economies. Overly aggressive growth strategies and poor governance rules resulted in some highly publicized business failures and critiques. Under these pressures, some cooperatives reacted by adopting either investor-owned firms (IOFs) strategies or hybrid forms of governance, management and capital structures. Although the effects of these strategies have been generally positive (Cook and Illiopoulos, 2000), there is a growing dissatisfaction (Bacchiega and De Fraja, 1999) with the way cooperatives deal with governance issues and take future decisions.

Previous models have shown that the capital structure of cooperatives is less efficient than the one of IOFs (Bonin *et al.*, 1993). Factors such as less "tradability" of ownership rights or a fixed capital contribution to the cooperatives' pool of capital seem to be the main reasons for this difference. It is argued in this paper that governance rules may be another factor that may explain the less efficient capital structure of cooperatives compared to IOFs. This paper deals with the relationship between regulatory governance and capital structure of cooperatives and investor-owned firms.

151

K. Karantininis & J. Nilsson (eds.), Vertical Markets and Cooperative Hierarchies, 151–167.
© 2007 *Springer.*

It examines the theoretical and empirical literature dealing with this issue and identifies the necessary conditions for a successful governance strategy which may increase the capital structure efficiency of cooperatives.

Section 2 reviews the literature on corporate governance and capital structure of cooperatives and IOFs and it sets out the theoretical and empirical outcomes in the context of globalization and the intensification of competition. Section 3 presents the traditional models of governance and highlights their strengths and weaknesses. Section 4 develops a unified framework of regulatory governance and establishes the link between governance structure and capital structure based on the traditional political and regulatory models of governance. Section 5 presents some successful governance strategies and capital structure efficiency for cooperatives and draws some policy recommendations. Lastly, Section 6 concludes.

2. THE THEORETICAL RELATIONSHIP BETWEEN GOVERNANCE AND CAPITAL STRUCTURE

One of the problems cooperatives have difficulties to deal with is their undercapitalization and therefore their sub-optimal capital structure.[1] Insufficient financial resources and relatively high capital cost make investments too expensive to realize. In that context, members are deprived of profitable opportunities. A number of arguments have been advanced to explain the capital constraints faced by cooperatives and their negative effects on members' wealth.[2] One of the most important of them has to do with the definition of the structure of property rights and the disincentives it provides to their members to invest. Indeed, traditional cooperatives depend entirely on the ability of their *current* members to invest, limiting thereby the capacity of a cooperative to find investment funds from all potential investors. Typically, members provide equity in direct proportion to the use of the cooperative. Equity does not appreciate or depreciate and there are no dividends attached to it. A cooperative's management may view equity as having zero cost and overuse it, relatively to debt. The capital structure of cooperatives may thus be less optimal than that of IOFs. By contrast, IOFs do not limit their equity to their current owners but, should investment opportunities be present, they can appeal to all potential investors within and outside the organization. Therefore, investment opportunities are not missed because of lack of capitalization.

These arguments are based on the assumption that the members of cooperatives are homogeneous. Because members are viewed as a unique group, so the argument goes, there are no conflicts of interest among themselves. The only conflict that may arise is between the *principal* (members) and the *agent* (the management). This principal-agent problem creates the need for adopting governance rules and regulations to safeguard the interests of all stakeholders.

Generally speaking, IOFs' objective is to maximize the share value of its investors. To this end, owners of IOFs devise internal governance rules appropriate to exercise control over the management of the corporation so that the latter's actions would coincide with the interests of owners. The owners may then choose to apply various channels to control the management either *ex ante* or *ex post*. For instance, while in some IOFs the control of the management by the owners may be exercised at an earlier stage of the decision process, i.e., ex ante,[3] in other IOFs the owners may leave the management to act freely and exercise their control ex post, i.e., after the management had acted and the owners have seen the results. Such governance rules may be equally applied to cooperatives. Nonetheless, cooperatives lack the tools the owners of IOFs use to control their management, especially the ones based on mechanisms outside the firm such as the capital markets and the market for corporate control. Both discipline the management but IOFs are accountable to a greater number of stakeholders than cooperatives, such as banks and financial intermediaries, management boards, shareholders and institutional investors and capital markets. By contrast, cooperatives are not subjected to the same capital market exigencies (Figure 1). This is particularly true when one considers the current complexity of markets.

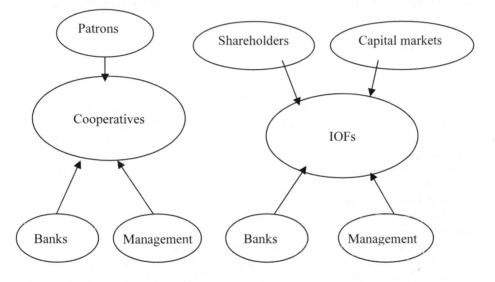

Figure 1. *Market exigencies for cooperatives and IOFs*

Indeed, the recent growth in *capital markets* and the proliferation of shareholding, sparked by deregulation and globalization, have spawned new channels of external control over the management of IOFs. Capital markets have become the main mechanism for the owners of IOFs to control their management. Advances in information and communication technologies (ICT) have increased the efficiency of the capital markets and with it the intensification of competition. Financial re-engineering and the inventive activity of major Stock Exchanges facilitated the role of institutional investors (pension and investment funds) and opened the way to the recognition of the importance of stock market information and regulatory governance. Whenever management performance is poorer than expected, dissatisfied investors can easily liquidate their investments and reduce thereby the risk of their portfolio. In that context, maximization of shareholder value has become one of the most important short run goals of IOFs. The management of these companies has to pay attention to the increase in the value of their shareholders by adopting strategies that increase the after-tax profits and distribute such profits as dividends and extraordinary redemptions to owners. Cooperatives lacking this market discipline may be less able to control the excesses of management and consequently the value of their investment.

The market for *corporate control* has been improved significantly, chiefly thanks to recent technological advances and the creation of more efficient capital markets. This has resulted in greater vulnerability of the management of modern organizations. For instance, poor performance may imply the disappearance of the firm and the replacement of the management by a more efficient firm through mergers and takeovers. Poor performance may result from the failure of the management to identify and realize profitable investment projects, wrong estimations of the market, bad timing and even bad decisions to finance its projects. Debt financing is more attractive than equity financing but an excessive debt financing may lead the company to bankruptcy and/or the replacement of the management by the management of the acquiring firm. The outcome is a more optimal capital structure for IOFs. *Debt financing* may then be deemed as a management control mechanism that forces managers to act efficiently on the decisions concerning the capital structure of the company and its operating costs. Market mechanisms are thus deemed to be the best channels by which the owners of IOFs may control their management. Nonetheless, in recent years, these mechanisms have become part of the problem since many well-known companies went bankrupt after pursuing such short term objectives. Management, in order to satisfy the pressing needs of owners for higher profitability, has increasingly entered into doubtful investment (and occasionally illicit) activities. Market mechanisms are not enough to guarantee that the management acts to the best interests of their owners. That's why there is a necessity for devising *internal regulatory mechanisms* to control the management. By contrast, cooperatives and their management are more reluctant to use debt than the managers of IOFs creating thereby a capital structure that is less efficient than that of IOFs.

Thus, capital markets are increasingly playing an important role in the control of IOFs' management while the role of banks and other financial institutions is gradually losing ground. Lately, new generation cooperatives started emulating IOFs to solve their equity problem and with it their performance. By changing the property right structure (Cook and Iliopoulos, 2000) cooperatives resemble more or less to IOFs and they are able therefore to apply governance structures that improve their performance. Nonetheless, the adoption of similar governance structures does not necessarily imply similar performance between these organizations. It is argued, in the next section, that cooperatives, despite their increasing resemblance to IOFs, are distinctive organizations and as such they tend to choose a regulatory governance structure which is different from that in IOFs. The dynamics of this structure may lead to the creation of powerful coalitions between the management and the members of the cooperative and among members themselves. This has as an effect to modify the capital structure of the cooperative and its cost of capital. The latter depends on the interplay of powerful coalitions and the way they succeed to dominate the unpowerful ones.

3. THE TRADITIONAL MODELS OF GOVERNANCE

There is no unified theory of corporate governance. Recent contributions on the subject identify the weaknesses of the existing models but they do not offer a convincing alternative framework of analysis capable to deal with the observed weaknesses. Further, they do not distinguish between governance models for IOFs and cooperatives. Without any refinement, it is difficult to argue that the existing governance models apply equally well to both organizations (despite the existence of new generation cooperatives). It is necessary, therefore, to clearly define the concept of governance and analyze the conditions under which governance rules determine the performance of cooperatives. The development of a unified framework of analysis is thus necessary. Before developing and presenting the unified framework, it is advisable to proceed with the review of the traditional models of governance and compare them. It should be stressed from the outset that the traditional governance models are merely an extension of the principal-agent theory and identify ways, i.e., governance rules, to improve the apparent strained relations between owners and managers of cooperatives and IOFs.

Hawley and Williams (1996) identified four models of governance presented in Figure 2: the simple finance model; the stewardship model; the stakeholder model and the political model.

The simple finance model is based on the well known agency theory. It recognizes from the start that the financial performance of a firm is not optimized whenever there is a conflict between the firm's owners' objectives and its management. This model is mostly applicable to IOFs, i.e., to firms having a distinctive separation of ownership from the management of the firm. The chief problem in corporate governance is to construct rules and provide incentives so that the managers (the agent) of the firm pursue the interests of the principal (the owner of the corporation) without major conflicts. The rules and incentives could be *implicit or explicit* contracts but they should be powerful enough to avoid any opportunistic behavior on either side of contracting parties. Any deficiencies or incompleteness in the contracts may provide an opportunity to the agent to behave in a manner which is not necessarily in the best interest of the principal.[4] Rules and incentives are set by a firm to control its managers. Recently, in countries like Canada and USA, where institutional investors (mutual funds, pensions, etc.) own the majority of a firm's shares, the usual agency problems and agency costs[5] are compounded by the creation of the so-called *two-tier agency* or double agency problem. The latter recognizes that the institutional owners and their investment managers are in fact agents themselves for the primary owner of the firm (beneficial ownership). Despite the existence of contracts and the rules and regulations to exercise control on agent's behavior, the financial performance of the firm may not be Pareto efficient and its value may not be maximized. The agent having more information than the two principals (double agency) is still able to act discretely and expropriate value for himself. As a result, the financial value of the firm cannot be maximized (finance model) and this has an impact on the firm's cost of capital. It seems that the governance rules and regulations are not adequate enough to control the management, especially when the double agency problem is present.

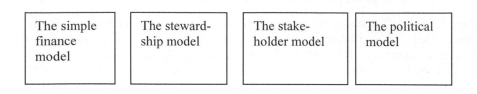

Figure 2. Models of governance for cooperatives and IOFs

The stewardship theory accepts the existence of the principal-agency problem but it builds upon incentive mechanisms that will steward the management of a firm to work to the best interests of the owners. According to this theory, cooperatives having strong incentive mechanisms built in the "collectively owned equity" should be able to perform better than IOFs. Indeed, cooperatives' owners-members participate more actively than IOFs' shareholders in the decision making process and this results in creation of value and the realization of high levels of return. Generally, this theory accepts the premise that cooperatives' management objective is: a) not to maximize its own goals but to reassure external investors (banks, regulators, etc.); b) to work to the best interest of the members and; c) to optimize the cooperative's value by stewarding its business activities to the right direction (stewardship theory). By influencing the cooperatives' constituencies, the managers are capable in attaining the goals of their members without the well-known agency problems. Given that trust is the basis for any business transaction particularly for cooperatives and the latter have no independent directors, a dynamic equilibrium is much easier to achieve than in IOFs.

Indeed, *trust,* the confidence one has in other's actions, leads to cooperation and this contributes in easing the conflict between the agent and the principal. It is true that the sentiment of trust is more pronounced in cooperatives than in IOFs because their members-owners are engaged in more durable transactions (repeated games) than in IOFs. In this type of games trust may be sustained as equilibrium behavior. Although this result may be desirable, it does not exclude inefficiencies.[6] Hart and Moore (1998) compared IOFs and cooperatives and found that, despite their differences in structure and governance, both organizations are indeed inefficient. The observed inefficiencies are at the production level though and they mostly depend on the prevailing market conditions. For instance, under normal competitive conditions, IOFs under-produce, depriving thereby some consumers the desire to consume while cooperatives overproduce leading their members to an over-consumption. Non cooperative members, who may value the cooperative's goods higher than that of its members, cross-subsidize (inter-finance) cooperatives' members' over-consumption. As competition intensifies, cross subsidies diminish and eventually disappear. Thus, as competition ratchets up cooperatives' viability is getting less sustainable (Hart and Moore, 1998) despite the fact that trust and cooperation are the fundamental elements of these organizations.

It can be argued therefore that from a theoretical point of view, globalization and the intensification of competition may be a major threat to the long run viability of cooperatives. Nonetheless, scant empirical evidence (Casadesus-Mansell and Khanna, 2003) shows that the performance of at least some well-known cases of successful cooperatives has increased after been exposed to a more competitive global environment (for instance, Irizar cooperative). This is attributable to the fact that trust, and especially trust as manifested in workplace settings, is an intrinsic cooperative value that is reinforced when global competition increases instability and therefore risk. In that context, trust makes the creation of governance rules unnecessary. Theoretically, cooperatives are in a far better position to achieve stability and a more efficient capital structure. It is obvious that this model does not take into account the coalitions and the conflicts of interest among powerful and non-powerful groups within cooperatives.

The stakeholder model is based on the belief that competitiveness of a cooperative, and as a matter of fact of any other economic organization, is possible to be improved should *strategic stakeholders* take part in the management of the cooperative. Members-owners of cooperatives manage to exercise control over their management by relinquishing part of their property rights to key stakeholders such as customers, suppliers, employees and community representatives. Control of cooperatives may be exercised by members-owners and stakeholders alike through multiple boards.[7] This governance structure eases the conflicts of interest and reduces the agency costs associated with the traditional, more vertical, governance structure. For example, the Montragon cooperative, by using all four institutional modes for governing transactions rather than markets and hierarchies, has achieved an enviable performance internationally (Turnbull, 1997).

The results of the stakeholder model have been criticized by Hill and Jones (1992). These authors have developed a "stakeholder-agency" model by recognizing the implicit and explicit contractual relationships governing a cooperative. Contrary to the results of Turnbull, (1997), Hill and Jones found that the usual inefficiencies encountered in the traditional principal-agent model are also present in their model. Nonetheless, neither Hill and Jones nor Turnbull establish the theoretical relationship between regulatory governance and capital structure of cooperatives, which is the subject matter of the next section.

The political model of governance assumes that the cooperative's constituencies do not necessarily have homogeneous objectives and some owners-members could create coalitions and try to change the cooperative's policies by developing voting support from other owners-members. The political model, as it was originally developed by Hawley and Williams (1996), does not necessarily imply a government role, rather it is dealing with the internal processes (non-market) used by owners-members of a cooperative to determine an outcome in their favor. This form of governance, which is based on politics rather than on finance, is a better way to exercise control of a cooperative's management in a more effective and less expensive way than the traditional corporate governance rules (Pound, 1992). This has been documented in an empirical study by Berstein (1980) and Turnbull (1995) for worker-governed cooperatives.

As it presently stands, the theoretical underpinnings of the political model of governance are not quite strong and they lack the analytical development and refinement of a model which aspires to explain some hard facts. Indeed, the formation of coalitions and the decision making process is quite complex within multi-agent organizations and the political model of governance is rather assertive than positive. It does not establish the link between regulatory governance and capital structure and it cannot adequately explain why such coalitions are generated. The next section establishes such a link by integrating the traditional theory of regulation and the main arguments of the political model of governance.

In sum, it is clear from the above that inefficiencies are present regardless of the governance model chosen by an IOF or a cooperative. In both types of organization, the principal-agency problem and the one of asymmetric information are present and this gives rise to a capital structure that is not necessarily optimal. Cooperatives seem to have more difficulties in choosing an optimal capital structure than IOFs. For instance, in a recent empirical study on Italian agricultural cooperatives Russo *et al.* (2000) found that cooperatives are undercapitalized relatively to IOFs by approximately 43%. Such an undercapitalization results in a performance which is not as good as the one in IOFs. This is mainly attributed to the existence of powerful groups (coalitions) within cooperatives and the way decisions are taken by these coalitions.

4. A UNIFIED APPROACH OF REGULATORY GOVERNANCE AND CAPITAL STRUCTURE FOR COOPERATIVES AND IOFS

The traditional models of governance are instructive and highlight the importance to devise explicit and implicit rules and regulations to alleviate the agency problem. The latter is present in both IOFs and cooperatives but at a different degree. Apparently, cooperatives with a "collectively owned equity" have built-in, i.e., structural incentives that make the principal-agent problem less acute. Nonetheless, none of the traditional models establishes adequately the link between regulatory governance and capital structure. *Regulatory governance,* in its strict sense, refers to rules and regulations adopted by stakeholders of an organization to discipline its management by offering incentives to ease the conflict that may arise in the pursuit of divergent individual interests. This definition refers to the *internal regulatory governance*[8] and its effectiveness depends on the way it makes explicit the rights and responsibilities of stakeholders (members, board, managers, shareholders, etc.) and on the way it specifies their role and spells out the rules and procedures for making decisions on business issues. Further, its precise form depends on the objectives and purposes of the organization. In this sense, it provides the structure through which the company objectives are set, and means to attain those objectives and monitor performance. By fixing different objectives, cooperatives and IOFs will necessarily adopt *different regulatory* structures to monitor performance. Although the regulatory governance is devised to increase efficiency, its degree of efficiency depends on the *dynamics* of managing the economic and financial aspects of the organization.

These dynamics depend on the relation and power that exist between managers and the diverse groups of members'/owners' of the organization. Two kinds of management may emerge; either a powerful management or a non-powerful one. *Powerful managers,*[9] the ones having more clout, may emerge naturally in both cooperatives and IOFs. By using their bargaining power, powerful managers are able to determine the course of an action and bring it closer to their own objectives than to their members/owners. In this context, powerful managers may pursue strategies to minimize the financial risk by emphasizing the use of more equity capital than debt. The capital structure is thus directly linked to the governance rules and the interplay of power that prevails within the organization. By contrast, non-powerful managers are less able to pursue their own objectives and act therefore more closely to the interests of their members/owners. This may result in a different capital structure between powerful and non-powerful cooperatives. The latter would emphasize a capital structure with less equity while the powerful cooperatives would have a capital structure that uses less debt than optimal. In both cases a sub optimal capital structure results. By contrast, the capital structure of IOFs would be closer to optimality despite the existence of powerful or non-powerful management. This is so because, as it was argued above, IOFs use more mechanisms to discipline their management and are accountable to a greater number of regulatory bodies than cooperatives. Yet the degree of homogeneity of members/owners of cooperatives and shareholders of IOFs play a deterministic role in the outcome of capital structure and efficiency of each organization.

It has long been recognized (Spulber, 1989) that heterogeneity creates incentives to form coalitions which are more able to pass rules and regulations in their favor. To develop the unified framework of regulatory governance, it is assumed in this paper that the members of a cooperative, and for that matter the owners of an IOF, are not homogeneous. Because of this heterogeneity, members' (shareholders') objectives cannot be the same. Minority coalitions are built and decisions are taken on the basis of the exchange of "votes" among members. More powerful groups get more often than not a confidence vote and they manage to pass their priorities first. As far as the management is concerned, it is hypothesized that it acts to its best interests. The agency problem is encountered at many levels; among the groups (coalitions) formed by the owners and the ones formed between the owners and the management. The power of each group to control the other's decisions determine the policies to be applied and the decisions to be taken. Thus, in some organizations, the management may be more powerful than the owners and in other the reverse may be true. It is possible that neither the management nor the owners have any superior power. Organizations with powerful management are thus called powerful organizations. Powerful cooperatives are thus the ones with strong management.

Cooperatives with more homogeneous members (less powerful cooperatives) will have fewer coalitions and therefore a stronger voice over management. In that context, members' decisions have higher chances to be passed and their interests have more chances to be pursued by the management. In more powerful cooperatives, management has more power than members (because of the presence of a high degree of heterogeneity and the formation of many but week coalitions) and it can pursue its own interests more freely. In contrast to cooperatives, IOFs' shareholders are necessarily heterogeneous. In this case, there will be more coalitions among themselves and therefore there are fewer chances to create strong majority coalitions. It is thus possible that the management of IOFs pursues its interests much easier than in the case of cooperatives.

Powerful groups may decide how costs and benefits are shared among other groups within the cooperative and each group decides which strategy to support based on the allocation of benefits and costs. Thus decisions are not taken using the rational economic criteria of rate of return on investment but rather on politics. Therefore, investments with low returns may be attractive as long as the most powerful coalition within the cooperative gets the maximum of benefits. The existence of high transaction costs among coalitions may thus lead to the adoption of Pareto-inefficient (non optimal) strategies. Cooperatives' overall performance may thus be less optimal than IOFs. Several techniques have been invented to overcome these negative effects such as *leverage and capital structure management* and *risk management technique.*

Cooperatives using leverage, i.e., debt to finance investments, are better equipped to mitigate the potential conflicts of interest of powerful coalitions. A realignment of interests contributes to the adoption of more efficient strategies and capital structure. This is also confirmed in Zhang's model (1998) which predicts that leverage increases when there is a controlling ownership (powerful coalitions) since the latter becomes more tolerant towards risk. Governance instruments applied as tools to control powerful coalitions enhance performance by decreasing the inefficiencies arising from a non optimal capital structure. When ownership is dispersed and coalitions are absent, risk sharing becomes much easier and fairer. In that case, cooperatives need to adopt a regulatory governance structure which takes into account the dynamics of cooperatives. When compensations for good management performance are not included in the regulatory governance rules then the managers of cooperatives would prefer risk-minimizing strategies rather than the maximization of members' returns.

Risk management, i.e., the identification and management of a cooperative's exposure to financial risk, can be seen as a surrogate to corporate governance. Risk may arise from the variability of cash flows due to changes in market conditions such as unpredictable changes in commodity prices, interest rates and exchange rates. Risk management techniques may be used to create value for the members of the cooperatives. Although risk management techniques are widely used by large IOFs, cooperatives are less prone to them. This may also result in a sub-optimal capital structure and therefore in an increase in cooperatives' cost of capital and/or the non adoption of profitable investment projects. Figure 3 depicts the link between regulatory governance, capital structure and overall performance.

As shown above the described relationship in Figure 3 is well established for IOFs but there is scant relevant literature on the subject for cooperatives. Additionally, there is even less evidence on how cooperatives develop successful governance strategies and how the latter affects their cost of capital. The next section deals with these issues.

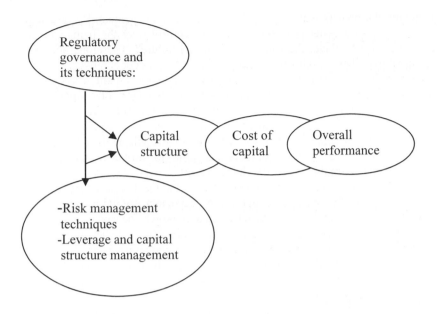

Figure 3. *The link between regulatory governance, capital structure and overall performance*

5. SUCCESSFUL GOVERNANCE STRATEGIES AND CAPITAL STRUCTURE EFFICIENCY OF COOPERATIVES

Capital structure management has increasingly become one of the most important researched subjects for both cooperatives and IOFs. Since Jensen's (1986) seminal work on the subject, considerable research output has been produced although there is not, as yet, a sound theoretical answer to the question of just how much financial leverage is enough. Nonetheless, Jensen extended the concept of agency costs and associated it to the subject of capital structure management by using the "free cash flow approach". The latter is defined as the cash flow "in excess of that required to fund all projects that have positive net present values when discounted at the relevant cost of capital". To be sure, the cost of capital may be different in cooperatives than in IOFs. If cooperatives use leverage less efficiently and their cost structure becomes non optimal, their cost of capital will be different (higher) than the one of IOFs. Using a higher interest rate to discount future cash flows will have as a result to lower future returns and to reject investment projects which would have been accepted otherwise.

According to Jensen, free cash flow can be used by management to satisfy its objectives instead of using it to finance profitable investment projects. Leverage, and therefore the use of debt, would provide the owners' of a firm a powerful tool to control more effectively its management team. The realization of profitable investment projects through the use of free cash and debt reduces the amount of free cash available to managers. The use of debt requires regular payments to service it providing thereby the owners with a heavy hand over the management. By levering up, shareholders are in a better position to exercise control over the management while management works under the "threat of financial failure". Therefore, according to this "threat hypothesis", IOFs work more efficiently than cooperatives.

When cooperatives determine their capital structure, they weight heavily the negative effects of risk on members' wealth. Thus, the managers of cooperatives show preference for equity rather than for debt because the latter increases the financial risk (Murray, 1983), especially for the cooperatives which are less diversified. The higher the preferences for equity, the lower will be the risk for the cooperative business. Thus, when managers are able to influence the capital structure through their bargaining power, the cooperatives will be less leveraged. This is also the hypothesis Russo et al. (2000) tested for the Italian cooperatives. They found that "powerful manager cooperatives [management with bargaining power] were less leveraged and had a long term strategy which focused on minimizing financial risk by increasing their equity/asset ratio" (p. 27). Therefore, the "threat hypothesis" is not working in powerful manager cooperatives as efficiently as in IOFs. Although risk is reduced in that way, this is not the best risk management strategy. Indeed, this strategy deprives cooperatives and their members the benefits of profitable investment projects.

Although in theory the issue of capital structure and governance may result in different outcomes for cooperatives and IOFs, in practice there are more similarities than one can expect from the beginning. For instance, a 1991 survey of chief financial officers of the largest nonfinancial, nonregulated U.S. firms about capital structure management, found that managers prefer by far the use of internal funds to finance their investment opportunities. They also prefer to forego seemingly profitable projects rather than to reduce shareholders' expected cash dividends. This was a way for IOFs' management to control risk. Indeed, the survey showed that in cases where management decided to use debt, its preferences were towards the use of short term debt instead of long term commitments. Short term solutions are thus viewed as the best strategy and a good way to wait out difficult market conditions. Thus, in practice even IOFs aim at minimizing the financial risk by using short term debt as much as possible. The "threat hypothesis" is less bounding in practice than in theory.

This is true despite the fact that in financial economics it is well established that the value of a levered firm is greater than the value of an unlevered one. Because debt is tax deductible, debt finance is cheaper than equity finance. In that context, debt may be overused and this may increase both financial distress (firm failure) and agency costs (costs of monitoring). Managers make the best possible decisions concerning a firm's optimal capital structure and therefore its optimal cost of capital by taking into account all the effects of leverage decisions. This is illustrated in Figure 4. At leverage level up to point A, the tax shield has the maximum effect. At point B, the actual market value of the levered firm is maximized while its overall cost of capital is minimized. At point C, leverage is overused and the cost of capital is high. The value of the firm decreases because the rating agencies downgrade the quality of its bonds, i.e., the debt capacity of the firm is overstretched. Beyond this point, the firm starts having a lesser ability to pay its bills on time. Its cash flows would become deficient and in case of adverse economic conditions, it may face bankruptcy. Its optimal capital structure should be set at the point where the cash flows the firm could expect to receive would be enough for the worst outcomes. In this context, the firm has to set its leverage at a level that is not threatening its financial viability under the worst scenarios. Its net cash balances during adverse circumstances must not be too risky for management to accept. Applied to cooperatives, Barton *et al.* (1996), determined the optimal solvency ratio (s) which depends on the difference between the return on assets and the going interest rate. The smaller the difference, the higher will be the solvency of the cooperative.[10]

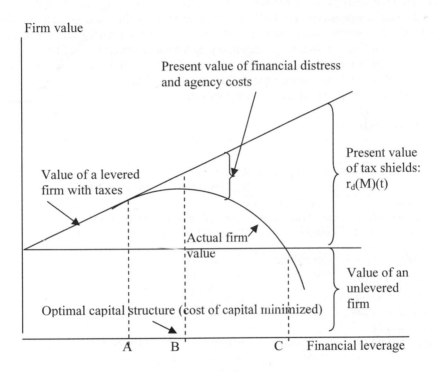

Figure 4. The cost of capital and the value of cooperatives and IOFs with taxes, agency and financial distress costs

The empirical evidence confirms the results of our unified framework of analysis. Indeed, Russo *et al.* (2000) found that powerful manager cooperatives (managers with great discretionary power over members) follow a more conservative approach to leverage and they focus their strategies in the minimization of financial risk. The equity/asset ratios are thus higher for powerful manager cooperatives than for non-powerful manager cooperatives in the Italian agricultural cooperatives. In powerful manager cooperatives, management seems to satisfy its own objectives by focusing on higher equity/asset ratios and therefore the minimization of financial distress. For the non-powerful manager cooperatives, members exercise a better control over management but members prefer to provide a minimum capital to cooperatives. These cooperatives are undercapitalized and this has a negative effect on long term prospects of the cooperative. Given that the equity/asset ratios of most cooperatives is quite low and significantly lower than IOFs both cooperatives and the government should find more efficient tools to encourage members to invest. The dilemma of members' investment minimizing behavior and managers' financial risk minimizing behavior, need to be reconciled with better governance rules and risk management strategies. Such a discrepancy in attitude should be fully understood so that better governance rules should be employed to provide incentives for strong membership and sound capital structure for the cooperatives.

In sum, cooperatives and IOFs have not necessarily the same objectives. Therefore, their regulatory structures to monitor management's performance will necessarily be different. Generally, regulatory governance increases efficiency but its degree of efficiency depends on the structure of power and the *dynamics* of coalitions that are formed within powerful and non-powerful organizations. Table 1 resumes the theoretical findings of our analysis.

Table 1. *Governance rules, financial risk management and capital structure for cooperatives and an IOFs*

	Governance model	Risk minimizing approach	Capital structure	Cost of capital
Powerful				
- Cooperatives	- political model	- financial risk management	- sub-optimal (less leverage)	- high
-IOFs	- stewardship model	- financial risk and agency costs management	- optimal (due to a balanced mix of finance)	- moderate (due to a balanced mix of finance)
Non-powerful				
- Cooperatives	- stakeholder model	- risk management to protect member capital	- sub-optimal (less equity)	- high (due to less leverage)
- IOFs	- the simple finance and/or stewardship model	- financial risk management	- optimal and/or sub-optimal	- low (due to more leverage)

It can be said from Table 1 that our unified approach of regulatory governance offers a good way to integrate the four models of governance and analyze their effects on risk, capital structure and the cost of capital for both IOFs and cooperatives.

6. CONCLUSIONS

Cooperatives increasingly compete with IOFs in an international and more aggressive business environment. The chase of growth opportunities, the acquisition of new technologies, the improvement in the quality of their goods and services, the satisfaction of their members and clients and the adoption of profitable strategies, require funds and access to capital. According to the traditional arguments, cooperatives have difficulties in getting an optimal capital structure because of the existing limits in the "tradability" of ownership rights (less access to capital markets) and of an equity capital that is limited to the fixed capital contributions of their members. It is argued in this paper that governance rules may be another factor that may explain the less efficient capital structure of cooperatives compared to IOFs. This paper, by combining the arguments of the political model of governance and the traditional theory of regulation, developed a unified approach that made the link between regulatory governance and capital structure explicit. It was argued that cooperatives' members are not necessarily homogeneous and as such they may pursue different objectives which may result in the formation of powerful coalitions. The stronger the homogeneity of members, the lower will be the number of coalitions and therefore the stronger the members over the management. Cooperatives with weak management are called non-powerful manager cooperatives. By contrast, powerful manager cooperatives are the ones with strong management.

The distinction between powerful and non-powerful manager cooperatives makes a difference in the ability of management to pursue its interests and in strategies adopted by each type of cooperative. Powerful manager cooperatives follow the strategy of financial risk minimization and they use less leverage. For the non-powerful manager cooperatives, members exercise a better control over management but members prefer to provide a minimum capital to cooperatives. These cooperatives are undercapitalized and this would have a negative effect on the cooperative's cost of capital in the long term. The equity/debt ratios are thus higher for powerful manager cooperatives than for non-powerful ones. In powerful manager cooperatives, management seems to satisfy its own objectives by focusing on higher equity/debt ratios and therefore the minimization of financial distress. Given that the equity/asset ratios of most cooperatives is quite low and significantly lower than IOFs both cooperatives and the government should find more efficient tools to encourage members to invest. The dilemma of members' investment minimizing behavior and managers' financial risk minimizing behavior, need to be reconciled with better governance rules and risk management strategies. Such a discrepancy in attitude should be fully understood so that better governance rules should be employed to provide incentives for strong membership and sound capital structure.

NOTES

*   I am grateful to Jerker Nilsson, Kostas Karantininis, and an anonymous referee for helpful comments and suggestions. Any remaining errors and omissions are my own.
**   This article was written while on sabbatical at the University of Crete.
1   Broadly speaking, the capital structure of a company is its ratio of debt to equity.

[2]   These include: equity capital depends on internally generated funds; incentives to invest by
      cooperatives' members are limited because of cooperatives' property rights structure; equity capital is
      not permanent; cooperatives' ability to get external finance is limited.
[3]   The adoption of stringent measures of surveillance *ex ante* is necessary to exercise control over the
      actions of the management.
[4]   The recent major US bankruptcies (Enron, Global crossing, etc.) are illustrative.
[5]   The agency costs are the ones associated with monitoring the management, the compensation of the
      management from the profits of the owners, and any residual losses.
[6]   Inefficiencies are defined relatively to the first-best.
[7]   Apparently this is the structure of the Mondragòn cooperative. The existence of three or more boards
      safeguards the smooth functioning of the cooperative because these boards introduce a division of
      power with checks and balances.
[8]   By contrast, *external regulatory governance* encompasses the rules and regulations adopted by
      governments to determine the way IOFs and cooperatives operate in the general framework of domes-
      tic and international economy.
[9]   Powerful managers are considered to be the ones who are able to pursue their own interests.
      Cooperatives with powerful management are thus defined as powerful cooperatives. It should be
      noted, however, that powerful cooperatives do not necessarily have a good *overall* performance.
      Although their capital structure may be more optimal than the one for non-powerful cooperatives,
      their overall performance may be less efficient than the one for non-powerful cooperatives. Thus, a
      better capital structure is a necessary but not a sufficient condition for better overall performance.
      Other strategies such as marketing, pricing, R&D, etc., are all essential ingredients for good overall
      performance.
[10] Mathematically, the optimal solvency ratio (s) for a cooperative is the ratio of the difference between
      Pratt-Arrow's relative risk-aversion coefficient (ρ) and the variability of the return on assets (σ^2_A) and
      the difference in the return on assets (r_A) and interest rate, i.e., $s = (\rho - \sigma^2_A)/(r_A - r)$.

REFERENCES

Bacchiega, A. and De Fraja, G. 1999. "Constitutional design and Investment in Cooperatives and
      Investor-owned Firms." *Working paper No. 05,* Dept. of Economics and Related Studies, University
      of York, York.

Barton, D., Parcell, J., and Featherstone, A. 1996. "Optimal Capital Structure in Centralized Agricultural
      Cooperatives." *Working paper.*

Berstein, P. 1980. *Workplace Democratization: Its Internal Dynamics*, Transaction Books, New
      Brunswick, New Jersey.

Bonin, J. P, D. C. Jones and L. Putterman. 1993. "Theoretical and Empirical Studies of Producer
      Cooperatives: Will Ever the Twain Meet?" *Journal of Economic Literature*, 31 (3):1290–1320.

Casadesus-Mansell, R. and Khanna, T. 2003. "Globalization and Trust: Theory and Evidence from
      Cooperatives." *Working paper No. 592,* William Davidson Institute, University of Michigan,
      Stephen M. Ross Business School.

Cook, M.L. 1995. "The Future of U.S. Agricultural Cooperatives: A Neo-Institutional Approach."
      American Journal of Agricultural Economics 77(4):1153–59 (December)..

___. and Iliopoulos, C. 2000. "Ill-defined Property Rights in Collective Action: The Case of Agricultural
      Cooperatives." *Institutions, Contracts, and Organizations: Perspectives from New Institutional
      Economics,* C. Ménard (ed.). London: Edward Elgar.

Hart, O.D. and Moore, J. 1998. "The Governance of Exchanges: Members' Cooperatives versus Outside
      Ownership." *Oxford Review of Economics and Politics* 12:53–69.

Hawley, J.P. and Williams, A.T. 1996. "Corporate Governance in the United States: The Rise of
      Fiduciary Capitalism – A Review of the Literature." *Working Paper,* Saint Mary's College of
      California, Moraga, California.

Hill, C.W.L. and Jones, T.M. 1992. "Stakeholder – Agency Theory." *Journal of Management Studies, 29 No 2*:131–54.

Jensen, M.C. 1986. "Agency Costs and Free Cash Flow, Corporate Finance, and Takeovers." *American Economic Review* 76:323–29 (May).

___. and Meckling, W.H. 1979. Rights and Production Functions: An Application to Labor-Managed Firms and Codetermination. *Journal of Business.* 52:469–506 (October).

Murray, G. 1983. "Management Strategies for Corporate Control in British Agricultural Cooperatives." *Agricultural Administration*, 14:51–63.

Russo, C., D. Weatherspoon, C. Paterson and M., Sabbatini. 2000. "Effects of Managers' Power on Capital Structure: A Study of Italian Agricultural Cooperatives." *International Food and Agribusiness Management Review* 3:27–39.

Spulber, D. 1989. *Regulation and Markets,* MIT Press, Boston.

Turnbull, S. 1995. "Innovation in Corporate Governance: The Mondragon Experience." *Corporate Governance: An International Review* 3(3):167–80 (July).

___. 1997. Corporate Governance: Its Scope, Concerns and Theories, *Working paper, Corporate Governance: An International Review, Blackwood, Oxford* 5(4):180–205 (October).

Zhang, G. 1998. "Ownership, Concentration, Risk Aversion and the Effect of Financial Structure on Investment Decisions." *European Economic Review* 42:1751–1778.

CHAPTER 10

COOPERATIVE FORWARD INTEGRATION IN OLIGOPSONISTIC MARKETS

A Simulation Analysis of Incentives and Impacts

JEFFREY S. ROYER

Dept. of Agricultural Economics, University of Nebraska, Lincoln, Nebraska, USA

Abstract. A model of a two-stage vertical market structure consisting of producers, processors, and a cooperative is developed to analyze the market incentives agricultural cooperatives may have for integrating forward into processing activities and the comparative impacts of cooperative forward integration on producers and consumers when processors are alternately characterized by Cournot, competitive, and collusive behavior. Results suggest that cooperatives do not have an incentive to integrate forward in competitive markets. In markets with some degree of market power, the potential for cooperative forward integration is linked to the cooperative's ability to restrict the output of its members to optimal levels.

1. INTRODUCTION

Agricultural cooperatives are typically involved in first-stage marketing and processing activities as a result of their role as vertical extensions of the farming operations of their members. Consequently, the marketing and processing activities in which cooperatives participate are generally associated with low margins and little market power (Rogers and Marion 1990). Economists have offered several explanations for why more cooperatives have not integrated forward into the later stages of the marketing channel where the amount of processing and product differentiation is usually greater. Most of these explanations are based on organizational characteristics of cooperatives that are considered to place them at a disadvantage in competing with other firms in processed product markets. Explanations include arguments that: (*a*) the production orientation of directors restricts the ability of a cooperative board to supervise and assist management as the organization's scope grows vertically and increasingly involves consumer-oriented merchandizing activities (Jamison 1960), (*b*) cooperatives are disadvantaged by scale economies associated with complex organizational

K. Karantininis & J. Nilsson (eds.), Vertical Markets and Cooperative Hierarchies, 169–194.
© 2007 *Springer*.

tasks (Caves and Petersen 1986), and (*c*) cooperatives are often insufficiently capitalized to make the substantial investments in research and development and in advertising that are necessary to be successful in processed markets (Rogers and Marion 1990).[1]

Only a few studies have analyzed the market power incentives cooperatives may have for integrating forward into processing activities within imperfectly competitive market structures. Most of those studies (Masson and Eisenstat 1978; Royer and Bhuyan 1994a and 1995) have focused on analyzing the integration incentives of cooperatives in market structures characterized by bilateral or successive monopoly rather than oligopolistic or oligopsonistic market structures in which cooperatives compete with other firms. Only the Royer and Bhuyan (1994b) study has analyzed the incentive of a cooperative to integrate forward in markets in which there are several firms. A limitation of that study is that it assumes that all firms hold Cournot conjectures, i.e., each firm sets its output as if the output of other firms is fixed. This paper extends that analysis by assuming that the other firms in the market are alternately characterized by Cournot, competitive, or collusive behavior. The model employed in this paper is also simpler than the one used in the Royer and Bhuyan analysis. Whereas that earlier model is based on a three-stage vertical market structure consisting of producers, assemblers, and processors, the model in this paper is based on what is essentially a two-stage vertical market structure consisting only of producers, processors, and a cooperative. This framework allows the analysis to focus directly on the relationships between producers and processors.

Incentives for vertical integration may arise from the existence of technological or transactional economies or from market imperfections (Perry 1989).[2] Because there are no *a priori* reasons to assume that the technological or transactional incentives for cooperatives to integrate forward differ from those of other firms, this paper focuses only on the incentives that may result from market imperfections. Specifically, this paper examines the incentives for integration that may arise from the ability of an integrated cooperative to maximize the joint profits of its members in both producing and processing a raw product and to abate the market power of oligopsonistic processors. As Perry observes, market imperfections are an important determinant of vertical integration. Vertical integration in response to technological or transactional economies can be expected to increase economic welfare. Thus the primary focus of transaction cost economics is explaining and predicting patterns of vertical integration. On the other hand, vertical integration in reaction to market imperfections raises questions of public policy because integration may either increase or decrease welfare (p. 189). Consequently, this paper also examines the effects of cooperative integration on prices, output, and welfare.

2. PREVIOUS RESEARCH

Masson and Eisenstat (1978) analyzed the ability of dairy cooperatives to countervail various types of monopsony power through bargaining or vertical integration and evaluated the expected impacts of these strategies on producers and social welfare. They concluded that forward integration by an open-membership coopera- tive would benefit both producers and consumers when the processor experienced constant returns to scale and possessed market power in the final product market. Integration by the cooperative would countervail the processor's monopsony power in the intermediate product market and eliminate the exercise of market power in the final product market. However, they also concluded that the cooperative would lack an incentive to acquire the processor if its price included the capitalized value of its monopsony returns.

Royer and Bhuyan (1994a and 1995) developed a model of a three-stage vertical market structure consisting of agricultural producers, an assembler, and a processor to analyze the market incentives cooperatives might have for integrating forward into processing activities and to evaluate the comparative impact of cooperative forward integration on prices, outputs, and welfare. That analysis considered both fixed- and variable-proportions production technology at the processing stage in addition to both assembler and processor dominance in the determination of the assembled raw product price. It concluded that both producers and consumers would benefit from forward integration by cooperatives but that those benefits would not ensure that a cooperative would have an incentive to integrate. Cooperatives that are successful in restricting producer output to optimal levels may have an incentive to integrate because forward integration would enable them to capture monopoly profits in the processed product market. On the other hand, a cooperative that is unable to restrict output may not have an incentive to integrate because it would act as a price taker in the processed product market.

Only a few works on vertical integration within oligopolistic market structures exist. These include articles by Greenhut and Ohta (1979) and Abiru (1988). Greenhut and Ohta constructed a two-stage model of successive oligopoly, assuming fixed-proportions production technology, constant costs, and linear demand. They demonstrated that vertical integration by a subset of firms increased industry output and decreased the final product price. Although the profits of the integrated firms increased, overall industry profits decreased, reversing the results of successive monopoly models, in which vertical integration is beneficial to the merging monopolists as well as consumers. Abiru built a successive oligopoly model based on a variable-proportions technology, which he used to isolate the pure effect of vertical integration from the effect of horizontal merger. He concluded that the pure vertical integration effect results in an unambiguous decrease in the final product price as well as increases in industry output and consumer surplus.

More recently, Wu (1992) published a treatise on oligopolies and vertical inte- gration that provides a useful framework for analyzing the incentives for cooperative forward integration and the expected price, output, and welfare impacts of coopera- tive integration in the context of oligopolistic market structures. Wu analyzed a two- stage successive oligopoly structure in which upstream firms produce an intermedi- ate input used by downstream firms in the production of a final product. The intermediate input market is characterized by Cournot competition among the upstream firms, i.e., each firms sets its output by assuming that the output of other firms is fixed. The downstream firms accept the price of the intermediate input as given but engage in Cournot competition with one another in the final product market. Like Greenhut and Ohta, Wu assumed fixed-proportions technology, constant costs, and linear demand. To avoid confusing the effects of vertical and horizontal mergers, Wu assumed an identical number of upstream and downstream firms.

Adapting the framework developed by Wu, Royer and Bhuyan (1994b) analyzed the incentives agricultural cooperatives may have for integrating forward into processing activities in an oligopolistic market structure. That analysis assumed a three-stage vertical market structure consisting of producers, assemblers, and processors to analyze the market incentives a cooperative assembler might have to integrate forward by acquiring a processor and compared those incentives and the expected impacts of cooperative integration on prices, outputs, and welfare to the incentives and impacts for a noncooperative assembler. The analysis considered both successive oligopoly, in which the assemblers set the output level of the assembled raw product, and the situation in which the processors exercise oligopsony power in the assembled raw product market.

The results of that analysis suggest that cooperatives in oligopolistic market structures frequently may have market incentives to integrate forward into processing activities. A cooperative assembler that is able to restrict output to optimal levels may always have an incentive to integrate regardless of the number of firms in the market and the current level of integration although the incentive is never as great as for a noncooperative assembler. A cooperative assembler that does not or cannot restrict output to optimal levels may also have an incentive to integrate forward, particularly when there is a large number of firms in the market or the level of integration is already high. An unexpected result of the analysis is that the net welfare gain from integration by a noncooperative assembler often exceeds the gain from integration by a cooperative assembler. Indeed, integration by a cooperative that does not restrict producer output can actually reduce total economic welfare unless there is a small number of firms in the market and the degree of integration is low.[3]

Because the analysis presented in this paper is based on a two-stage vertical market structure consisting only of producers, processors, and a cooperative, we are unable to compare forward integration by a cooperative to integration by noncooperative firms or to take the degree of existing vertical integration in the industry into account. However, this simpler framework allows us to consider the effects of competitive and collusive behavior, in addition to Cournot behavior, on the part of processors, which is the primary objective of the paper. This paper also focuses exclusively on an oligopsonistic market structure, which is probably the most realistic structure for most agricultural industries.

3. CONCEPTUAL FRAMEWORK

In this model, r identical producers (designated level A) sell a single raw product to n identical processors (level B), which manufacture a processed product they sell to consumers. Following Greenhut and Ohta (1979) and Wu (1992), it is assumed that processors face upward-sloping linear supply functions and a downward-sloping linear demand function. In addition, it is assumed that processors are subject to a fixed-proportions production technology, i.e., they employ one unit of the raw product in fixed proportion with other intermediate inputs in producing a unit of the processed product, and that the cost of processing the raw product is constant.

In addition to the producers and processors, there is a single cooperative that assembles and markets the raw product of m members who are contractually bound through marketing agreements to deliver their product to it. Initially, this cooperative does not process the raw product of its members. We analyze the incentives the cooperative may have to integrate forward by acquiring one of the processors by comparing the *ex ante* profits of the cooperative, its members, and the processor with the *ex post* profits of the integrated cooperative and members. We consider the cooperative to have an incentive to integrate forward if the *ex post* profits exceed the *ex ante* profits, i.e., the integrated cooperative and members are better off after paying the owners of the processing plant its *ex ante* profits than they were before integration. In order to isolate the effects of integration on the cooperative and its members, it is assumed that the cooperative does not have a cost advantage in assembling the raw product or any bargaining power in marketing it to processors.

The *ex post* analysis of the cooperative is conducted under two alternative behavioral assumptions. Under the first assumption, the cooperative (which we will label an *active* cooperative) maximizes the total profits of its members, including patronage refunds, by setting the quantity of raw product it handles. Under the second, the cooperative is *passive* in that it does not or cannot set the quantity of raw product it handles. Instead, it accepts whatever quantity of output its members choose to market.[4] This assumption conforms to the classic Helmberger and Hoos model of a marketing cooperative, in which the objective of the cooperative is to maximize the raw product price for the quantity set by producers. In the Helmberger-Hoos model, equilibrium occurs where the raw product price equals the cooperative's average net return, and the cooperative breaks even because its net return is exhausted by payments to producers. It frequently has been argued that cooperatives will be unsuccessful in restricting producer output to lower levels because the receipt of patronage refunds provides producers an incentive to expand output.[5]

The *ex ante* market structure is illustrated in Figure 1. The $r-m$ producers who are not members of the cooperative provide their raw product to a market that supplies the n processors. The m producers who are members of the cooperative deliver their raw product to the cooperative in accordance with their marketing agreements, and the cooperative in turn provides the raw product to the same raw product market as the nonmember producers. The processors are alternately assumed to exhibit Cournot, competitive, or collusive behavior in the raw product and processed product markets given the respective supply and demand functions.

In the *ex post* market structure illustrated in Figure 2, the cooperative has integrated forward by acquiring one of the processing firms, leaving $n-1$ noncooperative processors. These processors continue to participate in the raw product market, which is now supplied only by the $r-m$ nonmember producers. The m member

174   J.S. ROYER

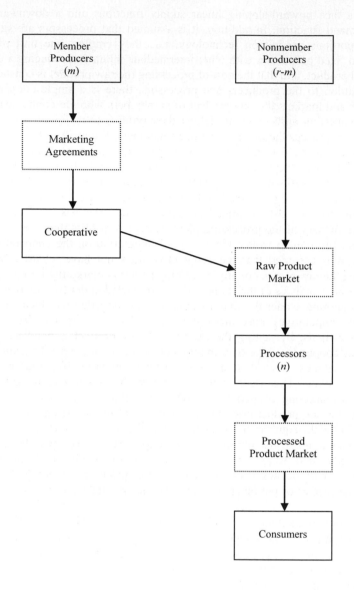

Figure 1. Ex ante industry structure

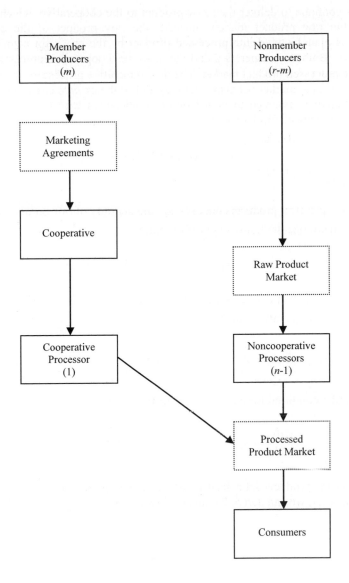

Figure 2. *Ex post industry structure*

producers continue to deliver their raw product to the cooperative, which no longer supplies the raw product market. Instead, the raw product of the cooperative members is manufactured into processed product by the processor acquired by the cooperative. Both the cooperative and the $n-1$ noncooperative processors participate in the processed product market. The noncooperative processors are assumed to maintain the same market behavior that they did in the *ex ante* case. For simplicity, the cooperative is assumed to hold Cournot conjectures with respect to the other firms in the processed product market.

4. EX ANTE MODELS

4.1 Producers

Each of the r identical producers chooses x_i, the quantity of raw product to produce, in order to maximize the following profit function:

$$\pi_i^A = p_A x_i - F_i \qquad i = 1, 2, \ldots, r \tag{1}$$

where p_A represents the price set by the raw product market and F_i represents the cost of producing the raw product:

$$F_i = e x_i + \frac{1}{2} f x_i^2 + g \qquad e \geq 0, f \geq 0, g \geq 0 \qquad i = 1, 2, \ldots, r. \tag{2}$$

The first-order condition for maximization of the profit function:

$$\frac{dF_i}{dx_i} = p_A + e + f x_i = 0 \qquad i = 1, 2, \ldots, r \tag{3}$$

requires that the producer set marginal cost to the raw product price. Aggregating (3) over r producers, we can derive the inverse raw product supply function faced by the n processors:

$$p_A = e + \frac{f}{r} \sum_{i=1}^{r} x_i, \tag{4}$$

which is linear due to the quadratic form of the cost function in (2).

4.2 Processors

Each of the n identical processors chooses q_i, the quantity of processed product to manufacture, in order to maximize its profit function, which can be represented as

$$\pi_i^B = (p_B - p_A - c)q_i \qquad i = 1, 2, ..., n \qquad (5)$$

where p_B is the processed product price and c is the constant per-unit cost of processing the raw product. The processed product demand function can be represented by the linear form:

$$p_B = a - b\sum_{i=1}^{n} q_i \qquad a > 0, b > 0. \qquad (6)$$

By substituting (4) and (6) into (5) and recognizing that $\sum_{i=1}^{n} q_i = \sum_{i=1}^{r} x_i$, the following first-order condition can be derived for the ith processor:

$$\frac{d\pi_i^B}{dq_i} = a - e - \left(b + \frac{f}{r}\right)\sum_{j=1}^{n} q_j - (1+\lambda)\left(b + \frac{f}{r}\right)q_i - c = 0 \qquad i = 1, 2, ..., n \quad (7)$$

where the parameter λ represents the processor's conjecture regarding how the other $n-1$ processors will respond to a change in its output.[6]

If we set $\lambda = 0$, it is assumed that the processor holds a Cournot conjecture and believes that the output of the other firms is invariant with respect to its own. If $\lambda = -1$, the processor is assumed to hold a Bertrand conjecture and to believe that the other firms will decrease their output to offset any increase in its output. The Bertrand conjecture can be used to represent competitive behavior on the part of the n processors because when $\lambda = -1$, the first-order condition represented by (7) reduces to that of a competitive firm. If $\lambda = n-1$, the processor holds a symmetric conjecture and believes that the other firms will match any increase in its output. The symmetric conjecture can be used to represent collusive behavior on the part of the n processors because when $\lambda = n-1$, (7) is equivalent to the first-order condition for maximizing the joint profits of the processors.[7]

By aggregating (7) over the n processors, and without specifying a value for λ, the aggregate reaction function for the n processors can be derived:

$$a - e - \left(1 + \frac{1+\lambda}{n}\right)\left(b + \frac{f}{r}\right)\sum_{i=1}^{n} q_i - c = 0. \qquad (8)$$

Solving (8) for $\sum_{i=1}^{n} q_i$, we can derive the equilibrium industry output:

$$\sum_{i=1}^{n} q_i = \left(1 + \frac{1+\lambda}{n}\right)^{-1}\left(b + \frac{f}{r}\right)^{-1}(a - e - c). \qquad (9)$$

Substituting this value into (4) and (6), we can determine the equilibrium raw product and processed product prices. From those values, additional information on revenues, costs, profits, and consumer surplus can be calculated.

5. *EX POST* MODELS

5.1 Noncooperative Processors

After the cooperative integrates forward by acquiring one of the processors, each of the $n-1$ remaining processors seeks to maximize its profit function:

$$\pi_i^B = \left(p_B - p_A - c\right)q_i \qquad i = 1, 2, \ldots, n-1, \tag{10}$$

which is a simply a restatement of the *ex ante* profit function in (5). However, the raw product price p_A must now be redefined to account for the absence of the cooperative members in the raw product market. In a manner similar to that described above, the raw product supply function facing the $n-1$ noncooperative processors can be derived and expressed as

$$p_A = e + \frac{f}{r-m}\sum_{i=m+1}^{r} x_i \,. \tag{11}$$

It is also useful to restate the processed product price p_B to reflect the cooperative's acquisition of one of the processors. Arbitrarily assume that the cooperative acquires the nth processor. Then the processed product demand function can be rewritten as

$$p_B = a - b\left(\sum_{i=1}^{n-1}q_i + q_n\right) \tag{12}$$

where q_n represents the quantity of processed product manufactured by the cooperative.

Given that the processing industry is no longer homogeneous with respect to the processors' objectives, it is convenient to dispense of the conjectural variations notation used in the *ex ante* case. Instead, we will successively derive the reaction functions for the $n-1$ noncooperative processors under Cournot, competitive, and collusive assumptions.

Under the Cournot assumption, the first-order condition for the ith noncooperative processor can be derived by substituting (11) and (12) into the profit function (10) and recognizing that $\displaystyle\sum_{i=1}^{n-1}q_i = \sum_{i=m+1}^{r}x_i$:

$$\frac{d\pi_i^B}{dq_i} = a - e - \left(b + \frac{f}{r-m}\right)\left(\sum_{j=1}^{n-1} q_j + q_i\right) - bq_i - c = 0 \qquad i = 1, 2, \ldots, n-1. \quad (13)$$

After aggregating (13) across the $n-1$ firms, we obtain the aggregate reaction function for the noncooperative processors given Cournot behavior:

$$a - e - \left(\frac{n}{n-1}\right)\left(b + \frac{f}{r-m}\right)\sum_{i=1}^{n-1} q_i - bq_n - c = 0. \quad (14)$$

For the competitive assumption, the ith noncooperative is assumed to produce the quantity of processed product for which p_B, the price the firm receives for the processed product, is equal to its marginal cost, which consists of p_A, the price it pays producers for the raw product, plus the per-unit processing cost c. After consolidating terms, the following condition can be derived:

$$a - e - \left(b + \frac{f}{r-m}\right)\sum_{i=1}^{n-1} q_i - bq_n - c = 0, \quad (15)$$

which serves as the aggregate reaction function for the noncooperative processors when competitive behavior is assumed.

Given the collusive assumption, each of the $n-1$ noncooperative processors is assumed to act so as to maximize their joint profits. By taking the derivative of joint profits, $(p_B - p_A - c)\sum_{i=1}^{n-1} q_i$, with respect to the quantity of processed product, the following first-order condition can be derived:

$$a - e - 2\left(b + \frac{f}{r-m}\right)\sum_{i=1}^{n-1} q_i - bq_n - c = 0, \quad (16)$$

which serves as the aggregate reaction function for collusive behavior.

5.2 Active Cooperative

After the active cooperative acquires the nth processing firm, its objective function can be expressed as

$$\pi^* = \pi_n^B + \sum_{i=1}^{m} \pi_i^A = (p_B - c)q_n - \sum_{i=1}^{m} F_i \quad (17)$$

where π_n^B represents the cooperative's profits at the processor level and $\sum_{i=1}^{m} \pi_i^A$ represents the profits of the m members at the producer level. It follows that the first-order condition of the integrated active cooperative is

$$\frac{d\pi^*}{dq_n} = a - e - b\sum_{i=1}^{n-1} q_i - \left(2b + \frac{f}{m}\right)q_n - c = 0, \tag{18}$$

which serves as the cooperative's reaction function.

5.3 Passive Cooperative

In this model, cooperative members recognize the existence of patronage refunds and take them into account in determining output. Accordingly, the profit function of the ith cooperative member can be written

$$\pi_i^A = \left(p_A^* + s\right)x_i - F_i \qquad i = 1, 2, \ldots, m \tag{19}$$

where p_A^* and s are respectively the cash price and the per-unit patronage refund the cooperative pays its members for the raw product. The first-order condition is

$$\frac{dF_i}{dx_i} = p_A + s - e - fx_i = 0 \qquad i = 1, 2, \ldots, m, \tag{20}$$

which requires that the producer set marginal cost equal to the net raw product price, $p_A^* + s$.

The per-unit patronage refund is determined by dividing the cooperative's net earnings by the quantity of raw product members deliver to it:

$$s = \frac{(p_B - c)q_n - \sum_{i=1}^{m} p_A^* x_i}{\sum_{i=1}^{m} x_i}. \tag{21}$$

Recognizing that $q_n = \sum_{i=1}^{m} x_i$, (21) can be reduced to

$$s = p_B - p_A^* - c. \tag{22}$$

Substituting this result into (20) for s, we obtain

$$p_B = e + \frac{f}{m} q_n + c,$$ (23)

which is the cooperative's inverse processed product supply function. Setting this equal to the inverse processed product demand function in (12), we obtain the following equilibrium condition:

$$a - e - b \sum_{i=1}^{n-1} q_i - \left(b + \frac{f}{m}\right) q_n - c = 0,$$ (24)

which takes the place of a reaction function for the passive cooperative.

By combining one of the aggregate reaction functions for the noncooperative processors, (14), (15), or (16), depending upon the assumption made about the firms' competitive behavior, with either (18), the reaction function for the active cooperative, or (24), the equilibrium condition for the passive cooperative, a system of two linear equations in two variables can be constructed. When solved simultaneously, these equations produce values for the two variables, $\sum_{i=1}^{n-1} q_i$, which is the aggregate output of the $n-1$ noncooperative processors, and q_n, which is the output of the integrated cooperative processor. Substituting these values into the appropriate relationships, information on prices and other economic variables can be determined for the *ex post* case.

6. SIMULATION ANALYSES

The systems of equations derived in the previous section and their solutions are complex, and they resist comparative statics analyses based on differential calculus (Wu 1992, 89). Consequently, we must resort to using simulation techniques to analyze the incentives cooperatives have for integrating forward and to evaluate the effects of cooperative forward integration on economic welfare.

Tables 1–5 report the results of simulations conducted for both active and passive cooperatives under four different scenarios. In three of the scenarios, the noncooperative processors are characterized by either Cournot, competitive, or collusive behavior in both the raw product and processed product markets. In the fourth scenario, termed the *quasi-collusive* scenario, the noncooperative processors are characterized by collusive behavior in the raw product market and Cournot behavior in the processed product market.[8] The quasi-collusive scenario is of interest because we are primarily concerned with the market power relationship between processors and producers in the raw product market and this scenario allows us to isolate the effect of collusive behavior in that market. Nonetheless, the scenario in which processors exhibit collusive behavior in both the raw product and processed product markets also is analyzed to determine if forward integration by the cooperative is of further benefit when there is an additional degree of collusion.

The integration incentive shown in the tables is calculated by subtracting the sum of the *ex ante* profits of the cooperative's members (equation (1) summed over *m*) and the *ex ante* profits of one of the *n* processors (equation (5)) from the *ex post* profits of the integrated cooperative and its members (equation (17)).[9] The net welfare gain is the difference between the *ex post* and *ex ante* values of total economic welfare, which is calculated by applying the conventional definitions of profits and consumer surplus to the mathematical relationships described earlier in this paper. The parameter values used in the simulations are shown at the foot of each of the tables. These are the same values used in the Royer and Bhuyan (1994b) analysis of the integration incentives of cooperatives in a three-stage vertical market structure and were chosen to enable direct comparisons with those results.

Table 1 shows industry output and the cooperative market share for each of the four scenarios in the *ex ante* case. Under the competitive scenario, industry output is 291.02 units, a benchmark by which the other simulation results can be compared. Cooperative members provide a proportionate share of the raw product, as in the other three scenarios. Under the Cournot scenario, industry output is substantially less than that for the competitive scenario when the market size, as defined by the number of processors, is small. As expected, output approaches that of the competitive scenario as the number of processors is increased.

Industry output is further restricted in the quasi-collusive and collusive scenarios. In both scenarios, processors seek to maximize their joint profits by acting as a monopsony in the raw product market; in the collusive scenario, they also act as a monopoly in the processed product market. As a result, industry output in the quasi-collusive scenario is less than that in both the competitive and Cournot scenarios. Although industry output in the quasi-collusive scenario increases as market size is increased, output in the collusive scenario is fixed at half the output of the competitive solution regardless of market size.

Table 2 shows industry output and the cooperative market share for the *ex post* case in which an active cooperative has integrated forward by acquiring a processor. Under the competitive scenario, industry output is less than in the *ex ante* case. This reduction in output occurs because the cooperative restricts its output by setting its perceived marginal revenue in the processed product market, less the processing cost, to its members' marginal cost of producing the raw product. As a result, the cooperative's members produce only a very small share of total industry output and both the cooperative's incentive to integrate forward and the corresponding net welfare gain are negative regardless of market size, as shown in Table 3.

Given the Cournot scenario, forward integration by the active cooperative marginally increases industry output and its market share when market size is small.[10] This can be attributed to the fact that the cooperative acts like a competitive firm with respect to the price it pays its members for the raw product. Consequently, the cooperative's integration incentive and the corresponding net welfare gain are both positive. However, both diminish as market size is increased and the Cournot solution approaches the competitive benchmark.

Table 1. *Industry output and cooperative market share given various market sizes and behavioral assumptions,* ex ante *case*

Market size (*n*)	Behavioral assumption for noncooperative processors			
	Competitive	Cournot	Quasi-collusive	Collusive
2	291.02	194.01	192.51	145.51
	0.50	*0.50*	*0.50*	*0.50*
3	291.02	218.26	215.73	145.51
	0.33	*0.33*	*0.33*	*0.33*
4	291.02	232.81	229.58	145.51
	0.25	*0.25*	*0.25*	*0.25*
5	291.02	242.51	238.78	145.51
	0.20	*0.20*	*0.20*	*0.20*
6	291.02	249.44	245.33	145.51
	0.17	*0.17*	*0.17*	*0.17*
7	291.02	254.64	250.24	145.51
	0.14	*0.14*	*0.14*	*0.14*
8	291.02	258.68	254.05	145.51
	0.13	*0.13*	*0.13*	*0.13*
9	291.02	261,91	257.09	145.51
	0.11	*0.11*	*0.11*	*0.11*
10	291.02	264.56	259.58	145.51
	0.10	*0.10*	*0.10*	*0.10*
15	291.02	272.83	267.34	145.51
	0.07	*0.07*	*0.07*	*0.07*
20	291.02	277.16	271.40	145.51
	0.05	*0.05*	*0.05*	*0 05*
25	291.02	279.82	273.90	145.51
	0.04	*0.04*	*0.04*	*0.04*

Note: Industry output in roman; cooperative market share in italic.
Parameters: $a = 150$, $b = 0.5$, $c = 1$, $e = 0$, $f = 1.2$, $m = 100/n$, $r = 100$.

J.S. ROYER

Table 2. *Industry output and cooperative market share given various market sizes and behavioral assumptions, active cooperative,* ex post *case*

Market size (*n*)	Behavioral assumption for noncooperative processors			
	Competitive	Cournot	Quasi-collusive	Collusive
2	284.92	194.04	194.04	194.04
	0.04	*0.51*	*0.51*	*0.51*
3	287.97	218.28	217.05	194.01
	0.03	*0.34*	*0.35*	*0.50*
4	289.01	232.82	230.72	193.52
	0.03	*0.26*	*0.27*	*0.49*
5	289.54	242.52	239.78	192.93
	0.03	*0.20*	*0.22*	*0.49*
6	289.86	249.45	246.23	192.31
	0.02	*0.17*	*0.18*	*0.48*
7	290.07	254.64	251.05	191.69
	0.02	*0.15*	*0.16*	*0.47*
8	290.22	258.68	254.79	191.07
	0.02	*0.13*	*0.14*	*0.47*
9	290.33	261.92	257.78	190.46
	0.02	*0.11*	*0.13*	*0.46*
10	290.42	264.56	260.22	189.87
	0.02	*0.10*	*0.12*	*0.46*
15	290.66	272.83	267.82	187.04
	0.02	*0.07*	*0.08*	*0.44*
20	290.78	277.16	271.79	184.59
	0.02	*0.05*	*0.07*	*0.42*
25	290.84	279.82	274.22	182.38
	0.02	*0.04*	*0.05*	*0.40*

Note: Industry output in roman; cooperative market share in italic.
Parameters: $a = 150$, $b = 0.5$, $c = 1$, $e = 0$, $f = 1.2$, $m = 100/n$, $r = 100$.

Table 3. *Integration incentive and net welfare gain for active cooperative given various market sizes and behavioral assumptions*

Market size (n)	Behavioral assumption for noncooperative processors			
	Competitive	Cournot	Quasi-collusive	Collusive
2	(174.35) *(404.35)*	106.98 *1.69*	71.96 *83.23*	(445.85) *4,354.76*
3	(124.03) *(204.45)*	59.61 *0.51*	89.21 *55.60*	1,218.60 *4,377.11*
4	(91.81) *(133.11)*	37.49 *0.21*	90.33 *40.06*	2,019.89 *4,336.69*
5	(71.39) *(96.70)*	25.54 *0.11*	86.46 *30.49*	2,470.78 *4,281.84*
6	(57.53) *(74.72)*	18.40 *0.06*	81.18 *24.15*	2,746.68 *4,222.48*
7	(47.60) *(60.09)*	13.81 *0.03*	75.76 *19.70*	2,923.36 *4,161.87*
8	(40.17) *(49.69)*	10.70 *0.02*	70.62 *16.43*	3,038.80 *4,101.38*
9	(34.43) *(41.95)*	8.50 *0.01*	65.92 *13.95*	3,114.12 *4,041.65*
10	(47.60) *(60.09)*	6.89 *0.00*	61.67 *12.00*	3,161.95 *3,983.00*
15	(16.71) *(19.52)*	2.97 *0.00*	45.90 *6.42*	3,194.13 *3,709.30*
20	(10.64) *(12.29)*	1.59 *0.00*	36.09 *3.81*	3,092.37 *3,468.06*
25	(7.31) *(8.41)*	0.96 *0.00*	29.49 *2.32*	2,955.59 *3,255.28*

Note: Integration incentive in roman; net welfare gain in italic.
Parameters: $a = 150$, $b = 0.5$, $c = 1$, $e = 0$, $f = 1.2$, $m = 100/n$, $r = 100$.

Under the quasi-collusive and collusive scenarios, forward integration by the active cooperative increases both industry output and the cooperative's market share due to its competitiveness relative to the other firms. Although the increases in industry output and the cooperative market share are minimal in the quasi-collusive scenario, the integration incentives and net integration gains are positive for all market sizes. The values of both the integration incentive and the net welfare gain decrease as market size is increased, as does the difference between the *ex post* and *ex ante* values for industry output and the cooperative market share.

The increases in industry output and cooperative market share due to forward integration by the cooperative are more pronounced in the collusive scenario under which the other processors act as a cartel in both the raw product and processed product markets. Although the cooperative market share declines as market size is increased, the cooperative's share is substantially greater than under the other scenarios and in the *ex ante* case. The cooperative's integration incentive and the net welfare gain from integration are typically positive and substantially higher than under the other scenarios, even for relatively large markets.

Generally, although cooperative integration increases industry output, corresponding increases in the cooperative's market share are also associated with a decrease in the output of the other processors. In addition, competition by the cooperative decreases the processed product price, increases the raw product price received by members, and decreases the raw product price received by nonmembers. As a result, consumer surplus generally increases and there is a redistribution of profits from noncooperative processors and producers to the cooperative and its members.

There is also an increase in the average cost of producing the raw product due to the shift of production to member producers and the increasing marginal cost function facing individual producers ($e + fx_i$). Whether total economic welfare is increased will depend on the increase in consumer surplus relative to the increase in raw product cost. Under the collusive scenario, the increase in consumer surplus outweighs the additional raw product cost.[11] However, the situation is considerably different in the case of the passive cooperative.

Industry output and the cooperative market share are shown in Table 4 for the *ex post* case in which a passive cooperative has integrated forward. Forward integration by the passive cooperative has no impact whatsoever under the competitive scenario. The cooperative and the other processors all act like competitive firms in terms of both the price they pay for the raw product and the price they receive for the processed product. Consequently, the cooperative maintains a proportionate market share, and the integration incentive and net welfare gain are both zero regardless of market size (Table 5).

Because of the competitive behavior of the passive cooperative, integration increases industry output and the cooperative market share in all three of the other scenarios. Moreover, both industry output and cooperative market share are greater after integration by a passive cooperative than in the *ex post* case for the active cooperative. Under the Cournot scenario, these increases are minimal for large

Table 4. *Industry output and cooperative market share given various market sizes and behavioral assumptions, passive cooperative,* ex post *case*

Market size (n)	Behavioral assumption for noncooperative processors			
	Competitive	Cournot	Quasi-collusive	Collusive
2	292.02 *0.50*	284.90 *0.96*	284.90 *0.96*	284.90 *0.96*
3	291.02 *0.33*	280.15 *0.88*	280.09 *0.89*	279.17 *0.94*
4	291.02 *0.25*	276.83 *0.80*	276.61 *0.81*	273.88 *0.92*
5	291.02 *0.20*	274.74 *0.71*	274.27 *0.72*	269.00 *0.90*
6	291.02 *0.17*	273.59 *0.62*	272.80 *0.64*	264.48 *0.88*
7	291.02 *0.14*	273.10 *0.54*	271.96 *0.57*	260.28 *0.86*
8	291.02 *0.12*	273.06 *0.48*	271.55 *0.51*	256.36 *0.85*
9	291.02 *0.11*	273.30 *0.42*	271.43 *0.45*	252.70 *0.83*
10	291.02 *0.10*	273.72 *0.37*	271.51 *0.41*	249.28 *0.81*
15	291.02 *0.07*	276.53 *0.22*	272.99 *0.25*	234.98 *0.74*
20	291.02 *0.05*	279.03 *0.14*	274.68 *0.18*	224.15 *0.69*
25	291.02 *0.04*	280.91 *0.10*	276.05 *0.13*	215.66 *0.64*

Note: Industry output in roman; cooperative market share in italic.
Parameters: $a = 150$, $b = 0.5$, $c = 1$, $e = 0$, $f = 1.2$, $m = 100/n$, $r = 100$.

Table 5. *Integration incentive and net welfare gain for passive cooperative given various market sizes and behavioral assumptions*

Market size (n)	Behavioral assumption for noncooperative processors			
	Competitive	Cournot	Quasi-collusive	Collusive
2	0.00	(4,036.86)	(4,071.88)	(4,589.70)
	0.00	*(5,596.45)*	*(5,577.24)*	*(3,253.72)*
3	0.00	(1,698.93)	(1,750.86)	(2,424.01)
	0.00	*(4,462.57)*	*(4,525.26)*	*(2,540.30)*
4	0.00	(648.60)	(693.14)	(1,227.20)
	0.00	*(3,291.74)*	*(3,425.15)*	*(1,932.19)*
5	0.00	(47.90)	(172.67)	(441.69)
	0.00	*(2,285.96)*	*(2,561.27)*	*(1,408.64)*
6	0.00	87.37	85.78	122.89
	0.00	*(1,734.97)*	*(1,927.82)*	*(955.66)*
7	0.00	189.35	209.14	551.01
	0.00	*(1,276.92)*	*(1,471.37)*	*(562.25)*
8	0.00	224.38	261.56	886.91
	0.00	*(954.78)*	*(1,141.85)*	*(219.53)*
9	0.00	226.67	276.81	1,156.49
	0.00	*(726.13)*	*(901.48)*	*79.86*
10	0.00	213.88	272.99	1,376.25
	0.00	*(561.60)*	*(723.63)*	*342.01*
15	0.00	120.91	189.63	2,026.60
	0.00	*(192.82)*	*(297.05)*	*1,247.25*
20	0.00	66.14	124.94	2,292.12
	0.00	*(85.86)*	*(156.05)*	*1,730.50*
25	0.00	38.78	86.74	2,386.40
	0.00	*(45.08)*	*(95.55)*	*1,987.15*

Note: Integration incentive in roman; net welfare gain in italic.
Parameters: $a = 150$, $b = 0.5$, $c = 1$, $e = 0$, $f = 1.2$, $m = 100/n$, $r = 100$.

markets because the *ex ante* output approaches the competitive benchmark as the number of processors is increased. However, the cooperative maintains a disproportionately high market share in the *ex post* case, even in large markets. As a result, the cost of the raw product increases and both the integration incentive and net welfare gain are negative for small markets although consumer surplus increases because of greater industry output. The integration incentive is positive for large markets, but the net welfare gain remains negative.

Integration by the passive cooperative produces similar effects under the quasi-collusive and collusive scenarios. As the competitiveness of the cooperative relative to the other firms is increased (i.e., as we move from left to right in Table 4), the cooperative's market share becomes progressively larger. Consequently, the concentration of raw product production among cooperative members is increased and the raw product cost increases. As a result, the integration incentives and net welfare gains are substantially negative for small markets. However, the integration incentives are positive for large markets under the quasi-collusive scenario, and both the integration incentives and net welfare gains are positive for large markets under the collusive scenario. Indeed, their values are relatively large for larger market sizes.[12]

7. POLICY IMPLICATIONS

In considering the public policy implications of cooperative forward integration, it is useful to summarize the information on integration incentives and net welfare gains in Tables 3 and 5. In Figure 3, the entries in the two tables are grouped according to the values of the integration incentive (INT) and net welfare gain (NWG). Each group is associated with specific implications for market performance and potential government intervention.

From a public policy perspective, forward integration by a cooperative would be desirable if the net welfare gain from integration is positive. In almost all the cases in Figure 3 for which the net welfare gain is positive, the integration incentive also is positive (INT > 0, NWG > 0). In other words, in most cases where forward integration by a cooperative would be socially desirable, the cooperative has an incentive to integrate. Thus it would be unnecessary for the government to offer a subsidy to the cooperative to encourage it to integrate. Instead, it probably would be more effective to educate the cooperative's management and membership about the economic benefits of integration. In cases for which the net welfare is positive but the integration incentive is negative (INT < 0, NWG > 0), government subsidization of integration would seem to be justified in order to maximize total economic welfare. However, there is only one such case in Figure 3, that corresponding to an active cooperative, the collusive scenario, and $n = 2$. For larger markets ($n \geq 3$), the cooperative would have an incentive to integrate without government subsidization.

Integration by a cooperative would be of no social benefit in those cases for which the net welfare gain is zero and would be socially undesirable in the cases for which it is negative. As Figure 3 indicates, there are situations for both the active

Market size (n)	Behavioral assumption for noncooperative processors			
	Competitive	Cournot	Quasi-collusive	Collusive
Active cooperative				
$n = 2$	INT < 0 NWG < 0 No incentive exists and integration is not desirable.	INT > 0 NWG > 0 Incentive exists and integration is desirable.		INT < 0 NWG > 0 No incentive exists but integration is desirable. Subsidy is justified.
$n \geq 3$				
Passive cooperative				
$n \leq 5$	INT = 0 NWG = 0 No incentive exists and integration is of no social benefit.	INT < 0 NWG < 0 No incentive exists and integration is not desirable.		
$6 \leq n \leq 8$		INT > 0 NWG < 0 Incentive exists but integration is not desirable.		
$n \geq 9$				INT > 0 NWG > 0 Incentive exists and integration is desirable.

Figure 3. *Summary of integration incentives (INT) and net welfare gains (NWG) for active and passive cooperatives*

and passive cooperatives in which total economic welfare either would not increase or would decrease due to integration. However, in many of these cases, integration would not be expected to occur because the incentive to integrate is not positive (INT $\leq$ 0, NWG $\leq$ 0). The cases for which the net welfare gain is negative and the integration incentive is positive (INT > 0, NWG < 0) are more problematic. Those cases are limited to the passive cooperative under the Cournot, quasi-collusive, and collusive scenarios when market size is relatively large ($n \geq 6$). Moreover, they may not be particularly relevant given that the markets in which agricultural cooperatives operate typically do not include that many processors. However, additional analysis would be necessary to secure this result under different parameter values.

The potential for cooperative forward integration in smaller markets appears to be limited to those markets in which firms have some degree of market power (i.e., the Cournot, quasi-collusive, and collusive scenarios) and the cooperative is able to restrict the output of its members to optimal levels. Thus, to the extent that cooperatives cannot limit the output of their members, there may not be an opportunity for them to integrate forward. This result may provide an additional explanation, based on market power, for the relatively low incidence of forward integration by cooperatives into processing activities.

8. CONCLUSIONS

Cooperatives do not have an incentive to integrate forward in competitive markets, and forward integration by cooperatives in such markets can be expected to decrease total economic welfare if member output is restricted. In markets characterized by some degree of market power (i.e., the Cournot, quasi-collusive, and collusive scenarios), cooperatives are more competitive than their noncooperative rivals, and integration by a cooperative can be expected to increase both total industry output and the cooperative's market share. Cooperative integration can also be expected to decrease the processed product price, increase the raw product price received by members, and decrease the raw product price received by nonmembers. This will result in an increase in consumer surplus and a redistribution of profits from noncooperative processors and producers to the cooperative and its members. It will also result in an increase in the cost of producing the raw product due to the concentration of production among member producers and the increasing marginal cost function facing individual producers.

The incentive of the cooperative to integrate will depend in part on the value of the redistributed profits relative to the increase in the raw product cost. Whether total economic welfare is increased will depend on the increase in consumer surplus as well as the increase in raw product cost. In general, the potential for cooperative forward integration is linked to the ability of cooperatives to restrict the output of their members to optimal levels. This may help explain the low incidence of forward integration by cooperatives into processing activities.

NOTES

[1] Consider the marketing operations of U.S. dairy cooperatives as an example of the extent to which cooperatives have integrated forward into processed product markets. In 2002, milk and milk products accounted for 33.1 percent of total farm products marketed by cooperatives in the United States (Adams *et al.* 2004, 20). The cooperative share of total milk delivered to plants and dealers was 86 percent. Cooperatives sold 62 percent of the milk they marketed as raw milk and used 38 percent in processing or manufacturing dairy products. The cooperative share of the U.S. market was substantial for several products but typically quite low for products sold to consumers. The cooperative market share was 85 percent for dry milk products, 52 percent for dry whey products, 53 percent for bulk condensed milk, 34 percent for condensed buttermilk, and 6 percent for ice cream mix. Although the cooperative share was 40 percent for natural cheese and 71 percent for butter, it was only 7 percent for packaged fluid milk products, 2 percent for yogurt, 9 percent for cottage cheese, 3 percent for ice cream, and 13 percent for sour cream (Ling 2004).

[2] Technological economies of integration are based on physical interdependencies in the production process. The usual example is the heating and handling economies that lead to integration in the production of iron and steel. Transaction costs are associated with the process of exchange instead of production. In some situations, the market may fail as an efficient means of coordinating economic activity. As a result, a firm may be able to reduce its transaction costs by integrating. For example, in the case of a bilateral monopoly, either firm may be able to eliminate the costs of negotiating and enforcing a contract with the other through integration. Market imperfections that may produce incentives for vertical integration include imperfect competition in addition to imperfections caused by externalities and imperfect or asymmetric information (Perry 1989).

[3] Hendrikse and Bijman (2002) have taken an alternative approach to analyzing the incentives for forward integration by a marketing cooperative. In their model, which is based on the theory of incomplete contracts, there is a single producer, a processor, and a retailer. The producer may have an incentive to acquire the processor to avoid a lower return on an idiosyncratic investment due to opportunistic behavior by the processor. Whether integration represents the optimal ownership structure depends on the relative costs of the investments at the producer and processor levels and the quasi-surplus generated by each of the investments. If the producer's investment is large relative to that of the processor, acquisition of the processor by the producer may be optimal.

[4] Given the assumptions of a fixed number of firms and of static cost and demand functions, the class of vertical integration models, such as Greenhut and Ohta (1979) and Wu (1992), from which this model is ultimately derived are essentially short run in nature. For that reason, the distinction between active and passive cooperatives is preferred to that of open and closed membership policies. Use of the former allows us to abstract from the issue of changing membership, which is more of a long-run notion.

[5] See, for example, Cotterill (1987, 190–92), Schmiesing (1989, 159–62), Staatz (1989, 4–5), or Buccola (1994, 437–38).

[6] The author acknowledges various shortcomings of conjectural variations models. Chief among the criticisms of these models is the problem of "inconsistent conjectures," which refers to the inconsistency between the conjectures and rational strategies of firms, except in equilibrium. For example, if the Cournot model is interpreted as multiperiod in nature, a firm would observe the responses of competing firms to a change in its output and would be irrational to maintain the false conjecture that the output of other firms is invariant with respect to its actions. Consequently, a firm's reaction function would be more accurately called its "equilibrium locus" (Dixit 1986, 110), and conjectural variations models do not represent dynamic theories of oligopoly. However, they do provide a convenient means for parameterizing oligopoly behavior that is useful in comparative statics analyses (Shapiro 1989, 352–54).

[7] Alternatively, the ith processor's conjectures can be expressed in terms of how the output of each of the $n-1$ individual rivals will respond to a change in its output. If v is used to represent the conjecture regarding the jth identical firm, where $j \neq i$, $v = 0$ represents the Cournot conjecture, $v = -1/(n-1)$ represents the Bertrand conjecture, and $v = 1$ represents the symmetric conjecture.

[8] The behavior of the noncooperative processors can, of course, be modeled separately for the raw product and processed product markets. For example, equation (8), which is the *ex ante* aggregate reaction function for the processors, can be replaced with

$$a-e-\left[\left(1+\frac{1+\lambda_1}{n}\right)b+\left(1+\frac{1+\lambda_2}{n}\right)\frac{f}{r}\right]\sum_{i=1}^{n}q_i-c=0$$

in which there are two parameters, λ_1 and λ_2, for representing the conjectural variations. If $\lambda_1 = 0$ and $\lambda_2 = n-1$, the firms exhibit Cournot behavior in the processed product market while behaving in a collusive manner in the raw product market.

[9] Implicit in this calculation are the assumptions that the owners of the acquired processing plant are willing to sell it for the capitalized value of its profits and that current profits are proportional to the capitalized values.

[10] The reader may observe that both *ex post* industry output and cooperative market share are identical under the Cournot, quasi-collusive, and collusive scenarios when $n=2$. If $n=2$, the value of $n/(n-1)$ in equation (14) for the Cournot scenario is two, which is the same as the corresponding coefficient in equation (16) for the collusive scenario. Similar logic can be used to demonstrate the equivalency of the analogous condition for the quasi-collusive scenario. These results hold for the passive cooperative as well.

[11] In the simulations reported in this paper, r, the number of producers, is set at 100 to reflect a fixed production capacity and m, the number of cooperative members, is set at $100/n$ so that membership is proportional to the number of processors. Recognition that these restrictions could result in a substantial increase in the average cost of the raw product as production is increasingly concentrated among cooperative members motivated additional experiments employing alternative assumptions. In those experiments, the number of producers was allowed to increase with the number of processors by setting r at $10n$ and m at r/n. Qualitatively, the results of those experiments do not differ materially from the results reported in Tables 1–5. The only notable difference is that the integration incentive and net welfare gain for the passive cooperative in the collusive scenario are positive for relatively smaller markets.

[12] These results are generally consistent with those reported in Royer and Bhuyan (1994b) to the extent they are comparable. In particular, these results confirm that active cooperatives always have a positive integration incentive under Cournot assumptions, regardless of market size. They also confirm that under Cournot assumptions, passive cooperatives may have a positive integration incentive and a negative net welfare gain when market size is large. These results cannot confirm the existence of positive net welfare gains for passive cooperatives in small markets, but that discrepancy can be attributed to the existence of at least one integrated noncooperative assembler in the other analysis.

REFERENCES

Abiru, M. 1988. "Vertical Integration, Variable Proportions and Successive Oligopolies." *Journal of Industrial Economics* 36:315–25.

Adams, C., K.C. DeVille, J.E. Penn, and E.E. Eversull. 2004. *Farmer Cooperative Statistics, 2002.* Washington DC: U.S. Department of Agriculture, RBS Serv. Rep. 62, June.

Buccola, S.T. 1994. "Cooperatives." In C.J. Arntzen and E.M. Ritter, eds. *Encyclopedia of Agricultural Science*, vol. 1. San Diego: Academic Press, pp. 431–40.

Caves, R.E., and B.C. Petersen. 1986. "Cooperatives' Shares in Farm Industries: Organizational and Policy Factors." *Agribusiness* 2:1–19.

Cotterill, R.W. 1987. "Agricultural Cooperatives: A Unified Theory of Pricing, Finance, and Investment." In J.S. Royer, ed. *Cooperative Theory: New Approaches.* Washington DC: U.S. Department of Agriculture, ACS Serv. Rep. 18, July, pp. 171–258.

Dixit, A. 1986. "Comparative Statics for Oligopoly." *International Economic Review* 27:107–22.

Greenhut, M.L., and H. Ohta. 1979. "Vertical Integration of Successive Oligopolists." *American Economic Review* 69:137–41.

Helmberger, P., and S. Hoos. 1962. "Cooperative Enterprise and Organization Theory." *Journal of Farm Economics* 44:275–90.

Hendrikse, G., and J. Bijman. 2002. "Ownership Structure in Agrifood Chains: The Marketing Cooperative." *American Journal of Agricultural Economics* 84:104–19.

Jamison, J.A. 1960. "Coordination and Vertical Expansion in Marketing Cooperatives." *Journal of Farm Economics* 42:555–66.

Ling, K.C. 2004. *Marketing Operations of Dairy Cooperatives, 2002.* Washington DC: U.S. Department of Agriculture, RBS Res. Rep. 201, February.

Masson, R.T., and P. Eisenstat. 1978. "Capper-Volstead and Milk Cooperative Market Power: Some Theoretical Issues." In B.W. Marion, ed. *Agricultural Cooperatives and the Public Interest.* North Central Regional Research Publication 256, University of Wisconsin–Madison, September, pp. 51–66.

Perry, M.K. 1989. "Vertical Integration: Determinants and Effects." In R. Schmalensee and R.D. Willig, eds. *Handbook of Industrial Organization*, vol. 1. Amsterdam: North-Holland, pp. 183–255.

Rogers, R.T., and B.W. Marion. 1990. "Food Manufacturing Activities of the Largest Agricultural Cooperatives: Market Power and Strategic Behavior Implications." *Journal of Agricultural Cooperation* 5:59–73.

Royer, J.S., and S. Bhuyan. 1994a. "Market Incentives for Cooperative Forward Integration into Processing Activities." In R.W. Cotterill, ed. *Competitive Strategy Analysis for Agricultural Marketing Cooperatives.* Boulder CO: Westview Press, pp. 35–57.

__. 1994b. "Vertical Integration by Farmer Cooperatives: Incentives, Impacts, and Public Policy." Paper presented at "Interactions between Public Policies and Private Strategies in the Food Industries," NE-165/WRCC-72 research conference, Montréal, Québec, 27–28 June.

__. 1995. "Forward Integration by Farmer Cooperatives: Comparative Incentives and Impacts." *Journal of Cooperatives* 10:33–48.

Schmiesing, B.H. 1989. "Theory of Marketing Cooperatives and Decision Making." In D.W. Cobia, ed. *Cooperatives in Agriculture.* Englewood Cliffs NJ: Prentice-Hall, pp. 156–73.

Shapiro, C. 1989. "Theories of Oligopoly Behavior." In R. Schmalensee and R.D. Willig, eds. *Handbook of Industrial Organization*, vol. 1. Amsterdam: North-Holland, pp. 329–414.

Staatz, J.M. 1989. *Farmer Cooperative Theory: Recent Developments.* Washington DC: U.S. Department of Agriculture, ACS Res. Rep. 84, June.

Wu, C. 1992. *Strategic Aspects of Oligopolistic Vertical Integration.* Amsterdam: North-Holland.

CHAPTER 11

EUROPEAN DAIRY COOPERATIVE STRATEGIES: HORIZONTAL INTEGRATION VERSUS DIVERSITY

LAURENCE HARTE

School of Agriculture, Food Science and Veterinary Medicine, University College Dublin, Ireland

JOHN J. O'CONNELL

School of Agriculture, Food Science and Veterinary Medicine, University College Dublin, Ireland

Abstract. *Horizontal integration has been widely used by cooperative dairy processors in an effort to reduce costs. This is seen as a necessary condition for the payment of higher farm-gate milk prices. However, the observation that farm-gate milk prices are not consistently correlated with degree of horizontal integration raises questions about other factors. The aim here is to investigate the relationship between the farm-gate milk price and three variables, namely, degree of horizontal integration, degree of diversification and size irrespective of volume of milk processed or degree of diversification. A positive relationship with farm-gate milk price was found for all three variables but was relatively weak especially after a certain scale of operation in the case of horizontal integration.*

1. INTRODUCTION

A 2003 strategic study of the Irish dairy industry recommended further rationalization of dairy processing to the extent of having one large player processing 70% of Irish manufacturing milk (Department of Agriculture and Food, 2003). This level of concentration is recommended on countervailing grounds as food distribution and retail becomes more concentrated and on competitive grounds by citing the examples of dairy industries in Denmark, the Netherlands and New Zealand, in which dairy processing is dominated by one or two firms.

These recommendations are not new in the Irish case. Consolidation and rationalization of the dairy industry to build a small number of large firms with the scale, cost efficiency and resources to develop new products and compete in foreign

195

K. Karantininis & J. Nilsson (eds.), Vertical Markets and Cooperative Hierarchies, 195–211.
© 2007 *Springer.*

markets was the organizational strategy urged on Irish cooperatives in the mid- to late 1980s by the Irish Cooperative Organisation Society (ICOS) (Moloney, 1988). In 2000, ICOS conducted a further strategic review of the Irish dairy sector and again urged the industry to implement structural changes favoring, to the extent allowed by competition authorities, the establishment of a single large-scale processing business for the country's main dairy products.

While the Irish dairy industry has restructured considerably over the years and is now well structured by general industry standards, it has not consolidated in the ways or to the extent consistently recommended. Accordingly, a key issue for the industry is whether it is behaving perversely and losing out by not following the strategies recommended, which are also those which were followed in the Danish, Dutch and New Zealand cases, or that the benefits of these strategies are overstated.

The emphasis on horizontal integrations and on achieving economies of scale and countervailing power is no doubt heavily influenced by the dominance of the cooperatives and the cooperative ethos in the dairy industries of the northern European countries concerned. Horizontal integration has been the growth path of the large farmer controlled dairy cooperatives that dominate dairy processing and marketing, particularly in the Netherlands, Denmark, Sweden and Germany. It is becoming more widely recognized in cooperative literature that this strategy may have limitations, that placing heavy emphasis on scale and geographical concentration to countervail the power of buyers and sellers is very much a production as distinct from a market orientation and that it is insufficient to serve the needs of the modern food market (Kyriakopoulos and van Bekkum, 1999, and Nilsson, 1998).

The aim here is to widen the scope of the debate and analysis. While the relationship between scale of operation, in terms of volume of milk processed, and performance is examined, so too is the relationship between other variables and performance. These other variables are the degree of business diversity and scale of business where scale is not confined to milk volume processed.

2. THEORETICAL BACKGROUND AND HYPOTHESES

This discussion of strategy relies on a few basic concepts from economics of the firm and economics of industrial organization, including economies of scale associated with horizontal integration and economies of scope in product and market diversification.

2.1. Economies of scale

Economies of scale are present when large-scale production is more efficient than small scale. It is associated with some elements of fixed or common costs, such as capital costs and management costs that may be spread over ever-greater volumes of production. The result is lower average or per-unit costs for larger scales of operations. Scale effects tend toward a limit in that the rate of cost decline diminishes with increasing size. The relationship between scale and costs is often illustrated in terms of a firm's average cost curve (ACC), which plots scale (output volume) against cost per unit of output. The typical curve shows average costs falling at a declining rate as scale increases to become almost horizontal beyond a certain operation level. The shape of the ACC provides important insight into the extent to which economies of scale prevail in a business or process. The scale that must be reached before the curve becomes horizontal is referred to as the minimum efficient scale (MES) of production. Beyond the MES the benefits of scale have practically all been exhausted, and while firms that expand above this level continue to be efficient, their cost advantages, if any, over smaller firms also producing at or above the MES tend to be small.

The contemporary economic perspective is that for many industries long-run ACCs tend to be L-shaped, whereby above some critical output level, costs are minimized (the MES) with constant returns to scale at output levels above this (Lowes, B. *et al.,* 1994). The critical issue for individual businesses, therefore, is to have a scale that is close to or above the MES, and the main determinant of optimum industry structure is the magnitude of the MES compared with the size of the market served. Where the market is small compared with the MES, the industry structure will tend to be concentrated and most efficiently served by a small number of larger firms. Examples of industries that have this kind of structure include aircraft and motor manufacturing, steel and aluminum industries, oil refining etc. At the other extreme, in industries such as farming, the MES can be very small compared with the size of the market and the market may be efficiently served by a large number of small firms. The food processing industry can be considered somewhere between these two extremes with an industry structure comprising both large and small firms.

According to the L-shaped ACC model, above the MES neither small nor large firms have a cost advantage, i.e., each competes effectively on an equal footing. An important implication of this is not just that smaller firms can compete successfully with larger firms, but that above the MES both scales of operation can be equally efficient. Applying this to the dairy industry, a key issue is the extent to which firms in the industry have operation levels that are at or above MES and, if not, whether they are sufficiently below it to make a difference.

Ideally this could be resolved empirically by determining the MES for dairy firms, but it would be a daunting task in terms of the variables to be considered and the data requirements. However, an indication of MES in the industry may be gleaned from the scales of operations that have emerged in different countries. In the recent analysis conducted on behalf of the Irish industry, comparative data on plant sizes for butter, cheese and milk powder were collected for the Dutch, Danish, New Zealand and Irish dairy processing industries. These are summarized in Table 1. New Zealand, followed by the Netherlands, had the largest average size of butter plants in 2001 at 35,200 metric tons and 21,700 metric tons, respectively. Average plant size in Ireland was estimated at 11,600 metric tons, with the smallest average plant size recorded for Denmark at 5,700 metric tons. The authors of the study, however, caution that the average size of butter plant in Denmark is influenced by a large number of small plants and that the average size of the three largest is 12,941 tons. No distribution of plants by size is given for the other countries, although a range of sizes must be presumed. For example, the average output of the two largest plants in Ireland is three times greater than the output of the average butter plant.

In the case of cheese, again New Zealand had the largest average size followed by the Netherlands, next the Irish, with the Danes again having the smallest average size of plant. The authors again caution that the average size of cheese plants in Denmark is influenced by a large number of small plants in the system and that the average of the 14 largest plants that account for 75% of production is 17,000 metric tons compared with the industry average of 8,900 tons. In the case of milk powder, the New Zealand plants are by far the largest, with an average output of 69,600 tons compared with 18,300 tons in Denmark and 9,900 tons average in Ireland.

Assuming efficiency in each market, an interpretation of this data is that there is a wide range of plant sizes that can be efficient depending on the circumstances, and that the MES for these processes may be relatively small. The data suggest that plant size may be more associated with the scale of national production for the commodity concerned than with any characteristic of plant cost structure. It is interesting that plant size in Denmark is not larger in view of the dominant position of Arla Foods in this market. If there were significant economies of scale to be achieved by further increasing plant size, it would probably have already been captured by internal rationalization of the firm's production. On this basis, the data cast doubt on the perspective that there are considerable additional economies to be gained from horizontal integration at plant level.

Table 1. *Average output per plant for butter, cheese and skim and whole milk powder in Ireland, Denmark, Netherlands and New Zealand (2001)*

'000 metric tons	Butter	Cheese	Skim and whole milk powder
Ireland: Average of all plants	11.6	12.0	9.9
Average of two largest plants	33,0	24.0	19.5
Total production	128.0	120.0	109.0
Denmark: Average of all plants*	5.7	8.9	18.3
Total production	46.6	317.9	129.0
Netherlands: Average of all plants	21.7	24.7	16.0
Total production	130.6	641.0	175.9
New Zealand: Average of all plants	35.2	31.3	· 69.6
Total production	258.0	289.9	766.0

* Excludes private dairy production.
Source: Department of Agriculture and Food, 2003, *Strategic Development Plan for the Irish Dairy Processing Sector,* prepared by Prospectus and Promar International, Department of Agriculture and Food, Dublin, www.agriculture.gov.ie, pp. 27–28 and pp.124–127.

Motives for horizontal integrations go much wider than the capturing of economies of scale in processing. It is generally accepted that dairy firms need to be large to compete successfully against scale competitors in domestic and international markets and to effectively serve and countervail the power of the modern highly concentrated retail sector. In this respect firms exploit the economies of scale of other resources such as research and development, marketing and management. This is another reason why firms would wish to expand horizontally, and in the modern food industry, leveraging these assets is probably much more important and rewarding than achieving the lowest processing costs. These assets probably also require a relatively larger scale of business to be fully exploited.

In terms of horizontal integration in the dairy processing industry, therefore, economies of scale at processing level may well be all but exhausted at relatively small plant size but scale economies associated with other resources such as research and development, marketing and management continue as firms expand. On this basis the following is hypothesized:

H1: Cooperatives that process higher volumes of milk outperform firms that handle smaller volumes of milk.

2.2. Product and international diversification

Resources such as research and development, marketing and management are not nearly as product specific as, say, a cheese manufacturing plant or a milk drier, and scale can also be achieved for such resources by extending the business into other related products and markets. Accordingly, a dairy company can leverage its non-manufacturing resources by diversifying into other food products and extending its reach geographically. In this way the firm is relying more on economies of scope rather than scale. Economies of scope arise when the combined total cost of producing and marketing two or more products or services in one firm is less than producing them at separate firms (Panzar and Willig, 1975 and 1981).

It is well known, however, that such diversification does not come without danger, especially if it takes an organization away from its core area of capability. There is much evidence of past failures and many prescriptions for successful diversification (Rumelt (1982), Palepu (1985), Johnson and Thomas (1987) and Gruca et al., 1997). The main danger is taking diversification too far: getting into businesses that managers do not understand (Campbell, 1992). The main general prescription is to diversify only into activities that are related to current products, markets or processes, the so-called concentric diversification strategy (Lowes et al., 1994). It is postulated here that if firms confine themselves to related product and market diversifications then this extension of the scope of the firm can complement or even substitute for pure horizontal integration.

However, some have questioned whether cooperatives, as distinct from corporations, do pursue coherent diversification strategies. Van Oijen and Hendrikse (2002) found that Dutch cooperatives tended to be less diversified than corresponding Dutch corporations, and that when they diversify, cooperatives diversify relatively more into unrelated activities than corporations do, and further that this unrelated diversification has a negative influence on performance of cooperatives, whereas it is neutral for corporations.

A further dimension of expanding the scope of a firm is international expansion. There has long been evidence that international companies are more profitable than domestic businesses (see examples: Grant 1987, Buhner 1987, and Kim et al.1989). The higher profitability comes from four main sources: (i) exploiting country-specific advantages by siting production or other facilities in cost and fiscal efficient locations; (ii) better market servicing by being closer to the customer; (iii) the benefits of an international scale for existing products and the development and marketing of new products; and (iv) the competitive benefits derived from international business experience. The underlying theory of internationalization is that the business has acquired some firm-specific advantage, a core competence, which it exploits on an international scale and decides that the best way to do this is by foreign direct investment (FDI) rather than arms-length exporting.

Furthermore, choosing not to participate in international markets may no longer be an option in many industries. With ever-freer trade, deregulation of markets, new technologies and modern communication, companies cannot avoid international competition even on their own doorsteps. Domestically focused firms deal with relatively fewer competitors and customers, have a more narrow range of experience and mental models because they confront a more limited range of challenges. This narrow focus hurts performance in the long run and leaves a domestically based enterprise very vulnerable as conditions change (Miller and Chen, 1994 and 1996). Internationalization therefore may be necessary as a defensive strategy as much as addressing performance objectives.

It is argued, therefore, that dairy firms that progress further down the route of internationalization, with or without product diversification, gain advantages that add to or compensate for purely horizontal integration. More generally it is argued that related product diversification and internationalization can be strategic complements or substitutes for pure horizontal integration, and that the performance of dairy firms that focus more on product and international diversification and less on horizontal integration can be at least as high as firms that favor horizontal integration. The following hypothesis is made:

H2: Dairy cooperatives that grow their businesses by product or international diversification can perform better than specialized, geographically confined cooperatives.

Combining H1 and H2, it can be further hypothesized that:

H3: Larger dairy cooperatives, irrespective of the volume of milk processed or degree of diversification, outperform smaller dairy cooperatives.

3. DATA AND METHOD OF ANALYSIS

These strategic issues are examined in the analysis by attempting to evaluate the merits of the general strategies pursued by leading European dairy cooperatives on the farm-gate milk price paid by each firm. Data relating to 12 dairy cooperatives from eight Northern European countries were used in the analysis. The firms included were drawn mainly from the set of cooperative firms for which farm-gate milk prices are compiled and monitored by the Dutch Dairy Board on behalf of LTO-Nederland, with additional firms added in the Irish case by drawing on data from the Irish Farmers' Journal/KPMG Milk Price Audit. Other data relating to the firms concerned were drawn from the Annual Reports and other institutional, official and website sources. Farm-gate milk prices were based on a three-year average for the 2001–2003 period and data relating to other characteristics of the cooperatives relate to the year 2003. Details of the data set are shown in an Appendix.

3.1 Farm-gate milk price as a performance indicator

Assessing the effect on farm-gate price is by no means a comprehensive method of evaluating dairy firms' strategies, and very much a milk producer's perspective of industry performance. A more complete assessment would embrace effects on financial performance in terms of return on investment and returns to other stake-holders such as employees and non-farmer service providers. Nevertheless, farm-gate price does have merits as a performance indicator, especially in the case of cooperatives. Dairy farmers are farther upstream from consumers than are proces-sors and tend to have relatively weak bargaining positions. Milk producers are very much price takers, and to a great extent farm-gate milk price represents the residual after dairy cooperatives have paid for all other resources and compensated all the non-farm stakeholders. Accordingly, the efficiency with which the firm combines the necessary resources influences the price (performance element) that can be paid to its milk suppliers.

Accepting that the farm-gate price is a valid – if partial – measure of dairy coop-erative performance, it is still a rather crude means of comparing the performances of firms, especially across countries and even within countries where major regional differences in milk production conditions and market opportunities prevail.

While it is recognized that many factors determine producer prices, it seems reasonable to suggest as a generalization that countries that have relatively high levels of self-sufficiency in milk will also have lower producer prices. Possible reasons for this include greater transport costs involved in supplying export markets, greater investment in storage capacity in foreign markets for servicing those markets, more costly communications, and domestic production preference.

Self-sufficiency data relating milk production and milk equivalent consumption are not readily available. For this analysis these were estimated by taking milk production data from Eurostat supply balances as published and using conversion factors to convert butter, cheese, drinking milk and whole milk powder consumption into milk equivalents. Total milk equivalent thus estimated was compared with milk production to give self-sufficiency. The exercise is capable of refinement. Producer prices were taken from "Dairy Facts and Figures – 2002 edition" published by the British Dairy Council but relying on Eurostat data. Table 2 shows results.

While at the extreme there is coincidence between low self-sufficiency and high prices in the cases of countries such as Italy, Greece and Germany and between high self-sufficiencies and low prices in Ireland and France, there are notable anomalies such as the lower price levels for net importers UK and Belgium and the good performances of Denmark and the Netherlands in view of their relatively high exports.

Table 2. Milk self-sufficiency and producer prices by country: EU-15, 2001

Country	Self-sufficiency (%) (Production/consumption)	Producer prices (Euro/100kg)
Italy	85	36.6 *
Greece	81	34.6
Finland	Na	34.0
Germany	97	32.8
Denmark	178	32.3
Portugal	101	32.2
Austria	96	31.8
Luxembourg	Na	31.4
Holland	173	31.3
Sweden	Na	31.2
Spain	86	30.3
France	109	30.0
UK	85	29.2
Belgium	88	28.6
Ireland	454	28.6

*Italian price data are not available for 2001. The price shown was estimated as the ratio of the Italian to Irish price in 1999 x the Irish price in 2001.
Source: Eurostat

Perhaps the main difference in price levels between countries is the differences between prices in continental European countries and those achieved in the UK and Ireland. The simple average of the British and Irish prices is 10% lower than the simple average of prices for the other 13 countries, and only the Belgian price is as low as British and Irish levels. It not unexpected that the Irish price is significantly lower than the rest on the basis of Ireland's offshore location and its very high degree of self-sufficiency. Irish milk which to date has been based more on a grass production system also has a significantly lower constituent content (especially protein and fat) and has a more seasonal supply profile than milk produced in other EU countries (see for example LTO Nederland, 2002). The differential between Irish and continental European milk prices has been the subject of study for many years. A study conducted in the early 1980s estimated a price difference of between 10 and 20 percent that the researchers sought to explain in terms of extra transport and storage costs and marketing performance factors (Keane and Pitts, 1981).

It is more difficult however to rationalize the relatively poor price achieved in the UK. The UK price is lower than the authors would intuitively expect and may be related to the effects of institutional arrangements both past and present in relation to milk marketing in the UK and residual effects of the Foot and Mouth outbreak. It has been estimated that UK farm-gate milk prices were between 8% and 13% below average EU prices over the four years 1998 to 2001 (Dairy Development Council, 2003).

3.2. Delineating between alternative dairy firm strategies

Volume of milk handled in Europe was adopted as the indicator of the extent to which dairy firms are horizontally integrated. An alternative proxy, used by other researchers is the share of the milk supply handled by the firms in their domestic markets (van Bekkum and Nilsson, 2000). However, since many European dairies now extend across borders into neighboring countries, and may even regard these as part of their domestic markets, it was felt that the wider European base was more appropriate.

Finding a suitable indicator or indicators of the extent to which firms are diversified by product and geographically is more difficult. Ideally one would like to be able to examine the product ranges of each firm and assess the extent to which these represent a diversification from the core dairy business. This would be an onerous task and well beyond the scope of the current analysis.

Similar issues arise in estimating the extent to which firms are internationalized. While many dairy firms do provide good information on the extent of their international activities, others do not. For example, many report turnover by geographic destination, but few provide an analysis by origin of production. Neither is good information provided by dairy firms on the geographic distribution of employees or of assets, each of which is an indicator of the extent of internationalizations. For these reasons, much more simplistic measures of the extent of diversification were sought.

One of the more reliable items of data readily available for all of the dairy firms is turnover. Since volumes of milk processed in Europe and the corresponding farm-gate prices paid for this milk are also available, a ratio of the extent to which turnover (total sales) exceeds the farm gate value of milk was calculated for each firm. This ratio provides an indicator of the extent to which firms' activities are wider than their core milk activities. This ratio is neutral in relation to the volume of milk handled and therefore excludes the scale effects associated with horizontal integration in dairy processing.

However, this is not a perfect measure of degree of diversification. Firstly it combines the two dimensions of diversification: product and geographic, and secondly it includes the element of 'value-added' by the firm to its core milk supply (the extent to which the firm is vertically integrated in dairy processing and marketing and produces, for example, more highly branded and differentiated dairy products). However, it was felt that since the data concern mainly the leading dairy firms in Europe which have a good deal of similarity in their core dairy businesses, most of the variation in this variable would be associated with product and geographic diversification rather than differences in dairy value-added. For example, in his evaluation of the extent to which dairy cooperatives pursue a strategy of product differentiation, Van Bekkum (2001) grouped the four European dairy cooperatives: Campina Melkunie, Arla Foods, Glanbia and Friesland, close together and in that order at the top end of the scale in terms of the extent to which they pursue product differentiation strategies.

Nevertheless, the presence of the value-added element remains and would reflect itself in variation in this ratio when contrasting for example first handling dairy firms such as First Milk in the UK with more vertically integrated dairy firms such as Campina Melkunie. Accordingly, to avoid misinterpretation, this ratio will be referred to as the diversity ratio so as not to imply that it reflects product and geographic diversifications only. It is therefore a measure of the extent to which dairy firms are diversified away from first handlers of milk whether downstream into further processing and marketing or through diversification into other products, markets or internationally. Figure 1 is an attempt to present the situation in diagrammatical form.

4. ASSESSMENT OF THE RESULTS

The results of this analysis are presented in a somewhat descriptive format. Although a large share of the milk processed in the eight northern European countries is accounted for by the firms included in the analysis, the number of cases at 12 is too small for any meaningful statistical analysis. Accordingly the data are presented mainly in terms of descriptive associations between variables using a simple bivariate scatter diagram and fitting curves, linear or curve-linear, with estimated R^2 to give some idea of degree of association between the two variables.

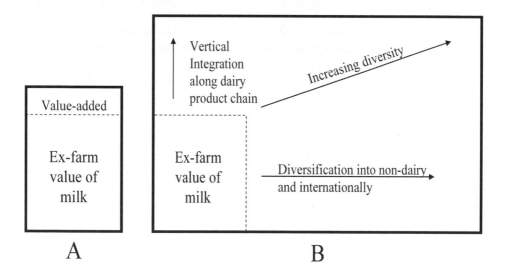

Figure 1. *Conceptual representation of the diversity ratio*

In Figure 1, 'A' represents a first handler dairy firm with low diversity ratio and 'B' represents a diversified dairy firm with high diversity ratio. The size of firm turnover is represented by the area of the diagram in each case. Ex-farm value of milk handled is represented by the area below and to the left of the dashed lined.

The diversity ratio is calculated as 1- (the ex-farm value of milk where such value is expressed as a fraction of firm turnover)

4.1 Association between volume of milk handled and farm-gate milk price

Figure 2 presents a scatter-diagram of the association between volume of milk handled by the individual dairies and the ex-farm price they paid to their milk suppliers. Farm-gate prices range from a low of €26 to a high of €32 per 100 kg, and scale of firms' operations in Europe range from 700 to 7,200 million liters. The data do indicate a general tendency of milk price increasing with scale of operations up to a limit at about €32 per 100 kg. Fitting a linear curve to the data estimates the rate of price improvement at about €0.80 per 100 kg for every extra 2,000 million liters of scale, but the linear relationship explains only 27% of the variation.

Accordingly the data is supportive of the proposition that firms that progress furthest in terms of horizontal integration perform best on milk price. It is therefore supportive, if not strongly so, of hypothesis H1: Firms that process higher volumes of milk outperform firms that process smaller volumes of milk.

At the same time it can be observed from the data points that it is by no means necessary for a firm to be a very large processor to pay high prices. For example, there are very small differences between the prices paid by Sodiaal handling 2.2 billion liters and Arla Foods handling 7.2 billion.

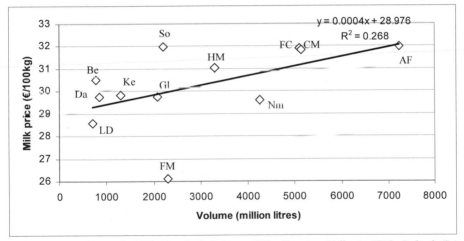

Abbreviations: *Arla Foods (AF), Friesland Coberco (FC), Campina Melkunie (CM), Sodiaal (So), Humana Milchunion (HM), Nordmilch (Nm), Belgomilk (Be), Glanbia (Gl), Kerry (Ke), Dairygold (Da), Lakeland Dairies (LD) and First Milk (FM)*

Figure 2. *Association between volume of milk handled and farm-gate milk price*

A further examination of where individual companies are positioned in Figure 2 reveals that the lower prices prevailing in the UK and Ireland, where dairy firms tend to be smaller scale than their continental European counterparts, account for much of the trend. Already it was observed from official statistics that milk prices in continental Europe are about 10% higher than the average for UK and Ireland. While the reason for this difference is not known, it is plausible, at least in the Irish case, that its prices are lower because of Ireland's high surplus production and its offshore position compared with the main deficit markets in continental Europe. Since the issue under investigation is whether scale influences price, it seems reasonable that some account should be taken of this difference between the continent and the UK and Ireland, on the basis that it is partly at least attributable to exogenous factors such as location and excess of supply over demand in the Irish case and institutional structures perhaps and other special circumstances in the case of the UK.

If an upward adjustment is made to the UK and Irish prices of 7.5% (about half of which, in the Irish case, could be justified on additional cost of transport alone) to allow for these 'special' factors, the relationship between volume of milk processed and price is very significantly weakened. It is acknowledged that the 7.5% adjustment is purely subjective and the issue will not be further pursued here.

4.2 Association between diversity and farm-gate milk price

A ratio of the excess of a firm's total turnover over what it pays for its milk supply is used as an indicator of the extent to which dairy firms are diversified from their core dairy businesses. Figure 3 presents the association between this diversity and farm-gate milk prices for the unadjusted data. There is a positive relationship between the two variables with increases in the ratio associated with increasing milk price, but the relationship is very sensitive to the outlier First Milk in the UK.

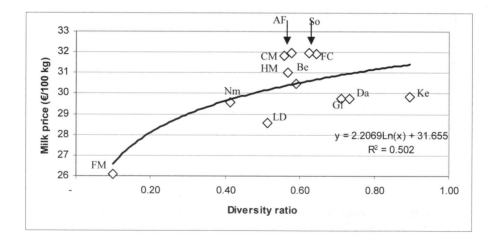

Figure 3. *Association between diversity ratio and farm-gate milk price*

A difficulty with these data is the cluster of observation for six cooperatives of rather similar diversity and paying rather similar milk prices at the centre of the range with few observations of the more specialized or more diverse. Lack of diversity in the strategies of the continental European dairy companies limits the capacity of the analysis to assess the value of diversity. Of the seven continental European cooperatives, only Nordmilch (Nm) differs significantly from the rest.

If the same upward adjustment of 7.5% as was made previously is made here also to the UK and Irish prices, the positive association between milk price and diversity is strengthened considerably, thus lending more weight to the value of diversification strategies. Neither is it so sensitive to the low ratio for outlier First Milk, the relationship remaining strongly positive with its exclusion.

4.3. Association between overall dairy firm size and farm-gate milk price

Do larger firms, irrespective of their degree of specialization or diversity pay higher prices to producers than smaller cooperatives? As shown in Figure 4 the answer is yes, but as in the case of horizontal integration, this is partly because of the lower farm-gate prices in the British and Irish markets coinciding with the prevalence of the smaller scale dairy cooperatives in these regions. When the levels of milk price in the UK and Ireland are adjusted upward as before, the positive relationship is less but still remains, and less of the variation in price is explained by change in firm size.

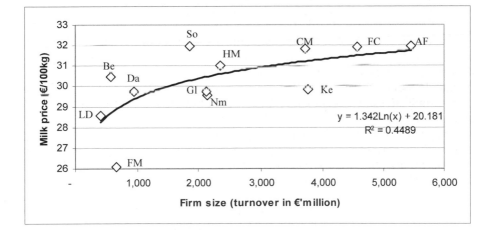

Figure 4. Association between overall firm size and farm-gate milk price

On this basis it is reasonable to accept H3: larger dairy firms, irrespective of their degree of horizontal integration or diversification, outperform smaller dairy businesses in terms of paying better prices to producers.

5. DISCUSSION AND CONCLUSIONS

This analysis set out to compare two growth strategies of European dairy cooperatives: growth by horizontal integration in dairy products, which has been the favored
strategy amongst northern European dairy firms, and a more diversified growth path
which includes product and geographic diversification as well as horizontal
expansion. In general, the analysis questions the degree of emphasis on horizontal
integration and argues that cooperatives that diversify can perform as well if not
better than specialized dairy firms.

Evidence on plant size structure was presented which cast doubts on the need for
very large scale at milk processing level. The literature was used to argue that, while
large scale is still necessary to leverage other resources such as research and
development, marketing and management, this can also be achieved through
exploiting economies of scope by diversification into related products and markets.

Data from 12 dairy cooperative cases were presented to compare outcomes in
terms of ex-farm milk prices of the two main strategic approaches. Three hypotheses
were tested against this evidence:

H1: Cooperatives that process higher volumes of milk outperform firms that handle
smaller volumes of milk.

H2: Dairy cooperatives that grow their businesses by product or international
diversification can perform better than specialized and more geographically
confined cooperatives; and

H3: Larger dairy cooperatives, irrespective of their degree of horizontal integration
or diversification, outperform smaller dairy cooperatives.

For H1 the relationship between horizontal expansion in core dairy business and
prices paid for milk was found to be weak especially when account is taken of
differences in market conditions between continental Europe and the UK and
Ireland. In particular dairy firms that are already handling of the order of two billion
liters of milk annually, seem to have little to gain from further horizontal expansion,
at least as reflected in prices paid to milk producers.

The evidence did provide tentative support for H2 and the proposition that dairy
cooperatives that pursue more diverse growth paths can perform better than
specialized and more geographically confined cooperatives. The evidence is
strongest when differences between continental European and UK and Irish market
conditions are recognized.

The data also provide support for H3: that large dairy cooperatives, irrespective
of their degree of horizontal integration or diversity, outperform smaller dairy
business. The implication is that firm size is important, but that it can be achieved by
increasing the diversity of the business as an alternative to or in conjunction with
horizontal expansion in core dairy activities.

The implications of these conclusions are substantial. Apart from the effect on
milk price, which has been the metric used in this assessment, growth in business
size also offers wider industry benefits. It increases the opportunities for firms to
pursue growth strategies that may be closed off when activities are confined to core

dairy. In this way the cooperatives can become more progressive and effective food industry competitors, providing greater opportunities for other stakeholders such as employees, investors and non-farmer suppliers. This strategy increases the industry development potential of dairy cooperatives. For example, three of the Irish dairy firms included in this analysis, Glanbia, Kerry and Dairygold, together employed almost 27,000 people in 2003 but handled only 4.2 billion liters of milk. By contrast the German cooperative Nordmilch, which also had a milk supply of 4.2 billion liters of milk, operated with only about 3,500 employees.

The data set used in this analysis has severe limitations, not least of which is the small number of observations, the limited strategic range of the cooperative and convergence between milk prices paid by some of the leading dairy processors. The topic would benefit from further work to increase the number of cases studied and to widen the performance criteria to include other aspects of performance including financial and market security.

NOTES

[1] Annual reports and website information for each dairy firm.
[2] Annual reports, personal communications and other sources including data on comparisons of European milk processors compiled by Rabobank, Netherlands.
[3] Estimates computed using national milk supply data from ZMP.
[4] Farm-gate milk prices: taken from the 'International Comparison of Producer Prices for Milk' compiled by the Dutch Dairy Board (Productschap Zuivel) on behalf of the Dutch Farmers Union (LTO Nederland). Prices are expressed in €/100 kg of standardized milk of 4.2% fat, 3.35% protein, total bacterial count of 24,999 per ml, somatic cell count of 249,999 per ml and a yearly delivery of 350,000 kg. VAT and levies are excluded and end of year profit distributions related to milk are included. Prices shown are averages for the three years 2001–2003. The LTO Nederland data provided the prices for all Arla Foods Denmark and Sweden, Friesland Coberco Dairy Foods, Campina Melkunie, Sodiaal, Humans Milchunion, Nordmilch, Belgomilk, Glanbia and First Milk. Prices paid by the other Irish cooperatives were scaled with reference to prices for Glanbia using data from the Irish Farmers' Journal/KPMG Milk Price Audit for prices paid by the Irish dairy firms.

REFERENCES

Bekkum van, O.-F., and J. Nilsson. 2000. "Liberalization of International Dairy Markets and the Structural Reform of European Dairy Cooperatives", paper presented to Agribusiness Forum of the International Food and Agribusiness Management Association, Chicago, June 2000.

Bekkum van, O.-F. 2001. *Cooperative Models and Farm Policy Reform,* Van Gorcum, Assen.

Buhner, R. 1987. "Assessing International Diversification of West German Corporations", *Strategic Management Journal* 8:25–37.

Campbell, A. 1992. "Brief Case: Why Do Companies Over-Diversify", *Long Range Planning* 25, 5:114–116.

Dairy Development Council. 2003. Price and Profitability in the British Dairy Chain, Report by KPMG for Dairy Development Council, UK.

Department of Agriculture and Food. 2003. Strategic Development Plan for the Irish Dairy Processing Sector, Prepared by Prospectus and Promar International, Department of Agriculture and Food, Dublin, www.agriculture.gov.ie, pp. 12–13.

Grant, R.M. 1987. "Multinationality and performance among British manufacturing companies" *Journal of International Business Studies,* Fall, pp 79–89.

Gruca, T.S., D. Nath, and A. Mehra. 1997. "Exploiting Synergy for Competitive Advantage, *Long Range Planning* 30, 4, 605–611.

ICOS. 2000. *A Strategic Review of the Irish Dairy Sector,* Dublin: Irish Co-operative Organisation Society.

Johnson, G., and H. Thomas. 1987. "The Industry Context of Strategy, Structure and Performance: The UK Brewing Industry", *Strategic Management Journal* 8:343–361.

Keane, M., and E. Pitts. 1981. A Comparison of Producer Milk Prices in EEC Countries, Marketing Department, Economics and Rural Welfare Research Centre, An Foras Taluntais, Dublin, pp. 57–62.

Kim, W.C., P. Hwang, and W.P. Burgers. 1989. "Global Diversification Strategy and Corporate Profit Performance", *Strategic Management Journal*

Kyriakopoulos, K., and O.-F. van Bekkum. 1999. "Market Orientation of European Agricultural Cooperatives: Strategic and Structural Issues", paper presented to the IXth Congress of the European Association of Agricultural Economists, "European Agriculture Facing the 21st Century in a Global Context", Warsaw, Poland, 24–28 August 1999.

Lowes, B., C.L. Pass, and S. Sanderson. 1994. *Companies and Markets: Understanding Business Strategy and the Market Environment,* Oxford: Blackwell Business.

LTO Nederland, 2002, "International Comparison of Producer Prices for Milk, 2000 Milk Prices", prepared for LTO-Nederland by the Productschap Zuivel in cooperation with the European Dairy Farmers, www.milkprices.nl, pp 20.

Miller, D., and M.J. Chen. 1994. "Sources and Consequences of Competitive Inertia: A Study of the US Airline Industry", *Administrative Science Quarterly,* 39:1–23.

___. 1996. "The Simplicity of Competitive Repertoires: An Empirical Analysis", *Strategic Management Journal,* 17:419–439.

Moloney, J., 1988, "Rationalisation of the Irish Dairy Industry" Proceedings of the Agricultural Economics Society of Ireland, 1987/88 pp. 205–210.

Nilsson, J. 1998. "The Emergence of New Organisational Models for Agricultural Co-operatives", *Swedish Journal of Agricultural Research* 28:39–47.

Van Oijen, A.A.C.J., and G.W.J. Hendrikse. 2002. Governance Structure, Product Diversification, and Performance, ERIM Report Series 2002-34-ORG, Rotterdam.

Palepu, K. 1985. "Diversification Strategy, Profit Performance and the Entropy Measure", *Strategic Management Journal* 6:239–255.

Panzar, J.C., and R.D. Willig 1975. "Economies of Scale and Economies of Scope in Multioutput Production" Economic Discussion Paper No. 33, Bell Laboratories.

___. 1981. "Economies of Scope", *American Economic Review*, papers and Proceedings 71:268–272.

Rumelt, R.P. 1982. "Diversification Strategy and Profitability", *Strategic Management Journal* 3:359–369.

APPENDIX. BASIC DATA FOR COOPERATIVES

	Turnover[1] m€	Milk m liters '03[2]	Share of national supply[3]	Employ- ment[1] (total)	Milk price[4]	Diversity ratio
Arla Foods Dk/S (AF)	5,462	7,241	79%	17,791	31.96	0.58
Friesland Coberco (FC)	4,575	5,200	NA	18,000	31.90	0.64
Campina Melkunie (CM)	3,707	5,148	32%	6,872	31.83	0.56
Sodiaal (So)	1,870	2,200	9%	6,627	31.97	0.62
Humana Milchunion (HM)	2,359	3,300	12%	3,200	31.02	0.57
Nordmilch (Nm)	2,146	4,256	16%	3,467	29.59	0.41
Belgomilk (Be)	572	770	25%	NA	30.49	0.59
Glanbia (Gl)	2,141	2,075	29%	5,052	29.75	0.71
Kerry (Ke)	3,755	1,310	21%	18,869	29.83	0.90
Dairygold (Da)	950	850	16%	3,000	29.75	0.73
Lakeland Dairies (LD)	411	700	9%	NA	28.56	0.51
First Milk (FM)	668	2,300	16%	367	26.11	0.10

Notes and sources:

[1] Annual reports and website information for each dairy firm.

[2] Annual reports, personal communications and other sources including data on comparisons of European milk processors compiled by Rabobank, Netherlands.

[3] Estimates computed using national milk supply data from ZMP.

[4] Farm-gate milk prices: taken from the 'International Comparison of Producer Prices for Milk' compiled by the Dutch Dairy Board (Productschap Zuivel) on behalf of the Dutch Farmers Union (LTO Nederland). Prices are expressed in €/100 kg of standardised milk of 4.2% fat, 3.35% protein, total bacterial count of 24,999 per ml, somatic cell count of 249,999 per ml and a yearly delivery of 350,000 kg. VAT and levies are excluded and end of year profit distributions related to milk are included. Prices shown are averages for the three years 2001–2003. The LTO Nederland data provided the prices for all Arla Foods Denmark and Sweden, Friesland Coberco Dairy Foods, Campina Melkunie, Sodiaal, Humans Milchunion, Nordmilch, Belgomilk, Glanbia and First Milk. Prices paid by the other Irish co-operatives were scaled with reference to prices for Glanbia using data from the Irish Farmers' Journal/KPMG Milk Price Audit for prices paid by the Irish dairy firms.

CHAPTER 12

SALES DISTORTION IN HETEROGENEOUS COOPERATIVES

PETER BOGETOFT

The Royal Veterinary and Agricultural University (KVL), Copenhagen, Denmark

HENRIK BALLEBYE OLESEN

Copenhagen Economics, Copenhagen, Denmark*

Abstract. We show that the internal conflicts in cooperatives can distort sales and reduce the marketing of high-quality products. The conflicts arise because modern agricultural marketing cooperatives must implement farm-level differentiation to meet requirements from high-quality market segments, e.g. consumers focusing on animal welfare. When standard producers hold the majority vote in the cooperatives, they are reluctant to promote the sales of specialty products to first best levels even though this does not affect the sales of standard products. The cooperatives will therefore tend to under-produce specialty products.

1. INTRODUCTION

Traditionally, agricultural marketing cooperatives have had relatively homogeneous memberships producing the same standard product, e.g. milk, cf. Hansmann (1996). The cooperatives then processed the standard product into different products, aimed at different market segments, e.g. butter and non-fat milk. Product differentiation in the processing that could increase sales would generally be in the interest of all members. Recent trends in consumer demand, however, have changed this. Many of the product qualities that are now in demand, e.g. animal welfare, originate at farm-level and must be documented throughout the production chain. In order to satisfy such demands from different market segments, production must be diversified at farm-level. Therefore, many marketing cooperatives now have more heterogeneous memberships; cf. Giannakas and Fulton (2001) and Cook (1995).

Cooperatives with heterogeneous memberships often have a number of common characteristics:

K. Karantininis & J. Nilsson (eds.), Vertical Markets and Cooperative Hierarchies, 213–223.
© 2007 *Springer.*

First, the differentiation often takes the form of vertical quality differentiation, where certain quality attributes are added to the product. This creates a marketing asymmetry because high-quality products can be sold at the specialty market as well as at the standard market. There are numerous examples of this: organic milk can be sold as conventional milk, non-GM crops can be sold on the market for GM crops, and pork satisfying high animal welfare constraints can be sold as standard pork.

Second, the specialty producers are normally a minority in the cooperative. Hence, the standard producers can determine the conditions for the specialty producers. The standard producers must, however, respect that the specialty producers can leave the cooperative and use other marketing channels, e.g. establish their own cooperative. This gives the specialty producers some bargaining power.

In this paper, we focus on the sales and production decisions in a heterogeneous cooperative with standard producers and high-quality producers. We show that a cooperative will sell too few specialty products when the cooperative is controlled by standard producers. The result is an over-production where specialty products are sold as standard products with no price premium. We also show that typical payment schemes do not give the standard producers incentive to solve the problem of over-production. Hence, the over-production will be a permanent problem for the cooperative when the standard producers hold the majority. The cooperative will therefore suffer from two problems: too little marketing of high-quality products, and persistent over-production.

These problems are often raised in the debate about cooperatives. Cooperatives are criticized for investing too little in product and market innovation, cf. Cook (1995), Fulton (1995), Nilsson (1999), and Hendrikse and Bijman (2002). The two biggest cooperatives in Denmark, Danish Crown and Arla Foods, both have significant over-production of specialty products. In Arla, only 40 percent of the organic milk is used for organic products, the remaining 60 percent is sold as standard milk with no price premium. In Danish Crown 30–40 percent of the specialty pigs produced under additional animal welfare requirements were sold as standard pigs, cf. Danish Crown (2001). In this paper we show that the payment schemes do not provide incentives to the standard producers (with majority power) to solve the problem of over-production.

The remainder of this paper is organized as follows. In Section 2, we introduce the problem of influence costs. In Section 3, we describe and formalize the bonus system. In Section 4, we analyze the sales and marketing of specialty products. Section 5 analyzes the production levels for specialty products. In particular, we discuss why the bonus will tend to be set too high ex ante and show that the standard producers have no incentives to solve the over-production ex post. In Section 6, we combine the sales and production decisions and describe the resulting distortions. Finally, we conclude the paper in Section 7.

2. INFLUENCE COSTS

Influence costs play an important role in cooperatives, cf. Cook (1995), Hansmann (1996) and Bogetoft and Olesen (2000). Influence costs come up whenever organizational decisions affect the allocation of wealth. Influence costs are created by selfish activities, e.g. activities aiming at increasing the benefits for one particular producer group. Influence activities are costly, directly because they divert resources from productive tasks and indirectly because they may lead to sub-optimal decisions.

A cooperative with standard and specialty producers will suffer from internal conflicts of interests between the producer groups. This will generate influence costs, in particular with respect to production levels and sales. The design of the payment scheme determines the details of the conflict.

The by-laws of cooperatives reduce the direct influence costs, e.g. lobbying efforts, by limiting the payment and profit sharing that is consistent with the cooperative form. Specifically, the usual by-laws suggest that surplus shall be shared in proportion with production levels. Likewise, the by-laws traditionally guarantee free entrance and exit from the cooperative and allocate the production decisions to the members. On the other hand, these very rules and restrictions may increase the indirect influence costs by leading to sub-optimal decisions.

In this paper we study a bonus scheme often used against specialty producers. Profits are shared proportional to production levels with a marginal bonus compared to the standard production. The bonus depends on the sales of specialty products.

The focus on sales rather than production may limit the direct influence costs since the latter may involve changes in the production practices at the farms while the former "only" concerns the discussion of the cooperative's strategic marketing decisions.

In terms of indirect influence costs, the bonus serves dual purposes. On the one hand, it will coordinate the production level and on the other it will attract the right number of producers. We will demonstrate how these roles will be balanced and how the result is too high production and too low sales of specialty products.

3. BONUS SYSTEM

It is more costly to produce specialty products than standard products. Therefore, the specialty producers require a bonus in addition to the base payment received by the standard producers. Typically, the bonus depends on the supply and demand of the specialty production. There can be many motivations for this. One is to give the specialty producers incentives to increase (decrease) production when demand is increasing (falling). We consider a model where the bonus depends linearly on the sales of specialty products

$$B(S,Q) = \alpha S/Q \qquad (1)$$

i.e., as the sales/production ratio S/Q increases, the bonus increases linearly to α. S/Q measures the utilization of the specialty production, i.e. the fraction of the production that is sold at a price premium on the specialty market. The bonus structure in (1) is used widely in practice. For examples, see Bogetoft and Olesen (2004). It is often combined with a lower bound on the bonus. In equilibrium, however, such combined systems generate either the outcome of this paper or the fixed bonus outcome, and it therefore does not facilitate the exposition to include a lower bound here. The bonus system can be interpreted either as an explicit contract[1] or an implicit contract describing bargaining outcomes in the cooperative.

We assume that there are no positive or negative synergies between specialty and standard products in the processing and sales. Hence, the specialty products do neither affect the costs of processing standard products nor the demand for standard products. In particular, note that we are not modeling the trivial conflicts that arise when the products are substitutes such that more specialty products make the standard products less profitable. In terms of applications, the cost and demand independences across products are also quite realistic. For example, one can think of standard products that are sold on the world market and specialty products that are sold to special consumer segments in local markets.

4. SALES

A cooperative has to make a number of sales and marketing decisions. Specialty products can be sold at different markets, and the marketing budget can be allocated to different markets. In our model, we compress this complex problem into one of selling the specialty products at the specialty market or at the standard market at the price P_w. In our model, we do not distinguish between a poor sale due to low marketing investments and a poor sale caused by direct sales decisions.

The sales decisions depend crucially on the allocation of decision rights. We consider two scenarios. The first is the ideal case, where the members agree to maximize the sum of the profits to all members – the integrated profit. In practice, this scenario can only serve as a benchmark, because the actual sales and marketing decisions will reflect the interests of the decision-makers rather than idealistic concerns. The second scenario is when standard producers hold the majority and make the sales decisions that maximize their profits.

The sales and production quantities $\left(S^{FB}, Q^{FB}\right)$ that maximize the integrated profit are given by

$$\left(S^{FB}, Q^{FB}\right) \in \underset{S,Q}{\arg\max}\left[R(S,Q) - C(Q)\right] \qquad (2)$$

where $R(S,Q)$ is the sales revenue, net of any processing costs, from the specialty production, when the quantity S is sold as specialty products and the quantity Q-S is sold as standard products, i.e. $R(Q,S) = P_S(S)S + P_w(Q-S)$. Note that we assume that the standard products are sold in a perfectly competitive market with price P_w (the world market price) such that there are no synergies on the demand side. The primary production costs[2] from a specialty production of Q is $C(Q)$. The production costs include the opportunity costs, e.g. foregone profits from standard production.

Specialty products can be sold as standard products. However, this is not optimal since the standard products make the same price in the standard market but is assumed to be less costly to produce. Therefore, the production of specialty products shall equal the sale $\left(S^{FB} = Q^{FB}\right)$ and (2) can be rewritten as

$$S^{FB} = \arg\max_{S}\{R(S,S) - C(S)\} \tag{3}$$

Consider now the second scenario where the standard producers hold the majority and make the sales decisions that maximize the profit to the standard producers. When the standard producers determine how to sell the specialty production, they consider the effects on the total revenue and on the allocation of the revenue. To understand this, note that if the cooperative increases the sales of specialty products, three effects come into play: (i) The sales revenue changes (increases if the marginal revenue on the specialty market exceeds the world market price); (ii) The bonus increases (at least weakly); (iii) The specialty production increases as a consequence of higher bonus.

To optimize their profit, the standard producers choose S by solving

$$\max_{S}\left[R(S,Q) - B(S,Q)Q; \ \text{st.} \ Q \geq S\right]$$

or equivalently

$$\max_{S}\left[SP_s(S) + (Q-S)P_w - \alpha\frac{S}{Q}Q; \ \text{st.} \ Q \geq S\right] \tag{4}$$

The first order condition for this problem is

$$P_s(S) + \frac{\partial P_s(S)}{\partial S}S - P_w - \alpha = 0 \tag{5}$$

The first two terms equal the marginal revenue from selling at the specialty market, MR(S). The majority therefore chooses S as the value S so that

$$MR(\underline{S}) = P_w + \alpha \tag{6}$$

For the standard producers, the shadow price on specialty products sold on the specialty market is the world market price P_w plus the increase in bonus payment α. That is, when the standard producers sell at the specialty market, P_w is forgone by not selling on the world market and α is foregone by increasing the bonus to the specialty producers. The revenue maximizing sale, on the other hand, would be to sell on the specialty market until $MR(S) = P_w$. We refer to this solution as $\overline{S}$. The outcomes are illustrated in Figure 1.

We now summarize our finding about the sales level. Let $S(Q)$ be the sales of specialty products when Q is produced.

Proposition 1: When standard producers hold the majority in the cooperative they choose the sale of specialty products as follows

$$S(Q) = \begin{cases} Q & \text{if } Q < \underline{S} \\ \underline{S} & \text{otherwise} \end{cases} \tag{7}$$

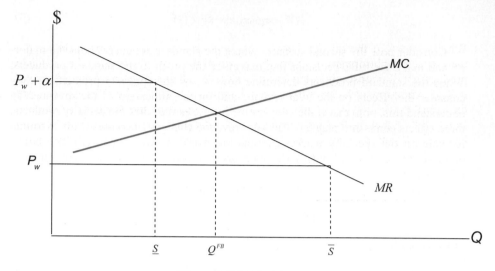

Figure 1. *Sales decisions*

Notice that the sales only increase with production when $Q < \underline{S}$, i.e. when the utilization rate is $S/Q = 1$ such that all products are sold on the specialty market. Changes in production level will not affect the sales of specialty products when the production exceeds $\underline{S}$. Hence, higher specialty production will only lead to more sales on the standard market, i.e. more over-production.

Inserting $S(Q)$ into $B(S,Q)$ gives us the following expression for the bonus payment to specialty producers

$$B\bigl(S(Q),Q\bigr) = \begin{cases} \alpha & \text{if } Q < \underline{S} \\ \alpha\,\underline{S}/Q & \text{otherwise} \end{cases} \qquad (8)$$

Figure 2 illustrates the sales (left figure) and the bonus payment (right figure) as a function of the production level.

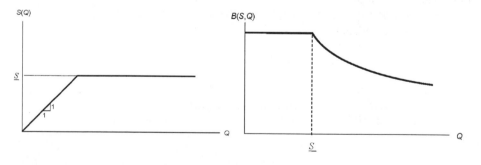

Figure 2. *The sales and the bonus as a function of production*

5. PRODUCTION

We have derived the relation between production and bonus payment above. It is therefore straightforward to find the production level $Q(B)$ that the specialty producers will choose given the bonus system B. Their marginal revenue from one unit of extra product is the base payment, assumed for simplicity to be P_w here, plus the bonus payment taking into account the response of the standard producers,[3] $B(S(Q),Q)$. Equating marginal revenue with marginal costs gives the production level as in Figure 3.

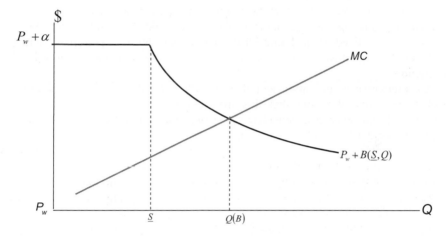

Figure 3. *Determination of specialty production level*

We have hereby shown how the sales distortions of the majority will lead to an under-utilization of the specialty production, $S<Q(B)$. This generates a social loss from the influence problem.

This presumes of course that the bonus α is relative large to begin with and that production level is not controlled via the number of contracts offered. We now discuss these possibilities.

To demonstrate the choice of a too high bonus α in the simplest possible setting, we assume that the costs of producing specialty products equals the costs of ordinary products except for a fixed cost A, i.e.

$$C(Q) = A + C_{s\,\tan\,dard}(Q) \qquad (9)$$

The fixed cost can for example be the costs of new stables. Also, we let the price in the specialty market at FB production level be p_{FB} .

To give the specialty producers the right production incentives, we must now have

$$\alpha = p_{FB} - p_W \qquad (10)$$

Also, to ensure that the right number of producers will choose to become specialty producers, we must have

$$\alpha Q_{FB} = A \tag{11}$$

since only then does the extra bonus covers the fixed costs.

However, this leads to a conflict unless specialty production is no more attractive than standard production which was the initial reason to differentiate. That is, assuming $\alpha Q_{FB} > A$, the cooperative is not able to ensure first best production level using the sales dependent bonus plan.

Intuitively, the problem is that the single bonus parameter tries to solve the dual problem of attracting the right number of producers and coordinating their production levels. The fixed costs should ideally be covered by intra-marginal payments, but this may conflict with cooperative sharing rules making payment proportional to production.

An alternative modification would be to allow for direct quantity control via production rights. We note that this may conflict with traditional cooperative principles. If, however, it is considered possible in a cooperative, the next question is if the majority has incentives to do so.

The advantage of reducing the excess production by reducing the number of production rights is that it will only hurt the producers who are no longer allowed to produce specialty products. This gives lower influence costs than reducing the bonus because all specialty producers are hurt by reduction in the bonus payment. In the remainder of this section, we therefore assume that the standard producers cannot reduce the maximum bonus payment, α, but that they can reduce the number of contracts.

We now formalize the standard producers' problem of determining the optimal production level for the specialty producers. The standard producers must pay the specialty producers the bonus plus the base payment. Hence, the standard producers solve

$$\max_Q \left[P_s(S(Q)) \cdot S(Q) + P_w [Q - S(Q)] - B(S(Q), Q)Q - P_w Q \right]$$
$$= \max_Q \left[P_s(S(Q)) \cdot S(Q) + P_w [Q - S(Q)] - \alpha S(Q) - P_w Q \right] \tag{12}$$

The first order condition for this profit function is

$$\frac{\partial P_s}{\partial S} \frac{\partial S}{\partial Q} S + P_s \frac{\partial S}{\partial Q} + P_w - P_w \frac{\partial S}{\partial Q} - \alpha \frac{\partial S}{\partial Q} - P_w = 0$$

$$\Updownarrow \tag{13}$$

$$\frac{\partial S}{\partial Q} \left[MR(S) - P_w - \alpha \right] = 0$$

Using (8) we see that $\dfrac{\partial S}{\partial Q} = 1$ for $Q \leq \underline{S}$ and (11) reduces to $MR(S) - P_w - \alpha = 0$,

hence the standard producers want the production to equate the optimal sales of specialty product, i.e. $Q = \underline{S}$. To see this, recall that $\underline{S}$ solves $MR(S) - P_w - \alpha = 0$

which implies that $MR(S) - P_w - \alpha > 0$ when $Q \leq \underline{S}$. Hence, when $Q \leq \underline{S}$ the standard producers want to increase the specialty production

When there is over-production, i.e. $Q \geq \underline{S}$, (8) gives us $\dfrac{\partial S}{\partial Q} = 0$ and the first order condition (11) is satisfied. Thus, the standard producers have no incentive to cut back on the specialty production to reduce the over-production. The reason is that the production level influences neither the sale of specialty products nor the total bonus payment.

We can summarize the analysis in the following proposition.

Proposition 2: Standard producers have no incentives to control the over-production of specialty products. The standard producers will neither increase sales nor reduce production.

6. DISTORTIONS

The analyses in Section 4 and Section 5 have demonstrated that both sales and production will be distorted. Figure 4 illustrates the distortions.

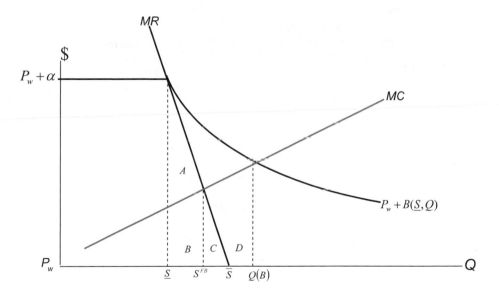

Figure 4. *Total distortions*

If the cooperative was able to choose the first best solution, the production costs would fall by $C+D$, and the revenue would increase by $A+B$. Hence, the total distortion in integrated profit is $A+B+C+D$.

Figure 4 also illustrates another important finding: the cooperative sells less on the specialty market than a profit maximizing investor owned firm would. This implies that the cooperative will be worse for the competition than a profit maximizing monopolist. This contradicts the standard assumption in the competitive yardstick school, where the standard intuition is that single-product cooperatives with quantity control problems will be better for competition than investor owned firms, cf. Sexton (1990), and Albæk and Schultz (1998). We find the opposite: a heterogeneous cooperative is worse for the competition than an investor owned monopolist. The reason is that the quantity control problem does not lead to more sales on the specialty market, since the over-production is dumped at the standard market, cf. Bergman (1997).

7. CONCLUSION

Many cooperatives have introduced differentiation at farm-level to satisfy high-quality demands from certain market segments. This development increases the internal conflicts within cooperatives, because the members become more heterogeneous. In this paper, we analyze a formal model of the influence costs that arise due to distortions in sales decisions in cooperatives with heterogeneous memberships.

We show that when the cooperative is controlled by standard producers, the sales of specialty products will be reduced below the first best level. The reason is that the standard producers take into account the fact that increased sale of specialty products will strengthen the bargaining position of the specialty producers. This makes the standard producers reluctant to promote the sales of specialty products. This critique has been raised without formal proof in the literature.

We also show that the standard producers do not have incentives to solve an over-production problem, where the production of specialty products exceeds the sales. Hence, the result will be a persistent over-production which generates distortions because products are being produced at high costs as specialty products but sold as standard products with no price premium.

These distortions suggest that a heterogeneous cooperative producing specialty products may result in lower social welfare than a pure profit maximizing monopolist. In particular, the competitive yardstick logic may not hold for heterogeneous cooperatives.

In conclusion, our model predicts a situation where the cooperatives are reluctant to promote specialty products because the internal control problems may distort sales and production levels and lead to a persistent over-production which is hard to escape.

NOTES

* This paper was written while Henrik Ballebye Olesen was assistant professor at the Royal Veterinary and Agricultural Unversity (KVL), Copenhagen, Denmark.
[1] In the cooperative slaughterhouse Danish Crown, the bonus system guarantees the special producers a minimum bonus of DKK 0.8 per kg. The bonus gradually increases to reach DKK 1.4 per kg. when all special pigs are sold as specialty products (Danish Crown, 2000).
[2] More precisely, $C(Q)$ is the lowest possible cost of producing Q, i.e. the production costs when the production Q is allocated efficiently among the special producers.
[3] Strictly speaking there is also a second order effect since an individual farmer i will realize that he may marginally reduce the bonus with $(\delta B/\delta Q)^*q_i = -(\alpha S/Q^2)q^i \sim 0$ and may therefore produce slightly less.

This effect is typically ignored in the cooperative literature since it is indeed a second order effect, cf. also Bogetoft and Olesen (2000).

REFERENCES

Albæk, S., and C. Schultz. 1998. "On the Relative Advantage of Cooperatives?" *Economic Letters* 59:97–401.

Bergman, M. 1997. "Antitrust, Marketing Cooperatives, and Market Power." *European Journal of Law and Economics* 4:73–92.

Bogetoft P., and H. B. Olesen. 2000. *Payment Schemes in Cooperatives: Theretical Models and Practical Examples from the Pig Industry.* In Danish. Copenhagen: DSR-Publisher.

Bogetoft, P., and H.B. Olesen. 2004. *Design of Production Contracts: Lessons from Theory and Agriculture.* Copenhagen: CBS Press.

Cook, M.L. 1995. "The Future of U.S. Agricultural Cooperatives: A Neo-Institutional Approach." *American Journal of Agricultural Economics* 77:1153–1159.

Fulton, M. 1995. "The Future of Canadian Agricultural Cooperatives: A Property Rights Approach." *American Journal of Agricultural Economics* 77:1144–1152.

Fulton, M., and K. Giannakas. 2001. "Organizational Commitment in a Mixed Oligopoly: Agricultural Cooperatives and Investor-owned Firms." *American Journal of Agricultural Economics* 83:1258–1265.

Hansmann, H. 1996. *The Ownership of Enterprises.* Cambridge, Mass.: Harvard University Press.

Hendrikse, G.W.J., and Bijman. 2002. "On the Emergence of New Growers' Associations: Self-selection versus Countervailing Power. *European Review of Agrigultural Economics* 29:255–269.

Milgrom, P., and J. Roberts. 1990. "Bargaining Costs, Influence Costs, and the Organization of Economic Activity." In J. Alt and K. Schepsle Eds. *Perspectives on Political Economy*, Cambridge UK: Cambridge University Press, pp. 57–89.

Nilsson, J. 1999. "Co-operative Organisational Models as Reflections of the Business Environments." *The Finnish Journal of Business Economics* 4:449–470.

Danish Crown. 2001. *Sales statistics for Gourmet and Porker.* Randers Denmark: Danish Crown.

Sexton, R.J. 1990. "Imperfect Competition in Agricultural Markets and the Role of Cooperatives: A Spatial Analysis." *American Journal of Agricultural Economics* 72:709–720.

CHAPTER 13

DO CONSUMERS CARE ABOUT COOPERATIVES?

*A Franco-Swedish Comparative Study of Consumer Perceptions**

JERKER NILSSON

Dept. of Economics, Swedish University of Agricultural Sciences, Uppsala, Sweden

PHILIPPE RUFFIO

Dept. of Rural Economics and Management, Agrocampus Rennes, Rennes, France

STÉPHANE GOUIN

Dept. of Rural Economics and Management, Agrocampus Rennes, Rennes, France

Abstract. The aim is to investigate the value that the cooperative ownership form might have in agricultural cooperative firms' relations to consumers. The empirical basis consists of interviews with 782 consumers in France and Sweden. Consumers have positive attitudes toward cooperatives while their level of knowledge is limited. Even though the concept of "cooperative" can be freely used by all cooperatives, it seems that nobody misuses its positive values. The main use could be made by well-established cooperatives, mentioning "cooperative" in conjunction with other attributes, and by local cooperatives trying to build a cooperative brand asset.

1. INTRODUCTION

Agricultural cooperatives exist in all countries where the markets for agricultural produce function imperfectly, and they have done so for more than a hundred years. These firms account for a large share of many markets – dairy, fruits, wine, eggs, etc. – although the market share varies greatly between product categories, stages in the value chain, and countries and regions. Nevertheless, it is safe to say that most consumers in almost all countries every day consume products that at one stage of the value chain have been processed by agricultural cooperatives.

225

K. Karantininis & J. Nilsson (eds.), Vertical Markets and Cooperative Hierarchies, 225–243.
© *2007 Springer.*

Still, it is not sure whether consumers think about the fact that agricultural coop-eratives account for many of the products they consume. It is also unclear if consumers in their choice of products take into account that some items are pro-duced by cooperatives and others by investor-owned firms. This study sets out to investigate these issues.

The aim of the study is to explore the value that the cooperative ownership form might have in agricultural cooperative firms' relations to consumers. This entails what the consumers know about cooperatives and their brands, what attitudes they have, whether they consider the individual manufacturer's ownership form, and whether their willingness to pay is affected by the manufacturer's characteristics. The empirical basis for the study is a consumer survey conducted jointly in France and Sweden.

The study applies only to cooperatives, which process their members' produce into consumer products, not those selling their produce to other processing firms. The focus is on the cooperatives' relations to consumers, while relations to farmer-members, retailers and all other stakeholder are discarded.

A literature search indicates that no researcher has previously investigated how consumers perceive agricultural cooperatives. Of course, the cooperative firms regularly conduct studies to investigate their markets, but these are not publicly available, nor do they have a scientific approach. There are numerous studies about how farmers perceive their cooperatives and a few about the general public's view, but these are not applicable here.

This study also has managerial implications. It is a general observation that rela-tively few agricultural cooperatives mention their ownership form when communi-cating with consumers. A tentative explanation is that the cooperatives do not consider this to be a strong sales proposition. However, as competition is becoming increasingly keen and all firms are searching for comparative advantages, insights about the consumers' view of cooperatives may be instrumental for the cooperative firms.

Next, the theoretical bases of the study are explained (Section 2), then the method employed (Section 3). Following, the results are presented (Section 4) and interpreted (Section 5), and conclusions are arrived at (Section 6).

2. THE NOTION OF "COOPERATIVE" AS A MARKET SIGNAL

2.1 Food products as experience goods

Economists distinguish between "search goods" and "experience goods", depending on the consumer's behavior in relation to the product attributes (Nelson, 1970).

> With search goods, the main characteristics of the product can be identified ex-ante (e.g., performances of computers, gas consumption of cars). ... Experience goods are goods with characteristics – particularly their quality – that cannot be fully identified and observed ex-ante by even well-informed consumers. They can be asserted only through "experience". Hence, reputation is a key factor. (Ménard, 1999:5–6)

Most agri-food products, whether fresh or processed, are experience goods. The product attributes of biological products are complex, and producers are challenged to maintain quality controls. Therefore, manufacturers of experience goods tend to put large efforts in creating strong brand names in order to differentiate their products from those of competitors.

> The reputation mechanism is based on the building up of a name during repeated identical transactions. Repetition creates a link between the quality of the product and the name of those who produce and/or sell it. (Ménard, 1999:6)

Expressed in marketing jargon, when the consumer exhibits low involvement buying behavior (Peter, Olson & Grunert, 1999:77), most manufacturers have problems with price sensitivity and poor market exposure. In order to avoid such problems, manufacturers try to influence the market so that they meet more highly involved consumers. This is achieved by a differentiation strategy (Porter, 2004), i.e., each manufacturer's product becomes different from other manufacturers' products. In these endeavors, branding the products is essential. An alternative strategy is a low-cost leadership strategy, but this is appropriate only for the manufacturer with the lowest cost level, selling to price sensitive consumers.

Most food products can be classified as experience goods, and most agricultural cooperatives manufacture food products. Hence, the reasoning explained above is relevant when analyzing cooperative firms' strategies on the consumer markets.

When differentiating a product through branding, the core issue concerns the so-called brand identity, i.e., the consumer's perception of the brand (Aaker, 1996). Part of the brand identity relates to the product's material attributes, such as taste, ingredients, price, and packaging. Another component involves immaterial, or symbolic, factors, such as whether the product expresses a certain lifestyle, belongingness to a specific community, or environmental or social status. These immaterial values are becoming more important as consumer affluence increases and as competition becomes more intense (Aaker, 1996).

If an agricultural cooperative signals the concept of "cooperative" to its market, this is an immaterial element in this firm's brand identity. Certainly, consumers' perceptions of material attributes of the cooperative firm's products (taste, ingredients, price, etc.) influence their perception of the immaterial brand component of "cooperative". Hence, the study must also include material brand elements, but only to the extent that these affect the consumers' perception of the immaterial brand component of "cooperative".

The question is: would the immaterial brand element "cooperative" enhance a cooperative's brand equity (Peter, Olson & Grunder, 1999:120)? Williamson (1985) uses the concept of brand name capital. The essence is that a brand constitutes an asset to the manufacturer that owns the brand. A brand is valuable as it reduces consumers' price sensitivity (raises the consumer's degree of involvement) whereby the manufacturer's revenues increase as well as the sales volume. Branding is a cost-efficient way of transferring large and complex sets of information to the potential buyers. On the negative side, building and maintaining brand consciousness in the minds of the consumers require large investments.

A brand component like "cooperative" has resemblance to many other brand elements such as organically produced, fair trade labels, country of origin, and regional brands. According to a large number of studies, such additions to a manufacturer brand could have positive effects on the consumer attitudes, though to a varying extent. Generally, when consumers in surveys state their knowledge of, attitudes towards and willingness-to-pay for socially accepted values they tend to exaggerate. By all probability, also the respondents of this study declare themselves to be more positive towards cooperatives than they would be in an actual purchasing situation.

2.2 Collective brands

If the consumers have the notion of "cooperative" associated with their perception of a food manufacturer's brand, this notion would function as if it were an element in a collective brand. A collective brand is a brand that is used jointly by several manufacturers, each of which is selling its own products (Ménard, 1999:12ff). There are both advantages and disadvantages connected to collective brands. One advantage is that the manufacturers do not have to invest in their own brands. Together, they can also get a stronger market impact. Each firm may benefit from the efforts of all other firms, using the same brand.

However, if a brand is owned by one firm but used by a number of other firms, property right problems may arise. This is a major weakness of collective brands. Each manufacturer becomes dependent on other manufacturers, using the same brand, as well as on the firm that owns the brand. If one manufacturer is deceitful, all will suffer. In order to discipline the various users of a collective brand, the brand owner is often a cooperative society, governed jointly by the users of the brand (Ménard, 1999:30). For a collective brand to function, the brand owner must also establish standards, which the brand users must adhere to, and it must have control mechanisms and power means to secure that every brand user performs adequately so that other brand users are not harmed.

There is, however, no firm or any other organization that has exclusive property rights to the concept of "cooperative", i.e., it can not be owned by any single organization, and it can neither be registered nor protected. The concept is generic, and it is common property. There is no one to establish product standards and to safeguard that the cooperative firms perform well. Hence, the consumers do not get any guarantee of what a cooperatively produced item stands for. A manufacturer can not design this "branding element" in the same way as other immaterial brand elements are designed. No cooperative firm can be prevented from using this brand element, irrespective of eventual deceitful behavior, and there are no possibilities of punishing the fraudulent user.

Hence, due to the similarity to a collective brand, the notion of "cooperative" is problematic. If it at one occasion gets a positive value, this will soon be challenged. That would give low-quality manufacturers an incentive to free ride on this good reputation, whereby their poor products would harm the goodwill (Tirole, 1996; Marette, Crespi & Schiavina, 1999; Winfree and McCluskey, 2005). So, provided that cooperative firms behave opportunistically and nobody controls the notion of "cooperative", the brand equity of this notion is by necessity low.

It should, however, be recognized that the free-riding problems are due to vary, depending on the attributes of the firms. The larger transaction specific investments a cooperative and its members have made, the less likely is opportunistic behavior. Firms, which plan to stay in the business for a long future, cannot send any false signals to the market without being punished by the consumers later on. "Fly-by-night" behavior can be expected by firms with small transaction specific investments and short-term perspectives; they are often smaller firms as well as intruding firms from other countries and regions.

2.3 Limited opportunism and alternative control mechanisms

One can imagine a few ways, whereby the free-rider problems could be overcome. Either the cooperatives are less inclined to act opportunistically (options 1-2 below), or there is some control of them, legally and/or socially (options 3-4):

(1) If *large cooperatives were to mention the concept of cooperative* in their communication to consumers, this concept would be only one element in their brand identity, the others being e.g. quality, freshness, healthiness, and environmental concerns. Therefore, these cooperatives become less vulnerable to eventual deceitful behavior of other cooperatives.

In a case like this, the consumers could be expected to have a positive image of the notion of "cooperative", connecting this to the other and more important brand elements of an established cooperative firm. So, "cooperative" in itself could not be a decisive factor in the consumers' assessment of the manufacturer's brands – only one element among several others.

(2) Some cooperatives adhere to *the traditional cooperative values* (honesty, solidarity, equity, etc.) (Craig, 1993). This may result in some social concerns, i.e., the risk for deceitful behavior decreases. Members of one cooperative may feel solidarity with colleagues who belong to another cooperative society.

This group of cooperatives can be expected to mention the ownership form in their market communication. This will increase the consumers' knowledge of the concept of "cooperative" but their attitudes are not necessarily improved – only if the product attributes are attractive. Hence, the "cooperative" market signal will not in itself have a strong impact.

(3) Through their *federative organizations* cooperatives may promote the concept of cooperatives. This is most likely to occur when a federative organization encompasses more or less all cooperatives in a region and/or an industry. For example, a federation of French winery cooperatives has exclusive property rights to the collective brand "Vignerons coopérateurs de France". The stronger this brand becomes, the larger number of winery cooperatives will belong to it – and the larger the number of member cooperatives, the stronger the brand will be.

These cooperatives tell consumers about their ownership form, but whether this will improve consumer attitudes depends on the product attributes. It is likely that products marketed under such a collective brand name are attractive, since there is no sense for an umbrella organization to provide a common brand only. For this brand to be valuable, the umbrella organization must also make sure that all products marketed under this brand are of high and even quality.

(4) There may be *cohesion within a group of cooperatives* without any federative organization. If so, everybody becomes dependent upon everybody else, and no one will misbehave. This is most likely to occur for small cooperatives, operating within a delimited region. In their attempts to differentiate themselves from the large manufacturers, they may emphasize their local connection, linking this to the fact that they are locally or regionally operating cooperatives.

Local cooperatives may be expected to get a positive reception by consumers, especially as these small firms probably follow a focus strategy, producing specialty products to less price-sensitive market segments. Hence, their brand names would be loaded with values like quality, local connection, and exclusivity, all of which will affect the consumers' perception of "cooperative" positively.

2.4 Hypotheses

Based on the discussions in the two preceding subsections, two hypotheses can be formulated.

(a) *The value that the cooperative business form has for agricultural cooperative firms' relations to consumers is generally limited.* Provided that at least some firms act opportunistically and that there are no control mechanisms, free-riding will prevent "cooperative" from being a valuable market signal.

(b) *In case that opportunism can be curbed and/or control mechanisms can be instituted to prevent free-riding, the notion of "cooperative" can have a value in cooperative firms' market relations.* This can occur (1) if well-established cooperatives include the concept of "cooperative" as one element in their brand identity, (2) if the cooperatives adhere to traditional cooperative values, (3) if the collective brand name is owned by a federation of cooperatives, and (4) if the cooperatives are small and regional, following a focus strategy.

3. METHODOLOGY

3.1 Samples

In order to empirically investigate the hypotheses presented in the preceding section, data of different kind are needed; about consumers' knowledge of agricultural cooperatives and their brands, about consumers' perception of these firms and these brands, and about their propensity to purchase the products. In order to make possible comparisons, such data are needed from at least two countries and at least two quite different regions, and a number of socioeconomic variables are required as background variables.

A survey was conducted in 2003, comprising interviews with a total of 782 consumers in three cities. One group (260 consumers) was interviewed in Paris and two other groups in medium-sized university cities – Rennes in Brittany, western France, (288 consumers) and Uppsala in Sweden (234 consumers). Rennes lies in a region with a strong agricultural and agri-food tradition, mostly for animal production (milk and meat). Uppsala is located in densely populated mid-Sweden and surrounded by arable land with crop production and some animal husbandry.

The cooperatives that the consumers meet in their supermarkets have quite different attributes. Both in France and in Sweden by far most cooperatives are large. In both cases their present structures are influence by governmental agricultural policies, but these policies are different in the two countries. The French cooperatives have for many years been subject to the Common Agricultural Policy (CAP) of the European Community. This has stimulated a large production of generic, low-processed products (butter, milk powder, etc.), which have been sold to the Community at so-called "intervention". Only during the last few decades, as the CAP is gradually liberalized, the French cooperatives have started to process their produce into high level added value products, whereby they also have had an impetus to invest in markets, for example by branding the consumer products.

The Swedish agricultural cooperatives were, until the country's accession to the European Community in 1995, protected by a national agricultural policy. As this was very generous the cooperatives had money to invest in products and markets. On the other hand, the cooperatives' connections to government fostered a negative image in the minds of the consumers. The cooperatives most of all adapted their operations to political demands, less so to market demands, and the negative image of cooperatives still prevails. This is in strong contract to France, where many consumers have sympathy for cooperatives.

The sample was based on a quota method using three criteria: geographical location, age, and gender (Table 1). Allowance was made for the judgment that groceries are more often purchased by women than by men. After one interview was completed, the interviewer asked a person close to the first one, so the sample was arbitrary though not random in a statistical sense.

Table 1. Quota distribution in the sample make-up

Location		Age		Gender	
Paris (F)	33%	15 – 30 years	33%	Women	65%
Rennes (F)	33%	31 – 50 years	33%	Men	35%
Uppsala (S)	33%	> 51 years	33%		
	100%		100%		100%

3.2 Data collection

Students interviewed consumers out shopping in supermarkets and shopping malls or waiting at railway stations. Data were processed with SPAD (Signalling Pathway Database) software using multivariate analysis methods mainly (principal components analysis and cluster analysis).

The questionnaire was divided into three parts:

A. A spontaneous approach to consumers' perception of cooperatives
Respondents were asked to give from three to five *names of agricultural cooperative enterprises* and three to five *names of brands* marketed by cooperatives. No aid was given to facilitate the respondents' recall.

In addition, for each country, consumers were asked to indicate which among a list of 14 brand names[1] are from cooperatives or from investor-owned firms. The brand names listed belong to a variety of food industries: dairy products, poultry, cooked pork, eggs, vegetables, etc. For comparative purposes data from France and Sweden are summarized as quantitative indicators.[2]

B. A guided approach to consumers' perception of cooperatives
Consumers were asked twelve questions about their attitudes to cooperatives, measured on Likert scales (See Table 3, left column). In order to get a good comprehension of consumer attitudes, a variety of cooperative facets were covered in the questionnaire: cooperative values, regional and local connections, attributes of the processing activity, and product quality. While most questions concern consumers' attitudes towards cooperative firms, some questions relate to cooperatively produced products, as the latter factors (material attributes) are due to affect the immaterial brand element of "cooperative".

Lastly, four questions concern consumers' willingness to pay 20% more for products with specific characteristics in respect of farmer incomes, employment, environmental protection, and the geographical location of decision-making power.

C. Respondents' socioeconomic characteristics (age; gender; professional category; home area; urban, rural or farming background)
The overall sample structure complied well with the quotas (Table 1) in terms of age and gender (Appendix A). The population was mainly town-dwellers (73%) and of urban background[3] (54%). Some 16% of the sample was from a farming background and 30% from a rural, non-farming background.

Compared to the French population as a whole, the two French samples contain a higher proportion of women, are markedly younger, belong to higher socioeconomic categories and include more people in the working population. Interviewees in Uppsala consist of younger persons and more women, but most of all they have higher education than Swedes in general.

Each sample has characteristics significantly different from the others (Table 2):
The Parisian sample comprises town-dwelling consumers from urban backgrounds. It consists mainly of managerial staff with rather poor unprompted knowledge of agricultural cooperatives. The sample has significantly fewer students and other occupations than the other two subpopulations.
The Rennes population typically lives in the country, are from rural or farming backgrounds, of average age, in intermediate occupations. This is without contest the subpopulation with the best spontaneous knowledge of cooperatives (Appendix B).
The respondents in Uppsala are mainly town dwellers with more students, engineering workers and others than in Paris or Rennes. They have fairly good

knowledge of cooperatives; better than the Parisians but not as well as people from Rennes.

Table 2. Main significant* features of each sample

Positively correlated characteristics (+)	Negatively correlated characteristics (-)
Paris (F)	
• town dwellers • managerial staff • urban background	• countryside dwellers • students, other occupations • rural and farming backgrounds
Cooperative knowledge: • names of cooperatives and cooperative brands given	Cooperative knowledge: • percentage of correct cooperative names given • percentage of correct cooperative brands given
Rennes (F)	
• countryside dwellers • administrative staff, manual workers • rural and farming backgrounds • 31 – 50 years	• town dwellers • other occupations • urban background • > 51 years
Cooperative knowledge: • percentage of correct cooperative names given • percentage of correct cooperative brands given • larger number of correct cooperative names given • large number of cooperative names (correct/incorrect) • larger number of brands correctly identified	Cooperative knowledge: • names of cooperative and cooperative brands given
Uppsala (S)	
• town dwellers • students, engineers, other occupations	• countryside dwellers • managerial, teachers, clerical, factory workers • 31 – 50 years old
Cooperative knowledge: • percentage of correct brands given • many cooperative names (correct or incorrect)	Cooperative knowledge: • percentage of 14 brands correctly identified • cooperative brands given

* p-value < 5%

4. FINDINGS

Two issues are analyzed more closely. First, the consumer perceptions of agricultural cooperatives are investigated in order to identify any regional differences. Next, different categories within the population are identified to unfold distinctive differences.

4.1 Consumer perceptions of cooperatives

According to Table 3 all three samples have an overall positive attitude to products from cooperative firms. The respondents think that such products are of better quality (Q1) and that they are no more expensive than other products (Q6).
The Parisian response is, however, less clear-cut. These two questions are the only ones where the responses from all three samples converge. Despite their positive

perception consumers do not have specific preferences for such products, particularly in Uppsala (where there is a majority opinion: 51%; 23%) and to a lesser extent in Rennes (40%; 25%). Parisians are more inclined to be persuaded (28%; 39%) even if this is not a majority opinion.

Table 3. Breakdown of responses (in %) to the questions (all three samples)

Question	Disagree entirely or partly (-)	Neither nor	Agree entirely or partly(+)	Significant* differences from average
Q1 Products made by cooperatives are of inferior quality	80	15	5	
Q2 If there is a product from a cooperative available, I prefer to buy that	40	31	29	Paris +; Uppsala (-)
Q3 Cooperatives mainly produce food that is not significantly processed (sugar, milk, flour)	34	24	42	Paris +; Uppsala (-)
Q4 Cooperatives guarantee long-term job security in the community	21	24	55	Paris +; Rennes +; Uppsala -
Q5 Cooperatives mainly produce food that is typical for the community	24	16	60	Paris +; Rennes +; Uppsala -
Q6 Food products from cooperatives are more expensive for consumers	50	26	24	Paris +
Q7 I trust food products from cooperatives more (food safety)	26	26	48	Paris +; Uppsala (-)
Q8 Working conditions and wages are not better in cooperatives	22	36	42	Rennes +; Uppsala (-)
Q9 Cooperatives protect small farmers better	19	17	64	Paris +; Uppsala (-)
Q10 Cooperatives produce mainly handmade products	51	21	28	Paris +; Uppsala (-)
Q11 Cooperatives do not pay higher prices to farmers for their output	37	37	26	
Q12 Cooperatives do not pay special care to environmental issues	23	31	45	Rennes (-); Paris +
Are you willing to pay 20% more if the firm making the product ...				
Q13 ... pays a higher price to farmers and protects small producers?	34	24	42	
Q14 ... secures jobs in the community in the long run?	25	21	54	Rennes + ; Uppsala (-)
Q15 ... particularly cares about environmental issues?	18	19	63	Uppsala (-)
Q16 ... is a firm where decision-making power is anchored locally?	32	25	43	

*p-value < 5%.

Most consumers in France (Paris and Rennes) think cooperatives make products that are typical for their region (Q5) (Paris: 77% agree; 9% disagree – Rennes: 71%; 18%) while the opposite opinion prevails in Uppsala (24%; 51%). Likewise, most French respondents believe that cooperatives provide lasting job security in their home regions (Q4) (Paris: 67%; 13% – Rennes: 63%; 15%) while consumers in Uppsala are doubtful or even disagree (32% agree; 30% uncertain; 39% disagree). The position is comparable with respect to cooperatives' ability to protect small farmers (Q9) although there is greater indecision among Swedish respondents on this point (34% agree; 22% uncertain; 34% disagree). Opinions are less clear, however, on cooperatives' ability to pay farmers more (Q11).

"Handmade" is an expression of high product quality in different respects. In Uppsala the majority of consumers disagree that cooperatives produce handmade products (Q 10: 11% agree; 73% disagree) and to a lesser extent in Rennes (21%; 51%). The Parisians tend to agree with this assertion (45%; 32%). For a range of other questions consumers' responses remain favorable but are not majority views in the population.

Most Parisians believe that cooperatives are concerned about environmental issues (Q12; 57% agree and 17% disagree). The respondents in Rennes tend to agree (42%; 27%), while many Swedes have doubts (26%). Likewise, French respondents tend to trust products made by cooperatives (Q7) (Paris: 49% agree; 17% disagree – Rennes: 45%; 25%) but Swedish respondents are uncertain (38% agree; 25% uncertain; 37% disagree). While many Swedish respondents are in doubt (34% agree; 33% uncertain; 32% disagree), French respondents and especially those in Rennes think that working conditions and pay are not better in cooperatives (Rennes: 50%; 21% – Paris 39%; 45%; 16%). Finally, French and particularly Parisian respondents (Paris: 52%; 25% – Rennes: 41%; 34%) think that cooperatives make products that are not significantly processed, for example few value-added products (Q 3) whereas Swedish respondents tend to disagree (21%; 44%).

On the questions about willingness to pay 20% more for a product made by a firm observing certain social values, only environmental issues (Q15) motivate the majority of the population in the three cities, even if a significant percentage (28%) of Uppsala respondents are against. Except for the final question (Q16), the majority of French respondents are generally prepared to pay more for products (Q14: Rennes: 63%; 18% – Paris: 58%; 20% – Uppsala: 38%; 39%) (Q13: Rennes: 53%; 27% – Paris: 50%; 29% – Uppsala: 21%; 45%). Swedish respondents are less attentive to employment and farmers' interests. While there is a hierarchy of criteria in France in favor of the environment, employment, farmers and local interests, this is markedly different from Uppsala where local interests seem more important (second position) and farmers' interests come last.

4.2 Identification of clusters

To go beyond an analysis of the average population and to take account of the complexity of the sample, a cluster analysis was conducted for responses to some questions (Q1, 3, 5, 7, 9, 10, 11), the others being considered illustrative variables (like the socioeconomic characteristics). The cluster analysis resulted in a division into four categories with a number of characteristics (Table 4):

Category 1: Idealists (279 respondents, 36% of the total population)
There are idealistic consumers who have *a positive view of cooperatives* in all respects and who agree with the questions asked. This is a French population (92% of respondents in this category), which does not have good unprompted knowledge of cooperatives. For example, more than half of the respondents failed to correctly identify cooperative names and brands. They consider cooperatives to make products that are not significantly processed, are handmade, are typical for their region of origin, and are of better quality. They trust the products, and they are prepared to buy preferentially even if the products were more expensive. Price is not an issue, and overall they are willing to pay more if manufacturers give them certain guarantees (environment, employment, local decision making). They think that cooperatives are alert to environmental issues, promote regional employment and protect small farmers. They do not, however, think that cooperatives provide any better pay and working conditions for their employees.

Category 2: Assenters (151 respondents, 19% of the total population)
This category of consumers does not have any specific socioeconomic characteristics. Overall they *trust cooperatives*. Products made by cooperatives are of better quality, are typical for the region, and involve some degree of processing (a divergence from category 1). Respondents trust these products and are ready to buy them. Cooperatives are believed to protect small farmers, pay them better and are concerned about the environment. Similarly they guarantee regional employment; hence, this category is ready to pay more.

Category 3: Detractors (165 respondents, 21% of the total population)
The detractor category, which includes more men, comprises consumers with a *negative view of cooperatives.* They see cooperatives as making products of inferior quality, in which they place no trust, and which they are not prepared to buy preferentially. These products are neither handmade nor typical for their region. Cooperatives do not pay farmers more nor protect them any better. Neither are they especially attentive to environmental issues, nor to guarantee regional employment. These consumers are not prepared to pay more for products made by firms which guarantee regional employment and keep decision-making power in the local area.

Category 4: Doubters (187 respondents, 24% of the total population)
More than 60% of the consumers in the category of doubters come from Uppsala. The category has significantly more engineering workers and fewer managerial staff than the others. It includes individuals with a *divided view of cooperatives.* They tend to disagree with the questions asked. They consider the products to be of better quality even if paradoxically they are not ready to trust them and the products are not more expensive. Similarly they think that pay and working conditions for employees and farmers are somewhat better.

Table 4. *Main features of the clusters of consumers*

Question*	1. Idealists	2. Assenters	3. Detractors	4. Doubters
Q1 Products made by cooperatives are of inferior quality	-	-	+	-
Q2 If there is a product from a cooperative available, I prefer to buy that	+	+	-	-
Q3 Cooperatives mainly produce food that is not significantly processed (sugar, milk, flour)	+	-		-
Q4 Cooperatives guarantee long-term job security in the community	+	+	-	-
Q5 Cooperatives mainly produce food that is typical for the community	+	+	-	-
Q6 Food products from cooperatives are more expensive for consumers	+			-
Q7 I trust food products from cooperatives more (food safety)	+	+	-	-
Q8 Working conditions and wages are not better in cooperatives	+			-
Q9 Cooperatives protect small farmers better	+	+	-	-
Q10 Cooperatives produce mainly handmade products	+		-	-
Q11 Cooperatives do not pay higher prices to farmers for their output	-		+	-
Q12 Cooperatives do not pay special care to environmental issues	+	+	-	-
Are you willing to pay 20% more if the firm making the product ...				
Q13 ... pays a higher price to farmers and protects small producers?				
Q14 ... secures jobs in the community in the long run?	+	+	-	-
Q15 ... particularly cares about environmental issues?	+			-
Q16 ... is a firm where decision-making power is anchored locally?	+		-	-
Cooperative knowledge	No cooperative name or brand given + % of correct cooperative brands (-)		No correct cooperative brands given (-)	No cooperative names or brands given (–)
City	Paris + Rennes + Uppsala (-)			Uppsala + Paris (-) Rennes (-)
Gender			Male + Female (-)	
Occupation				Engineering workers + Managerial (-)

*p-value < 5%.

However, consumers are not prepared to buy cooperative products preferentially. They do not believe that cooperatives produce handmade products, which are typical for a region or not significantly processed. For these respondents, cooperatives do not protect small manufacturers any better, are not particularly concerned about environmental issues and do not secure local employment. Likewise they are not willing to pay more to encourage firms to be sensitive to environmental issues or maintain decision-making power locally.

5. ANALYSIS

Hypothesis (a) declares that the notion of "cooperative" has only small importance for the brand equity of agricultural cooperatives. Given that cooperatives act opportunistically and there is no disciplining control, the value of this notion could not be high.

The findings do not support this hypothesis. Many consumers have fairly positive attitudes toward cooperatives, even though at the same time a large number of consumers have little knowledge of cooperatives. It seems rather that good attitudes and poor knowledge are related. The Parisian figures especially indicate that.

Swedish consumers are more skeptical than two French consumers, also their level of knowledge is only moderate. A plausible explanation is that in Sweden the concept of "cooperative" got negative connotations during the many years with a strongly protective national agricultural policy. Consumers interpret "cooperative" to mean bureaucracy, planned economy, collectivism, etc. Hence, the notion of "cooperative" contributes less to brand equity in Sweden than in France.

The fact that the notion of "cooperative" has some value for consumers indicates that few (or no) cooperatives try to exploit this value by selling inferior goods. Hypothesis (b) suggests four possible explanations, based on the assumptions that the cooperatives do not act opportunistically and/or that there are some control mechanisms to prevent free-riding. As hypothesis (a) is rejected, one or several of these four options can be expected to offer explanations to the findings.

1. Large cooperatives mention the concept of cooperative
Some large French cooperatives inform consumers about their ownership form, even though various product attributes constitute the core of their market communication. This is hardly found in Sweden. Hence, here is an explanation as to why so many French consumers have both better knowledge and a positive attitude towards cooperatives.

Observations indicate that the relatively positive view of cooperatives may be due to the large cooperatives, mentioning their ownership form as one element in their brand identity. Consumers tend to believe that cooperatives produce high quality products; to a large extent they would prefer to buy products from cooperatives; they have trust in cooperatively produced products; they don't find these products overly expensive, etc. Hence, there is reason to accept this part of hypothesis (b).

2. Traditional cooperative values

While cooperative ideology is little appreciated by Swedish consumers, a number of French consumers know this ideology and sympathize with it. The findings indicate so. Also, the number of consumers is not insignificant.

Among the French consumers with an ideological motivation, cooperatives are believed to protect farmers, guarantee local employment, provide better working conditions for employees, and care for environmental protection. Likewise, many consumers are willing to pay a higher price for products if they know that the manufacturer promotes certain social aims, such as paying farmers more, job security, environmental care and local decision-making power. This is to say that various ideologies tend to coincide – cooperative ideology, environmental, regional development, etc.

Evidently, many consumers are receptive to ideological arguments. However, this is probably not an effect of the cooperatives' communication to the consumer markets as the consumers' views are hardly based on reality. The conclusion is that this part of hypothesis (b) cannot be confirmed, but neither can it be rejected.

3. Federative organizations

Second-tier cooperatives with property rights to a collective brand name exist both in Sweden and in France, though in greater number in the latter country. The Swedish cooperatives however, do not market their brands as cooperatively made, so consumers have no knowledge of the ownership form. Anyhow, the number of cooperative brands, owned by a federation of cooperative and referring to the cooperative identity, is quite limited in both countries.

These cooperatives typically work to promote quality in their members' products. Hence, several of the findings may support the hypothesis that the positive consumer attitudes are influenced by these organizations. For example, consumers like the quality of cooperative-made products; many think these products are better processed; they believe that cooperative products are of local origin. Hence, this part of hypothesis (b) can at least not be rejected, but the data set is too limited to support it.

4. Cohesion within a group of cooperatives

The number of local cooperatives is significant in some French regions (southern and central France, for instance). Thanks to the attractive product features of these products it is likely that they get more attention by the consumers, compared to their actual market position. The fact that consumers believe that cooperatives to a large extent produce products which are typical for their region is an interesting observation in this context and also that the products are sometimes believed to be hand-made.

The positive Parisian consumer attitude is influenced by these organizations since consumers may have experienced this type of marketing strategy, for example when traveling across the country. Hence this part of hypothesis (b) can be accepted.

6. CONCLUSIONS

A large share of the *consumers have a positive view of agricultural cooperatives,* but the extent of this attitude varies greatly – more in France than in Sweden, and more in Paris than in Rennes.

This means that *the notion of "cooperative" is actually not misused* by firms, which want to free-ride by selling products of poor quality with reference to this concept. This would happen if there were firms acting opportunistically and if there were no control of the concept of "cooperative". So these two conditions do not apply.

Some large, *established cooperatives mention the ownership form in their market communication* together with information about the various product attributes. The most important marketing communication concerns the product attributes, while the notion of "cooperative" is a complementary and supporting element in the brand identity. Thereby these firms are not very vulnerable to free-riding, deceptive firms.

Furthermore, *there may be some control mechanisms*, which have the effect of assuring that the cooperative firms do not abuse the concept of cooperatives. It is possible that there is some degree of cohesion within groups of local cooperatives, and that some federative organizations serve to promote the collective brands that their members use, although the data set is too limited to confirm such a hypothesis in the latter case.

The positive attitude is not due to a consequence of deliberate action by the cooperative firms. On the contrary – only few cooperatives mention the ownership form in their marketing communication. Other observations also indicate that the consumer perceptions do not originate from the cooperatives; the consumers' level of knowledge is low and consumers often have unrealistic perceptions, for example, that cooperatives produce handmade products and provide both better conditions for employees and better pay to the farmers. Hence, the consumers' image of cooperatives is based on values of a different kind. It could be cooperative ideology but also values about environmental care, regional development, and product safety.

At a general level a conclusion is that an asset that is seemingly of a collective character ("cooperative" as a brand element) is not necessarily subject to widespread abuse by free riders. The number of potential free riders may be limited – many actors may have such large transaction-specific investments that they would hurt themselves if they were to act fraudulently. Some actors, which might be affected by free riders' fraudulent behavior, can take precautionary measures. There may be some monitoring mechanisms, controlling the collective asset to some extent.

A conclusion from a managerial perspective is that agri-food cooperatives would benefit from using the notion of "cooperative" as a market signal. In particular, the large, well-established firms may include this as one element in their brand identity. Small, local cooperatives can probably gain credibility in marketing themselves as cooperatives with local origin. It is questionable whether the cooperatives should stress cooperative ideology in their market communication – there might be a backlash if the consumers recognize that the real business world diverges from their ideological conceptions. Federations of cooperatives are often successful when using collective brands.

NOTES

* The authors gratefully acknowledge receipt of financial support from the Regional Organization of Western France Farmers' Cooperatives (CCAOF) as well as from Arla Foods amba, Division Sweden. Likewise, the authors are thankful to the two MSc students, Peter Brusvall (Swedish University of Agricultural Sciences – SLU, Sweden) and Caroline Hervé (Agrocampus Rennes, France) for their work with the collection of data (Brusvall, 2004; Hervé, 2003).

[1] For France: seven brands from cooperative firms (Yoplait, Matines, Paysan Breton, D'Aucy, Le Guérandais, Florette, Loué) and seven brands from non cooperative firms (Fleury Michon, Tipiak, Hénaff, Bonduelle, Père Dodu, Président, Danone). For Sweden: seven brands from cooperative firms (Yoggi, Kronägg, Ostkompaniet, Arla, Skogaholms, Scan, Kungsörnen) and seven brands from non cooperative firms (Kronfågel, Swegro, Carlshamn, Pågens, Finax, Pastejköket, Findus).

[2] Number of names given, number of correct names given, percentage of correct names given; number of brands given, number of correct brands given, percentage of correct brands given; number of brands known out of the 14, number of brands correctly identified out of the 14, percentage of brands correctly identified.

[3] "Urban background" means that the respondent comes from an agglomeration of more than 5000 inhabitants.

REFERENCES

Aaker, D.A. 1996. *Building Strong Brands*. New York: The Free Press.

Brusvall, P. 2004. "Is 'Co-operative' a Valuable Element in Market Communication? An Empirical Study of Consumer Perceptions." MSc thesis no. 357, Uppsala: Department of Economics, Swedish University of Agricultural Sciences.

Craig, J.G. 1993. *The Nature of Co-operation*. Montréal: Black Rose Books.

Hervé, C. 2003. "L'identité coopérative est-elle valorisante aux yeux du consommateur?" Mémoire de fin d'études. Rennes: Agrocampus Rennes, INSFA.

Marette, S., J.M. Crespi, and A. Schiavina. 1999. "The Role of Common Labelling in a Context of Asymmetric Information." *European Review of Agricultural Economics* 26:167–178.

Ménard, C., and E. Valceschini. 1999. "The Creation and Enforcement of Collective Trademarks." *Voprosi Economiki* (Economic Issues), Moscow, March 1999:74–87.

Nelson, P. 1970. "Advertising as Information." *Journal of Political Economy* 78:311–329.

Peter, J.P., J.C. Olson, and K.G. Grunert. 1999. *Consumer Behaviour and Marketing Strategy.* European Edition. Maidenhead: McGraw-Hill Book Co.

Porter, M. 2004. *Competitive Advantage: Creating and Sustaining Superior Performance.* New York: The Free Press.

Ruffio, P., C. Hervé, S. Gouin, F. Ledos, and E. Périnel. 2004. *L'image des coopératives agricoles vue par les consommateurs*. Rennes: Agrocampus Rennes & Cooperatives Agricoles de l'Ouest.

Tirole, J. 1996. "A Theory of Collective Reputations." *Review of Economic Studies* 63:1–22.

Winfree, J.S.,, and J.J. McCluskey. 2005. "Collective Reputation and Quality." *American Journal of Agricultural Economics* 87:206–213.

242   J. NILSSON, P. RUFFIO & S. GOUIN

APPENDIX A. FEATURES OF THE CONSUMER SAMPLES

		Paris	Rennes	Uppsala	Total
Number of consumers		260	288	234	782
Gender	male	35	35	39	36
(%)	female	65	65	61	64
Age	15–30 years	28	32	37	32
(%)	31–50 years	36	41*	31*	37
	>50 years	36	27*	32	31
Home	town	87*	56*	78*	73
area (%)	country	13*	44*	22*	27
Family	urban	66*	38*	59	54
background (%)	rural	25*	37*	27	30
	farming	9*	25*	14	16
Occupation	Farmer	0	2	3	2
(%)	Engineering worker	5	5	12*	7
	Shopkeeper and trades perdon	5	3	2	4
	Managerial staff	19*	8	1*	9
	Administrative staff	18	32*	12*	21
	Teacher	6	6	2*	5
	Student	13*	16	28*	18
	Manual worker	3	7*	0*	4
	Homemaker, or retired, or unemployed.	25	18	20	21
	Other	6*	3*	20*	9
Cooperative	% of correct cooperative names given	11.7*	62.8*	39.1	38.7
knowledge	% of correct cooperative brands given	9.4*	41.6*	43.5*	31.5
	% of the 14 brands correctly identified	65.6	66.0	62.8*	64.9

* p-value < 5%

APPENDIX B. SPONTANEOUS KNOWLEDGE OF COOPERATIVES

Number of correct answers to the question "give 3–5 names of cooperative firms"	Rennes	Paris	Uppsala
No answer	26%*	73%	16%
No correct answer	4%	13%	17%
1 correct cooperative name	24%	10%	40%
2 correct cooperative names	20%	3%	20%
3 correct cooperative names	14%	1%	7%
4 or 5 correct cooperative firms' names	12%	0%	0%
	100%	100%	100%

*26% of the Rennes sample did not mention any cooperative name at all.

Number of correct answers to the question "give 3–5 names of cooperative brands"	Rennes	Paris	Uppsala
No answer	36%*	71%	30%
No correct answer	8%	16%	11%
1 correct cooperative brand name	29%	9%	24%
2 correct cooperative brand names	18%	3%	23%
3 correct cooperative brand names	7%	1%	12%
4 or 5 correct cooperative brand names	1%	0%	0%
	100%	100%	100%

*36% of the Rennes sample did not mention any brand name at all.

Correct recognition of the 14 brands: breakdown (%) of correct answers														
	1	2	3	4	5	6	7	8	9	10	11	12	13	14
Rennes	0	0	0	1	5	5	11*	17	20	20	12	8	1	0	100
Paris	0	0	1	2	6	6	11	14	23	20	12	4	1	0	100
Uppsala	1	2	5	5	20	20	19	7	10	6	4	1	0	0	100

* 11% of the Rennes sample correctly identified seven brands (cooperative and non-cooperative brands)

CHAPTER 14

THE HORIZON PROBLEM RECONSIDERED

HENRIK BALLEBYE OLESEN

Copenhagen Economics, Copenhagen, Denmark[*]

Abstract. This paper challenges the general view in the literature that cooperatives underinvest, because some members will exit the cooperative before the full benefits from their investments are harvested (the horizon problem). This paper demonstrates that full equity redemption will solve the horizon problem. The majority of members will, however, bias the exit payment to their own advantage. This will lead to overinvestment. Thus, the main finding in this paper is that if there is a horizon problem, it will lead to overinvestment – not underinvestment.

1. INTRODUCTION

One of the important challenges for cooperatives is the ability to raise sufficient capital. In the agribusiness sector, the industrialization of agriculture, merger waves and increased R&D have led to bigger cooperative firms financed by fewer farmers. This development creates new challenges for the traditional cooperatives.

The literature argues that the ability to raise capital is one of the weaknesses of the cooperative organizational form. The literature lists a number of problems that will lead to underinvestment in cooperatives. One of the most important of these problems is the horizon problem.

Cook (1995) summarizes the literature on the horizontal problem in this way:

> The horizon problem occurs when a member's residual claim on the net income generated by an asset is shorter than the productive life of that asset. [...] The horizon problem creates an investment environment in which there is a disincentive for members to contribute to growth opportunities. [...] Consequently, there is a pressure on the board of directors and management to accelerate equity redemption at the expense of retained earnings.

This paper challenges the standard view in the literature that the horizon problem leads to underinvestment in cooperatives. The main finding in this paper is that if there is a horizon problem, it will most likely lead to overinvestment – not underinvestment.

K. Karantininis & J. Nilsson (eds.), Vertical Markets and Cooperative Hierarchies, 245–253.
© 2007 *Springer.*

The standard view of the horizon problem also suggests that compensating the members exiting the cooperative for their investments (exit payment) will improve the investment incentives in cooperatives. This view is, however, too simple. Basically the problem of determining an exit payment is zero sum game. The exit payment is paid by the continuing members. Therefore it is not obvious that redemption of equity to exiting members will improve investment incentives.

There are two main differences between the standard approach to the horizon problem and the approach in this paper. First, we analyze how an exit payment will affect the exiting members and the continuing members. The standard approach only focuses on the exiting members. Second, this paper focuses on the incentives of the majority in the cooperative. The standard approach uses the investment incentives for the exiting members as a benchmark for the investment level in the cooperative. However, this gives a wrong picture, because investments are decided by the majority and not by the exiting members.

This paper does not suggest that there will not be underinvestment in cooperatives, per se. The paper only claims that the horizon problem will not lead to underinvestment in cooperatives. In fact, the horizon problem may actually induce overinvestment. However, there may be many other problems leading to underinvestment in cooperatives.

Cook (1995) defines five problems caused by vaguely defined property rights in traditional cooperatives: Free Rider Problem, Horizon Problem, Portfolio Problem, Control Problem and Influence Costs. These problems are caused by the lack of a market for cooperative shares.

Free Rider Problems emerge, when individuals (new members, existing members, or outsiders) harvest benefits from investments, which they have not (fully) contributed to. The Portfolio Problem occurs, because the cooperative's investment portfolio may not match the preference of each member. Since there is no market for equity shares, the member cannot withdraw and reallocate the investment. The Control Problem is the problem of ensuring that the management follows the interests of the owners. In a cooperative, this problem is enhanced as there is no market for cooperative shares that provides market pressure on the management. Influence Costs are especially a problem in organizations (e.g. heterogeneous cooperatives) where the members have different interests. Influence costs include costs consumed in the decision process and distortions caused by special interests.

A large literature has expanded on how these problems affect cooperative behavior. However, only a small part of the literature is based on formal modeling. This makes it difficult to distinguish precisely between the five problems. In particular, the Horizon Problem and the Free Rider Problem are often mixed together in the literature, which creates some confusion.

This paper only analyzes the horizon problem, but it uses the distinction between the Free Rider Problem and the Horizon Problem defined in the literature (see e.g. Cook, 1995). There is no free-riding in our model, because no new members can enter the cooperative and because all members contribute fully to the investment. Hence, we avoid mixing the two problems.

The role of exit payment or equity redemption has been addressed specifically in various articles.

Hansmann (1999) discusses redemption policies. He argues that most cooperatives do not redeem the equity in full upon retirement, because the internal politics of the firm weigh against full equity redemption. Full redemption will benefit members who are going to retire shortly, while the members who are not retiring have an interest in a low redemption. The reason for this is that the benefits to the continuing members from a low redemption (the saved redemption) falls immediately, while their disadvantage in receiving a low redemption upon their own retirement will not occur for many years.

Rey and Tirole (2001) also analyze the problem of entry payments and exit payments in cooperatives. They develop a model of a cooperative with a constant member base, i.e. the number of members exiting the cooperative is equal to the number of members entering the cooperative. They show that there are first best investments incentives in cooperatives with free entry and exit (i.e. no exit payment). However, the equilibrium found by Rey and Tirole is not subgame perfect. Rey and Tirole do not allow the cooperative to change the redemption policy once the cooperative has been started – e.g. by charging an entry payment from new members even though the present members have not paid an entry payment themselves.

Hansmann (1999) raises a new problem in relation to exit payment. He points out that a full redemption may encourage too much exit. If there are economies of scale, exit will impose a negative externality on the continuing members. With full redemption of equity, the members do not take this into account, when they decide whether to exit or not.

Holmström (1999) adds another argument against full equity redemption. He argues that, over-pricing exit can be devastating for the cooperative, because it may encourage strategic exit, if the exit payment exceeds the expected payoff from continued membership. Thus, Holmström concludes that "Strategic exit and bankruptcy favour conservative pricing [of exit]".

Rey and Tirole (2000) expand these arguments in a formal model. They demonstrate that cooperatives are fragile institutions because member exit may start a snow-balling effect. They also discuss the optimal level of loyalty in cooperatives.

This paper does not include the problem of strategic exit where members exit the cooperative to avoid being the "last man on the boat". In our model exit is exogenous in the sense that it is not influenced by the successfulness of the cooperative. Hence, in our model exit is solely determined by external factors such as new outside opportunities, age, health, or the member may be forced out of business, etc.

The remainder of this paper is structured as follows. Section 2 discusses redemption policies in practices. This discussion is based on the current debate in leading Danish agricultural cooperatives. Section 3 introduces the model. Section 4 analyzes the horizon problem in a homogenous cooperative and Section 5 analyzes the horizon problem in a heterogeneous cooperative. Finally, Section 6 concludes the paper.

2. REDEMPTION POLICIES IN PRACTICE

Cooperatives meet the challenge of raising more capital in different ways. Some cooperatives choose to use the New Generation Cooperative model with closed membership and tradable production rights, etc. Other cooperatives make more modest adjustments to the traditional cooperative model.

In Denmark, traditional cooperatives have been characterized by free entry and exit, and unallocated equity obtained through retained earnings – i.e. no redemption of equity (Federation of Danish Cooperatives, 1998). Members lost their share of the equity, when they exited the cooperative. This model has actually proven to be quite successful, for instance one of Europe's biggest dairy companies, Arla Foods, does not pay out equity to exiting members.

Many cooperatives in the Danish agribusiness sector have modified the financial structure of their cooperative. In particular, a number of leading cooperatives have allocated some of the equity to member accounts, while other big cooperatives, including Arla, are considering introducing allocated equity. The equity on the member accounts is paid out, when a member exits the cooperative.

3. MODEL

In this paper, we use a simple model to analyze how the redemption policy affects investment incentives in a cooperative. In particular, we analyze how the compensation to members exiting the cooperative, affect the incentives to invest.

We consider a cooperative with N members, who have to decide whether or not to make a joint investment at the cost I. For simplicity, we normalize N so that $N=1$.

The investment decision is made, knowing that some members will exit the cooperative before the payoff falls. The decision about exiting the cooperative can be caused by internal or external factors. We use a survival rate s to model the exit. Hence, with probability $(1-s)$ a member will exit the cooperative before the payoff falls.[1]

When members exit the cooperative before the payoff falls, they may receive a compensation, which we refer to as *exit payment X*. The amount on the personal equity account corresponds to X in our model.

The members make the decision about the exit payment before they make the investment decision. Hence, the exit payment cannot depend on the success of the investment. This is an important assumption. There are three strong arguments supporting this assumption. First, the cooperative is not valued (i.e. priced) on the market, as there are no tradable ownership rights. Therefore, the value of the cooperative and thus the equity is determined through accounting procedures in stead of market evaluation. Second, the success and the expected payoffs may be non-verifiable before the payoffs actually fall. Third, adjustments in the personal equity may cause double taxation. In Denmark, increases in the amounts on the personal equity accounts would be considered as personal income and both the cooperative and the members would be taxed (Federation of Danish Cooperatives, 1999).

The payoff from the investment may depend on the number of members remaining in the cooperative (N_t), when the payoff falls. If the cooperative makes a purely financial investment, e.g. buys stocks, the payoff is independent of the number of members in the cooperative. On the other hand, if the cooperative invests in marketing or in a processing plant, the payoff will depend on the number of members in the cooperative. Both types of investments are covered in our model. In principle, the expected payoff depends on the number of members, $V=V(N_t)$. However, our results do not depend on the functional form of $V(N_t)$. We therefore suppress N_t to simplify the presentation.

4. HOMOGENOUS COOPERATIVE

First we consider a homogeneous cooperative where all members have the same survival rate s. The total payoff in this situation is $V-(1-s)X$, which gives a payment to each remaining member of $V/s-X(1-s)/s$. The members foresee this and they will support the investment if

$$s\left(\frac{V}{s}-\frac{1-s}{s}X\right)+(1-s)X \geq I \Leftrightarrow V \geq I \tag{1}$$

This shows that the members will support an investment if, and only if, it is profitable. This is the first best investment level. We can thus conclude:

Proposition 1: *in a homogenous cooperative all members support the first best investment level, regardless of the exit payment and the survival rate.*

This means that there is no horizon problem in a homogeneous cooperative. The intuition behind this result is simple. The risk of exogenous exit means that some members will not get their share of the payoff. The flipside of the coin is that there is more left for the continuing members. In other words, the exit merely transforms the setup into a lottery. The lottery is a fair odds lottery, since all members have the same survival rate. With risk neutral members, this does not influence the value of the investment.

5. HETEROGENEOUS COOPERATIVES

We now turn to a cooperative with heterogeneous members. For simplicity, we assume that there are only two types of members, certain members and uncertain members.

We introduce heterogeneity in the model by assuming that a fraction, α, of the members face no risk of exogenous exit and have a survival rate of 1. We refer to this group as the *certain members*. The rest of the members, $1-\alpha$, may exit the cooperative before the pay-off falls and have a survival rate below one, i.e. $s<1$. We refer to this group as *uncertain members*. The model can be interpreted as a model of generational conflict, if one thinks of certain members as young members and uncertain members as old members.

The total payoff to continuing members in the heterogeneous cooperative is $V-(1-\alpha)(1-s)X$. Hence, the payment to each of the certain member is

$$\frac{V-(1-\alpha)(1-s)X}{1-(1-\alpha)(1-s)} = \frac{V-X}{\alpha+s(1-\alpha)} + X \cdot \tag{2}$$

The investment cost is the same for certain and uncertain members. The certain members will therefore support an investment if

$$\frac{V-X}{\alpha+s(1-\alpha)} + X \geq I \tag{3}$$

If there is no exit payment, $X=0$, certain members will support some unprofitable investments with $I>V$. This is because the investment cost threshold given by (3), below which all investments are supported, is higher than the expected value of the investment. To see this, observe that the number of remaining members, $\alpha+s(1-\alpha)$, is less than 1.

There are two reasons why the certain members are willing to overinvest if $X=0$. First, exit of uncertain members leaves more payoffs to the certain members, i.e. there will be a transfer of payoff from the uncertain to the certain members. This is easiest to see if we assume that the total payoff is independent of the number of members, $V(N_t)=K$. Second, the certain members do not take into account the pay-off that is lost because some uncertain members exit the cooperative. Exit of uncertain members may reduce the expected total payoff. To see this, assume that the payoff depends linearly on the number of members, such that $V(N_t)=vN_t=v(1-s)$. Exit of uncertain members will reduce the expected total payoff from v to $v(1-s)$, but the certain members are willing to support any investment with $I \leq v$.

To give the certain members incentives to support the first best investment level, the exit payment must be equal to the investment costs – i.e. *full redemption*,[2] i.e.

$$X=I. \tag{4}$$

An alternative solution is to set the exit payment equal to the expected payoff.[3] This result is not surprising since, in principle, this is the way ownership is valued on the stock market or at a market for tradable delivery rights.

Now we turn to the uncertain members, who will support an investment if

$$s\left(\frac{V-X}{\alpha+s(1-\alpha)} + X\right) + (1-s)X \geq I \tag{5}$$

$$\Leftrightarrow \frac{s(V-X)}{\alpha+s(1-\alpha)} + X \geq I$$

If there is no exit payment $(X=0)$, the uncertain members will not support all profitable investments.[4] The reason for this is that the exogenous exit implies a transfer of payoff from uncertain to certain members.

Again, the uncertain members will have incentive to support the first best investment level, if the exit payment is equal to the expected pay-off[5] or equal to the investment costs

$$X=V. \tag{6}$$

We summarize these findings in Proposition 2.

Proposition 2: *in a heterogeneous cooperative, the horizon problem can be solved either by full equity redemption, i.e. setting the exit payment equal to the investment costs, or by setting the exit payment equal to the expected payoff from the investment.*

A closer look at the investment criteria for certain and uncertain members reveals an interesting finding.

A low exit payment means that the investment threshold for the certain members will be high.[6] Hence, the lower the exit payment, the more costly investments will be supported by the certain members. The reason is that the certain (continuing) members will pay less to the exiting members, thus obtaining a higher payment for themselves. Hence, if the certain members hold the majority, they have incentive to set a low exit payment, $X<V$. This gives the certain members incentive to support some unprofitable investments with $I>V$.

On the other hand, a high exit payment means that the investment threshold for the uncertain members will be high. The higher the exit payment, the more costly investments will be supported by the uncertain members. The reason is that a high exit payment implies a transfer from certain members to uncertain members, due to the exogenous exit. If the uncertain members hold the majority, they have incentive to set a high exit payment, $X>V$. This gives the uncertain members incentive to support unprofitable investments with $I>V$.

Hence, we have the following result:

Proposition 3: *in a heterogeneous cooperative, the majority will bias the exit payment to their own advantage. This may lead to overinvestment.*

This result contradicts the general view that cooperatives suffer from underinvestment due to horizon problems. The result is, however, not that surprising, if one follows the logic in Hansmann (1999) that the exiting members are exploited by the majority. This will give the majority incentive to increase the equity to obtain an even larger transfer of equity from the exiting members.

The result means that horizon problems cannot explain underinvestment in cooperatives. Instead, underinvestment must be explained by other problems, e.g. free rider problems, portfolio problems, or limited access to capital.

There are two important comments to be made about the result that the majority will distort the exit payment and induce overinvestment in cooperatives.

First, the overinvestment *(I>V)* is not individually rational for the minority members. The minority members are better off if they do not participate in these investments. However, investment decisions cannot be seen in isolation. A member can only avoid participating in an investment if he exits the cooperative – and this may impose greater losses than staying and participate in an unprofitable investment.

Second, a high exit payment (*X>V*) implies de-capitalization of the cooperative. Hence, our model suggests that cooperatives dominated by uncertain members (perhaps old members) will tend to de-capitalize. This is not surprising from a theoretical perspective, because de-capitalization is in fact a completely rational for these members – they have no incentive to give up equity to the continuing members. However, the de-capitalization is not in the interest of the management who will push for unallocated equity (low redemption) to ensure capital accumulation. This conflict is analyzed in Murray (1983a, 1983b).

6. CONCLUSION

The ability to raise sufficient capital is an important issue for cooperatives. This paper analyzes how compensation to members exiting the cooperative, affects the incentives to invest in a cooperative.

The literature points to a number of general problems that reduce the incentive to invest in a cooperative. One of these problems is the horizon problem, which states that cooperatives will underinvest, because the members evaluate investment according to a shorter horizon than the economic lifetime of the investment. The problem is that the members expect that some of the payoff will fall after they have exited the cooperative.

This paper shows that this view is incorrect. In a cooperative with homogenous members, the horizon problem only transforms the investment problem into a fair odds lottery with the same expected payoff, because the members do not know ex ante who will exit the cooperative before the payoff falls. The horizon problem can easily be solved in a cooperative with heterogeneous members by full redemption such that the members are compensated for their investment costs when they exit the cooperative. The majority will, however, bias the exit payment to their own advantage. This will lead to *overinvestment*.

This means that horizon problems cannot explain problems of underinvestment in cooperatives. Instead underinvestment must be explained by other factors, e.g. free rider problems. This suggests that the literature needs to distinguish more precisely between free rider and horizon problems.

NOTES

* This paper was written while the author was assistant professor at the Royal Veterinary and Agricultural University, Copenhagen.
[1] Using a survival rate to model the exit from the cooperative reflects that members can change their decision to exit the cooperative at any point in time. Therefore, it would be inappropriate to use a model imposing a fixed retirement date on the members.

[2] Proof: when $X=I$ the expected payment to the certain members is

$$\frac{V}{\alpha + s(1-\alpha)} + I\left(1 - \frac{1}{\alpha + s(1-\alpha)}\right) = \frac{V-I}{\alpha + s(1-\alpha)} + I .$$

Hence, the certain members will support the investment if and only if $V \geq I$.

[3] Proof: when X=V the certain members will get an expected payment of

$$\frac{V}{\alpha + s(1-\alpha)} + V\left(1 - \frac{1}{\alpha + s(1-\alpha)}\right) = V .$$

Hence, the certain members will support the investment only if $V \geq I$.

[4] Note that $\dfrac{s}{\alpha + s(1-\alpha)} = \dfrac{s}{s + \alpha(1-s)} < 1$.

[5] Proof: If X=V the uncertain members will get an $\dfrac{s(V-X)}{\alpha + s(1-\alpha)} + X = V \Leftrightarrow X = V$.

[6] The investment threshold defined by formula (2) will decrease as X increases because $\dfrac{1}{\alpha + s(1-\alpha)} < 1$.

REFERENCES

Borgen, S.O. 2004. "Rethinking Incentive Problems in Cooperative Organizations". *Journal of Socio-economics.* 33(4):383–393.

Cook, M. 1995. "The Future of U.S. Agricultural Cooperatives: A Neo-institutional Approach". *American Journal of Agricultural Economics* 77:1153–1159.

Diamond, D.W., and P.H. Dybvig. 1983. "Bank Runs, Deposit Insurance, and Liquidity". *Journal of Political Economy* 91:401–419.

Federation of Danish Cooperatives. 1998. *Cooperatives' Financing by means of Equity Capital, Structure of Models with Personally Allocated Equity Capital.* Federation of Danish Cooperatives Copenhagen.

Fulton, M. 2001. *New Generation Co-operative Development in Canada.* Centre for the Study of Co-operatives. University of Saskatchewan, Saskatoon, Saskatchewan, Canada.

Hansmann, H. 1999. "Cooperative Firms in Theory and Practice". *The Finnish Journal of Business Economics* 4:387–403.

Holmström, B. 1999. "Future of Cooperatives: A Corporate Perspective". *The Finnish Journal of Business Economics* 4:404–417.

Murray, G. 1983a. "Management Strategies for Corporate Control in British Agricultural Co-operatives – Part 1", *Agricultural Administration* 14:51–63.

Murray, G. 1983b. "Management Strategies for Corporate Control in British Agricultural Co-operatives – Part 2". *Agricultural Administration* 14:81–94.

Porter, P.K and G.W. Scully. 1987. "Economic Efficiency in Cooperatives". *Journal of Law and Economics* 30:489–512.

Rey, P. and J. Tirole. 2000. "Loyalty and Investment in Cooperatives". Working paper IDEI Toulouse.

Rey, P. and J. Tirole. 2001. "Financing Access in Cooperatives". Working paper IDEI Toulose.

CHAPTER 15

THE HORIZON PROBLEM IN AGRICULTURAL COOPERATIVES – ONLY IN THEORY?[*]

ERIK FAHLBECK

Dept. of Economics, Swedish University of Agricultural Sciences, Uppsala, Sweden

Abstract. Modern agricultural cooperatives need considerable amounts of capital. Theoretically the financing of cooperatives has been identified as one problem area for their future success. In part, the difficulties associated with raising capital are asserted to stem from heterogeneity among cooperative members, not the least of which is the so-called horizon problem. Here a number of potential heterogeneity dimensions are empirically investigated, in relation to financing and ownership of cooperatives. Almost all the hypotheses surrounding conflicting interests in relation to ownership and financing building on heterogeneity must be rejected. Reported answers provide no support for a horizon problem in agricultural cooperatives.

1. INTRODUCTION

Modern agribusiness and food processing industries are often portrayed as heading towards an increasingly diversified demand, a higher degree of product differentiation, and a much broader scale of parameters to consider, both in production technology and consumer preferences (for an enlightening discussion see Antle, 1999). In this development we see a high pace of change in the food chains. In the U.S. as well as in Europe we have recently witnessed a process of rapid structural change in agribusiness. Many cooperative researchers have discussed the consequences of this transformation for agricultural cooperatives (see e.g. Cook, 1995, Nilsson, 1998, Nilsson, 2001, and Chaddad and Cook, 2004). For a cooperative to be an active and successful partner in the future, capital is needed, e.g. to develop and communicate new products and new markets.

Over the years agricultural cooperatives have been highly successful in food processing, and in most developed economies cooperatives have substantial market shares in many relevant markets. However, recently traditional agricultural cooperatives have had problems keeping their market shares and adapting to new market conditions (see e.g. Nilsson, 1997).

255

K. Karantininis & J. Nilsson (eds.), Vertical Markets and Cooperative Hierarchies, 255–274.
© 2007 *Springer.*

One reason for the traditional cooperatives' financial problems is often hypothesized to be their ill-defined property rights and conflicting interests due to increasing heterogeneity of the members (see e.g. Cook and Iliopoulos, 2000). In this article this hypothesis is tested empirically. The article is organized as follows; some of the theoretically identified problems with agricultural cooperatives are summarized in Section 2, concluding with an identification of certain theoretical problems and related hypotheses. Section 3 describes the hypotheses tested and the data used. In Section 4 results are reported. In the last section these results are discussed and conclusions are drawn.

2. THEORETICAL FRAMEWORK AND PROBLEMS WITH COOPERATIVES

For some time, cooperatives have been analyzed in a neo-institutional framework (see e.g. Cook, 1995, Nilsson, 2001, Sykuta and Cook, 2001, and Srinivasan and Phansalkar, 2003). Within this framework agency problems and ill-defined property rights are often seen as potential obstacles for cooperative growth and progress. The development of this theoretical understanding of cooperatives builds partly on general observations of agency problems and property rights, as analyzed by e.g. Jensen and Meckling (1976) and Fama and Jensen (1983). One of the cornerstones of this theory is that the ownership of cooperatives is unclear, in the sense that the members don't have individual unrestricted ownership rights to the residual of the cooperative. Members are therefore supposed to have weak incentives to control the management.

Another aspect is that the individual ownership in traditional cooperatives is untradable. Hence, the members are not able to achieve the future income stream of investments in cooperatives. Compared to shareholding companies, cooperative owners therefore have restrictions in relation to the possibility to transfer as well as to exchange their ownership.

As discussed in e.g. Chaddad and Cook (2004) the ownership rights in traditional cooperatives still give the member the right to influence both how the cooperative is managed and how the result should be used. Even if these ownership rights may be seen as being weaker than the ownership in joint-stock companies, they are frequently seen as one important rational for cooperatives, i.e. although the profit interests of farmers' and the activities in the cooperative might appear to conflict, members will have trust in the cooperative since they have the right to information about and collective control over the cooperative business. As discussed below, the access to information and collective control does not, however, overcome conflicting interests among member groups.

Traditionally agricultural cooperatives have had two sources for raising capital – direct investments from its members or investments in the form of retained profits, i.e. unallocated capital. The modern development of new organizational forms among cooperatives, as discussed in e.g. Nilsson (2001) has resulted in a number of alternatives for the organization of ownership. Chaddad and Cook (2004) present an analytical framework and categorization with examples that can be seen as reactions to the claimed problem with fundraising.

The market conditions in modern agribusiness require large investments and organizational changes in many agricultural cooperatives, but as traditional cooperatives have unclear residual claims, problems may arise. Consistent with cooperative theory and agency theory, traditional cooperatives are prone to problems adopting to these changes, not the least the often discussed horizon problem (see e.g. Vitaliano, 1983, Porter and Scully, 1987, Cook, 1995, Nilsson, 2001, Sykuta and Cook, 2001, and Cook and Iliopoulos, 2000). Porter and Scully (1987, p. 495) define horizon problems as follows: "A horizon problem arises when an owner's claim on the net cash flow generated by an asset is shorter than the productive life of the asset."

Vitaliano (1983, p. 1082) states that horizon problems "...can be expected to give rise to additional differences in subgroup preferences among members, based on differences in such horizons, with a general tendency for them to favor investment decisions with short payoff horizons."

In his PhD thesis Condon (1990) discusses, in part, the same issues. Condon presents a broad discussion under the terms of "the investment portfolio problem," "the common-property problem" and the "residual-horizon problem". Based on traditional assumptions on economic behavior Condon illustrates some of the theoretically identified horizon problems in his model, i.e. members of cooperatives must see themselves as long-term members in order to find economic motives to accept certain investments in cooperatives. Owners of IOFs will not have the same problem.

Staatz (1989) discusses the horizon problem and stresses the link between the lack of secondary markets for cooperative membership and the horizon problem. Both Staatz, (1987, 1989) and Condon (1987) identify conditions that might reduce the horizon problem. Most of the arguments for less severe horizon problems are linked to the potential of secondary markets for membership. The main argument is that the value of members' fixed resources, e.g. farmland, might depend on the future income stream on investments in cooperatives, i.e. that the future value of cooperative investments may be capitalized in the value of farmland or other fixed resources among members. Another condition, identified by Condon (1987) and Staatz (1987), that may overcome the horizon problem is if membership can be transferred to the heirs within farm families.

Staatz (1987, p. 46) also points to one more factor that may reduce the horizon problem: "On the other hand, in smaller cooperatives, especially those in which the members have strong ties to one another (e.g., because of a common religion or set of social beliefs) and in which there is a strong tradition of family farming the horizon problem may pose fewer difficulties."

Staatz (1987, p. 46) summaries five characteristics that may increase the horizon problem:

1. The per-member capital invested in the cooperative is large;
2. The cooperative has a closed membership;
3. Few of the member firms are legally incorporated;
4. The intergenerational transfer of membership within families is prohibited, and
5. The cooperative has a large, diverse membership.

The potential horizon problem has been the focus of more current studies and its importance in relation to investments is stressed by e.g. Cook (1995, p. 1157), "The severity of this problem intensifies when considering investment in research and development, advertisement, and other intangible assets." Iliopoulos (1998) discusses the horizon problem in detail; his empirical analysis is claimed to support a number of related problems. In other words, modern cooperatives ought to have augmented difficulties with an increased need to raise funds for investments in order to develop the business in relation to changed market conditions.

As identified above the problem with investments can be expected to be more severe in cooperatives with a large share of elder members as compared to cooperatives with a more uniformly distributed age structure. Conflicting interests between elder and younger members have been recognized in empirical work (see e.g. Hakelius, 1999, who identified a number of differences in attitudes towards cooperatives in a comparison of young and old farmers in Sweden). Richards *et al.* (1998) investigated potential principal-agent related problems in cooperatives in Alberta, in Canada. In particular, they looked at members' opinions about what is important for the cooperative and their ideas of what board members find important for the cooperative. In these investigations age is one parameter that is significant in explaining differences in opinions among members. Education is also significant for a number of aspects.

The group of elder farmers becomes increasingly important to cooperatives. Elderly farmers have had a longer time to establish positions within the cooperatives, i.e. to establish a real influence; therefore their interests ought to dominate the cooperative. Long-term investments are e.g. not in the interest of farmers that will remain members only for a short time.

In this article the theoretically identified horizon problem is tested on a sample of Swedish farmers. Among Swedish farmers the median age in 2003 was 53 years (Statistics Sweden 2004a). The share of farmers at an age of 55 and over increased from 37 percent to almost 44 percent between 1996 and 2003 (Statistics Sweden 2004b and 2000), so prerequisites for conflicting interests based on age seem to exist.

From a theoretical point of view not just age but the degree of heterogeneity in general among members is seen as a potential problem for the cooperative. LeVay (1983, pp. 18–19) stresses the point that: "The membership cannot be assumed to be homogeneous, so that it may be made up by a number of conflicting groups, each wanting different solutions, making its interest as a whole difficult to discern."

Additionally, Staatz (1987, pp. 37–38) discusses the problem of heterogeneous membership, especially in relation to potential conflicts in pricing and cost allocation, and problems in raising capital. Such conflicting groups might be very costly for the cooperatives. In a game theory setting Staatz (1983) illustrates the fact that subgroups of cooperative members may have the incentive to leave a cooperative and form a new cooperative. If such subgroups choose to stay in the cooperative Staatz's model suggests that "bargaining over allocation of costs and benefits can be intensive and bruising" (Staatz, 1983, p. 1088).[1]

In most Western countries we have seen a development where the number of full-time farm entrepreneurs is declining at a higher rate than the decline in membership in cooperatives, i.e. the share of members with other income sources is increasing. Also, it can be expected that the degree of homogeneity within cooperatives have been reduced during recent years. As in other areas of society more diverse patterns of education levels should be common among members in cooperatives. Well-educated farmers can be expected to understand complex financial structures and new organizational needs better than less educated farmers.[2]

Market conditions and regional cultural differences might also be reasons for conflicting interests among cooperative members. Intensified competition ought to be followed by a stronger need to adapt, hence a stronger need for investments and organizational change. Using Sweden as an example, the EU membership in 1995 changed market conditions substantially. It seems fair to say that competition has been strongest in the Southern regions of Sweden, while the Northern regions didn't show as much change. This is certainly true in the area of agricultural support, where national support in combination with the implementation of environmental and rural development schemes under the CAP gave farmers in the North relatively stable conditions. For decades the level of governmental support has been higher in Northern parts of Sweden. Farmers in the North might therefore have a different view of a number of issues related to the organization of cooperatives, as compared to farmers in the South.

In many countries agricultural cooperatives face increased competition and this is very much the case in Sweden. Theoretically it is easy to see the arguments for new investments and the need to find new organizational forms. (See e.g. Nilsson 1997 for a discussion that to a large degree is still valid.) Differences in market competition in the Northern and Southern parts of Sweden might be reflected by members' opinions in relation to ownership issues in cooperatives.

Farmers' ages, education and geographical location are all possible reasons for conflicting interests. It can also be assumed that farmers who are members of several cooperatives have interests that differ from farmers who are members of only one or two cooperatives, since the first group e.g. ought to have a better understanding of needs for new organizational and financial structures. There may also be differences between genders although no theoretical basis for such discrepancies is identified in this article.

In Sweden the main theoretical arguments against the horizon problem, i.e. the condition that the value of the cooperative is capitalized in farmland or the value of the individual farm, and the opportunity to transfer membership over generations seem to have very limited relevance. Cooperative membership cannot be transferred and, as Condon notes (1987, p. 26), it is very difficult to empirically test the hypothesis that "...farmland values may fluctuate with relative performance of the local marketing or supply cooperative, ceteris paribus." Traditionally most farms have not been strongly specialized. More important for the value of the farm is the housing dimension, the distance to larger cities etc.[3] Neither do we have any support for the fact that the price of farmland varies with local cooperative performance.

The investigated Swedish cooperatives are relatively open for new members and in most cases they do not have high per-member capital investment, but the other conditions for serious problems identified by Staatz are certainly relevant. In combination with the low importance for the arguments relaxing the problem potential problems are expected.

With a more diverse membership we expect more conflicting interests, i.e. significant differences in attitudes in relation to ownership, property rights, residual claims and financing of the cooperatives. Based mainly on the theoretical arguments discussed above the following hypotheses can be identified:

- Younger farmers ought to be more interested in investing in cooperatives than their elderly counterparts.
- Younger farmers are expected to prefer high returns on investments, rather than low input prices and high payments for products sold.
- Young farmers are expected to feel that they have less influence over the cooperative business, as compared to elder farmers.
- Farmers in areas with less intense competition, i.e. the North in this case, are expected to be less interested in opening cooperatives to outsiders, as compared to farmers in areas with higher market pressure, i.e. the South.
- Better educated farmers are supposed to be more interested in new financial solutions and therefore are also more open to new ownership solutions.
- Farmers that are members of many cooperatives are supposed to be more interested in new financial solutions and are also more open to new ownership solutions.
- Farmers that are members of many cooperatives are supposed to pay more attention to ownership compared to farmers that are members in only one or two cooperatives.

If the horizon problem and heterogeneity among members is as important as theory indicates for the financial conditions of cooperatives, significant differences among members ought to be an important barrier for a successful development of agricultural cooperatives. It is therefore theoretically and empirically relevant to investigate potential conflicting interests among cooperative members, especially in relation to a growing need to finance new investments.

3. HYPOTHESIS TEST AND DATA

The null hypothesis, according to the theoretically identified horizon problem, is that significant differences exist between young and old farmers in relation to their interest in investing in cooperatives. Similar differences are supposed to exist also among the other member groups. The hypotheses are tested with a simple Chi-square test of independence between groups,

$$\chi^2 = \sum_{i=1}^{r} \sum_{j=1}^{c} \frac{\left(A_{ij} - E_{ij}\right)^2}{E_{ij}}$$

where A_{ij} = observed frequency in i^{th} row and j^{th} column and E_{ij} = expected frequency in i^{th} row and j^{th} column, r = number of rows and c = number of columns.

3.1 Data

A questionnaire was sent out to 300 farmers, 150 classified as old and 150 classified as young.[4] Age, education, geographic location, memberships in agricultural cooperatives and gender are investigated as potential reasons for heterogeneity among members in relation to ownership and financing of investments.

Out of 145 answers more than 20 were highly incomplete. On most questions there are about 120 useful answers,[5] which gives a response rate of 40 percent. Since the response rate is about the same in both groups the sample has a younger average than the total population.[6] None-respondents have not been investigated so there is no information indicating to which extent the sample is biased.

The respondents were asked a number of questions related to ownership, ownership rights, the financing of the cooperatives and organizational forms. Respondents were asked to consider 13 statements[7] and give their opinions on a six-grade Likert scale, from strongly agree to strongly disagree.[8] One group of statements related to the respondents' opinion about the importance of influence and ownership and about their beliefs concerning their role as owners and their influence over the cooperative. Another group of statements related to the respondents' opinion about the financing of cooperatives, cooperative ownership and investments in the cooperatives.

The Chi-square test of independence can be used to identify significant differences in how various groups answer such questions. Because of too few answers in some categories the six categories of answers were merged, i.e., strongly agree and agree as well as strongly disagree and disagree were merged into a four-grade scale. Even at this level some statements had few observations and, perhaps more relevant, some significant differences are explained by the fact that the groups differ only in the distribution of answers that agree or disagree more or less strongly, i.e. within both groups the general opinion is the same. For this reason, all potential differences were investigated also for only two categories of answers, such that all levels of agree and disagree where merged into a two-graded scale.

Answers were transformed into a scale from strongly agree = 1, to strongly disagree = 6. Average marks for the statements are reported in Table 1. Since the scale goes from 1 to 6 anything below 3.5 indicates that the average opinion is an agreement of some kind. Table 1 describes the average degree of agreement to the statements for the entire sample.

4. FINDINGS

According to the theoretically important horizon problem and previous Swedish (Hakelius, 1999) as well as North American (Richards, *et al.,* 1998) studies, it was expected to find most significant differences between old and young farmers. According to Hakelius' study the two groups differ on a number of issues, not the least with relation to economic aspects of cooperative business.

There is, however, almost no support at all for the null hypothesis that different age classes within the cooperative memberships have different opinions about ownership issues (see Table 2). At a 10 percent level of significance we can say that younger farmers think that the organizational form of their business partners is less important compared to what elder farmers think. It is, however, worth noting that, on average, young farmers also disagree with this statement.

Table 1. Average marks on the statements

Statement	Average point
Considered owner	3.25
Ownership is important	2.49
Believed influence	4.24
Influence is important	2.88
Overview of the business is important	2.22
Influence over profit disposal is important	2.61
Financing of cooperatives is OK	3.36
Unallocated capital is OK	3.19
Invest in cooperative is OK	1.93
Partly open ownership is OK	3.94
Fully open ownership is OK	4.36
High dividend important	3.99
Organizational form unimportant	3.47

The full questionnaire is presented in Appendix A.

Since the average age in the sample is lower than the population average we also changed the category of "old" farmers age 36 and older to those elder than 55, i.e. pensioners and those that reasonably soon will become pensioners, the idea being to see if such a categorization could give support to the horizon problem hypothesis. The only significant difference is that with these new categories, older farmers agreed significantly more with the statement that the financing of cooperatives works satisfactorily (a 5 percent level). On the other hand there is no significant difference in the statement concerning the organizational form and trading partners in this case. So even if we focus on the elder farmers and define "old" as 55 years or more, we find no support for the horizon problem hypothesis.

Highly educated farmers are supposed to have a better understanding of the need for new organizational forms of ownership and new financial solutions than less educated farmers. With an increasing discrepancy in educational level significant differences can be expected also on other issues related to the complex financial needs.

Table 2. Chi-square test of independence between young and old farmers

Statement	P value for four categories	P value for two categories
Considered owner	0.68	0.67
Ownership is important	0.79	0.43
Believed influence	0.17	0.48
Influence is important	0.40	0.25
Overview of the business is important	(0.76)	(0.54)
Influence over profit disposal is important	0.77	0.84
Financing of cooperatives is OK	0.87	0.67
Unallocated capital is OK	0.73	0.32
Invest in cooperative is OK	(0.92)	0.49
Partly open ownership is OK	0.57	0.80
Fully open ownership is OK	0.01*	0.71
High divided important	0.40	0.52
Organizational form unimportant	0.22	0.07**

* Significant on a 5 percent level   ** Significant on a 10 percent level
Numbers in parentheses have too few observations to be fully reliable, i.e. the spread of answers is too low to give reliable interpretations.
Young farmers are < 36 years old.

No support for the hypothesis of heterogeneity in members' opinions about ownership can be found (see Table 3). The significant differences in relation to the statements if they considered themselves as owners and the statement that outsiders should be offered ownership to a limited part of the cooperative only relates to differences in how strongly the minorities agree with each statement. When comparing the two merged categories "agree" and "disagree", answers within the two groups are instead very homogeneous in both cases and a majority disagrees with the statements. The only existing significant difference is in relation to the organizational form of trading partners where members with higher education disagree to a higher extent, i.e. well educated members think that the organizational form of their trading partners is more important than do members with a lower level of education.

Farmers that are members in many cooperatives ought to be more aware of the requirements for future investments and new financial needs, as compared to farmers that are members in only one or two cooperatives. Also, with relation to other aspects of cooperatives those that are members of many cooperatives can be expected to pay more attention to the cooperative organizational form.

Table 3. Chi-square test of independence between farmers with "high" and "low" level of education

Statement	P value for four categories	P value for two categories
Considered owner	0.04*	0.69
Ownership is important	0.23	0.16
Believed influence	0.61	0.54
Influence is important	0.27	0.30
Overview of the business is important	(0.32)	(0.44)
Influence over profit disposal is important	(0.84)	(0.47)
Financing of cooperatives is OK	0.67	0.23
Unallocated capital is OK	0.44	0.83
Invest in cooperative is OK	(0.64)	(0.90)
Partly open ownership is OK	0.09**	0.88
Fully open ownership is OK	(0.04*)	0.21
High dividend important	(0.08**)	0.28
Organizational form unimportant	0.37	0.08**

* Significant on a 5 percent level   ** Significant on a 10 percent level
Numbers in parentheses have too few observations to be fully reliable, i.e. the spread of answers is too low to give reliable interpretations.

The pattern is the same; almost no significant differences are found (see Table 4). The only question where a clear difference exists is in the statement that it is more important to have higher dividends on investments in the cooperative than to have high prices for sold raw material and low prices on inputs. Farmers that are members in many cooperatives strongly disagree to this statement; the average mark is 4.52, while those that are members of only few cooperatives are rather neutral to the statement, with an average of 3.42.

Increased competition ought to make farmers more sensitive to coping with new investment needs and financial constraints. A similar argument may be that farmers in areas where governmental support has been a fundamental part of the income for decades are less responsive to such needs. Even if the Swedish market used to be protected differences between Northern and Southern parts exist, both in relation to competition after the EU accession and in relation to the amount of public support.

Here the only statement with significant differences is if the members perceive themselves as owners to the cooperative(s) where they are member(s) (see Table 5). Farmers in the North, where public support is higher and the competition may be lower, disagree to this statement to a higher extent than their colleges in the South. Southern farmers have an average mark of 3.09, while farmers in the North on average disagree slightly, 3.60. In relation to financial aspects and the option to open the ownership of cooperatives to outsiders no difference exists.

Table 4. *Chi-square test of independence between farmers that are members in "many" agricultural cooperatives and those that are members in "few"*

Statement	P value for four categories	P value for two categories
Considered owner	0.83	0.51
Ownership is important	0.16	0.02
Believed influence	0.99	0.96
Influence is important	0.25	0.20
Overview of the business is important	(0.20)	(0.17)
Influence over profit disposal is important	(0.35)	0.71
Financing of cooperatives is OK	0.12	0.42
Unallocated capital is OK	0.72	0.54
Invest in cooperative is OK	(0.75)	(0.46)
Partly open ownership is OK	0.86	0.88
Fully open ownership is OK	0.68	0.75
High dividend important	0.00*	0.00*
Organizational form unimportant	0.02*	0.79

* Significant on a 5 percent level   ** Significant on a 10 percent level
Numbers in parentheses have too few observations to be fully reliable, i.e. the spread of answers is too low to give reliable interpretations.

Table 5. *Chi-square test of independence between "Southern" and "Northern" farmers*

Statement	P value for four categories	P value for two categories
Considered owner	0.07**	0.01*
Ownership is important	(0.24)	0.44
Believed influence	0.77	0.37
Influence is important	(0.45)	0.90
Overview of the business is important	(0.19)	(0.07)
Influence over profit disposal is important	0.79	0.87
Financing of cooperatives is OK	0.23	0.23
Unallocated capital is OK	0.23	0.26
Invest in cooperative is OK	(0.28)	(0.07)
Partly open ownership is OK	0.81	0.88
Fully open ownership is OK	(0.87)	0.52
High dividend important	(0.54)	0.15
Organizational form unimportant	0.68	0.48

* Significant on a 5 percent level   ** Significant on a 10 percent level
Numbers in parentheses have too few observations to be fully reliable, i.e. the spread of answers is too low to give reliable interpretations.

Even if there is no identified theoretical basis for expecting significant differences between male and female farmers it is interesting to investigate such potential disparities, not the least because the share of female farmers is increasing and that divergences between genders exist in many other areas. The results are presented in Table 6.

Table 6. *Chi-square test of independence between "male" and "female" farmers*

Statement	P value for four categories	P value for two categories
Considered owner	0.86	0.68
Ownership is important	0.18	0.11
Believed influence	0.23	0.37
Influence is important	0.10**	0.02*
Overview of the business is important	(0.15)	0.22
Influence over profit disposal is important	0.56	0.83
Financing of cooperatives is OK	0.41	0.55
Unallocated capital is OK	0.17	0.37
Invest in cooperative is OK	(0.47)	0.63
Partly open ownership is OK	0.09**	0.01*
Fully open ownership is OK	0.45	0.93
High dividend important	0.80	0.58
Organizational form unimportant	0.44	0.35

* Significant on a 5 percent level　　** Significant on a 10 percent level
Numbers in parentheses have too few observations to be fully reliable, i.e. the spread of answers is too low to give reliable interpretations.

The general pattern is the same as above; there are almost no significant differences between male and female members as concerns ownership issues. Female members do, however, agree to the statement that it is very important to have the feeling that they can influence the decisions of the cooperative board. With this in mind it might be surprising to find that females, on the other hand, disagree less to the statement that it is a good idea to give outsiders ownership to parts of the cooperative business. On the statement that it would be good to accept full ownership by non-farmers there is, however, no significant difference.

5. ANALYSES AND DISCUSSION

Cooperative theory identifies a number of problems in relation to increased membership heterogeneity. In a time where the capital need ought to be large for many agricultural cooperatives the most obvious theoretical problem in this aspect is the horizon problem. Even if Swedish cooperatives don't qualify for all Staatz five conditions for serious horizon problems there certainly exist theoretical arguments for existing problems.

Based on the empirical findings in this study, one may be inclined to reject the hypotheses concerning significant differences between various member groups, thereby also rejecting the potential horizon problems and other principal agent problems based on conflicting interest among cooperative members. Before drawing such conclusions other explanations to the findings must, however, be considered.

One possible explanation to the lack of significant differences is that we might loose specific and relevant information when we treat all agricultural cooperatives in the sample equal. Disparities might exist if we focus on certain cooperatives instead of all cooperatives, not the least could there be differences between various kinds of cooperatives.

In order to check for such issues we investigated various types of cooperatives. "Forestry-members" were compared to "non-forestry-members", "meat-members" to "non- meat-members" and "grain and input-members"[9] to "non-grain and input-members".

Also here very few significant differences are found except for the comparison between members in forestry cooperatives and members in non-forestry cooperatives. Results are therefore only reported from that comparison (see Table 7).

Members of forestry cooperatives agree with the statement on experienced ownership – that it is important to perceive oneself as an owner and to have the feeling that they [members] can influence the board's decisions to a higher degree than other cooperative members. In relation to the statement of whether they feel they can influence the board's decision, the forestry members disagree to a lower extent than farmers who are members of other cooperatives. Farmers in forestry cooperatives also agree to a higher extent with the statement that the financing of cooperatives works well, while they disagree to a higher extent with the statement that it does not matter with whom they are trading.

An interesting observation is that no differences in statements directly related to open ownership are found. At the same time it seems as if forestry farmers perceive themselves as cooperative members to a higher extent and in a more conventional sense than members in other cooperatives. In their answers they seem to agree with traditional cooperative values to a higher degree than members in other cooperatives.

Members in forestry cooperatives must have a long-term perspective on their business. Issues related to horizon problems ought to be most relevant for these cooperatives, but the sample indicates no such problems. Instead, answers indicate that forestry members see themselves in more traditional cooperative terms than members of other cooperatives.

When comparing other member categories with one another very few significant differences are found. Both members of meat cooperatives and members of grain and input cooperatives disagree to a higher degree with the statement that it is more important to get high dividends, rather than high prices of products sold to and low prices on inputs bought from the cooperative. Apart from this, no significant differences are found for members in grain and input cooperatives, slaughter cooperatives or bank cooperatives.[10] Looking at the findings when comparing different cooperatives, it is obvious that there is no support for conflicting interests among various groups.

Table 7. Chi-square of independence between members in forestry cooperatives and farmers that are not members of such cooperatives

Statement	P value for four categories	P value for two categories
Considered owner	0.16	0.06**
Ownership is important	(0.03)	0.01*
Believed influence	0.04*	0.00*
Influence is important	0.13	0.02*
Overview of the business is important	(0.11)	(0.25)
Influence over profit disposal is important	(0.08)	0.19
Financing of cooperatives is OK	0.07**	0.03*
Unallocated capital is OK	0.56	0.88
Invest in cooperative is OK	(0.57)	(0.62)
Partly open ownership is OK	0.73	0.31
Fully open ownership is OK	0.59	0.42
High dividend important	0.49	0.30
Organizational form unimportant	0.01*	0.03*

* Significant on a 5 percent level   ** Significant on a 10 percent level
Numbers in parentheses have too few observations to be fully reliable, i.e. the spread of answers is too low to give reliable interpretations.

Another explanation for the lack of the theoretically motivated differences might be that the respondents did not understand the questions and therefore gave non-representative answers. With the aim of investigating this potential explanation correlation between answers to the statements were calculated, in order to see if there is any support for the suggestion that respondents answered inconsistently. A correlation matrix reporting the significant correlations is presented in Appendix B.

Positive correlations can be expected between questions 6 to 11. If the respondents see themselves as owners and having influence, they can also be expected to think that these aspects are important and that having full insight into the business is important. Respondents that view themselves as owners and having influence also should agree to the statement that the present cooperative financial solutions are good and those who think the financial models are good can be expected to agree to the statement that the amount of unallocated capital is satisfactory.

Negative correlations can be expected between statements 6 to 11 and 14 and 15 respectively. If respondents think that influence and ownership is important then it is logical that they also disagree with the statements concerning the widening of cooperative ownership. Negative correlations can also be expected between statements 6 to 11 and statement 18. On the other hand, those who agree with the statement that cooperatives should have outsiders as co-owners can also be expected to agree with the statement that the organizational form of the trading partners is unimportant, i.e., we ought to have a positive correlation between 14 and 18 and 15 and 18 respectively.

As can be seen in Appendix B, most of the significant correlations have the expected sign and there is no support for the hypothesis that respondents systematically give inconsistent answers.

A third explanation for the unexpected findings may be that the investigated parameters are not relevant in relation to the statements included. OLS regressions, in which the answer to each statement depends on the parameters, are presented in Appendix C. Since these regressions have low explanatory power and most parameters are insignificant, this may be partially true. In no case is the R^2 higher than 12 percent, and only a few parameters are significant in a very limited number of cases. Significant parameters are those that could be expected from the Chi-square tests. However, compared to Richards, *et al.,* 1998, the explanatory powers of these regressions are not especially low.

Some other findings can also be reported. Even if the investigation was not set up in order to identify farmers' opinions towards such issues as non-member ownership, or low input prices and high prices on products sold vs. high dividend, it is shown that in many cases members in forestry cooperatives hold traditional cooperative attitudes and they do not seem to experience a need for change.

We also see that members in meat cooperatives and grain and input cooperatives disagree to the statement that it is more important with dividends than with good prices to a significantly higher degree than those that are not members in such cooperatives. Members in cooperatives for meat, and grains and inputs, support the traditional view that the boards of cooperatives feel pressure from members to focus on prices for inputs and raw materials, i.e., there is a tendency to under-finance the cooperative.

Maybe Staatz' argument (1987, p. 46) that "...strong ties to one another..." among members reduce the horizon problem is relevant to the Swedish case. Even if Hakelius (1999) found a number of conflicting ideas between young and old farmers it might still be the case that there exists a relatively strong common ground among Swedish farmers. For a long period the Federation of Swedish Farmers exhibited a strong dominance in areas such as political influence, negotiations with the government, etc. During this period it seems reasonable that the "social beliefs" within the farming community were relatively homogeneous. Even if conditions in this area have changed a lot during the past 10 years the Swedish farming community may still be relatively homogeneous in this respect.

After investigating various alternative explanations to the findings, the overall conclusion from this investigation is that there is no empirical support for conflicting interests among various member categories in relation to their opinions on ownership and financial issues in cooperatives. The theoretically identified horizon problem seems in reality to be nonexistent. These conclusions seem to be true at least for Swedish agricultural cooperatives.

270 E. FAHLBECK

NOTES

* The author wants to express his gratitude to Dr. Karin Hakelius for collaboration in a previous project, where the present questionnaire was used, as well as to the participants at the conference, where this paper was presented.

[1] Mainly for reasons of imperfect information Staatz says that in reality such problems "…may not be so harsh" (Staatz, 1983, p. 1088).

[2] This is at least what teachers' and researchers at universities can hope for.

[3] This hypothesis will not be tested in this study. A limited number of estate agents were contacted, but none offered any relevance to this hypothesis in Sweden.

[4] In this study the term 'young' was defined as a farmer being registered within the youth organization of the Federation of Swedish Farmers. "Youth" in this context is a farmer no more than 35 years old.

[5] We had between 118 and 122 useful answers and in most cases more than 120 on the statements.

[6] The average age in the sample is 45 years old compared to a median in the total population of 53 years (Statistics Sweden 2004a).

[7] The complete list of statements is found in Appendix A.

[8] The possible answers were: strongly agree, agree, slightly agree, slightly disagree, disagree and strongly disagree.

[9] Members of Svenska Lantmännen (Swedish Farmers' Supply and Crop Marketing Association). This cooperative mainly deals with grain marketing and supplying members with farm inputs.

[10] The number of dairy members is too low for interesting statistical analysis, particularly since most dairy members who responded are young.

REFERENCES

Antle, J.M. 1999. "The New Economics of Agriculture." *American Journal of Agricultural Economics*, 83:993–1010.

Chaddad, F.R., and M.L. Cook. 2004. "Understanding New Cooperative Models: An Ownership-Control Rights Typology." *Review of Agricultural Economics*, September 2004, 26 (3):348–360.

Condon, A.M. 1990. "Property Rights and the Investment Behavior of U.S. Agricultural Cooperatives". PhD dissertation, Department of Agricultural and Applied Economics, Virginia Polytechnic Institute and State University.

___. 1987. "The Methodology and Requirements of a Theory of Modern Cooperative Enterprise," in J. S. Royer, ed *Cooperative Theory: New Approaches*, Washington DC: U.S. Department of Agriculture, ACS Service report 18, July 1987.

Cook, M.L., 1995. "The Future of U.S. Agricultural Cooperatives: A Neo-Institutional Approach," *American Journal of Agricultural Economics*, 77:1153–1159.

___. and C. Iliopoulos. 2000. "Ill-Defined Property Rights in Collective Action: The Case with US Agricultural Cooperatives," in C. Ménard, ed. *Institutions, Contracts and Organizations*, Edward Elgar, Cheltenham, U.K., 335–348.

Fama, E.,E., and M.C. Jensen. 1983. "Agency Problems and Residual Claims", *Journal of Law and Economics*, XXVI:327–349.

Hakelius, K. 1999. "Farmer Cooperatives in the 21th Century; Young and Old Farmers in Sweden". *Journal of Rural Cooperation*; 27(1):31–54.

Iliopoulos, C. 1998. "Study of the Property Rights Constraints in US Agricultural Cooperatives: Theory and Evidence". Ph.D. Dissertation, University of Missouri - Columbia.

Jensen, M.C., and W.H. Meckling. 1976. Theory of the Firm: Managerial Behavior, Agency Costs, and Ownership Structure, *Journal of Financial Economics*, 15(2):305–60.

LeVay, C. 1983. Agricultural Cooperative Theory: A Review. *Journal of Agricultural Economics*, XXXIV(1):1–44.

Nilsson, J. 1997. Inertia in Cooperative Remodelling. *Journal of Cooperatives*, 12:62–73.

__. 2001. "Organizational Principles for Co-operative Firms". *Scandinavian Journal of Management*, 17:329–356.

__. 1998. "The Emergence of New Organizational Models of Agricultural Cooperatives", *Swedish Journal of Agricultural Research*, 28:39–47.

Porter, P.K. and G.W. Scully. 1987. "Economic Efficiency in Cooperatives", *Journal of Law and Economics*, 30:489–512.

Richards, T.J., K.K. Klein, and A. Walburger. 1998, "Principal-Agent Relationships in Agricultural Cooperatives: An Empirical Analysis from Rural Alberta", *Journal of Cooperatives*, 13:21–34.

Srinivasan, R. and S.J. Phansalkar. 2003. "Residual Claims in Cooperatives: Design Issues". *Annals of Public and Cooperative Economics*, 74(3):365–395.

Staatz, J.M. 1989. *Farmer Cooperative Theory: Recent Developments*, Washington D.C: U.S. Department of Agriculture, ACS Research Report No. 84, June.

__. 1983. "The Cooperative as a Coalition: A Game-Theoretic Approach". *American Journal of Agricultural Economics*, 65:1084–1089.

__. 1987. "The Structural Characteristics of Farmer Cooperatives and their Behavioral Consequences", in J. S. Royer, ed. *Cooperative Theory: New Approaches*, Washington DC: U.S. Department of Agriculture, ACS Service report 18, July 1987.

Statistics Sweden. 2004a. JO 34 SM 0401.

__. 2000. Yearbook of Agricultural Statistics, Örebro.

__. 2004b. Yearbook of Agricultural Statistics, Örebro.

Sykuta, M.E., and M.L. Cook. 2001. "A New Institutional Economics Approach to Contracts and Cooperatives". *American Journal of Agricultural Economics*; 83:1271–1277.

Vitaliano, P. 1983. "Cooperative Enterprise: An Alternative Conceptual Basis for Analyzing a Complex Institution". *American Journal of Agricultural Economics*, 65:1078–1083.

APPENDIX A. QUESTIONNAIRE

To each statement the respondent marked within the following categories: Strongly agree, agree, agree slightly, slightly disagree, disagree, strongly disagree. The in the questionnaire are:

2. I consider myself as an owner to the agricultural cooperatives where I am a member.
3. It is important for me that I consider myself as an owner to the cooperatives where I am a member.
4. I believe that I can influence the decisions taken by the boards in the cooperatives where I am a member.
5. It is conclusive for my engagement in the agricultural cooperatives that I think that I can influence the decisions of the board.
6. It is important for me that I can take in the whole picture of what happens in the agricultural cooperatives.
7. It is conclusive for my engagement in the agricultural cooperatives that I get an influence over the disposal of the profit.
8. In my opinion the financing of the agricultural cooperatives works fine.
9. In my opinion the member's individual capital should increase and the unallocated capital should be reduced.
10. For me it is more important to invest money into my own business compared to putting investing them agricultural cooperatives.
11. In my opinion it is a good idea to open ownership also to outsiders to those parts of the agricultural cooperatives that are not core activities.
12. In my opinion it is a good idea that outsiders can own parts of all cooperative businesses.
13. To me it is more important to get a dividend on money that I have invested in cooperatives than that I get a high price for products sold and low price for products bought.
14. I am indifferent to the organizational form of my business partners.

APPENDIX B. CORRELATIONS BETWEEN ANSWERS AND STATEMENTS

	6	7	8	9	10	11	12	13	14	15	16
6	0.373*										
7											
8	0.588*	0.327*									
9		0.603*	0.325*								
10		0.585*	0.427*	0.505*							
11	0.508*			0.425*	0.608*						
12	0.357*	0.261*	0.417*								
13											
14											
15		-0.281*					-0.268*				
16		-0.321*		-0.213**	-0.248*		-0.266*			0.693*	
17							0.191**				
18	-0.297*	-0.338*	-0.246*			-0.222**	-0.227**		0.224**	0.316*	0.231**

* Significant at a 1% level
** Significant at a 5% level

APPENDIX C. OLS-REGRESSIONS

Question	Regression equation
6 (7/2.4)	= 2.28 + 0.0411 county - 0.122 sex + 0.147 educ + 0.0268 membership + 0.00179 age (0.003*) (0.024**) (0.670) (0.108) (0.732) (0.833)
7 (74/2.8)	= 4.45 - 0.0003 county - 0.567 sex - 0.0706 educ - 0.137 membership - 0.0153 age (0.000*) (0.987) (0.061) (0.459) (0.098) (0.087)
8 (2.2/0.0)	= 3.83 + 0.0222 county - 0.185 sex + 0.0262 educ + 0.0642 membership + 0.00238 age (0.000*) (0.251) (0.547) (0.788) (0.447) (0.794)
9 (4.4/0.0)	= 3.98 - 0.0137 county - 0.557 sex - 0.041 educ - 0.0970 membership + 0.00270 age (0.000*) (0.517) (0.099) (0.699) (0.294) (0.787)
10 (11.9/7.4)	3.85 + 0.0102 county - 0.646 sex - 0.0381 educ - 0.116 membership - 0.0108 age (0.000*) (0.462) (0.004*) (0.585) (0.057) (0.099)
11 (10.1/5.6)	= 4.12 + 0.0182 county - 0.387 sex - 0.147 educ - 0.0268 membership - 0.0177 age (0.000*) (0.263) (0.144) (00.74) (0.705) (0.025)
12 (1.0/0.0)	= 3.71 - 0.0038 county - 0.032 sex + 0.0131 educ + 0.0284 membership - 0.00748 age (0.000*) (0.836) (0.913) (0.888) (0.724) (0.388)
13 (3.7/0.0)	3.57 - 0.0197 county + 0.000 sex - 0.0196 educ + 0.0984 membership - 0.0102 age (0.000*) (0.311) (1.000) (0.843) (0.251) (0.273)
14 (6.3/1.6)	= 2.65 - 0.0242 county + 0.115 sex - 0.0198 educ - 0.0071 membership - 0.0133 age (0.000*) (0.092) (0.612) (0.785) (0.909) (0.050)
15 (4.3/0.0)	= 5.21 + 0.0032 county - 0.689 sex - 0.033 educ + 0.0226 membership - 0.0085 age (0.000*) (0.886) (0.056) (0.771) (0.817) (0.416)
16 (1.7/0.0)	= 4.30 - 0.0104 county + 0.191 sex - 0.058 educ + 0.0851 membership - 0.0049 age (0.000*) (0.642) (0.592) (0.611) (0.378) (0.640)
17 (10.2/5.6)	= 3.07 + 0.0187 county - 0.111 sex + 0.024 educ + 0.292 membership - 0.00131 age (0.001*) (0.384) (0.744) (0.827) (0.002**) (0.895)
18 (9.5/4.9)	= 1.02 - 0.0057 county + 0.675 sex + 0.123 educ + 0.121 membership + 0.0218 age (0.243) (0.785) (0.045**) (0.247) (0.182) (0.028**)

The two numbers under each question is the R^2 and the adjusted R^2 respectively. The other figures in the parentheses are P-values for each parameter.
* Significant at a 1 % level.
** Significant at a 5 % level.

CHAPTER 16

PERFORMANCE OF COOPERATIVES AND INVESTOR-OWNED FIRMS: THE CASE OF THE GREEK DAIRY INDUSTRY*

OURANIA NOTTA

Dept. of Farm Management,
Technological Educational Institute of Thessaloniki, Thessaloniki, Greece

ASPASSIA VLACHVEI

Dept. of International Trade,
Technological Educational Institute of West Macedonia, Kastoria, Greece

Abstract. This paper examines factors that might affect performance of cooperatives and investor-owned firms (IOFs). The empirical work tests whether significant profitability differences between the two groups exist, in the case of the Greek dairy industry, over the period 1990–2001. The relevant descriptive statistics show that IOFs are more profitable, while results suggest that profitability differences between cooperatives and IOFs can be attributed mainly to the greater effectiveness of IOFs' capital structure determinants and market share.

1. INTRODUCTION

The increasing competition in many sectors of most modern economies forced the cooperatives to improve their performance in order to secure their survival. Both cooperatives and investor-owned firms (IOFs) coexist and compete for market share. One of the major goals in current cooperative research is to identify the sources and determinants of performance differences between cooperative and investor-owned firms. There are many ways one can view the performance differences between a cooperative and an IOF.

Some economists (according to Schrader *et al.*, 1985) feel that there are significant differences between the goals of the two forms of organization and these differences in goals caused differences in business strategies. An IOF's objective is the maximization of the value of the firm, which means that firm will try to maximize

K. Karantininis & J. Nilsson (eds.), Vertical Markets and Cooperative Hierarchies, 275–285.
© 2007 *Springer.*

the profitability at a given risk level (Copeland and Weston, 1983). Cooperatives, on the other hand, are expected to have a lower rate of return than IOFs, since profit maximization is not their primary aim.

Other economists believe that it is more useful to view the differences among these two business entities in terms of property rights. Thus, "the residual claimants to the income generated by the cooperative are its users, whereas in an IOF the capital owners are the residual claimants" (Fulton, 1995). According to this theory, this fundamental difference creates several problems for the cooperative resulting from the conflict over residual claims: the horizon problem, the non-transferability and the control problem (Oustapassidis *et al.*, 1998).

Although profit maximization is not the cooperatives' primary goal and differences concerning property rights do exist between cooperatives and IOFs, in the long run it is crucial for cooperatives to be competitive and successful in order to survive within markets where the intensity of competition is steadily increasing. The factors underlie a firm's sustainable competitive advantage and hence profitability is of particular interest. Since competitiveness is the sustained ability to profitably gain and maintain market share (Martin *et al.*, 1991), one approach to evaluate the issue of cooperative competitiveness is to investigate the relationship between profitability, market share and capital constraints.

The purpose of this work is to contribute to this ongoing discussion by studying the factors that can increase the performance of cooperatives and IOFs in a particular market – the Greek dairy sector. More specifically, in this paper we develop a model of firm profitability and test the significance of various factors affecting profitability and whether there are differences in the way these factors affect cooperatives and IOFs, using a panel data econometric analysis.

The paper is organized as follows. In Section 2 a review of other empirical studies of cooperatives relative to the question under investigation is presented. In Section 3 a model of firm performance is developed. Data and variable definitions are presented in Section 4, while the results for both IOFs and cooperatives are presented in Section 5, and conclusions in Section 6.

2. PERFORMANCE OF COOPERATIVES AND INVESTOR-OWNED FIRMS

As noted in a comprehensive review by Sexton and Iskow (1993), there are two categories of empirical studies regarding the performance of cooperatives – those based on concepts of economic efficiency and those involving financial ratios.

Porter and Scully (1987) utilized a production function approach to conclude that dairy cooperatives were less efficient than the dairy IOFs. Sexton *et al.* (1989) tested the allocative efficiency of cotton ginning cooperatives and rejected the argument that cooperatives tend to under-utilize capital. Akridge and Hertel (1992) used a multiproduct variable cost function to compare the efficiency of cooperative and investor-oriented grain and farm supply firms. Their results suggest that cooperatives are no less efficient in a variable cost sense than their investor-oriented counterparts. Sexton and Iskow (1993) noted that these studies failed to consider the ancillary services often provided by cooperatives (field services, market information, lobbying services etc.) which will increase a cooperative's production costs, leading to the incorrect conclusion that cooperatives are inefficient. They found that no credible evidence exists to support the proposition that cooperatives are inefficient relative to investor-owned businesses. Katz (1997) examined the influence of owners on strategies employed to achieve competitive advantage in owner-influenced IOFs, cooperatives and manager-controlled IOFs. The evidence indicates that firm performance is affected by the influence owners have over the strategies available to the firm.

Another stand of the cooperative performance literature focuses on financial ratios concepts. Schrader *et al.* (1985) found that large diversified agribusiness IOFs had significantly higher rates of return on assets, significant less leverage, and were more efficient than comparable cooperatives. Venieris (1989) tested whether statistically significant differences exist in the financial structure, as measured by financial ratios, between cooperatives and IOFs within the Greek wine industry. The main conclusion of the paper is that agricultural cooperatives and IOFs differ significantly in terms of liquidity, in the percentage of total capital employed used to finance fixed assets, in gearing and in total profitability. Lerman and Parliament (1990) determined that in both the fruit and vegetable processing and dairy sectors, cooperatives and IOFs were leveraged similarly and generated similar rates of return to equity. Both the liquidity and asset efficiency of fruit and vegetable processing IOFs were greater than that of cooperatives, but these results were reversed in the dairy sector. Parliament, Lerman and Fulton (1990) compared the financial performance among the dairy cooperatives and investor-owned dairy firms. In their sample, the cooperatives performed significantly better than the IOFs when compared by leverage, liquidity, asset turnover, and coverage ratios, while the rate of return to equity was not found to be significantly different. They also reviewed a broad range of non-market benefits that cooperatives can provide to their members. Sexton and Iskow (1993) pointed out that a cooperative could be less profitable than an IOF and still desirable to a member, so long as the member's discounted stream of returns from the cooperative were greater than those from marketing the commodity directly or through an IOF.

Oustapassidis and Notta (1997) compared the profitability among the dairy co-operatives and investor-owned Greek dairy firms. Their results show that cooperatives were not able to apply effectively competitive strategies such as advertising and diversification, in contrast to IOFs. Oustapassidis *et al.* (1998) examined the determinants of the annual growth and tested whether significant differences between IOFs and cooperatives exist. Their results showed that both advertising and diversification strategies were important determinants for IOF growth, while the cooperative growth depends on capital structure and intensity and these organizations do not effectively apply competitive strategies.

Hardesty and Salgia (2004) compared the financial ratios for profitability, liquidity, leverage and asset efficiency in four US sectors – dairy, farm supplies, fruits and vegetables, and grain. Cooperatives demonstrated lower rates of asset efficiency, except in the dairy sector. Cooperatives in all four sectors were less leveraged, while results regarding the relative profitability and liquidity of cooperatives were not conclusive.

As discussed above, there are numerous behavioral differences between cooperatives and IOFs that are attributable to the cooperative principles. The majority of the
studies compare financial characteristics – particularly profitability, capital structure,
liquidity and asset efficiency indices between cooperatives and IOFs. There is a very
limited work (Ananiadis et al., 2003; Oustapassidis and Notta, 1997) that used a
comprehensive analysis to test the effects of financial, behavioral and other structural variables on both the cooperative and IOF profitability.

In the following section we develop a model of firm profitability, based on Industrial Organization literature, to investigate which are the main determinants
affecting performance of cooperatives and IOFs, in the case of a manufacturing
industry – the Greek dairy industry, by applying modern econometric techniques.

3. SPECIFICATION OF THE PROFIT MODEL

Following the relevant Industrial Economics literature (Martin, 1993) an expression
for firm level price-average cost margin equation is given below:

$$\frac{pq_i - wL_i - \rho K_i}{K_i} = \frac{s_i}{\varepsilon_{QP}} \frac{pq_i}{K_i} \qquad (1)$$

The left-hand term is equal to the net profits to total assets ratio. The term on the
right is equal to the market share s_i, the ratio of the firm's sales (pq_i) over its total
assets (K_i) and the price elasticity of demand (e_{QP}). Data for price elasticity of
demand are not easily available but the empirical studies (Martin, 1993) ordinarily
use other variables to express the elasticity of demand. The elasticity of demand in a
competitive market is determined mainly by competitive strategies such as advertising intensity, R&D, market channels and other strategies. Given that the above are
expensive strategies depending on the availability of capital it is reasonable to
express the elasticity of demand as a function of the capital structure determinants.

Thus we include in the model a number of financial indices describing the capital
structure along with the two variables appeared in (1) (e.g. Scherer and Ross, 1990;
Martin, 1993 and 1994). Thus the specified empirical model is

$$NRT = a_0 + a_1 MS + a_2 SK + a_3 LEV + a_4 FATA + a_5 NPCP \qquad (2)$$

where NRT is the annual profitability, MS is the firm's market share, SK is the ratio
of sales over total assets, LEV is the leverage index, FATA is the ratio of fixed assets
to total assets, and NPCP is the internal finance index.

Following the relevant literature (Martin, 1993; Shepherd, 1994; Lev, 1974;
Chen et al., 1985; Copeland, 1983; Parliament et al., 1990; Oustapassidis, 1998),
market share is expected to have a positive effect on profitability since it shows the
superior performance of large firms. When the market is an oligopolistic, with few
firms dominating the market, then the leaders apply their own strategies and the
lesser firms follow. This provides a comparative advantage to the leading firms that
results in an increase of their profit margin which is greater than the smaller ones

(a_1>0). The ratio of sales over total assets shows the efficient utilization of a firm's assets to generate sales and is expected to affect profitability positively (a_2>0).

The higher the leverage ratio, the greater the risks associated with the probability of default by the firm, while lower leverage generally indicates greater financial security. So, the higher the leverage ratio, the lower the level of profits expected. However, there are cases where the firm needs financial support to invest in modern technology. Value-maximization theory suggests the existence of optimal leverage for a firm (Copeland and Weston, 1983), which is determined by the trade-offs between the benefits of borrowing and the associated risks. Theoretical consideration suggests that moral hazard behavior in cooperatives and equity "starvation" induced by horizon problems and the non-marketability of cooperative stock will cause cooperatives to rely more heavily on debt than IOFs. (a_3><0). The fixed assets to total assets ratio is expected to affect firm's profitability negatively. This can be attributed to the reduced level of current assets which could lead to a lower level of sales, since the firm will be short of the necessary materials, stocks, etc., with a reduced level of activity overall (a_4<0). The extent of internal finance is expected to have a positive impact on profitability, due to the firm's financial independence (a_5>0).

4. DATA AND VARIABLES

The dairy sector was chosen mainly because of its significance in the food industry and the co-existence of dynamic firms of both types. The latest available data shows that the contribution of the dairy industry to the total gross production value of the food sector increased from 12.4% in 1990 to 17.1% in 1999, while the contribution of dairy to the production value added to the food sector increased from 12.0% in 1990 to 17% to 1999 (NSSG, 2000).

The study uses panel data from the 39 largest firms covering a period of 12 years (1990–2001). This is sufficient to give a reliable evaluation of the factors influencing profit. The sample includes cooperatives and IOFs comprising 90% of total turnover in the sector (the rest is covered by a large number of small local firms). Thirty-four of the companies are IOFs; the rest are cooperatives. We collected data from both the balance sheets and the income statements of the large dairy companies in Greece. It is important to note that all Greek firms are obliged to publish their annual balance sheets and income statements which are available on an annual basis by a proprietary service company called ICAP (ICAP, 1990–2001). The authors calculated the profit ratios, structural variables and financial indices used.

Following the relevant financial economics and accounting literature (e.g. Kim, 1978; Haugen and Senbet, 1978; Parliament *et al.*, 1990) we calculate and study the mean values of the annual financial indices, which are expected to affect profitability, for the full sample and the two groups (cooperatives and IOFs). The profitability variable is measured as the ratio of net profits over assets, while market share is the ratio of a firm's sales over industry sales. The efficiency index *SK* is measured as the ratio of sales over total assets, while *LEV* is the ratio of liabilities over total assets. The *NPCP* variable is measured as the ratio of reserve capital (retained or undistributed

profits) to the share capital showing the annual contribution of the retained profits to
the capital formation.

Table 1 shows the mean values of all variables included in the models for each of
the group of firms and overall for the sample used. The indices for profitability show
that IOFs are more profitable than cooperatives, which may be attributed to the
hypothesis that cooperative members do not expect to earn a rate of return on their
investment, while they do expect to receive benefits through services and in the form
of higher product prices or lower costs. However, it is interesting to note that IOFs
also have a mean market share higher than cooperatives. According to the literature,
profitability along with market share are measures of competitiveness, which means
that IOFs increase their superiority against cooperatives in terms of their competitiveness. The value for the sales to total assets ratio (1.36) for cooperatives show that
they utilize their assets to generate sales less efficiently than IOFs (1.48). The latter
supports the hypothesis of cooperatives' tendency to over invest. The leverage ratio
for dairy cooperatives is higher than that for IOFs. It appears that the cooperatives,
in contrast to the IOFs, are indebted.

Table 1. *Mean values of variables by group, 1990–2001*

Variables	Definition	All		IOFs		Cooperatives	
		Mean	SD	Mean	SD	Mean	SD
NRT	Net profits / Total assets	0.04	0.13	0.05	0.12	0.003	0.16
Market share	Firm sales / Industry sales	0.04	0.06	0.05	0.07	0.03	0.03
SK	Sales / Total assets	1.46	0.84	1.48	0.84	1.36	0.85
LEV	Total liabilities / Total assets	0.61	0.36	0.57	0.30	0.88	0.51
FATA	Fixed assets / Total assets	0.46	0.20	0.47	0.20	0.38	0.18
NPCP	Reserve capital / Capital	0.40	12.12	0.92	1.60	-2.61	31.36

Sources: ICAP HELLAS (1990–2001) (Annual Balance Sheet Data of the Greek Manufacturing
Companies).

The fixed to total assets ratio for both IOFs and cooperative dairies seems to be
favorable (0.47 and 0.38, respectively). The value of the internal finance index for
this period for the investor-owned dairies is 0.92, and shows the extent to which
undistributed profits are made available to finance the firm's activity. In contrast the
value of the internal finance index for the cooperatives is negative (-2.61).

In order to examine the possible degree of colinearity among our variables we
have obtained the correlation matrix of variables, as shown in Table 2. As we
observe in Table 2, both the coefficients of the correlation matrix and the evidence

of their significance prove that the correlations among the independent variables are weak.

Table 2. Correlation Matrix for Variables, 1990–2001

	Definition	MS	SK	LEV	FATA
MS	Market Share				
SK	Sales Total assets	0.04960 (0.339)[a]			
LEV	Total liabilities Total assets	0.00966 (0.852)	0.12407 (0.016)[b]*		
FATA	Fixed assets Total assets	0.06390 (0.213)	0.22391 (0.000)**	0.33226 (0.000)**	
NPCP	Reverse capital Capital	0.10332 (0.045)*	0.09392 (0.069)	0.34218 (0.000)**	0.09414 (0.068)

a. Sig. 2-tailed in parentheses
b. * Correlation is significant at the 0.05 level (2-tailed) and
** Correlation is significant at the 0.01 level (2-tailed).
Sources: ICAP HELLAS (1990–2001) (Annual Balance Sheet Data of the Greek Manufacturing Companies).

5. RESULTS

The application of Hausman-test for fixed effects or random effects shows that the fixed effect model is the advisable estimation method for the model (14.60 for 5 df, prob value =.0122). The method provides a dynamic evaluation of the effects of the financial variables included in the model of the profitability changes and it is able to isolate the particularities of certain companies (Judge *et al.*, 1988). Table 3 shows the results of the Fixed Effect method[1] for the full model, the IOFs and cooperatives separately.

The results for the full model show that the main factors affecting profitability in case of the Greek dairy sector are market share and financial variables: efficient index, leverage and internal finance index. Furthermore, the results show that the two variables (the efficient index and the internal finance index) have all the expected positive and statistically significant effect on profitability while the leverage index has negative and statistically significant effect on profitability. As we expected, the effect of market share is positive and significant, while the coefficient of the ratio of the fixed to total assets is insignificant.

In order to examine if cooperatives and IOFs behave differently we estimated the same model for each group separately. Then we applied Chow-test to examine whether the respective coefficients obtained from the two samples are statistically different. The estimated value for the Chow-test is found $F^* = 3.92$ while the theoretical value of F for $v_1=6$ and $v_2=376-(28x6) =364$ degrees of freedom is 2.80.

Thus, $F^*>F_{.01}$ shows that, the coefficients of the variables are different in the two groups.

Table 3. Fixed Effects Estimates of Profitability by Sample, 1990–2001

Variables \ Sample	ALL	IOFs	Cooperatives
	FE	FE	FE
MS Market share	0.013 (4.37)*[b]	0.02 (5.66) *[a]	0.10 (0.07)
SK Sales Total assets	0.023 (2.98)*	0.025 (3.33)*	0.013 (0.44)
LEV Total liabilities Total assets	-0.081 (-4.08)*	-0.031 (-1.44)	-0.16 (-3.19)*
FATA Fixed assets Total assets	-0.026 (-0.61)	0.014 (0.33)	-0.12 (-0.79)
NPCP Reserve capital Capital	0.002 (4.05)*	0.013 (3.41)*	0.001 (1.26)
SSR	2.55174	1.63110	0.789255
F* test (Chow Test)		3,29	
R^2	0.58	0.64	0.47
Number of Observ.[c]	376	320	56[d]

a. t-values in parentheses

b. * denotes statistical significant results at 5% (or less) level of significance.

c. There are 39 annual observations with no complete data for all variables.

d. The size of this sample is rather small but the model for cooperatives is estimated just for comparison with the IOFs.

The main factors affecting positively and significantly IOFs' profitability are market share, efficient index, and reserves-to-capital ratio. As was expected, an increase in market share has positive effect on profitability. It was also found that the relationship between efficient index and profitability is positive and significant, which shows that dairy IOFs use their assets efficiently.

In contrast, the results for the cooperative dairy firms show that only one variable (leverage index) has the expected negative and significant effect on net profits and explains profitability differences among the cooperatives. This result shows that cooperatives financing their assets formation by borrowed capital are less profitable than other cooperatives depending more on their own funds (capital and reserves).

The coefficients of the other introduced variables are not found to significantly affect the profitability of cooperative dairy firms. The latter shows either that these factors are not the main determinants of cooperatives' performance due to their different behavior, or that future research should include a different set of variables such as managerial decision variables, conduct strategies, etc.

6. CONCLUSIONS

The discussion of whether cooperatives and IOFs differ, in which aspect and to what extent, has occupied economists' thinking for a long time. Nowadays, where there is an increasing competition in food markets, the debate has focused on whether cooperatives perform as well as their IOF counterparts. The factors underlie cooperatives' sustainable competitive advantage; hence profitability is of particular interest.

This paper uses data for the 39 largest Greek dairy firms for the period 1990–2001 to examine the factors that affect profitability differences between IOFs and cooperatives. A comprehensive panel data analysis (fixed effects) is used to test the relationship between profitability and market share, leverage, internal finance index and two efficiency measures. The sample is divided into two groups' cooperatives and IOFs. The application of Chow test shows that there are significant differences between the two groups.

The comparison between cooperatives' and IOFs' descriptive statistics reveals a number of interesting results. First of all, cooperatives have a lower rate of return on assets and lower market share than IOFs for the study period, while cooperatives are found to relying on borrowed capital more than private firms. The latter is consistent with the moral-hazard behavior and "equity starvation" induced by horizon problems and non-marketability of cooperative stock, which cause cooperatives to rely more heavily on debt than IOFs.

The regression estimates suggest that dairy companies, irrespective of their type of ownership, can increase their profits by increasing their size (market share), their efficiency (efficient use of assets) and their contribution of retained profits to capital. In contrast to the IOFs, market share, efficiency index and internal finance index are not found to have any significant effect on cooperatives' profitability. The profitability of cooperatives is found to be affected only by leverage negatively.

These findings suggest that if cooperatives' aim is to improve their competitiveness against IOFs, then Greek dairy cooperatives should increase the contribution of retained profits to capital along with a better exploitation of efficient use of capital and economies of scale. Further research is required to investigate the cooperative comparative disadvantages against IOFs, in terms of dynamic competition aspects such as differentiation, advertising, innovation rates and mergers, along with quality and capacity of cooperative management.

NOTES

* This work is dedicated to the late Prof. K. Oustapassidis' memory. The authors wish to express their special thanks to Prof. J. Nilsson and Prof. K. Karantininis and to an anonymous referee for their useful suggestions and comments on an earlier draft of this paper.
[1] The estimation of the Fixed Effect method was made by the use of the program "LIMDEP 7.0, 1999".

REFERENCES

Akridge, J.T., and T. Hertel. 1992. "Cooperative and Investor-Oriented Firm Efficiency: A Multi-Product Analysis." *Journal of Agricultural Cooperation* 7:1–14.

Ananiadis, I., O. Notta, and K. Oustapassidis. 2003. "Cooperative Competitiveness and Capital Structure in the Greek Dairy Industry." *Journal of Rural Cooperation* 31 (2):95–109.

Chen, K., E.M. Babb, and L.F. Schrader. 1985. "Growth of Large Cooperatives and Proprietary Firms in the US Food Sector." *Agribusiness* 2:201–210.

Copeland, T.E., and J.F. Weston. 1983. *Financial Theory and Corporate Policy*. Reading, MA: Addison-Wesley Publishing Co.

Fulton, M.E. 1995. "The Future of Cooperatives in Canada: A Property Rights Approach." *American Journal of Agricultural Economics* 77:1144–52.

Hardesty, S.D., and V. D. Salgia. 2004. Comparative Financial Performance of Agricultural Cooperatives and Investor-Owned Firms. Paper presented at *NCR-194 research on Cooperatives Annual Meeting*. Nov. 2–3, Kansas City, Missouri.

Haugen, R., and L. Senbet. 1978. "The Insignificance of Bankruptcy Costs to the Theory of Optimal Capital Structure." *Journal of Finance* June: 383–394.

ICAP Hellas. 1990–2001. *Annual Balance Sheet Data for the Greek Manufacturing Companies*, Athens, 1990–2001 (series).

Judge, G., C. Hill, W.Griffiths, H. Lutkepohl, and T. Lee. 1988. *Introduction to the Theory and Practice of Econometrics*. New York: John Wiley and Sons.

Kim, H. 1978. "A Mean Variance Theory of Optimal Structure and Corporate Debt Capacity." *Journal of Finance* March:45–64.

Lerman, Z., and C. Parliament. 1990. "Comparative Performance of Cooperatives and Investor-Owned Firms in US Food Industries." *Agribusiness* 6:527–40.

Lev, B. 1974. On the Association between Operating Leverage and Risk. *Journal of Financial and Quantitive Analysis* 9:627–42.

Martin, L., R Westgren and E. VanDuren. ,1991. "Agribusiness Competitiveness across National Boundaries." *American Journal of Agricultural Economics* Dec 1991, 1456–1464.

Martin, S. 1993a. *Advanced Industrial Economics*. Oxford, UK: Blackwell Publishers.

____. 1993b. *Industrial Economics*. New York: Macmillan Publishing Co.

Nielsen Hellas. 1990–2001. *Advertising Expenditures Directory,* Athens.

NSSG. 2000. *National Statistical Service of Greece 2000. The Annual Industry Survey*, Athens.

Oustapassidis, K. and O. Notta. 1997. "Profitability of Cooperatives and Investor-Owned Firms in the Greek Dairy Industry." *Journal of Rural Cooperation* 25 (1):33–43.

___. 1998. Performance of Strategic Groups in the Greek Dairy Industry. *European Journal of Marketing* 32, (11/12):962–973.

___., A. Vlachvei, and K. Karantininis. 1998. "Growth of Investor Owned and Cooperative Firms in Greek Dairy Industry." *Annals of Public and Cooperative Economics* 69:399–417.

Parliament C., Z. Lerman, and J. Fulton. 1990. "Performance of Cooperatives and Investor-Owned Firms in the Dairy Industry." *Journal of Agricultural Cooperation* 5:1–16.

Porter P.K., and G.W Scully. 1987. "Economic Efficiency in Cooperatives." *The Journal of Law and Economics* October, 30:489–512.

Scherer, F.M., and D. Ross. 1990. *Industrial Market Structure and Economic Performance*. Boston: Houghton Mifflin Company.

Schrader, L., F. Babb, E.M. Boynton, R.D. and M.G. Lang. 1985. Cooperative and Proprietary Agribusiness: Comparison of Performance. *Agri. Exp. Stat. Bull.* 982, Purdue University.

Sexton, R., B.M. Wilson, and J.J. Wann. 1989. "Some Tests of the Economic Theory of Cooperatives: Methodology and Application to Cotton Ginning." *Western Journal of Agricultural Economics* 14:55–66.

__., and J. Iskow. 1993. "The Competitive Role of Cooperatives in Market-Oriented Economies." In C. Csaki and Y. Kislev, eds. *Agricultural Cooperatives in Transition.* Boulder CO: Westview Press.

Shepherd, W. G. 1994. *The Economics of Industrial Organization.* Englewood Cliffs, NJ: Prentice-Hall International Editions.

Van Bekkum, O.F., and G. van Dijk. 1997. *Agricultural Co-operatives in the European Union: Trends and Issues on the Eve of the 21st Century.* Van Gorcum: Assen.

Venieris, G. 1989. "Agricultural Cooperatives vs. Public Companies in the Greek Wine Industry." *European Review of Agricultural Economics* 16:129–135.